Green economy and good governance for sustainable development

Green economy and good governance for sustainable development: Opportunities, promises and concerns

Edited by Jose A. Puppim de Oliveira

United Nations University Press

TOKYO · NEW YORK · PARIS

© United Nations University, 2012

The views expressed in this publication are those of the authors and do not necessarily reflect the views of the United Nations University.

United Nations University Press
United Nations University, 53-70, Jingumae 5-chome,
Shibuya-ku, Tokyo 150-8925, Japan
Tel: +81-3-5467-1212   Fax: +81-3-3406-7345
E-mail: sales@unu.edu   general enquiries: press@unu.edu
http://www.unu.edu

United Nations University Office at the United Nations, New York
2 United Nations Plaza, Room DC2-2062, New York, NY 10017, USA
Tel: +1-212-963-6387   Fax: +1-212-371-9454
E-mail: unuony@unu.edu

United Nations University Press is the publishing division of the United Nations University.

Cover design by Andrew Corbett

Printed in Hong Kong

ISBN 978-92-808-1216-9

Library of Congress Cataloging-in-Publication Data

Green economy and good governance for sustainable development: opportunities, promises and concerns / edited by Jose A. Puppim de Oliveira.
   p. cm.
 Includes bibliographical references and index.
 ISBN 978-9280812169 (pbk.)
  1. Economic development—Environmental aspects. 2. Sustainable development. 3. Environmental policy. I. Puppim de Oliveira, Jose Antonio, 1966–
HD75.6.G736   2012
338.9'27—dc23   2012010918

Endorsements

"This is a book that must be read by everyone who still believes that the world can change its development patterns towards a more sustainable path. With a critical perspective, the book examines the obstacles and opportunities for greening the economy and improving governance in several important sectors, and greatly contributes to advance the debates on sustainable development and its implementation beyond Rio+20."

Cristovam Buarque, *Senator of the Brazilian National Congress, Head of the Rio+20 Senate Commission, Brazil, and member of the United Nations University Council*

"The transition to a green economy will require a truly transformational change, analogous to the transition economies underwent with the industrial revolution. Effective governance is a prerequisite for driving this complex and sensitive process. This publication is a very timely contribution to the dialogue underway on the role of good governance for a green economy."

Yannick Glemarec, *Director of Environmental Finance, Environment and Energy Group, United Nations Development Programme (UNDP)*

"This is indeed a very timely publication since it addresses major problems that are on the agenda of the UN Rio+20 Conference in Brazil, but also points out some of the other real challenges to be faced by all mankind in the next 40 years, at least. A must-read book, in my opinion."
Heitor Gurgulino de Souza, *Vice-President of the Club of Rome and former Rector of the United Nations University*

"This well-timed book deserves a broad readership. It addresses a wide range of critically important governance issues relating to green economy transitions. The contributors offer many significant arguments and insights valuable to anyone who is interested in sustainable development."
Henrik Selin, *Boston University*

Contents

Figures x

Tables xi

Boxes xii

Contributors xiii

Acknowledgements xv

Introduction 1

1 Introduction: Framing the debate on the green economy and
   governance from different angles. 3
   Jose A. Puppim de Oliveira

2 Sustainable development: A changing paradigm 23
   Sam Johnston

Part I: Green economy 45

3 Towards equity and sustainability in the "green economy" 47
   Manu V. Mathai and Govindan Parayil

4 The political economy of green growth: Food, fuel and
   electricity in southern Africa 71
   Danielle Resnick, Finn Tarp and James Thurlow

5 Learning for a green society: Towards sustainable
   consumption and production 94
   *Zinaida Fadeeva, Abel Barasa Atiti, Unnikrishnan
   Payyappallimana, Aurea Tanaka, Mario Tabucanon, Sachiko
   Yasuda and Kazuhiko Takemoto*

6 Revitalizing socio-ecological production landscapes through
   greening the economy 117
   Kaoru Ichikawa, Robert Blasiak and Aya Takatsuki

7 Governance challenges for promoting the green economy in
   Africa 136
   Timothy Afful-Koomson

8 Geothermal energy and the Millennium Development Goals.. 160
   Ingvar B. Fridleifsson

9 Enabling green economic transitions through biodiversity
   conservation: Potential and challenges 181
   M. S. Suneetha and Alexandros Gasparatos

Part II: Governance 197

10 Visioning transformative sustainable development
   governance 199
   Norichika Kanie

11 Oceans and sustainability: The governance of marine areas
   beyond national jurisdiction 221
   Marjo Vierros, Anne McDonald and Salvatore Arico

12 The role of indigenous peoples in global environmental
   governance: Looking through the lens of climate change 245
   *Kirsty Galloway McLean, Sam Johnston and Ameyali Ramos
   Castillo*

13 Global environmental health governance for sustainable
   development 267
   Jamal Hisham Hashim and Zailina Hashim

14 Good governance in cities for promoting a greener economy.. 286
   *Jose A. Puppim de Oliveira, Aki Suwa, Osman Balaban,
   Christopher N. H. Doll, Ping Jiang, Magali Dreyfus, Raquel
   Moreno-Peñaranda, Puspita Dirgahayani and Erin Kennedy*

Conclusion 325

15 Key issues and lessons learned for moving towards a greener
   economy and creating better governance for sustainable
   development 327
   Jose A. Puppim de Oliveira

Index 338

Figures

4.1	Alternative electricity sector investment plans for South Africa	79
4.2	Evolution in the financial cost of Malawi's Agricultural Input Subsidy Program	83
6.1	Conceptual framework of the *Satoyama* Initiative	122
7.1	A theoretical framework of green economy governance in Africa	154
8.1	World population showing historical development, 1850–1990, and World Bank projection to 2100: (a) by rural–urban and (b) by macro region	162
8.2	Installed capacity and energy production for geothermal electricity generation and direct use, by continent	166
8.3	The 14 countries with the highest percentage share of geothermal energy in their national electricity production	168
13.1	The "Environment of Health Model" of H. L. Blum	268
13.2	Health effects of global climate change	280
13.3	A theoretical assessment of the combined impacts of environmental and climate change on the environment and human health in the Mekong Delta	281
13.4	Environmental health governance within a national development plan	283

Tables

4.1	Summary of case studies	88
5.1	Case studies and ESD principles	108
8.1	Ranges of technical potential of renewable energy sources	164
8.2	Electricity from renewable energy resources in 2009	164
8.3	Top 16 countries utilizing geothermal energy	167
8.4	Number of countries in different economic categories using geothermal for electricity production and direct use, 2010	167
8.5	Levellized cost of renewable energy sources with commercially available technologies for electricity and direct use	172
8.6	Registered geothermal CDM projects as of January 2012	174
13.1	Deaths and DALYs attributable to five environmental risks and to all five risks combined, by region in 2004	274

Boxes

5.1	The United Nations Decade of Education for Sustainable Development	103
5.2	UNU's cross-sectoral multi-stakeholder initiatives on ESD	105
6.1	The *Satoyama* Initiative and its international partnership	119
6.2	Natural resource management in Western Siem Pang, Cambodia	124
6.3	Biomass power generation in the Gokase River Watershed, Nobeoka, Japan	126
6.4	Ankeniheny–Zahamena Corridor, Madagascar	127
6.5	Compensatory mitigation in Aichi Prefecture, Japan	128

Contributors

Timothy Afful-Koomson is an Environmental Policy Fellow at United Nations University Institute for Natural Resources in Africa (UNU-INRA).

Salvatore Arico is a Visiting Research Fellow at the United Nations University Institute of Advanced Studies (UNU-IAS) and a Programme Specialist at UNESCO.

Abel Barasa Atiti is a Research Fellow at UNU-IAS.

Osman Balaban is a Postdoctoral Fellow at UNU-IAS.

Robert Blasiak is a Communications Coordinator at UNU-IAS.

Puspita Dirgahayani is a Lecturer at the School of Architecture, Planning and Policy Development, Bandung Institute of Technology.

Christopher N. H. Doll is a Postdoctoral Fellow at UNU-IAS.

Magali Dreyfus is a Postdoctoral Fellow at UNU-IAS.

Zinaida Fadeeva is a Research Fellow at UNU-IAS.

Ingvar B. Fridleifsson is Director of the United Nations University Geothermal Training Programme (UNU-GTP).

Kirsty Galloway McLean is a Fellow at UNU-IAS.

Alexandros Gasparatos is a James Martin Research Fellow at the Biodiversity Institute, University of Oxford.

Zailina Hashim is a Professor at Universiti Putra Malaysia.

Jamal Hisham Hashim is a Research Fellow at the United Nations University International Institute for Global Health (UNU-IIGH) and a Professor at the National University of Malaysia.

CONTRIBUTORS

Kaoru Ichikawa is a Research Fellow at UNU-IAS.

Ping Jiang is a Postdoctoral Fellow at UNU-IAS.

Sam Johnston is a Senior Research Fellow at UNU-IAS.

Norichika Kanie is an Associate Professor at the Tokyo Institute of Technology and a Research Fellow at UNU-IAS.

Erin Kennedy is a Programme Assistant at UNU-IAS.

Anne McDonald is the Director of the UNU-IAS Operating Unit in Kanazawa (UNU-IAS/OUIK).

Manu V. Mathai is a Research Fellow at UNU-IAS.

Raquel Moreno-Peñaranda is a Postdoctoral Fellow at UNU-IAS.

Govindan Parayil is a UNU Vice-Rector and UNU-IAS Director.

Unnikrishnan Payyappallimana is a Research Coordinator at UNU-IAS.

Jose A. Puppim de Oliveira is Assistant Director and Senior Research Fellow at UNU-IAS.

Ameyali Ramos Castillo is a Research Fellow at UNU-IAS.

Danielle Resnick is a Research Fellow at the United Nations University World Institute for Development Economics Research (UNU-WIDER).

M. S. Suneetha is a Research Fellow at UNU-IAS.

Aki Suwa is a Research Fellow at UNU-IAS.

Aya Takatsuki is a Programme Associate at UNU-IAS.

Kazuhiko Takemoto is a Senior Fellow at UNU-IAS.

Aurea Tanaka is a Research Associate at UNU-IAS

Finn Tarp is the Director of UNU-WIDER.

James Thurlow is a Research Fellow at UNU-WIDER.

Marjo Vierros is an Adjunct Senior Fellow at UNU-IAS.

Sachiko Yasuda is a Programme Associate at UNU-IAS.

Acknowledgements

I would like to acknowledge several people and organizations that made this book possible. Firstly, I thank the United Nations University* for providing a multidisciplinary environment with a presence in several parts of the world. This was essential for generating such a diverse collection of chapters, particularly those institutes and programmes whose staff contributed to the chapters of the book: the UNU Institute of Advanced Studies (UNU-IAS), the UNU World Institute for Development Economics Research (UNU-WIDER), the UNU Institute for Natural Resources in Africa (UNU-INRA), the UNU International Institute for Global Health (UNU-IIGH) and the UNU Geothermal Training Programme (UNU-GTP).

I am also grateful to the United Nations University Press for giving its full support for the idea of the book and producing it in a timely manner. I especially thank Vesselin Popovski and Naomi Cowan for the confidence they placed in this book. Erin Kennedy and Makiko Arima were also key members who provided production support and timely proofreading. I thank all authors for producing their pieces and prioritizing the writing of the chapters over other tasks, as well as the anonymous peer reviewers for their comments. Finally, I thank UNU-IAS, particularly its director Govindan Parayil, for providing full support to make the book a reality.

* The opinions expressed in the chapters do not represent the position of the United Nations University, its institutes or any other UN organization. They are solely the responsibility of the authors.

Introduction

1

Introduction: Framing the debate on the green economy and governance from different angles

Jose A. Puppim de Oliveira

Introduction

The United Nations Conference on Environment and Development (UNCED) took place in the city of Rio de Janeiro, Brazil, in 1992 and put the concept of sustainable development definitively on policy agendas at all levels from global to local. It was one of the largest gatherings of world leaders and generated a series of important documents such as *Agenda 21*, the United Nations Framework Convention on Climate Change, the Convention on Biological Diversity and the United Nations Convention to Combat Desertification. Almost 20 years later, even though important progress has been made in several areas, the world still struggles to implement the decisions following up UNCED and to steer humanity towards a more sustainable path.

In order to advance further the implementation of the sustainable development agenda, the United Nations has set two broad themes for the United Nations Conference on Sustainable Development in 2012 (UNCSD, or Rio+20): the institutional framework for sustainable development and the green economy in the context of sustainable development and poverty eradication. These two themes will be the axes of the discussions in this book. The authors will analyse the themes from different perspectives, ranging from implications to development assistance to the role of indigenous people and cities. The debates on these two themes will permeate the discussions in the sustainability arena in the future.

Green economy and good governance for sustainable development: Opportunities, promises and concerns, Puppim de Oliveira (ed.),
United Nations University Press, 2012, ISBN 978-92-808-1216-9

The term "sustainable development" became popular in the 1990s, particularly after the release of the Brundtland Report and after UNCED. The term definitively broke the stalemate between environmental protection, economic development and social inclusiveness (called the three pillars of sustainable development), offering the possibility that all three could come together without a trade-off, at least in theory. Nevertheless, this has not always held true in practice. Even though environmental awareness has increased and there are many good examples to illustrate sustainable development around the world, the planet has become dangerously more unsustainable in several aspects, such as loss of biodiversity and climate change, which have also affected the most vulnerable populations. Thus, the question many raise is how to achieve environmental sustainability with reasonable economic growth that can lead to poverty alleviation and social inclusiveness at all levels (local, national and global). The key observation to answer this question is the difficulty of achieving sustainable development owing to the lack of institutions capable of translating the concept of sustainable development into practice.

One relevant policy question is how to translate global concerns into local action, and local concerns into global action. However, we still have a long way to go. We have to create effective and democratic institutional mechanisms to make sustainable development a reality in practice at the various levels. Many of the organizations and institutions at the different levels still operate in the old paradigm of development or are unable to bring the three pillars of sustainable development together in an effective manner. They have to be changed to create the capacity to move societies and the world effectively on a more sustainable path.

Moreover, institutions at the national and subnational level need to interact with global institutions to make societies work properly for sustainable development. Resources and knowledge have to be used effectively to address many of the global challenges. Economic institutions also have to be reformed to be greener and more socially inclusive so that they lead to poverty eradication and more sustainable development. However, we need to understand how they can be mainstreamed and make radical changes in the way the economy and organizations work to eradicate poverty and to be environmentally sustainable.

Thus, the challenges and opportunities for creating a greener economy and the institutional framework for sustainable development rest necessarily, or mostly, on how we can be effective in incorporating the challenges of sustainable development into our institutions and creating the implementation capacity to translate those concerns into practice. This book will analyse those challenges from different angles.

The authors of this book come from different programmes and institutes of the United Nations University (UNU) and contribute in several areas where their respective programmes and institutes have accumulated expertise. The idea is to have thematic discussions led by UNU experts to understand the achievements and obstacles in relation to sustainability in the last 20 years in order to propose new ideas and changes in economy and governance for a more sustainable future.

This chapter sets the stage for the debates that will be elaborated in the following chapters of the book. It starts with a short overview of the debates on sustainable development before and since UNCED, particularly the recent debates on the green economy and institutional frameworks for sustainable development. The chapter then highlights the main contributions of the book to the discussions on the green economy and sustainable development by giving perspectives from different angles. It concludes with a short summary of the main points of each chapter and a portrait of what the readers can expect from the following chapters.

Towards the limits

The world has faced massive changes in the last three centuries. Until the eighteenth century, humans had a limited form of energy for using in production and transportation, particularly their own energy and the energy from animals, wind and biomass. This limited human action in both intensity and scale, even though the great navigations in the East and West were the first step to globalization. However, the invention and dissemination of steam power on a large scale definitively changed the reach of human action, and consequently the world. Steam power catalysed the emerging industrial revolution and allowed humans to use the energy from abundant coal and other fossil fuels to increase their capacity to transform materials and to transport goods much more efficiently.

The industrial revolution was initially a technological revolution, but it led to huge transformations and consequences in the economy, society, politics and environment, both locally and globally. In economic terms, the revolution improved labour productivity and production, leading to a huge increase in the material wealth of societies. These economic changes implied a transformation of both urban and rural societies. Factories demanded labour, bringing people to live near them, and consequently led to urbanization. They also demanded raw materials, such as wool, from the rural areas, leading to pressure to increase production on farms and to the final break-up of some feudal systems. In the political economy, the industrial revolution consolidated market capitalism as a political system, but it also created an increasing degree of inequality in societies and led to the creation of a working class in the urban areas, which influenced political changes, such as a stronger labour movement, which in turn sparked many socialist revolutions around the world.

The possibilities from the industrial revolution expanded the capacity of humans to interfere with nature. First, there was a huge increase in the use of natural resources, both to produce inputs to the industrial processes and to feed the machines with fuel. In addition, the new, more efficient forms of transportation enabled industries to bring in inputs and to reach distant markets. However, the by-products of the increase in production, such as air and water pollution, were felt across the big industrial cities, as well as in the less evident degradation of ecosystems far away from the cities owing to an increase in agricultural production or the exploitation of natural resources.

Those rapid changes in the eighteenth and nineteenth centuries caused profound changes in the relationship between humans and nature. Many societies aimed to increase their material wealth in order to improve their well-being, and, indeed, society has been richer on average since the industrial revolution. "Development", which initially was synonymous with economic growth, was pursued at any cost. The social and environmental problems caused by rapid industrialization and urbanization – such as air pollution, income inequalities and lack of sanitation in the cities – were regarded as the price to be paid for "development". In the first quarter of the twentieth century, this seemed to be the universal view, and not only in the capitalist world. In the Soviet Union, industrialization without concern for the environmental consequences was also the motto for its development, as portrayed in a poster from the Soviet Era that says "the smoke of chimneys is the breath of Soviet Russia".[1] Environmental pollution was almost synonymous with "development" and even was something desirable. This was the economic development at any cost practised in modern society, in both capitalist and communist regimes, in the first half of the twentieth century.

The rise of the debates and the governance of sustainable development

The term "sustainable development" stemmed from many of the social movements in society demanding social and political changes, such as feminism, the civil and human rights movements and pacifism. The evolving discussions in the environmental conservation debate brought together the different movements when the term "sustainable development" was coined and popularized in the 1980s. Even though the "green" agenda is still dominant in the debates on sustainable development, this agenda has changed significantly since the voice of the other social movements joined the debates on sustainable development. Nevertheless, the history of the environmental movements over time is key to understanding how we reached the current discussions on sustainable development.

The conservationist movement in the United States in the nineteenth century could be considered the first "modern" environmental movement on a large scale. The American conservationists developed some of the core actions of the environmental conservation movement, which still exist today, such as national parks to protect certain natural areas from human action for the common good. They were concerned that the "expansion to the west" would have the same consequences for nature as they had in the eastern part of the United States. The conservation movement achieved important political landmarks, such as the creation of the first National Park (Yellowstone), and it was responsible for influencing conservation policies all over the world. However, this was not sufficient to make radical changes in the way human action affected nature. Conservationists tried to isolate (conserve) part of nature from human action, but this did not change human action, per se, which continued with economic and industrial growth at any cost. Moreover, the turbulent first half of the twentieth century, with two world wars, socialist revolutions and economic recessions, blurred the political relevance of the continuing environmental degradation.

After the Second World War, the big economic powers (the so-called "developed countries") reorganized their economies and industrial parks. Many of them, propelled by high rates of economic growth, soon achieved industrial production and per capita income higher than they had prior to the war. In the 1960s, their populations achieved significant levels of consumption and material wealth, which have not yet been achieved by large parts of the population in Asia, Africa and Latin America in the 2010s. Nevertheless, the high level of material wealth did not necessarily lead to other benefits in terms of the quality of life. Many city inhabitants in the developed countries were living in places with high levels of air and water pollution in the 1950s, as the result of the expansion of industrial activities. In rural areas, the "green revolution" (that is, the use of modern methods for agricultural production, such as machines, chemical fertilizers and pesticides) facilitated the expansion of agricultural fields and production, but caused contamination of the environment.

Intellectuals started to raise the alarm on the destruction of nature, for example Rachel Carson in her book *Silent Spring* (Carson, 1962). In many cities, high levels of contamination led to a lot of health problems and the appearance of diseases never before seen. In Japan, high levels of noxious pollutants, including heavy metals, contaminated entire populations, as was the case in Minamata or Yokkaichi (Puppim de Oliveira, 2011; Tsuru, 1999).

In the conceptual field, there was still a dilemma in the 1960s over how to combat environmental problems. Mainstream political, business and economic thinking claimed that environmental pollution was the natural consequence of economic development and the price to pay for increasing material wealth. Thus, there was a supposed trade-off between the economy and the environment (*Newsweek*, 1972). If a society wanted high levels of economic wealth, it had to put up with the high levels of environmental pollution caused by the new factories and cars that were the engines of economic growth. Businesses claimed that, if a city did not want the development they brought, they could move their factories to other cities or countries that were happy to accept the trade-off.

In the instrumental field, the state and society did not have the tools or the means to make economic development compatible with environmental quality. The few tools available were to zone areas for industrial development and to try to distance them from residential areas. Environmental Impact Assessment was incipient in most countries and still not completely institutionalized. The other alternative was to halt industrial development, or even to close down factories to stop pollution. However, industries generated a large part of the taxes on which the state depended, and they also provided services and jobs for the population, who might oppose any initiatives that would cut their jobs.

As neither businesses nor governments were willing to take action, environmental movements started to appear and become relevant in civil society. Initially, neighbourhood associations, small environmental groups, schools, universities and labour unions protested against environmental contamination and its consequences for specific populations and on environmental issues, such as nuclear energy. They were also interacting with a range of other social movements that were emerging in the industrialized countries, such as feminism, pacifism and the civil rights movements. Many of the environmental movements thought, in line with mainstream conceptual ideas, that there was a trade-off between environmental protection and economic development, and some claimed that it was vital to have zero or negative economic growth in order to have a better environment. Those movements became larger both in scale and in resources and more influential in politics, and were the seeds of the transnational environmental movements we have today.

At the international level, there were rising concerns as well. The 1972 report from the Club of Rome (Meadows et al., 1972), which comprised respected specialists, showed through modelling techniques that the increasing population and use of natural resources would strain the planet. The report had a big impact on policy-makers internationally, and was translated into several languages. Nevertheless, the economy–

environment trade-off was still the only major conceptual framework within which to consider solutions to the environmental crisis.

The growing environmental concerns, protests and reports at the beginning of the 1970s led to the organization of the United Nations Conference on the Human Environment in Stockholm, Sweden, in 1972. Led by an emerging environmental movement in those countries influenced by the conceptual framework of the trade-off between the environment and economic development, the conference had as its main concern the severe industrial pollution in developed countries. The agenda was driven by the developed countries, which were suffering from severe industrial pollution and internal political pressure from environmentalists. Developing countries had different views on environmental issues at that time. Some countries, such as India, expressed their concern that environmental problems might be caused by poverty and the lack of economic opportunities. Others were sceptical about the intentions behind the environmental concerns and the theories about zero economic growth that many proposed as a solution. They saw the international environmental movements as attempts to block developing countries from opportunities to develop their economies; many of these developing countries had rapid growth rates and were already showing signs of the same environmental problems as the developed countries.

The Stockholm conference was fundamental in institutionalizing the environmental debate on the global agenda and in the national policies of many countries, which started to create state institutions to cope with environmental concerns. It also led to the creation of the United Nations Environment Programme (UNEP). Nevertheless, the debates did not include issues such as inequality and poverty that were being raised by the various social movements and were of importance particularly to developing countries. The debates were shaped mostly by "Western" concerns and ideas.

During the 1970s and 1980s, the environmental agenda expanded to a large number of countries, which created national and subnational laws and organizations to control environmental problems. Nevertheless, the mainstream idea of the existence of an economy–environment trade-off was questioned. On the one hand, there were a lot of win–win situations involving environmental protection and economic gains, because many advances in environmental management reduced waste and led to improvements in economic efficiency, for example in some industrial processes. Moreover, tighter environmental standards in developed countries, for example in relation to car emissions, did not reduce the demand for cars or jobs in the automobile industry in the 1970s. On the other hand, lack of economic development, and not an excess of positive economic growth, was indeed at the root of some environmental problems, such as lack of sanitation or deforestation in some areas. The mainstream framework to combat environmental degradation was also lacking important dimensions, such as economic and development inequalities and poverty.

The continuing depletion of natural resources and the environmental pollution in some countries and their consequences for economic and social development led the United Nations to create the World Commission on Environment and Development (WCED), or the Brundtland Commission, chaired by Gro Harlem Brundtland (former Norwegian prime minister) in 1983. The Commission released its report *Our Common Future* in 1987. Widely known as the Brundtland Report, it popularized the concept of sustainable development and had a huge impact on international and national policies all over the world (WCED, 1987). Doubt was already being cast on the narrow focus of the concept of development on economic development, and the idea of the Human Development Index was being developed by the United Nations Development Programme (UNDP, 1990). The Brundtland Report consolidated the idea that economic and social development can go hand in hand with environmental protection. The Commission said it was also important to include the needs of future generations in the development equation, defining sustainable development as development that "meets the needs of the present without compromising the ability of future generations to meet their own needs". The environmental and development agenda after WCED changed definitively. It moved from being only "green" to trying to make environmental protection compatible with social and economic development for both present and future generations.

While the WCED was meeting and presenting its results, new environmental problems were emerging, such as the depletion of the ozone layer, biodiversity loss and global warming. The nature of these problems was different from that of previous problems related to local air and water pollution – they had global causes and consequences and needed global solutions. One country alone could not solve these problems.

The need to find solutions for global problems and the search for a new kind of development (sustainable development) led the United Nations to call for a second large global environmental summit, the United Nations Conference on Environment and Development, or Rio-92, in Rio de Janeiro, Brazil, in 1992. The conference produced important conventions and other documents such as *Agenda 21*, the Convention on Biological Diversity and the United Nations Framework Convention on Climate Change. *Agenda 21*, a blueprint for the implementation of sustainable development, was widely discussed around the world, and thousands of Agendas 21 were drafted at national, subnational and local levels.

Rio-92 was also a landmark conference in terms of participation and governance. The conference brought together the largest number of heads of state or government up until then. Civil society, particularly environmental groups, was also widely represented at the conference, and some held their own parallel meetings in the Global Forum organized by non-governmental organizations (NGOs). Some business leaders also eagerly joined the conference and proposed solutions for sustainable development (Schmidheiny, 1992). Civil society groups had a big influence on the discussions during Rio-92 and consolidated their participation in the official environmental meetings. The so-called "Major Groups" are now part of almost all environment and development discussions. On the other hand, international organizations and many governments realized that solutions and the policies to tackle environmental problems could be implemented only with the engagement of civil society, both businesses and environmental NGOs. The conference also brought non-environmental groups of interest to the table, such as non-environmental NGOs and social movements, development organizations and businesses.

One of the most important contributions of Rio-92 was the launch of a positive agenda that seemed achievable. There was a new concept of development (sustainable development) on which all were agreed as a basis. Many important documents and international laws were supported by almost all countries, laying down the blueprint of a set of international norms that could solve many of the global and local environmental problems. The large involvement of civil society signalled a new, more participative governance structure, indicating the broad support governments would receive in making the necessary changes to pursue sustainable development. The Commission on Sustainable Development (CSD) was created to follow up the decisions of Rio-92. Rio-92 changed the environmental discourse and politics forever. Environmental movements became more concerned about social and economic aspects and non-environmental organizations gained more awareness of environmental issues.

After Rio-92, the concept of sustainable development became popular in government policies, business projects and political discourses. *Agenda 21* was discussed and drafted in many places at different levels around the world. Several interesting projects emerged at the local and regional scale that could achieve environmental protection with economic and social benefits. These included the apparent control of global menaces of the 1980s, such as the destruction of the ozone layer, by controlling emissions of the most important ozone-depleting substances. The Rio conventions achieved important breakthroughs in follow-up international agreements, such as the Cartagena and Kyoto Protocols.

In 2000, the United Nations and world leaders launched the Millennium Development Goals (MDGs) at the Millennium Summit in New York, setting a series of goals to mitigate some of the major social and environmental problems around the world. Nevertheless, when government leaders and civil society met again in Johannesburg, South Africa, at the World Summit on Sustainable Development (or Rio+10) in 2002, they concluded that the environmental and social situation was in many respects worse than it had been 10 years earlier, and sustainable development was not being achieved in either developed or developing countries, even though there was an improvement in awareness and the institutional capacity to deal with sustainable development. Johannesburg and the MDGs also brought poverty and human development to the centre of the debate on sustainable development. Poverty was framed more strongly as a global problem that needed global solutions too. Developed countries promised more resources for international development. The main output of the meeting was the Johannesburg Plan of Implementation, in which the parties committed themselves to achieve the MDGs and to implement *Agenda 21* and the international agreements.

The green economy and governance for sustainable development

Twenty years after Rio-92 the same old problems, such as deforestation and air and water pollution, persist in many parts of the world and many global problems have been aggravated, including climate change and biodiversity loss. New problems have emerged, such as the degradation of the oceans and the increasing concentration of persistent organic pollutants. The agenda for sustainable development is more complex because the population keeps growing and economic crises have hit several parts of the world. Many of the problems are intertwined and win–win solutions are not always easy. Even when there is commitment, there are implementation gaps in the capacity of international regimes and governments to make changes happen on the ground on a large scale.

In this context, the United Nations set two main topics of discussion for Rio+20 and beyond: the institutional framework for sustainable development and the green economy in the context of sustainable development and poverty eradication (United Nations, 2010a, 2010b). Addressing these topics could lead to more sustainable development.

The concept of the green economy is not new. Discussions on how to value the environment and include environmental economic values in markets and in governmental policies have been occurring for more than three decades. The concept most notably includes the "polluter pays principle" of the 1970s. There is solid literature on environmental and ecological economics, as well as green debates in political economy (Constanza, 1991; Pearce, 1976). Many methods and tools have been developed to assess environmental values and bring them into economic and financial decisions at many levels; see, for example, the Stern Review (Stern, 2006) and the recent report from The Economics of Ecosystems and Biodiversity (TEEB) study (TEEB, 2010). Many initiatives involving green taxes or accounting have been introduced in public policies at the local, national and global level, for example the Clean Development Mechanism of the Kyoto Protocol. With the announcement of the green economy as a theme for Rio+20, the debates have evolved to encompass other dimensions such as trade (UNCTAD, 2010; UNEP/UNCTAD, 2010).

However, the green economy has been the target of several criticisms. It has not become part of the mainstream economy. Its effects have not been enough to stop continued environmental degradation. In addition, many are critical that the green economy has benefited large corporations and the rich, not the poor, and it has not emphasized discussions on inequalities; it has not been framed to work for the poor. Thus, the concept of the green economy set by UNEP (2011) now includes "in the context of sustainable development and poverty alleviation". However, reaching a consensus on these topics is not an easy task, including the green economy itself, which has been very controversial. For example, the term generated heated debate and alienated some countries, which asked to be left out of the declaration during the Latin American and Caribbean Regional Meeting preparatory to Rio+20 (UNSCD, 2011). In the discussions on the institutional framework for sustainable development, the idea of creating a global environmental agency is also very contentious, with no consensus or agreement. This book analyses the idea of the green economy in diverse contexts, particularly concerning its implementation. Mainstreaming the green economy may arouse resistance from different groups, including the poor, because it may conflict with short-term interests (see Resnick et al. in Chapter 4), but it may be an opportunity for Africa, if the countries in the continent can improve their governance (see Afful-Koomson in Chapter 7).

The institutional framework for sustainable development (IFSD) is the other main discussion theme set by the United Nations. At the global level, there have been several long-term research efforts and seminal works published on the global governance mechanisms that try to understand the effectiveness of international environmental regimes (Kallhauge et al., 2005; Oberthur and Stokke, 2011; Selin, 2010; Young et al., 2008; Young, 1999, 2010). Emerging patterns of environmental governance at the global level have been consolidated, but we still need to understand how they emerge and how to assess their effectiveness. However, the debates about the IFSD have focused mostly on reforms of international organizations, including the United Nations (UNEP, 2010; Bernstein and Brunné, 2011). Even though the discussions of the reforms and the multilateral regimes and laws are relevant, they are not sufficient to create all the necessary changes on the ground. This book covers many discussions on the IFSD from different angles, including the role of indigenous people and governance of the oceans.

The governance discussions have to include debates beyond the reform of international organizations and regimes. The work of Elinor Ostrom is an important landmark for understanding good governance of the environment and natural resources (Ostrom, 1990). Ostrom and others have challenged the previous assumptions of the "tragedy of the commons", which described the destruction of common managed resources (Hardin, 1968). Ostrom showed that there are many cases around the world of good governance of "common pool resources". Those resources are managed by local communities, which create the institutions (for example, rules and enforcement mechanisms) that lead to good governance in the use of the resources in the long term. Even though her theoretical work still has some limitations in terms of the assumed rationality of the social actors, she showed that common pool resources can be managed collectively and the tragedy of the commons can be avoided.

Ostrom also studied the challenges concerning the management of large-scale resources, such as marine ecosystems, and identified that "[i]nstitutional diversity may be as important as biological diversity for our long-term survival" (Ostrom et al., 1999). However, there is little understanding of this diversity of institutions and how they lead to patterns of good governance that cut across scales (local to global) in different environments. Thus, this book tries to understand the diversity of institutions that can lead to good governance of environmental resources at the different levels, connecting governance and socio-ecological outcomes and also connecting all the previous research that partners have undertaken at the local, governmental and global level in order to provide policy-relevant research outcomes to guide practices in the area.

About the book

This book analyses the green economy and environmental governance from different disciplines and through various lenses. Even though the debates on the green economy and IFSD are certainly relevant and can catalyse changes if they get enough political support, most of the debates on green growth and IFSD tend to be very general and are too conceptual or mono-disciplinary (for example, green growth is dominated by economists; IFSD is dominated by political scientists). The book presents the discussions on those themes from the angle of particular topics, where we make links between discussions and practice. This makes the book interesting for various fields of knowledge and practice and attractive to different groups of audience.

The United Nations University and the contributors to the book have developed a series of studies on the themes of the green economy and governance, trying to link global environmental changes and local impacts and policies. The UNU Institute of Advanced Studies (UNU-IAS) has a long history of work in the area of ecosystem governance, biodiversity and its relation with human well-being, particularly in the context of the Convention on Biological Diversity. Members of UNU-IAS played an important role in the Millennium Ecosystem Assessment (MA, 2005), because its former Director was co-chair of the MA. The book also brings the expertise of other institutes and programmes that have done research in this area: the UNU World Institute for Development Economics Research (UNU-WIDER), the UNU Institute for Natural Resources in Africa (UNU-INRA), the UNU International Institute for Global Health (UNU-IIGH) and the UNU Geothermal Training Programme (UNU-GTP).

Recent studies have continued the UNU work related to environmental governance and its links to human well-being. UNU-IAS and other partners have developed an indicator-based integrated assessment of ecosystem change and human well-being and tested it in several case studies in Indonesia, China and Japan (Suneetha et al., 2011). Contributors to the book have also conducted previous studies in global environmental governance, looking at the emergence of international environmental regimes (Kanie and Haas, 2004; Kanie et al., 2010), which will be particularly important for the discussions on IFSD. In addition, UNU-IAS has carried out research trying to link local action to global regimes, such as the work on cities and biodiversity, looking at the governance aspects related to the role of cities in the implementation of the Convention on Biological Diversity (Puppim de Oliveira et al., 2011) and the role of subnational governments in the implementation of global agreements (Puppim de Oliveira, 2009). This book brings together several research initiatives in different contexts and presents the research on governance and the green economy at the various levels (local, government and global). The aim is to bring lessons from different angles to move the agenda of the green economy and governance in diverse directions.

There is a need to consider how these topics play out in the discussions in different arenas, such as in education, or regionally, such as in Africa, and for particular themes, such as ocean governance, or for certain stakeholders, such as indigenous groups. Thus, the main objective of this book is to gather essays from authors across the UNU institutes in order to contribute to the debates on the two themes in several areas in which the programmes/institutes have accumulated expertise. Thematic discussions led by UNU experts will help us to understand the achievements and obstacles in relation to sustainability in the last 20 years so that we can propose new ideas and changes in economy and governance for a more sustainable future. Each group of experts will contribute to its specific area of expertise, having as a background the United Nations' crosscutting broad themes for Rio+20 and beyond.

In the next chapter, Sam Johnston of UNU-IAS discusses how the debates on sustainable development have evolved, particularly since Rio-92, and identifies the main achievements and challenges for moving the sustainable agenda forward. He examines advances in the implementation of sustainability, having as a background the global environmental processes that started in 1972 and looking at the best practices and lessons we can learn from more than 40 years of global environmental processes. Based on that, he identifies opportunities to scale those lessons and the necessary changes that could facilitate the achievement of a more sustainable future.

In Chapter 3, Manu V. Mathai and Govindan Parayil of UNU-IAS argue about the limitations of defining and applying the concepts of sustainable development and the green economy. Even though the two concepts are popular, they are both ambiguous and incomplete. The authors identify three attributes of sustainability that could clarify some of the ambiguities found in these concepts: having the economic system as a subsystem of the ecosystems, recognizing environmental injustices, and acknowledging the limitations and consequences of technological fixes to environmental problems.

In Chapter 4, the idea of the green economy is analysed critically. UNU-WIDER's Danielle Resnick, Finn Tarp and James Thurlow examine the concept of green growth to see if it is possible for general economic development objectives, such as job creation and poverty alleviation, to go hand in hand with "green" or environmental goals. Using the cases of Mozambique, South Africa and Malawi, they argue that the concept of green growth, and the reforms needed to achieve it, demands policy reforms similar to other reforms that require short-term adjustment costs in order to achieve long-term gains. They conclude that green growth strategies can lead to fierce opposition from some parts of society, including the poor.

Chapter 5 presents a discussion of the green economy in the context of education, particularly its role in changing patterns of consumption and production. The team of authors (Zinaida Fadeeva, Abel Barasa

Atiti, Unnikrishnan Payyappallimana, Aurea Tanaka, Mario Tabucanon, Sachiko Yasuda and Kazuhiko Takemoto), part of the UNU-IAS programme on Education for Sustainable Development (ESD), explain that *Agenda 21*, published in 1992, had already warned about the unsustainable trends in consumption and production, particularly in more developed countries. In the 20 years since, the situation has become worse. The authors argue that ESD has a critical role in moving society steadily to a more sustainable path regarding production and consumption. This would be achieved by transformative learning processes aligned to increasing awareness and advocacy that could lead to increased resource-use efficiency in different societies.

Chapter 6 then examines how the concept of the green economy plays out in the particular context of sociocultural landscapes. The team in the UNU-IAS's *Satoyama* Initiative (Kaoru Ichikawa, Robert Blasiak and Aya Takatsuki) analyses the diversity of sustainable production systems involved in the initiative. Those systems promote diverse linkages between humans and nature that can lead to environmental conservation. The concept of the green economy could be a framework for reinforcing the strategies aimed at sustaining ecosystems and the activities of people in such landscapes.

In the following chapter, the green economy and governance are examined in a regional perspective for Africa by Timothy Afful-Koomson from UNU-INRA in Ghana. He analyses the governance challenges that African countries face if they want to benefit from the green economy. He looks at the information provided by several national reports submitted to the United Nations by national coordinating institutions for sustainable development. He concludes that African nations are in a privileged position to benefit from the follow-up of the discussions in Rio+20 on the green economy, but they need to improve governance institutions in order to introduce more participation and representative voices into the processes.

Chapter 8 examines the issue of energy, which is key to moving society onto a more sustainable path. Ingvar B. Fridleifsson from UNU-GTP discusses how geothermal energy can provide a large part of the energy needs for development. One-third of the global population does not have access to modern energy services, which are fundamental to improve their living conditions and raise them out of poverty. Geothermal energy is available in many parts of the world and could provide clean affordable energy sources for the poor. However, several technical and institutional challenges need to be overcome to tap the potential of geothermal energy.

Chapter 9, by M. S. Suneetha of UNU-IAS and Alexandros Gasparatos of the Biodiversity Institute of the University of Oxford, examines ways to boost the green economy by local communities that manage and are dependent on biological resources, particularly in places with high biological diversity. There is an implementation gap in global environmental policies as a result of the limited involvement of local stakeholders who would be affected the most by and, theoretically, benefit most from those policies. However, trade tends to concentrate the benefits from biological resources in those who trade final products and services and much less in the primary producers and those responsible for managing the biological resources. For the green economy to work, we need to design mechanisms both nationally and internationally that could make a more equal distribution of the benefits from resources conservation.

Chapter 10 looks at the traditional discussion on international environmental governance but with a different analysis. The author, Norichika Kanie of UNU-IAS, examines the main problems of and alternatives to the current sustainable development institutional framework. Using the World Café workshop, a format of discussions where small groups rotate to address the same discussion points, he presents an analysis of the reforms that may be needed to make international processes more efficient, legitimate and effective in providing solutions to pressing global problems.

Chapter 11 analyses the governance challenges of the deep and open oceans beyond the limits of national jurisdiction. Marjo Vierros and Anne McDonald of UNU-IAS and Salvatore Arico of UNESCO argue that the principle of the "freedom of the sea" that prevails in the governance of ocean areas beyond national jurisdiction is leading to unsustainable use and an inequitable distribution of the benefits from marine resources. Oceans are the least protected ecosystems on the planet. One of the reasons is the lack of knowledge about their rich biodiversity, despite oceans accounting for the largest surface area. The authors believe that a better understanding of the richness of the oceans could boost governance and make oceans a real global commons, instead of almost an open access resource as they are now. The modern tools used for the conservation of coastal areas could also improve the management of conservation in the oceans.

Chapter 12 analyses the role of indigenous peoples in global environmental governance. Kirsty Galloway McLean, Sam Johnston and Ameyali Ramos Castillo of UNU-IAS look at how international processes have evolved in relation to the participation of indigenous people, who have brought important interests and knowledge to those processes. Local indigenous communities make direct links between environmental assets and human well-being, because many of them have depended on nearby ecosystems for their livelihood for many generations and have developed specific knowledge about keeping those ecosystems in good health. In this chapter, the authors examine the benefits and challenges of an effective engagement of indigenous groups in global environmental debates, particularly in the case of climate change.

In Chapter 13, Jamal Hisham Hashim of UNU-IIGH and Zailina Hashim of Universiti Putra Malaysia look at the governance of global environmental health. Environmental problems have severe impacts on health, including global problems such as climate change and biodiversity loss. A more effective institutional framework for sustainable development could have direct positive impacts on health. The chapter discusses how the governance of environmental health needs to be changed to adapt to the pressure of global environmental problems.

Chapter 14 is about the concept of the green economy in cities. The authors (Jose A. Puppim de Oliveira, Aki Suwa, Osman Balaban, Christopher N. H. Doll, Ping Jiang, Magali Dreyfus, Raquel Moreno-Peñaranda, Puspita Dirgahayani and Erin Kennedy), from the Sustainable Urban Futures team at UNU-IAS, argue that urbanization offers opportunities for greening the economy, because cities can offer economies of scale, knowledge and resources to move the economy to a more sustainable path. Moreover, the idea of greening the economy in cities includes decisions taken in cities that have far-reaching impacts. Thus, understanding the economic functions of and in cities, such as urban development, transportation, consumption and production, and knowledge generation, as well as ecosystem services, can provide important lessons for designing a more sustainable economy that affects the city within and beyond its boundaries.

Based on the analyses and the discussions in all the chapters of the book, we can identify the main points for understanding why and how progress has been achieved in certain areas and what the obstacles are to progressing the agenda of the green economy and good environmental governance to achieve more sustainable development.

Note

1. See at ⟨http://en.wikipedia.org/wiki/File:Smoke_of_chimneys_is_the_breath_of_Soviet_Russia.jpg⟩.

REFERENCES

Bernstein, S. and J. Brunné (2011) *Options for Broader Reform of the Institutional Framework for Sustainable Development (IFSD): Structural, Legal, and Financial Aspects. Report prepared for the Secretariat of the United Nations*

Conference on Sustainable Development (Rio+20). UNECA. Available at ⟨http://www.uneca.org/eca_programmes/sdd/events/Rio20/cfssd7/IFSD%20FIVE%20OPTIONS%20REPORT_31Oct11.pdf⟩ (accessed 10 January 2012).
Carson, R. (1962) *Silent Spring*. Boston: Houghton Mifflin.
Constanza, R. (1991) *Ecological Economics, the Science and Management of Sustainability*. New York: Columbia University Press.
Hardin, G. (1968) "The Tragedy of the Commons", *Science*, 162: 1243–1248.
Kallhauge, A. C., G. Sjöstedt and E. Corell (eds) (2005) *Global Challenges: Furthering the Multilateral Process for Sustainable Development*. London: Greenleaf Publishing.
Kanie, N. and P. M. Haas (eds) (2004) *Emerging Forces in Environmental Governance*. Tokyo: United Nations University Press.
Kanie, N., H. Nishimoto, Y. Hijioka and Y. Kameyama (2010) "Allocation and Architecture in Climate Governance beyond Kyoto: Lessons from Interdisciplinary Research on Target Setting", *International Environmental Agreements: Politics, Law and Economics*, 10(4): 299–315.
MA (Millennium Ecosystem Assessment) (2005) "Millennium Ecosystem Assessment", ⟨http://www.maweb.org/⟩ (accessed 9 February 2012).
Meadows, D. L., D. H. Meadows, J. Randers and W. W. Behrens (1972) *The Limits to Growth*. New York: Universe Books.
Newsweek (1972), "To Grow or Not to Grow", 13 March, pp. 102–103.
Oberthur, S. and O. S. Stokke (eds) (2011) *Managing Institutional Complexity: Regime Interplay and Global Environmental Change*. Cambridge, MA: MIT Press.
Ostrom, E. (1990) *Governing the Commons: The Evolution of Institutions for Collective Action*. Cambridge: Cambridge University Press.
Ostrom, E. et al. (1999) "Revisiting the Commons: Local Lessons, Global Challenges", *Science*, 284(5412): 278–282.
Pearce, D. W. (1976) *Environmental Economics*. London: Longman.
Puppim de Oliveira, J. A. (2009) "The Implementation of Climate Change Related Policies at the Subnational Level: An Analysis of Three Countries", *Habitat International*, 33(3): 253–259.
Puppim de Oliveira, J. A. (2011) "Why an Air Pollution Achiever Lags on Climate Policy? The Case of Local Policy Implementation in Mie, Japan", *Environment & Planning A*, 43(8): 1894–1909.
Puppim de Oliveira, J. A., O. Balaban, C. N. H. Doll, R. Moreno-Penaranda, A. Gasparatos, D. Iossifova and A. Suwa (2011) "Cities, Biodiversity and Governance: Perspectives and Governance Challenges for the Convention on Biological Diversity at the City Level", *Biological Conservation*, 144(5): 1302–1313.
Schmidheiny, S. (1992) *Changing Course: A Global Business Perspective on Development and the Environment*. Cambridge, MA: MIT Press.
Selin, H. (2010) *Global Governance of Hazardous Chemicals: Challenges of Multilevel Management*. Cambridge, MA: MIT Press.
Stern, N. (2006) *Stern Review on the Economics of Climate Change*. London: HM Treasury.

Suneetha, M. S., S. R. Joeni, K. Shoyama, X. Lu, S. Thapa and A. Braimoh (2011) "An Indicator-Based Integrated Assessment of Ecosystem Change and Human Wellbeing: Selected Case Studies from Indonesia, China and Japan", *Ecological Economics*, 70(11): 2124–2136.

TEEB (The Economics of Ecosystems and Biodiversity) (2010) "The Economics of Ecosystems and Biodiversity. Mainstreaming the Economics of Nature: A Synthesis of the Approach, Conclusions and Recommendations of TEEB". Available at ⟨http://www.teebweb.org/TEEBSynthesisReport/tabid/29410/Default.aspx⟩ (accessed 20 January 2012).

Tsuru, S. (1999) *The Political Economy of the Environment: The Case of Japan.* London: Athlone Press.

UNCED (United Nations Conference on Environment and Development) (1992) *Agenda 21: Earth Summit – The United Nations Programme of Action from Rio.* Available at ⟨http://www.un.org/esa/dsd/agenda21/res_agenda21_00.shtml⟩ (accessed 4 February 2012).

UNCTAD (United Nations Conference on Trade and Development) (2010) *The Green Economy: Trade and Sustainable Development Implications.* Geneva: UNCTAD.

UNDP (United Nations Development Programme) (1990) *Human Development Report.* New York: UNDP.

UNEP (United Nations Environment Programme) (2010) "Elaboration of Ideas for Broader Reform of International Environmental Governance", Second meeting of the Consultative Group of Ministers or High-level Representatives on International Environmental Governance, Helsinki, 21–23 November 2010, UNEP/CGIEG.2/2/2.

UNEP (United Nations Environment Programme) (2011) *Towards a Green Economy: Pathways to Sustainable Development and Poverty Eradication. A Synthesis for Policy Makers.* Nairobi: UNEP.

UNEP (United Nations Environment Programme) / UNCTAD (United Nations Commission on Trade and Development) (2010) *The Transition to a Green Economy: Benefits, Challenges and Risks from a Sustainable Development Perspective.* Geneva: UNEP/UNCTAD.

United Nations (2010a) *Progress to Date and Remaining Gaps in the Implementation of the Outcomes of the Major Summits in the Area of Sustainable Development, as Well as an Analysis of the Themes of the Conference.* Report of the Secretary-General, A/CONF.216/PC/2.

United Nations (2010b) *Objective and Themes of the United Nations Conference on Sustainable Development.* Report of the Secretary-General, A/CONF.216/PC/7.

UNSCD (United Nations Conference on Sustainable Development) (2011) "Conclusions of the Latin American and Caribbean Regional Meeting Preparatory to the United Nations Conference on Sustainable Development", 1 November. Available at ⟨http://www.uncsd2012.org/rio20/content/documents/600ECLAC.pdf⟩ (accessed 20 January 2012).

WCED (World Commission on Environment and Development) (1987) *Our Common Future.* New York, Oxford University Press.

Young, O. R. (ed.) (1999) *The Effectiveness of International Environmental Regimes: Causal Connections and Behavioral Mechanisms*. Cambridge, MA: MIT Press.

Young, O. R. (2010) *Institutional Dynamics: Emergent Patterns in International Environmental Governance*. Cambridge, MA: MIT Press.

Young, O. R., L. A. King and H. Schroeder (eds) (2008) *Institutions and Environmental Challenges: Principal Findings, Applications, and Research Frontiers*. Cambridge, MA: MIT Press.

2

Sustainable development: A changing paradigm

Sam Johnston

Introduction

The last couple of decades have seen dramatic changes and the rise of significant new challenges. The global financial crises, the significant shifts in political and economic power globalization, and the information and communications technology revolution have created opportunities and renewed receptivity for a new sustainable development paradigm. In this context, the Rio+20 Summit is timely and will be an opportunity for world leaders to motivate this change, chart a new course and reinvigorate the sustainable development paradigm.

The most important priority and intervention for the developing world is to tackle poverty. The experience of the past 40 years has demonstrated what a complex and difficult challenge this is, with poverty, inequity and environmental degradation being intertwined. The challenge over the next 40 years — or between now and 2050 — is to ensure that the expected tripling of economic growth also achieves social equity and reverses the unsustainable use of our natural resources.

There are no simple blueprints for addressing a challenge as vast and complex as this. Sustainable development at this level is a continuing process more than a plan or project. Tools, not rules, are what governments are calling for. Rio+20 represents an important opportunity to take stock of the actions undertaken at all levels to achieve sustainable development, to identify good practices that could be replicated and to reflect on innovative measures conducive to true change and a new development paradigm.

Green economy and good governance for sustainable development: Opportunities, promises and concerns, Puppim de Oliveira (ed.),
United Nations University Press, 2012, ISBN 978-92-808-1216-9

This chapter provides an overview of the concept of sustainable development and sets out some of the discussions that will be examined in the chapters that follow. Within this chapter the following are discussed:
- The current status of implementation of sustainable development, taking into account the international process that began in 1972
- The lessons learned and good practices at all levels
- The opportunities to promote these lessons and scale up the good practices
- The strategic interventions that need to be made to achieve sustainability

The current status of implementation of sustainable development

Key elements

The concept of sustainable development, with its economic, social and environmental pillars, is already well honed over more than 20 years through a series of international conferences and agreements. Important elaborations of sustainable development are contained in the 1972 Stockholm Declaration, the Brundtland Report (WCED, 1987), the 1992 Rio Declaration on Environment and Development and Agenda 21, the Millennium Development Goals (MDGs), the outcomes of the World Summit on Sustainable Development (WSSD) and the Rio Conventions. Sustainable development has been described in all these documents, and in other relevant documents, in different, albeit complementary, ways. There is an increasingly sophisticated debate about its definition, limits, usefulness and detail.

Even so the most widely used definition remains the one used in the 1987 Brundtland Report, which defined sustainable development as that which "meets the needs of the present without compromising the ability of future generations to meet their own needs" (WCED, 1987: 1). The 2002 WSSD formalized the notion that sustainable development needed to address the three pillars in a balanced way and that there was a "collective responsibility to advance and strengthen the interdependent and mutually reinforcing pillars of sustainable development – economic development, social development and environmental protection – at the local, national, regional and global levels" (WSSD, 2002).

The principles for promoting sustainable development are outlined in the Rio Declaration (United Nations, 1992), and include principles on good governance, subsidiarity, respect for the rule of law and secure property rights, intra- and inter-generational equity, reducing unsustainable consumption and internalizing externalities, respect for diversity, common but differentiated responsibility, special attention and support for the least able and most vulnerable, enfranchisement for all stakeholders, access to justice accountability and the precautionary principle.

Specific goals and targets to guide implementation of sustainable development are numerous and cover a wide range of issues. The most important set is the MDGs, which set out 21 targets and 60 indicators within the following goals:[1]
1. Eradicate extreme poverty and hunger
2. Achieve universal primary education
3. Promote gender equality and empower women
4. Reduce child mortality
5. Improve maternal health
6. Combat HIV/AIDS, malaria and other diseases
7. Ensure environmental sustainability
8. Develop a global partnership for development

The MDGs are the epitome or minimum set of core goals, targets and indicators that the international community developed and importantly agreed to through numerous conferences, processes and conventions.

As such the MDGs are a product of political and practical compromise and as a result are not complete or final. They are missing key elements for sustainable development, such as references to cultural diversity, minority rights, population stabilization or principles of good governance. The MDGs are also missing important targets and indicators, such as economic rights for women, action on chemical pollutants or renewable energy. Moreover, the internal structure of the MDGs is debatable. For example, it is not clear why four of the eight goals deal with human health.

Even though many of the targets are time bound – most referring to 2015 as the relevant date – the goals, the indicators and many of the targets are enduring. For example, eliminating extreme poverty and hunger are still important goals even for richer countries and will always be important goals for any government at any stage of development.

The institutional architecture for developing and implementing sustainable development, like the concept itself, is complex and multifaceted. As outlined in the General Assembly Resolution on Rio+20 (United Nations, 2010a), it centres on the General Assembly, the United Nations Economic and Social Council, the Commission on Sustainable Development and the member states, in particular their national sustainable development commissions. The UN Secretary-General, the United Nations Secretariat, the World Bank, the International Monetary Fund, the World Trade Organization, the United Nations Development Programme (UNDP), the World Health Organization, the United Nations

Environment Programme (UNEP) and the Multilateral Environmental Agreements are important parts of the international architecture as well.

This architecture has been developed in an ad hoc rather than a logical manner (UNEP, 2010a). It is beyond the scope of this chapter to propose major changes to the institutional architecture for a variety of reasons. One important reason is that a basic rule of institutional building is that "form should follow function" and, without consensus about what is required to reinvigorate sustainable development, there can be no clear idea about the role or function of the international architecture and whether and/or how it needs to be changed (UNEP, 2010a).

Implementation

Regardless of how well developed sustainable development may be intellectually, politically and legally, it will mean little if the idea is not implemented. A lack of implementation is the essential reason for concern amongst many governments and experts that the world is not developing sustainably and that the basic elements of the sustainable development paradigm are largely ignored by mainstream decision-making (United Nations, 2010b). The increasing pressures that humans are placing on the world's natural resources, manifested by decreasing fish stocks, anthropogenic climate change, nitrogen pollution, biodiversity loss and desertification, are cited as evidence to support these views (MA, 2005; UNEP, 2007).

Yet the record of implementation is more nuanced and from this record the important lessons emerge. Indeed, by most measures people are better off than they were 40 years ago, despite the near-universal lament that things were better before. Sustainable development has been used successfully in a wide range of ways and areas and it remains a relevant and vibrant paradigm. Recognizing and celebrating this success is an important – perhaps the most important – way of promoting change and development. The remainder of this section reflects on the experience of implementation, highlighting the most important successes of the past 40 years.

A dominant feature of development from 1972 has been the increase in economic wealth. In constant 2000 USD, global gross domestic product (GDP) increased from USD 13.4 trillion in 1972, to USD 25.1 trillion in 1992 to USD 40.2 trillion in 2009; in other words, a tripling since 1972 (World Bank, 2011a). In constant 2000 USD global, GDP per capita was USD 3,500 in 1972, USD 4,614 in 1992 and USD 6,007 in 2008 – an increase of 172 per cent since 1972. The World Bank and the International Monetary Fund estimate that global GDP will triple again over the next 40 years, increasing to USD 135 trillion by 2050 (World Bank, 2011a).

This economic growth has been widespread and its effects have been felt around the world, lifting many people out of poverty. As a result of this growth, the developing world as a whole remains on track to achieve the MDG poverty reduction target of halving – between 1990 and 2015 – the proportion of people whose income is less than USD 1 (United Nations, 2011).

Many developing countries have developed significantly since 1972. South Korea and many of the Southeast Asian economies led the way in the 1980s. China has developed dramatically since 1990. Over the last decade Brazil, Russia and India have also seen significant increases in development, forming with China the well-known BRIC. Now countries around the world are experiencing significant increases in living standards and improvements in their productivity, including most countries in Latin America, the Caribbean, Oceania, South Asia, Eastern Europe and North Africa. Sub-Saharan Africa has more lagging countries than any other region and has a higher percentage of extreme poverty than elsewhere, but even in this region a growing number of success stories are emerging, such as Botswana, Mali, Ghana, Mauritius and South Africa. Economic growth has picked up all across the continent in the past few years, with Kenya, Tanzania, Malawi and Zambia showing positive trends.

An important consequence of this economic growth is improved access to technologies, particularly information and communication technologies (ICTs). By the end of 2009, 67 per cent of the world's population had a mobile telephone and 25 per cent were using the Internet (United Nations, 2010c). Satellite maps are being used by local people in Australia, Kenya, Brazil, Botswana and South Africa to monitor the use of their ecosystems, enforce their land rights, develop human and technology capacities to support sustainable economic development and to promote biodiversity conservation and regional stability. Donors are accepting applications by video from semiliterate or illiterate communities.

Even from an economic perspective, growth has not been equitable, with many countries not properly benefiting and the gap between rich and poor within many, perhaps most, countries growing as well, causing social upheaval. That there remain 1.2 billion people who live in extreme poverty is the starkest indictment of the failings of the economic growth (World Bank, 2011a).

Importantly, this economic growth has not been socially balanced. Understanding what is socially balanced growth is a complex matter and will vary from society to society. The most important elaboration of its basic elements are contained within the 8 goals, 21 targets and 60 indicators of the MDGs. Goals such as universal education, decent employment, good health and shelter, and gender equality are, in the view of the

General Assembly and its member states, the cornerstones of the social pillar of sustainable development.

In September 2010, a High-Level Plenary Meeting of the General Assembly reviewed progress towards the MDGs. This meeting concluded that "developing countries have made significant efforts towards achieving the Millennium Development Goals". They have also had major successes in realizing some of the targets of the MDGS, particularly in "combating extreme poverty, improving school enrolment and child health, reducing child deaths, expanding access to clean water, improving prevention of mother-to-child transmission of HIV, expanding access to HIV/AIDS prevention, treatment and care, and controlling malaria, tuberculosis and neglected tropical diseases" (United Nations, 2010d).

The meeting acknowledged that "much more needs to be done in achieving the Millennium Development Goals as progress has been uneven among regions and between and within countries. Hunger and malnutrition rose again from 2007 through 2009, partially reversing previous gains. There has been slow progress in reaching full and productive employment and decent work for all, advancing gender equality and the empowerment of women, achieving environmental sustainability and providing basic sanitation, and new HIV infections still outpace the number of people starting treatment." Grave concern over the slow progress being made on reducing maternal mortality and improving maternal and reproductive health was also recorded (United Nations, 2010d).

The General Assembly concluded the following to be the most important lessons of the MDG experience:
- National ownership and leadership are indispensable in the development process
- National efforts need to be supported by an enabling international environment
- Good governance and the rule of law are essential for sustained, inclusive and equitable economic growth, sustainable development and the eradication of poverty and hunger
- Gender equality and the eradication of poverty are essential to economic and social development

An important message of the MDG experience is that the goals have offered a concrete vision and measurable targets to aspire and work towards, even if the record of achievement is mixed. They have mobilized action at all levels and have become an important focus for the international community. Providing this focus has allowed greater cooperation and a more efficient use of resources (United Nations, 2010c). The reaffirmation by the General Assembly of the validity of the MDGs and the relatively successful experience of their implementation since 2000 means they will remain an important focus for the international community after 2015.

However, economic growth has not been environmentally balanced (United Nations, 2010a). Climate change, declining water resources, degrading ecosystems and loss of biodiversity are undermining efforts in developing countries to develop economically (United Nations, 2010a). Perhaps more importantly, though, an increasing number of reports on the state of the environment, such as the Fourth Assessment Report of the Intergovernmental Panel on Climate Change (IPCC, 2007) and the third edition of the *Global Biodiversity Outlook* (CBD, 2010a), point out that we are closer to a number of irreversible environmental tipping points such as the collapse of the Greenland ice sheet, the turning off of the Gulf Stream and ocean acidification. Passing such tipping points would catastrophically reduce the ability of ecosystems to provide goods and services to humankind. The poor would suffer most immediately and most disproportionately, because they tend to be directly dependent on the environment and its resources for their livelihoods.

Even so, there are some important successes and more emerging ones. Tropical deforestation, a major problem in 1972, is finally beginning to slow at the global level (UNEP, 2007). Global pollution problems such as ozone-depleting substances (ODS) and organic pollutants are being tackled (UNEP, 2007). The global protected area estate grew from 4 per cent of the terrestrial surface in 1972 to 13 per cent in 2010 (UNEP, 2007). Concern about biodiversity loss is rising up the political agenda. Climate change has matured from an environmental problem into a genuine developmental problem. Certification schemes such as those run by the International Organization for Standardization, the Marine Stewardship Council, numerous coffee certification schemes and the Forest Stewardship Council have provided the consumer with the choice to use sustainably produced products and allowed them to promote sustainable development. The knowledge and the role of local and indigenous communities in addressing the issues within this pillar are increasingly being recognized.

Perhaps the best example of sustainable development at the international level is the move to post-ODS technologies. These efforts centre on the Montreal Protocol on Substances that Deplete the Ozone Layer (UNEP, 2010b).

Vital to the success of the Montreal Protocol was the Multilateral Fund, which provided financial assistance to developing parties (UNEP, 2010b). Contributions to the Fund come from developed countries. Unlike many other funds, the Multilateral Fund has had sufficient resources to assist developing countries to properly address the economic and social costs, as well as the technical and environmental costs, of phasing out

ODS. To date it has provided USD 2.5 billon to nearly 6,000 activities in over 140 developing countries (UNEP, 2010b).

Another critical element was the support and involvement of the private sector. Essential to this engagement was an alignment between the public and the private sectors. Both wanted to eliminate ODS, albeit for different reasons: the public sector to protect the ozone layer and address the potential health impacts of the ozone hole; the private sector to phase out the old ODS-reliant technologies and introduce new post-ODS technologies (UNEP, 2010b).

An important factor in the success of the Montreal Protocol was its early application of the concept of common but differentiated responsibilities. Special provisions for developing countries include the provision of financial and technical assistance and granting these countries a 10–15-year "grace period" for compliance with the control provisions applicable to developed countries. With developed countries showing leadership and building trust, developing countries were willing to follow (UNEP, 2010b).

Another important factor was that the Montreal Protocol had strong mechanisms for bringing science into policy-making. Scientific, Environmental Effects, and Technology and Economic Assessment Panels produce comprehensive and policy-relevant reports at least every four years to enable parties to adjust and amend control measures and to make informed decisions. These reports are recognized to be the most authoritative assessments in the arena of ozone layer protection and provide a clear scientific basis for action (UNEP, 2010b). A much overlooked factor was that the Montreal Protocol evolved a robust and supportive reporting and compliance procedure, which developed trust between the parties (UNEP, 2010b).

Broadening participation in international affairs has been a prominent characteristic of the past 40 years. This reflects the diminishing role of governments and the increasing role of the private sector, civil society groups and local communities. The benefits include more effective and efficient development, and increased transparency, diversity and resilience. An important attraction of the green economy is that it will directly engage the private sector and consumers, thereby broadening participation in sustainable development (UNEP, 2011).

An key aspect of this broadening participation has been the engagement of local and indigenous communities, which is considered in more detail in Chapter 12. Many local projects effectively balance the social, economic and environmental pillars. They connect the dots between climate change, food security, livelihoods and biodiversity. One reason they connect the dots is that for poor local communities there is a direct and immediate relationship between the health of ecosystems and economic opportunities, food security, health and the reduction of risks. For example, many local projects facilitate small-scale agriculture through better soil management and harvesting techniques and through improved markets and connections, which directly affect local food security and diet. Projects often develop local infrastructure, such as water and sanitation systems, schools and health clinics, which directly support education and health goals. Often the extra income is used to pay school fees. Many local projects centre on women. As a result, local actors in many areas are more dynamic, innovative and progressive than actors at the national or international level. Leadership at the international and the national levels often emerges from such "grassroots" activities.

Local actors also demonstrate the complexity of the challenges to sustainable development and of their solutions. The success of the Green Revolution and the power behind the Washington Consensus mean that global processes are susceptible to the big idea, the "silver bullet". The core challenges facing most countries are, however, complex and require many parallel actions, something that is very evident at the local level.

A critical question at the international level is how to link the ad hoc nature of these activities to global goals and needs. In particular, the issue is how to stop free-riding, whereby some countries derive an unfair advantage from the sacrifices of others (United Nations, 2010a).

Since 1992 there has emerged a more systematic approach to supporting these local-scale projects by the international community and donors. Programmes where international donors establish an international mechanism to directly support small local-scale projects have been an important success for sustainable development. Under these programmes, which offer financing and technical assistance, communities identify their own development priorities, hire assistance, manage project funds and manage and sustain the project. Many donors now have such programmes. The Small Grants Programme of the Global Environment Facility (GEF) was one of the leading initiatives in this regard. Many others have followed, including the Community-Driven Development Programme of the World Bank, the Community Based Adaptation of the United Nations Framework Convention on Climate Change (UNFCCC) and the Equator Initiative of the UNDP.

Despite their increasing popularity, local-scale projects are still a minor part of many organizations' work. Their success and potential warrant a scaling-up of support for these projects and programmes.

Key lessons

Sustainable development is well developed politically and legally, but implementation remains patchy and elusive, especially in relation to balancing the three pillars. As a result, governments are not looking for more rules but instead want the tools to implement sustainable development.

It is evident from the many successful examples of sustainable development that it is possible to achieve sustainable development in a wide range of circumstances. The diversity of these experiences also points to the difficulty in predicting where this spirit and ingenuity will emerge and provide the lessons worth learning, experiences worth scaling up and the path to take to promote sustainable development. This is especially true at the international level. Modern challenges are complex and do not have "silver bullet" answers, but require many varied actions often over long periods of time. One size will not fit all. Sustainable development solutions need to be adapted to the specific circumstances of each society.

Nevertheless, there are fundamental factors shaping our world and universal ideas evident in all of these success stories. Such ideas form the basis of any principle and of a reinvigorated, revalidated, re-energized concept of sustainable development. They include the following:
- The political and legal elements of sustainable development are well developed but are not implemented well enough.
- Economic growth will remain the dominant goal of the international community over the next 40 years.
- Economic growth needs to be more equitable and less damaging to the environment if it is to be sustainable.
- Challenges to development also create opportunities.
- The technologies, financial resources and incentives exist to address these challenges.
- National ownership and leadership are indispensable in the development process.
- Good governance and the rule of law are essential for sustained, inclusive and equitable economic growth, sustainable development and the eradication of poverty and hunger.
- Education, individual rights and equality for women are shown to be effective simple, affordable, practical steps that provide the basis for achieving not only the social pillars of sustainable development but also the economic and environmental pillars.
- Transparent targets are a powerful tool for mobilizing action, outreach and measuring progress. The MDGs will form the basis of many of the core goals after 2015 and provide the foundation for a new way of measuring development.
- The strong narrative of sustainable development needs to be communicated to inspire further action and to spread knowledge and lessons. Success will inspire more rapid and profound change than fear.

- New technologies, such as ICTs, are already having a great impact on poverty, efficiency, productivity and environment and they may well have a greater impact over the next few decades.
- Effective mechanisms for incorporating science into the policy-making processes are critical. Although the IPCC has become an effective process for climate change, other issues lack effective mechanisms.
- Bottom up approaches are more effective.
- Leadership is a vital ingredient for changing development pathways.

Opportunities and scaling up

Dramatic changes and significant new challenges have taken place over the last couple of decades. Events like the global financial crises, the enormous shifts in political and economic power, globalization and the ICT revolution have created opportunities and renewed receptivity for a new sustainable development paradigm. The Rio+20 Summit provides an opportunity for world leaders to motivate this change, chart a new course and reinvigorate the sustainable development paradigm.

This will require a degree of pragmatism. Vested interests and challenges will not disappear simply because of a good idea. Identifying the strategic issues that provide the most effective and influential interventions will be critical to implementing and mainstreaming sustainable development and reinvigorating the paradigm.

The green economy is one such prominent intervention that is being widely debated, discussed and considered in the lead-up to Rio+20. Proponents see it as a way to balance the three pillars of sustainable development (UNEP, 2011). Market tools are one aspect of this green economy that has received a lot of attention. For example, Working Group III of the Secretary-General's High-Level Panel on Global Sustainability addresses how market tools and investments could support sustainable development. It concluded that achieving the transformation towards a more sustainable future in the longer term would require significant shifts in terms of regulation, markets, consumer preferences and true cost pricing for sustainable development. Quantum change is needed to meet the objective that business and markets become an integral part of delivering sustainability, rapidly and at scale. Key proposals for reform include a global framework for public procurement for sustainability, profound capital market reform to advance sustainability-aligned investment activity, the development of fiduciary standards for extending corporate accountability, and the reduction of subsidies that harm the environment and slow poverty alleviation (GSP, 2011).

The most important priority and intervention for the developing world is tackling poverty. The experience of the past 40 years has demonstrated what a complex and difficult challenge this is, with poverty, inequity and environmental degradation being intertwined. The work of the Global Sustainability Panel shows that education, vocational training and employment are important means for the transformation towards an environmentally conscious and resilient society. Other options being considered by the Global Sustainability Panel include paying for ecosystem services, ensuring universal access to renewable energy, defining codes of conduct for investments related to natural resources, connecting social protection systems to sustainability outcomes, and pushing for agricultural research and development (R&D) that includes sustainable practices.

Building on this work for Rio+20, particularly the work of the Global Sustainability Panel, requires strategic interventions, which are highlighted in the next section.

Strategic interventions to help achieve sustainability

Climate change

Climate change is predominantly seen as a challenge. Yet the issue also creates significant opportunities for developing countries and for promoting sustainable development. Global energy demand is estimated to grow 55 per cent by 2030, which will require an investment of USD 22 trillion in energy infrastructure, with about half of that in developing countries (IEA, 2011). Significant mitigation opportunities for developing countries are being created, such as potentially USD 60 billion per year for halting deforestation (World Bank, 2011b). Under the UNFCCC, developed countries are considering how to provide financial assistance for adaptation costs in the developing world, which are expected to be USD 250 billion per year by 2020. Global investment in renewable energy projects will rise from USD 195 billion in 2010 to USD 395 billion in 2020 and to USD 460 billion by 2030, according to Bloomberg New Energy Finance analysis. Over the next 20 years this growth will require nearly USD 7 trillion of new capital (Bloomberg, 2011). Many of the world leaders in clean energy technologies are in the developing world.

At a more philosophical level, many parties to the UNFCCC have argued that atmospheric resources are the common wealth of human beings and should be shared equally, and that cumulative per capita emissions can be used as an indicator of equity. Scientists estimate that society will have emitted 600 gigatons of carbon (GtC) between the years 1800 and 2050. Equal per capita shares of that overall budget means developed countries would be entitled to 125 GtC and developing countries 475 GtC. By 2008, developed countries emitted 240 GtC, or 115 GtC more than their entitlement of 125 GtC. Even with a global cut in greenhouse gas (GHG) emissions, 50 per cent of developed countries will emit another 85 GtC between 2009 and 2050, bringing their total to 325 GtC between 1800 and 2050. Developing countries have argued in the UNFCCC negotiations that this is 200 GtC more than their equitable share and that the developed world needs to recognize this and compensate the developing world in some way for it. Even though these arguments are unlikely to be more than a negotiating position, they illustrate the inequity in the current use of the atmosphere and give an indication of the scale of the response if the atmosphere is to be used equitably in the future.

An important focus for promoting these opportunities will be the various funds being established by the UNFCCC to provide finance to developing country parties, in particular the Green Climate Fund, established at the sixteenth session of the Conference of Parties (COP16) of the UNFCCC. Ensuring that these developing countries are financed adequately and in a timely manner will be critical to the long-term future of the UNFCCC regime and of sustainable development in general.

Reducing Emissions from Deforestation and Forest Degradation

Despite the apparent conflicts about the nature of the next phase of the UNFCCC and the apparent lack of progress, there are a number of important issues where the three pillars are being balanced and progress is being made. Typically this is where, in addition to governments, the private sector and local and indigenous communities have been actively involved, because the economic and social incentives are more evident and more available. An important area where this is happening is REDD+ (Reducing Emissions from Deforestation and Forest Degradation).

REDD+ will remain an important mechanism for tackling climate change whatever the nature of the next phase of the UNFCCC. Forest loss and degradation contribute 17 per cent of global GHG emissions (IPCC, 2007). The IPCC in its last assessment (2007) noted that reducing deforestation is the mitigation option with the largest and most immediate carbon stock impact in the short term (IPCC, 2007). McKinsey & Co. calculated that it would cost around €9 per tonne of carbon dioxide equivalent (tCO_2e) to generate credits from reducing forest loss and degradation, whereas carbon capture and storage on power plants would cost around €40–55 per tCO_2e, and switching to solar would cost around €37 per tCO_2e (Nauclér and Enkvist, 2009). McKinsey & Co. also estimated that reducing forest loss and degradation could contribute as much as 6 Gt CO_2e per year, or one-third of the required total global reduction in GHG emissions by 2020 (Nauclér and Enkvist, 2009).

Consequently over USD 5 billion has been committed to REDD projects in the past few years and promises of many more billions have been made. As of September 2011, the main global REDD database had 480 registered projects in 36 countries, amounting to USD 3.35 billion (REDD+, n.d.).

The scale of the REDD experiment, combined with the lack of relevant experience with REDD+ projects, has meant that projects have encountered considerable problems and delays. A recent global review of REDD+ projects (Simula, 2011) noted that they face many challenges, including: criteria for sustainable forest management; monitoring, reporting and verification of GHG emissions; local tenure arrangements – permanence and baseline issues that can be effectively addressed only if local communities are able to participate properly in the REDD+ projects. It also found that, despite widespread recognition that local ownership is key to REDD+ success, the scope and intensity of participation by local communities have not always been adequate and often there is a lack of clarity about their role in implementation (Simula, 2011).

A strategically important aspect of REDD+ is that it represents the first significant international example of a payments for ecosystem services (PES) scheme – that is, payment for the carbon stored in forests in developing countries. In order to ensure that global needs for ecosystem services are secured on a long-term basis, payments need to be forthcoming to cover the economic and social costs of providing these environmental services. Securing public sources of funding has been slow. The GEF, the most obvious mechanism for delivering international PES, has, despite five replenishments, never been financed to fulfil this role; rather it has been restricted to a more experimental, catalytic role. The promised USD 30 billion in start-up funding for the Copenhagen Accord and USD 100 billion in long-term adaptation funding, which is in part a PES scheme, has not resulted in new or additional funds. International efforts over the last 40 years are littered with such unfulfilled promises.

The REDD+ projects are applying the PES concept in a real-world situation, at scale, for the first time. The lessons from this endeavour will pave the way for the PES to be applied to other global ecosystem services, such as water, food security and biodiversity.

Technology development

Another important example of how climate change has acted as an entry point for sustainable development is technology development. Technology has driven and defined most of the significant changes in human history. The Stone Age, the Bronze Age, the Iron Age, the industrial revolution and the ICT revolution were all created by advances in technology. Technology has the potential to address the climate change issues and transform how energy is produced as well.

Ensuring that developing countries have access to new energy technologies and can participate equally in the new energy markets is a vital element to a sustainable strategy for reducing GHG emissions and a strategic priority for developing the overall economies of developing countries. Facilitating access to new technologies to developing parties has been an integral part of the UNFCCC. The Bali Action Plan reaffirmed its centrality and COP15 called for the establishment of a mechanism to accelerate technology development and transfer.

The role of intellectual property rights (IPRs) in the transfer of climate change technologies has emerged as a particularly contentious issue in the past two years. UNEP, the European Patent Office (EPO) and the International Centre for Trade and Sustainable Development (ICTSD) recently undertook a database search of patents in clean energy technologies (CETs). They found that patenting rates for CETs have increased 20 per cent per annum since 1997 and have outpaced the traditional energy sources of fossil fuels and nuclear energy (UNEP–EPO–ICTSD, 2011). Patenting in the selected CET fields is currently dominated by countries of the Organisation for Economic Co-operation and Development (OECD). A number of developing countries are, however, showing specialization in individual sectors, providing further competition in the field and potentially changing the future of the CET patent landscape. For example, India features within the top five countries for solar photovoltaics, Brazil and Mexico share the top two positions in hydro/marine and China is one of the most important for CETs (UNEP–EPO–ICTSD, 2011).

Patent searches reveal only the supply side of technology development. Only a small percentage of patents cover processes that are commercialized, and an even smaller number become important, widespread or profitable technologies. Of more importance for developing countries is the demand side of technology, or accessing, using and developing technologies for local use. A consistent concern for many developing countries in the UNFCCC, as well as many other international discussions, is that patents and other IPRs block access to useful technologies. In a few important examples this has been the case. A more significant problem for many developing countries is the capacity to develop technologies suitable for their own circumstances and needs and to access technologies that are publically available. The emergence of Korea, China, Brazil and India as world-class leaders in various CETs has been driven not by facilitated access to IPRs and international assistance but by their own investment in R&D capacities.

Many developing countries have started to prioritize their R&D investments. China, a prominent example in recent years, doubled its gross domestic expenditure on R&D (GERD) to 1.54 per cent in 2011 compared with 2002 (UNESCO, 2011). China expects to invest USD 154 billion in R&D in 2011, second only to the United States in USD terms. GERD has remained stable in Brazil (0.9 per cent) and India (0.9 per cent), but this has resulted in significant new finds for R&D owing to strong economic growth. In 2011, India will spend USD 36 billion (eighth-highest in the world) and Brazil will spend USD 19 billion (eleventh-highest in the world). Mexico, South Africa, Argentina, Hungary, Romania, Turkey and Poland have billion dollar commitments to R&D and rank inside the top 40 countries in the world. Only China has a GERD above 1 per cent, whereas the OECD average is nearly 2 per cent, led by Japan (3.3 per cent), Sweden (3.3 per cent), Finland (3.1 per cent), South Korea (3.0 per cent) and the United States (2.7 per cent) (UNESCO, 2011). Additionally the ICT revolution has meant cheap and easy access to R&D and technologies.

The global financial crisis has also shifted relative investments in that it has had larger effects on R&D budgets in many developed countries than in the developing world and resulted in the speeding-up of developing countries' competitive edge. As the UNESCO *Science Report 2010* concluded:

> [A]chieving knowledge-intensive growth ... depends increasingly on a better use of knowledge, whatever the level of development, whatever its form and whatever its origin: new product and process technologies developed domestically, or the re-use and novel combination of knowledge developed elsewhere. This applies to manufacturing, agriculture and services in both the public and private sectors.... Knowledge accumulation and knowledge diffusion are able to take place at a faster pace, involving a growing number of new entrants and providing a threat to established institutions and positions. (UNESCO, 2010: 2, 26)

Governments nevertheless need to create the right policy environment to encourage people into R&D and private investment. For most developing countries, this will mean a significant long-term commitment of public funds to the tertiary education system, as in Korea, China, India and Brazil.

MDGs

As noted before, the MDGs have provided an important focus for the entire international community and will offer important goals for the international community beyond 2015. As such they will represent an important entry point for mainstreaming sustainable development. The reaffirmation by the General Assembly of the validity of the MDGs and the progress that has been made over the past decade mean that MDGs will remain an important focus for the international community after 2015.

The MDGs are based on goals, targets and indicators that the international community has agreed to through numerous conferences, processes and conventions. Moreover, they were initially developed on the basis of available statistics as much as fundamentally important goals. They are therefore a product of political and practical compromise and are not necessarily complete or final.

Important gaps in the MDGs are goals or targets for good governance, cultural rights and economic equality for women. Also, a number of targets have been overtaken by developments since 2000 and need revision. One example is Target 7.B: "Reduce biodiversity loss, achieving, by 2010, a significant reduction in the rate of loss". This is now obsolete in light of the new Strategic Plan for Biodiversity 2011–2020 of the Convention on Biological Diversity adopted at COP10 (Target 6.B also refers to 2010). The two new biodiversity targets that the MDGs will have to take into account are (CBD, 2010b):

> A world ... where ... "[b]y 2050, biodiversity is valued, conserved, restored and wisely used, maintaining ecosystem services, sustaining a healthy planet and delivering benefits essential for all people".

> "[T]o halt the loss of biodiversity in order to ensure that by 2020 ecosystems are resilient and continue to provide essential services."

Indicator 7.3 on ozone-depleting substances is also obsolete: owing to the success of the Montreal Protocol, ODS were banned as of 2010.

There is a need for a target on the use of chemicals to reflect the developments of the Rotterdam Convention on Prior Informed Consent and the Stockholm Convention on Persistent Organic Pollutants and the WSSD target to "use and produce chemicals by 2020 in ways that do not harm human health and the environment". Targets or indicators addressing renewable energy, organic pollutants, nitrogen pollution, desertification and/or degraded ecosystems, the elimination of illegal fishing (as called for in WSSD) and illegal trade in endangered species (i.e. the Convention on International Trade in Endangered Species), as well as planning indicators such as Nationally Appropriate Mitigation Action, National Biodiversity Strategies and Action Plans and REDD+, could all be included to reflect developments in international law and policy over the past decade.

The collection of data and statistics has significantly improved in the last decade and means that many of the indicators could be refined and improved. Examples include Indicator 7.1 on forest coverage, which could be refined to include natural habitat coverage or could be replaced by natural habitat coverage, and Target 7.6, which could be refined to be more accurate or meaningful so that it refers to eco-regions, biomes, ecosystems, Alliance for Zero Extinction sites or Important Bird Areas, rather than just protected marine and terrestrial areas.

The internal structure or logic of the MDGs could also be improved. For example, it is not clear why health issues have three separate goals (MDG4 – reduce child mortality; MDG5 – improve maternal health; and MDG6 – combat HIV/AIDS, malaria and other diseases). In addition, the relationship between several of the targets and their indicators is not clear or understandable. For example, the relationship between Targets 7.A and 7.B and their indicators needs revision. Moreover, many of the targets for MDG8 have a tangential relationship to the overall goal.

Conclusion

The challenge over the coming decades is to ensure that economic growth is equitable, rolls back unsustainable use of our natural resources and restores those ecosystems that have been degraded. There are no silver bullets or simple strategies for addressing a challenge as vast and complex as sustainable development. Sustainable development is a continuing iterative process, more than a plan or a project. Consequently, governments need more tools to implement sustainable development, not more rules.

The experience of the last 40 years and our existing needs for the future raise profound questions, including:
- Is the sustainable development model still relevant and should we focus on mechanisms for implementing it? Or should we change the paradigm for the coming decades?
- What is currently missing that needs to be put in place to ensure that the needs of current and future generations are met?
- What lessons can be drawn from recent experience to frame a new international "deal" for sustainable development at Rio+20?
- Who are the key parties and what are their respective interests and constraints?
- What is needed to ensure that development over the next 40 years is equitable?
- What are the key lessons from the record?

This chapter illustrates that there are a number of other key strategic contributions that can be made, including developing REDD+, promoting technology development and transfer, and revising the MDGs.

A recurring theme throughout this chapter is that we face a world of increasing complexity. One consequence of this complexity is that it is not possible for a piece such as this to develop a comprehensive list of contributions or even questions. Indeed, all that can realistically be hoped for is to highlight some key issues and trends, to provide a platform for an informed exchange of ideas, to prompt discussions and to point discussions towards identifying the right questions to ask.

Note

1. For information on the MDGs, see ⟨http://www.un.org/millenniumgoals/⟩ (accessed 1 February 2012).

REFERENCES

Bloomberg (2011) *Global Renewable Energy Market Outlook*. Available at ⟨http://bnef.com/free-publications/white-papers/⟩ (accessed 30 January 2012).

CBD (Convention on Biological Diversity) (2010a) *Global Biodiversity Outlook 3*. Montreal: Secretariat of the Convention on Biological Diversity.

CBD (Convention on Biological Diversity) (2010b) "COP 10 Decision X/2: Strategic Plan for Biodiversity 2011-2020", ⟨http://www.cbd.int/decision/cop/?id=12268⟩ (accessed 23 January 2012).

GSP (Secretary-General's High Level Panel on Global Sustainability) (2011) "Input to the High-level Panel on Global Sustainability: The Use of Market Tools and Investments to Support Sustainable Development". Available at ⟨http://www.un.org/wcm/content/site/climatechange/pages/gsp⟩ (accessed 23 January 2012).

IEA (International Energy Association) (2011) *World Energy Outlook 2011*. London: IEA. Available at ⟨http://www.iea.org/w/bookshop/add.aspx?id=428⟩ (accessed 23 January 2012).

IPCC (International Panel on Climate Change) (2007) *Fourth Assessment Report: Climate Change 2007*. Cambridge: Cambridge University Press.

MA (Millennium Ecosystem Assessment) (2005) "Millennium Ecosystem Assessment", ⟨http://www.maweb.org/⟩ (accessed 23 January 2012).

Nauclér, T. and P.-A. Enkvist (2009) *Pathways to a Low-Carbon Economy: Version 2 of the Global Greenhouse Gas Abatement Cost Curve*. McKinsey & Company.

REDD+ (n.d.) "Voluntary REDD+ Database". Available at ⟨http://reddplusdatabase.org/⟩ (accessed 23 January 2012).

Simula, M. (2011) *Analysis of REDD+ Financing Gaps and Overlaps*. REDD+ Partnership.

UNEP (United Nations Environment Programme) (2007) *Global Environment Outlook 4 (GEO 4): Environment for Development*. Available at ⟨http://www.unep.org/geo/geo4.asp⟩ (accessed 23 January 2012).

UNEP (United Nations Environment Programme) (2010a) "Elaboration of Ideas for Broader Reform of International Environmental Governance", Second meeting of the Consultative Group of Ministers or High-level Representatives on International Environmental Governance, Helsinki, 21–23 November, UNEP/CGIEG.2/2/2.

UNEP (United Nations Environment Programme) (2010b) "Brief Primer on the Montreal Protocol". Available at ⟨http://ozone.unep.org/Publications/MP_Brief_Primer_on_MP-E.pdf⟩ (accessed 23 January 2012).

UNEP (United Nations Environment Programme) (2011) *Towards a Green Economy: Pathways to Sustainable Development and Poverty Eradication. A Synthesis for Policy Makers*. Nairobi: UNEP.

UNEP–EPO–ICTSD (United Nations Environment Programme – European Patent Office – International Centre for Trade and Sustainable Development) (2011) *Patents and Clean Energy: Bridging the Gap between Evidence and Policy*. Available at ⟨http://ictsd.org/i/publications/85887/⟩ (accessed 23 January 2012).

UNESCO (United Nations Educational, Scientific and Cultural Organization) (2010) *UNESCO Science Report 2010*. SC-2010/WS/2. Available at ⟨http://www.unesco.org/new/en/natural-sciences/science-technology/prospective-studies/unesco-science-report/unesco-science-report-2010/⟩ (accessed 23 January 2012).

UNESCO (United Nations Educational, Scientific and Cultural Organization) (2011) *Global Education Digest 2011*. Montreal: UNESCO Institute for Statistics. Available at ⟨http://www.uis.unesco.org/Library/Documents/global_education_digest_2011_en.pdf⟩ (accessed 23 January 2012).

United Nations (1992) *Report of the United Nations Conference on Environment and Development (Rio de Janeiro, 3–14 June 1992). Annex I: Rio Declaration on Environment and Development*. A/CONF.151/26 (Vol. I).

United Nations (2010a) "Implementation of Agenda 21, the Programme for the Further Implementation of Agenda 21 and the outcomes of the World Summit on Sustainable Development", Resolution Adopted by the General Assembly, A/RES/64/236, 31 March.

United Nations (2010b) *Progress to Date and Remaining Gaps in the Implementation of the Outcomes of the Major Summits in the Area of Sustainable Development, as Well as an Analysis of the Themes of the Conference*. Report of the Secretary-General, 1 April, A/CONF.216/PC/2.

United Nations (2010c) *The Millennium Development Goals Report 2010*. New York: United Nations. Available at ⟨http://www.un.org/millenniumgoals/pdf/MDG%20Report%202010%20En%20r15%20-low%20res%2020100615%20-.pdf⟩ (accessed 23 January 2012).

United Nations (2010d) "Keeping the Promise: United to Achieve the Millennium Development Goals", Resolution Adopted by the General Assembly, A/RES/65/1, 19 October.

United Nations (2011) *The Millennium Development Goals Report 2011*. New York: United Nations. Available at ⟨http://www.un.org/millenniumgoals/11_MDG%20Report_EN.pdf⟩ (accessed 23 January 2012).

WCED (World Commission on Environment and Development) (1987) *Our Common Future*. New York: Oxford University Press.

World Bank (2011a) *The World Development Report 2011: Conflict, Security, and Development*. Washington, DC: World Bank. Available at ⟨http://wdr2011.worldbank.org/⟩ (accessed 23 January 2012).

World Bank (2011b) "State and Trends of the Carbon Market Report 2011". Available at ⟨http://web.worldbank.org/WBSITE/EXTERNAL/TOPICS/ENVIRONMENT/EXTCARBONFINANCE/0,,contentMDK:22928492~pagePK:64168445~piPK:64168309~theSitePK:4125853,00.html⟩ (accessed 23 January 2012).

WSSD (World Summit on Sustainable Development) (2002) *Johannesburg Declaration on Sustainable Development*, adopted at the 17th plenary meeting of the World Summit on Sustainable Development, 4 September 2002, Johannesburg, A/CONF.199/20, Paragraph 5. Available at ⟨http://www.un-documents.net/jburgdec.htm⟩ (accessed 23 January 2012).

Part I
Green economy

3
Towards equity and sustainability in the "green economy"

Manu V. Mathai and Govindan Parayil

Introduction

In his remarks to the General Assembly on the priorities of the United Nations for 2011, the UN Secretary-General identified eight areas for the year. The first was "advancing action on inclusive and sustainable development" (Ban, 2011a). The second strategic priority, addressing climate change, is closely related to advancing inclusive sustainable development. Remarks like these are high points in the evolution of contemporary public discourse on environmental and economic issues being pursued around the world. The twentieth anniversary of the landmark 1992 United Nations Conference on Environment and Development (Earth Summit) in Rio de Janeiro contributes further to the attention given to these matters.

Sustainable development has been a long-cherished, but elusive goal. In recent years, marked by various crises, many influential thinkers and policy-makers have called for a dramatic rethink of humanity's economic arrangements. Various stakeholders, including the UN Secretary-General, have sought to articulate how the goals of "inclusive *and* sustainable development" can be advanced. The basic premises of these articulations converge invariably on an absolute and non-negotiable commitment to enhancing economic growth, with a focus on technological innovation as a means to improve efficiencies across the energy and material use spectrum. As the Secretary-General noted in his Preface to the *World Economic and Social Survey 2011*: "Rather than viewing growth and

---

Green economy and good governance for sustainable development: Opportunities, promises and concerns, Puppim de Oliveira (ed.),
United Nations University Press, 2012, ISBN 978-92-808-1216-9

sustainability as competing goals on a collision course, we must see them as complementary and mutually supportive imperatives. This becomes possible when we embrace a low-carbon, resource-efficient, pro-poor economic model" (Ban, 2011b: iii).

It is this low-carbon, resource-efficient, pro-poor economic model that is being offered as the basis for the so-called "green economy". Such vocabulary, however, is not new, and it echoes the prescriptions of *Our Common Future*, the report of the World Commission on Environment and Development (WCED, 1987), for pursuing sustainable development; but the green economy has nevertheless gained popularity as an easy point of reference. It seems to have captured the attention of policy-makers and the wider policy community, and appears to offer a more tangible set of prescriptions than the ideal of sustainable development. The phrase itself is not very new (Pearce et al., 1989) but its recent use appears to have furnished an evocative rallying point a generation after the Rio Earth Summit. Endorsements of the green economy are forthcoming from various quarters. The Asia-Pacific Youth Position Paper on Rio+20, for instance, states that the "Green Economy is the stair-case to achieve sustainable development" (Asia-Pacific Youth Forum, 2011).

Notwithstanding such endorsements, core assumptions of sustainable development, as outlined and popularized by *Our Common Future*, remain questionable (for example, Byrne et al., 2006; Daly, 1990; Martinez-Alier et al., 2010) and the green economy runs the risk of being a "stair-case" to the same inconsistencies that have rendered sustainable development a largely failed ideal in practice. Thus, there remains room for clarifying the central ideas being discussed and asking if they can bring about an arrangement of the relationship between nature and society that is both ecologically viable and socially equitable (or development that is "sustainable" and "inclusive", to borrow the Secretary-General's words).

The evolution of sustainable development

The modern environmental movement is nearly two generations old.[1] The articulation and subsequent popularization of the idea of sustainable development, which culminated in *Our Common Future*, was a negotiated settlement, a victory of sorts, won by the first generation of the environmental movement. For its time and the discourse that preceded it, its ideal and the political consensus it was able to garner were remarkable.

By the middle of the twentieth century, the evolution of industrial society had culminated in articulations of modernization theory such as those by W. W. Rostow (1960). In Rostow's influential version, offered in the throes of the Cold War, all countries in the world were arranged along the same economic development trajectory and differed merely in where they were located on this path. Countries, he suggested, starting off as "traditional societies", progressed through the stages of "pre-take-off", "take-off" and "maturity" before becoming "high-mass consumption" societies. Putting aside the amusing metaphor of an airplane ride, this view has deep ramifications for sustainability.

Offered explicitly as "a non-communist manifesto" (the book's subtitle), Rostow (1960) emphasized, and further entrenched, an evolving political consensus around the idea that the solution to humankind's conflicts was an abundance of consumption and asserted that the market economy (fighting in the stark dualism of his day) offered the most efficient path to this cornucopia. In essence, peace and stability in the social and political realm depended on material plenty. Calling it the "politics of productivity", Charles Maier (1977) offers an insightful analysis of the evolution of this position in the domestic policy of the United States and eventually in US foreign policy, a not insignificant development given the country's post-war global reach and influence. Indeed, the ideas elaborated by Rostow are echoed around the world; for instance seen here almost verbatim in India's seventh Five-Year Plan (1985–1990), which "intended to provide by the year 2000 plentiful mass consumption goods at reasonable prices" (Planning Commission of India, 1985).

Although visible because of his academic and policy affiliations, W. W. Rostow was not the originator of these ideas. The underlying relationship between an expanding economy and social stability that he uses goes back to the founders of classical economics. Making observations on the then nascent modern industrial society, Adam Smith ventured to speculate:

> It deserves to be remarked, perhaps, that it is in the progressive state, when the society is advancing to the further acquisition, rather than when it has acquired its full complement of riches, that the condition of the laboring poor, of the great body of the people, seems to be the happiest and the most comfortable. It is hard in the stationary, and miserable in the declining state. The progressive state is in reality the cheerful and hearty state to all the different orders of society. The stationary state is dull; the declining melancholy. (Smith, [1776] 1994: 93)

By the middle of the twentieth century this pursuit of the "progressive state" had reached a watershed in its evolution. Its social and ecological impacts became increasingly visible and untenable to a generation coming of age. It was during this time that contemporary environmentalism was born in various hues around the world. Informed by diverse ideologies, cultural predispositions and life circumstances, environmentalism was voiced in a variety of shades: "agrarianism", "wilderness thinking", "eco-Marxists", "neo-Malthusians", "technological optimists", "scientific industrialism", "environmentalism of the poor" and "environmental justice" (Byrne et al., 2002; Guha, 2006; Guha and Martinez-Alier, 1997; Martinez-Alier, 2002). Despite this multitude of perspectives, the institutionalization of environmentalism from the 1970s onwards relied on a sliver of this variety. Two broad approaches came to dominate, of which sustainable development was the second.

Initial reaction to the now iconic events of that period of churning, such as the London smog, the Love Canal disaster, the Minamata disease and *Silent Spring*, sought to rein in the business corporations that despoiled nature and undermined human health. In this telling of the story, governments responded to public pressure through newly instituted environmental bureaucracies that sought to manage the problem by regulating businesses. The adversarial relationship that followed marked a phase of grudging adaptation by businesses to environmental regulations (Huber, 2000). These efforts were under pressure from two other problems. First, regulating end-of-pipe effluents did not involve systemic measures and did little to address the causes upstream. Thus, regulation in this form was accused of simply problem displacement across time and space. The second, perhaps more damaging, allegation was that regulation dampened economic growth. The costs imposed in, say, installing air filters or effluent treatment plants to adhere to pollution limits were allegedly undermining the economic viability of businesses (Weale, 1998).

The ideal of sustainable development emerged from this adversarial milieu. Given this background, perhaps its most notable success was the political consensus that it was able to garner. It succeeded in recasting the previous adversarial relationship between business and environment and also in calming the purported conflict between development and environment voiced by developing countries.[2] It did this by adopting the conventional economic growth and development discourse but also acknowledging that the status quo was not ecologically viable. In addition, it enshrined the principles of inter- and intra-generational equity. All people, those living today and those yet to live in the future, had the same right to pursue economic development to "meet their needs". Or, as the now famous definition presented in *Our Common Future* proclaimed, "development that meets the needs of the present without sacrificing the ability of future generations to meet their own needs" (WCED, 1987: 8).

The report said perhaps everything that everyone wanted it to say. It tackled head-on the consumption vs. population debate and recognized the obvious, that a free ride for either side was untenable. The report recognized underlying structural problems in the organization of the global economy. It acknowledged that many aspects of the economic development status quo were "leaving increasing numbers of people poor and vulnerable, while at the same time degrading the environment" (WCED, 1987: 4). For instance, addressing the debt crisis, this report recognized that countries are often forced to deplete their ecological wealth by trading in primary commodities to service their loans and not necessarily to invest in their human capital. In these and similar instances, *Our Common Future* was a remarkable document and marked an important destination at that time.

A crucial aspect of the report is how it dealt with the issue of biophysical limits. How did it reconcile its support of the conventional growth-based development discourse with its acknowledgement that the status quo was not ecologically viable? It is clear that achieving such reconciliation was crucial to the political consensus it was able to build, which was important, but it did so on the basis of a tenuous relationship. We argue that the compromises required for holding the two positions together are at the core of its failure in practice, and remain its chief weakness. Ultimately this issue is the non-negotiable core of the environmental problem, and how the report chose to deal with it reveals the interests and forces it had to accommodate to win consensus and the questionable assumptions and lacunas that remain.

The report is explicit in its recognition of biophysical finitude: "ultimate limits there are, and sustainability requires that long before these are reached, the world must ensure equitable access to the constrained resource and reorient technological efforts to relieve the pressure" (WCED, 1987: 45). Further, the report flags sustainability as ultimately a normative question: "perceived needs ... are socially and culturally determined, and sustainable development requires the promotion of values that encourage consumption standards that are within the bounds of the ecologically possible and to which all can reasonably aspire" (WCED, 1987: 44).

Although such crucial spaces were opened, they have found few takers. Instead, the policy proposals and practical strategies that are offered have largely emphasized technological optimism and scientific management in the pursuit of efficiency. The report's calls for sufficiency, an undeniable requirement in any finite system, tended to be caricaturized as an individualistic, altruistic "strategy of self-limitation" (Huber, 2000) and set aside as being impractical. This even while advocates of "efficiency" and "industrial ecology" explicitly acknowledge that "certain limitations, thus sufficiency, must finally be respected" (Huber, 2000). The question of how sufficiency can be approached creatively, practically *and institutionally* is the important tone of green that was missing from prescriptions for sustainable development and appears to be absent from today's green economy proposals as well.

The reissued green economy

As already noted, the green economy, despite the recent attention it has attracted, has long been a strategy for pursuing sustainable development. Nevertheless, at this juncture, at its reissuing of sorts, it is useful to look at how it is being defined and proposed. The policy world is rife with efforts to define or at least demarcate the meaning of a green economy and to offer prescriptions for its realization (for example, UNDESA, 2011; UNEP, 2011). The starting point for these efforts is often disillusionment with the status quo, especially after the great recession of 2007–2008 emanating from the industrialized countries. After noting that something is deeply awry with prevailing economic arrangements, and focusing on the financial system and anaemic growth in OECD countries, these reports highlight entrenched environmental degradation, persistent deprivation and destitution, and gross inequality. The green economy is presented as an ideal response, a solution even, to these multiple problems.

The green economy is understood as an economic arrangement that enhances "growth, social progress and environmental stewardship". These are recognized as complementary goals and it is asserted that the "trade-offs among them en route to their realization can be overcome" (UNDESA, 2011: v). Beyond such an assertion, however, it is not apparent how these trade-offs are to be overcome. The UNDESA (2011: vi) survey explicitly recognizes ecological limits and notes that the "objective of the green economy is to ensure that those limits are not crossed" (as an aside, it is important to clarify that humanity has *already* crossed those limits and is in the territory of using up the planet's stocks; see, for example, Global Footprint Network, 2011). To avert this situation and to change course, a technological revolution – "Great Green Technological Transformation" – is proposed. The primary goal of this technological overhaul will be to "become more efficient in the use of energy and other resources and minimize the generation of harmful pollutants" (UNDESA, 2011: vi). The survey acknowledges that efficiency improvements in energy and material use often result in greater overall throughput. Although it cautions about the need to protect against this trend, known widely as "Jevon's Paradox" or the "Rebound Effect", it does not reveal how the green economy will address this concern.

Another report, *Towards a Green Economy* (UNEP, 2011), approaches the problem with a slightly different emphasis. In its analysis, the multiple crises of today are the result of consistent gross misallocation of capital (over the past two decades). Thus, "property, fossil fuels and structured financial assets with embedded derivatives" received the lion's share of capital investment, whereas relatively little was invested in "renewable energy, energy efficiency, public transportation, sustainable agriculture ... etc." (UNEP, 2011: 14). This trend, the report reveals, has brought significant achievements in terms of physical, financial and even human capital but came at the cost of severely undermining "natural capital" (UNEP, 2011).

The responses proposed by UNEP (2011), which the green economy will embody, is a project for reorienting the system of economic incentives and disincentives in order to shift the allocation of capital from "brown industries" of the past to green industries of the future. The resulting green economy is envisaged as one in which "growth in income and employment should be driven by public and private investments that reduce carbon emissions and pollution, enhance energy and resource efficiency, and prevent the loss of biodiversity and ecosystem services" (UNEP, 2011: 16). The following efforts are identified as crucial to bring about this transition.

Incomplete or even non-existent valuation of natural capital and ecosystem services and the failure to count externalities of economic activity have long been recognized as lacunas in environmental and economic policy-making. Thus, the report urges that blind spots in the economic valuation of ecosystems and their attributes, which essentially render them invisible to economic decision-making, be removed. *The Economics of Ecosystems and Biodiversity* (TEEB, 2010) is an example of efforts to make ecosystem services and the imposition of externalities economically visible.[3] In addition, the UNEP report stresses the role of better information on the state of the environment and biodiversity. It suggests that more complete information on the status of ecosystems, along with better economic valuations, will lead to better decision-making that alleviates the prevailing misallocation of capital. Finally, the report stresses the need for a multidisciplinary approach to better monitor and understand changes that are under way and their consequences and to develop efforts to reverse the current unsustainable course (UNEP, 2011).

Overall, it appears that the green economy and efforts to move towards it emphasize the following key themes. An emphasis on economic growth and expansion is seen as the route to alleviate poverty, pursue equality and arrive at sustainability. The primacy of a "green technological revolution" to improve efficiencies and open up biophysical space for more growth is highlighted. To support this process, a range of measures, primarily related to better valuation and information and more appropriate (multidisciplinary) expertise, is proposed. These are expected to inform the policy process and aid in the design of more suitable institutional mechanisms.

There is much of value in these proposals, as far as they go. In a world where poverty and destitution plague the lives of billions of people, growing the overall pot of wealth appears, intuitively, to be the correct policy prescription. After all, proponents can point out that the *average* Indian or Chinese citizen is today considerably wealthier in terms of cash income than they were only a decade or two ago. Energy efficiency, for instance, is recognized as the cheapest form of energy. The ability of efficiency improvements to reduce resource or energy use per unit of gross domestic product has long been recognized. The highly successful energy service company business model is built on this recognition and uses well-established mechanisms to capture and monetize energy savings and use them as revenue streams to amortize initial investments in efficiency.

As the old adage goes, "you cannot manage what you cannot measure"; thus, more quantified information about the environment examined from multiple disciplinary perspectives is likely to furnish better understandings of reality and inform more effective management strategies. Having a better handle on the value of the ecosystem services lost by, say, the cycle of oil exploration and eventual combustion, would rationally be expected to produce policy measures that commensurately disincentivize these activities. At the same time, such valuations will incentivize energy options that avoid the imposition of such costs. Thus, considered as a whole, the package of measures that characterize the green economy can be thought to be the right prescription for these troubled times.

The missing shades of green

The green economy is a useful improvement on the status quo. Nevertheless, it has not addressed arguments that its proposals are premised on some assumptions that are flawed, perhaps fatally. The discourse has avoided fully engaging with the implications of the limits imposed by the quantum of energy and material throughput that the biosphere can sustain. Instead, it has preferred to unequivocally recognize that such limits exist (WCED, 1987; UNDESA, 2011) and assert that greater efficiencies across the economic system will ensure that biophysical limits are not breached. This reasoning reflects a rejection of (or at the least a reluctance to acknowledge) an elementary understanding of the difference between ratios and absolutes and its implications for scale in the ecological context.

Further, the discourse frames the question of limits in the future tense, whereas natural scientists have for long recognized that the human economy is now functioning beyond the material limits imposed by a biosphere amenable to life as we know it (Global Footprint Network, 2011; Metz et al., 2007; Vitousek et al., 1997). Thus, just as it becomes increasingly imperative that societies recognize the limitations of efficiency to offset the absolute scale of throughput and engage, conceptually and practically, with proposals for a "steady-state economy" (Daly, 1991) or "sustainable de-growth" (Martinez-Alier et al., 2010), the green economy discourse presses ahead oblivious of these urgent necessities for the present and future mediation of the relationship between nature and society.

This failure to acknowledge that, "in an absolute sense, modernization leads to supermaterialization rather than dematerialization" (York and Rosa, 2003: 282) remains a fundamental weakness of its proposals. Such silence, however, is expected from the green economy discourse, situated as it is within "ecological modernization theory" (Mol and Spaargaren, 2000), or at least a version of it, which valorizes efficiency and has logically become embedded in the liberal economic ideology. The problem with this approach to addressing the environmental problem is thus, ultimately, a function of the unresolved problem within liberal economic thinking.

The pursuit of justice or equality in society has, since the Enlightenment at least, been enshrined as a political ideal for the organization of society. Although the rhetoric has existed for a long time, it is relatively recently that practical strategies to realize that high ideal were applied. As recounted above in the quote from Adam Smith, it is the "progressive state" that is seen as enabling the well-being of "different orders of society" (Smith, [1776] 1994). What is being announced here is that equality in society is now seen less as a function of political arrangements arrived at to organize social and economic intercourse, and instead as the *managed* outcome of applying putatively apolitical modern science, technology and economic ideas to liberate individuals from the shackles of "stingy nature" or oppressive tradition (Byrne and Yun, 1999). Thus, in terms of a practical strategy in the face of the environmental crisis emanating from exceeding the planet's limits, efficiency is allegedly the only path that is available for redress, because "the stationary state is dull; the declining melancholy" (Smith, [1776] 1994). This perspective transmits a powerful legacy (whatever the doubts of this early voice articulating it) that we experience even today.

A prominent and influential illustration of this economic thinking in twentieth-century public policy was seen in the framing of US foreign policy after the Second World War. Masterfully characterized by Charles Maier (1977) as the "politics of productivity", the consensus forged on domestic economic policy in the United States (before it was exported) was built on the theme that the "coinage of politics – power and coercion – was minted only in the kingdom of necessity and would have no function in the realm of material abundance" (Maier, 1977: 613). The stated purpose of this approach, which apparently was validated during the decades of the post-war "gilded age", was to set aside the difficult questions of pursuing a more equitable social order through political and economic reform. As noted by Maier (1977: 607): "American blueprints for international monetary order, policy toward trade unions, and the intervention of occupation authorities in West Germany and Japan sought to transform political issues into problems of output, to adjourn class conflict for a consensus on growth." Thus, when the responsibility of delivering an equitable and peaceful world was wrested from politics and laid exclusively on the shoulders of "material abundance", efficiency, writ large, became the most legitimate policy strategy in the face of the environmental crisis.[4]

The second major lacuna, quite surprising for a project that is decidedly reliant on a great deal of technological innovation, is the absence of reflection on technology and its interrelationship with society and the environment. In the green economy discourse, technology is an inert mediator between nature and society. Despite widespread study and commentary on technology that recognizes its social and political ramifications, the green economy discourse assumes that responding to the environmental crisis is limited to retooling the technological infrastructure for greater efficiencies by policy-makers guided by rational experts.

That efficiency is a useful tool in the pursuit of sustainability is only a half-truth, and the half that is missing is profoundly important. Specifically, technology is also a social construct, imagined, designed and built to carry out the political and economic priorities of society. This is crucial because the underlying political and economic priorities could be ones that undermine the efficacy of reductions in throughput produced by efficiency. The growth imperative highlighted above is one such political economic priority; indeed, considerable empirical evidence highlights the Jevon's Paradox or the rebound effect whereby, despite efficiency-induced savings, the overall scale of energy and material throughput grows unsustainably (for example, Wilhite and Norgard, 2004). Thus, building a "green economy" on a retooling of infrastructure for efficiency improvements alone will remain a half-measure, with some gains to be had no doubt, but one that has been found to be counterproductive as well.

The third area of concern about the green economy discourse is its refusal to engage with remarkable insights into human development that have emerged in the past couple of decades. The fallacy of a non-negotiable commitment to economic growth and expansion as an end in itself has been outlined by various scholars (for example, Daly, 1989, 1996; Jackson, 2009; Rogoff, 2012; Sen, 1987, 1992, 1999) and is also recognized by many religious and secular traditions. For instance, in the intellectual realm, the human development and capability approach conceives of the purpose of economic organization as expanding the "freedom to do and to be as one values" (Sen, 1999).

> Focusing on human freedoms contrasts with narrower views of development, such as identifying development with the growth of gross national product, or with the rise in personal incomes, or with industrialization, or with technological advance, or with social modernization. (Sen, 1999: 3)

This insight has profound implications for addressing the environmental crisis, which ultimately results from exceeding the planet's boundaries. For starters, it helps untangle the Gordian Knot that has greatly hampered attempts to address the growth imperative of conventional development thinking (Jackson, 2009; Mathai, 2004). Although a deeply useful insight is offered, the challenge of operationalizing the ideas remains. The questions that have to be dealt with range from normative ones such as which "freedoms to do and to be" (Sen, 1992) are valuable, to practical policy ones about how to answer such questions and which architectures of technological infrastructure are conducive to addressing such questions democratically. There is clearly a great deal of work to be done, "but it should not be given up lightly. It may well offer the best prospect we have for a lasting prosperity" (Jackson, 2009: 36). In this context, refusing even to acknowledge such possibilities and to consider their implications is a critical failure of the green economy discourse.

A further touch of green that is missing from the green economy discourse is its inability to recognize and address the problem of (ecological) injustice. The green economy discourse fails to engage the question of equality at two levels. First, as discussed above, equality within this discourse is premised on the success of scientific and technological advances and management in producing an era of "material abundance". That over the past two centuries humanity has witnessed unprecedented economic growth and material abundance and yet is far from the "cheerful and hearty state to all the different orders of society" (Smith, [1776] 1994) is evidence that something is awry in this policy position. At the very least, we must recognize that a reduction in inequality in, say, the space of cash income has failed to become a reality.

Second, the green economy discourse fails to recognize a form of inequality – ecological injustice – induced by the growth ideology. Ecological injustice reflects the iniquitous impacts in modern society of the acquisition of energy and material resources and the disposal of their effluvia. Emerging from revelations of inequality along axes such as race, class and gender, ecological injustice now encompasses evidence of "environmental colonialism" and "ecological imperialism" (see Byrne et al., 2002). At its core, ecological injustice arises from the usurpation by the privileged of the ecological space that rightly belongs to the less privileged. The phenomenon of ecological refugees, for instance, is a result of degradation and the resultant loss of ecological services crucial to the livelihoods of those who now are forced to move. Although increasing efficiency helps limit the ecological space that is usurped per unit of output, the sum of the ecological space that is occupied is, necessarily, a product of throughput per unit of output and the total number of units. And, given that the liberal economic predisposition appears unable to address inequality without continuous economic expansion, the green economy discourse seems, perhaps unwittingly, bound to further ecological injustice.

Towards the right shade of green

As an exercise in evaluating the green economy discourse, which is a prescription for reorganizing our world, this chapter cannot merely be an examination of its ideas. In addition to engaging with those ideas, we must match the objectives of the protagonists of the green economy and propose strategies for social change that overcome its limitations.

The missing shade of green in the "green technological revolution" is the ability to imagine a green economy that fosters the societal dynamics required by a nature–society relationship that is unsustainable. What is needed is the valorization of sufficiency, which can complement efficiency. The green economy as it is presently envisaged does not engage normative questions and it conducts its business of shaping discourse and public policy in the monochromatic vocabulary of efficiency.[5] Thus, the pressing question is how are such alternative values, and the structures of political economy conducive to such values, to be enabled? To that end, some further reflection on the dynamic interrelationships between the realms of technology and society is helpful.

It is often asserted that developing countries and economies in transition can leapfrog to a green economy.

> Developing countries, especially low-income ones, with relatively low rates of electricity usage, may be able to "leapfrog" into electricity generation based on renewable forms of primary energy, for instance. The question is how to enable those countries to access, utilize and, above all, afford green technologies. (UNDESA, 2011: ix)

As seen in this quote, leapfrogging to a green economy is supposed to be evidenced through the adoption of renewable energy technologies. In addition, more efficient technologies, processes and protocols are also considered indicative of leapfrogging to a green economy. The concern to be recognized here is that this "leapfrogging" towards more efficiency or renewable energy content need not necessarily lead to equitable or sustainable outcomes. It is possible that the social and ecological gains from renewables or efficiency will be overwhelmed by a parallel advance of the conventional growth logic, its conventional technology infrastructure and the attendant relationships of production and consumption.

Consider the evolution of solar photovoltaic (PV) in relation to the broader energy sector. This relationship is marked by two notable trends. Solar PV capacity has grown remarkably in the last decade and is expected to continue to do so in the years ahead.[6] The problem arises when we consider how everything else (coal, oil, gas and nuclear) has fared and is expected to perform. The evidence so far and projections for the next two decades suggest that, in absolute numbers, the growth in demand for conventional sources (or the failure to reduce their demand) could overwhelm sustainability gains from renewable energy sources and energy efficiency improvements.[7] Despite the promise of technological leapfrogging, what appears lacking is a commensurate transformation of institutionalized political and economic values and norms towards sufficiency.

The second trend in the evolution of solar PV pertains to the abandonment of the promise of a "soft energy path" (Lovins, 1977), which renewables were supposed to be harbingers of (Glover, 2006). That path envisioned a decentralized solar energy infrastructure that was socially integrated and reflective of values and practices commensurate with an energy supply that is in practice infinite, dispersed and variable but less energy intensive than fossil fuels or nuclear power. The evolution of solar PV, although it started out with and still retains this distributed character, is being overwhelmed by the growth in centralized utility-scale solar plants,[8] which, much like large centralized fossil fuel and nuclear power infrastructures, are more representative of elite interests and lack the promise of deeper social reflexivity that a distributed and renewable energy infrastructure is inherently capable of. Thus, the green economy's faith in leapfrogging, which is blind to the institutionalized norms overseeing such transformations, could result in technological change that is of limited value for pursuing equity or sustainability.

Lessons from another illustration of slightly longer vintage are also relevant to the green economy discourse. Modern society's encounter with fossilized energy set in motion unprecedented social, political and economic dynamics. When the scope of the changes unleashed is assessed by their impact on the biosphere, this encounter and society's reaction to it are epoch making (Crutzen, 2002). Lewis Mumford cogently and eloquently captured the dynamism of this encounter, the norms that emerged and their technological legacy (1934: 157–158).

> Now, the sudden accession of capital in the form of these vast coal fields put mankind in a fever of exploitation: coal and iron were the pivots upon which the other functions of society revolved. The animus of mining affected the entire economic and social organism: this dominant mode of exploitation became the pattern for subordinate form of industry.... Mankind behaved like a drunken heir on a spree. And the damage to form and civilization through the prevalence of these new habits of disorderly exploitation and wasteful expenditure remained, whether or not the source of energy itself disappeared.

Two crucial attributes of the relationship between technology and society are evident here. First, they have a reciprocal influence on each other, wherein a portfolio of technical capabilities "put mankind in a fever of exploitation" and subsequently the "animus of mining affected the entire economic and social organism". Second, the very important phenomenon characterized as "technological momentum" (Hughes, 1994) meant that "the damage ... through the prevalence of these new habits of disorderly exploitation and wasteful expenditure remained, whether or not the source of energy itself disappeared". Whether we consider a specific instance, such as reducing dependence on oil or the considerable difficulties in figuring out a steady-state economic arrangement, the momentum of past choices is evident. It is crucial to recognize that "momentum" does not mean "determinism"; instead it captures the weight of the challenge at hand to change course.

The pervasive understandings of technology as socially "neutral" (its impacts are largely accidental and therefore society is limited to tinkering) and of society as being "technologically determined" (its social impacts are inherent to its design) are half-truths that reduce technology to a spectator sport controlled only by the key players in the field. Technology policy often proceeds in this manner (consider, for example, civilian nuclear power, genetically modified crops or, more generally, the preference for socially isolated technology innovation in both the public and private sectors). Yet the evolution of technology choices ought to be anything but a spectator sport. Technology can be on a par with, or perhaps on occasion more influential than, politics and legislation in shaping society and in certain forms holds the potential to be liberating and emancipatory. Thus it is imperative for society to have commensurate influence on technology's evolution and form.

Andrew Feenberg (1991: 3) has insightfully suggested that "the design of technology is thus an ontological decision fraught with political consequences. The exclusion of the vast majority from participation in this decision is the underlying cause of many of our problems." Capturing the essence of his argument with great clarity, he notes that "technology is not a thing in the ordinary sense of the term, but an ambivalent process of development suspended between different possibilities". This characterization of technology–society relations, read along with the missing shades of green discussed above, offers ideas for moving the green economy discourse towards an improved shade of green.

Fundamentally, then, what appears to be needed is the ability of society to influence the evolution of technology and to impart to it values of sufficiency visible in alternative conceptions and practices of human development and economic organization. The notion of *Development as Freedom* (Sen, 1999), as considered above, and discussion of the *Subsistence Perspective* (Mies and Bennholdt-Thomsen, 1999) are illustrations of concepts and practices that are not wedded to the ideology of continuous economic growth. Similar ideas and practices are available, even in contexts where their presence is not immediately apparent (for example, Grigsby, 2004). Conversations and social deliberations about norms and practices, such as these, are constantly ongoing and evolving in response to the challenges faced by conventional development thinking. The crucial need is for emerging green technology infrastructure to be able to reflect these changes from the status quo. Thus an essential requirement for green technology innovation is that it be "democratic" as opposed to being "authoritarian" (Mumford, 1964).

In addition to addressing the question of scale, discussed above, a democratic technological infrastructure is also crucial for pursuing equality. The conventional economic development paradigm that emerged from the industrial revolution has followed a peculiar process of wealth production and accumulation by tying it to the availability of concentrated finance capital and then seeking to redistribute wealth. This idea, that a rising tide will raise all boats, has now proven itself to be less than adequate, even before its environmental consequences are considered. In this context, democratic technologies allow for a reorganization of the relationships between production and consumption. Specifically, they have the potential to shift agency from concentrated capital to community. Stated differently, democratic technologies strive not so much to redistribute wealth but rather to distribute the means to generate wealth, a theme that was central to Mahatma Gandhi's critique of modern technology (Gandhi, [1909] 1938). This vision was eloquently captured by the extraordinarily gifted scholar D. D. Kosambi, in the context of debates over the choice of civilian nuclear power in India. In a lecture to the Rotary Club of Pune in 1960, Kosambi reasoned:

> The most important advantage of solar energy would be decentralisation. To electrify India with a complete national grid would be difficult, considering our

peculiar distribution of hydropower and thermal resources. With solar energy, you can supply power locally, with or without a grid. Solar power would be the best available source of energy for dispersed small industry and local use in India. If you really mean to have socialism in any form, without the stifling effects of bureaucracy and heavy initial investment, there is no other source so efficient. (Kosambi, 1960)

Adam Smith, writing in the wretched context of forced enclosures and proletarianization that marked capitalist industrialization (not that the later socialist version was very different in practice), speculated that the expanding economy is the "happy state" for all social classes. Going forward, an unconditionally expanding economy is no longer feasible, not least because of the biosphere's energy and material limits and the inequality it presupposes. Thus, as the world economy seeks to realign its material infrastructure, the focus must move to designs that can internalize and engage valuations of sufficiency and shift power over production and consumption arrangements from capital to community. A truly green economy, in short, must be a revolution of democracy and equality reflected in the technology infrastructure that society shapes, and that, in turn, shapes society.

Towards the right shade of green: Illustrative directions and priorities

Where the green economy discourse ought to have embraced sufficiency along with efficiency, it notes merely that "doing so would complicate efforts to meet the development objective and would thus not be in the interest of developing countries" (UNDESA, 2011: vi). In the process, the green economy discourse has unhelpfully restricted its frame of reference to the mundane task of "innovating" more efficient technologies and recommending policy tools to facilitate the adoption of these technologies. It has left out a hugely creative realm of imagining, innovating and adopting efficient, but also socially enmeshed, technological means that might foster sufficiency within ecological limits and equity. Yet such creative realms do exist in our world. Let us consider two trends from two different settings, one a less industrialized country (India) and the other a highly industrialized or even post-industrial country (the United States).

India

India is home to remarkable civil society initiatives directed at equity and sustainability in arrangements for economic development. We focus on two such initiatives: the Solar Electric Light Company (SELCO), a commercial business enterprise concentrating on "underserved households and livelihoods";[9] and the Honey Bee Network, which connects, documents and helps further develop the innovations of grassroots innovators (Gupta, 2009).

Since 1995, when it was founded, SELCO has won more than 100,000 customers through products such as customized solar-powered home appliances, including lighting, transistors and mobile phone chargers, water heating systems and biomass cooking stoves. In addition to being a commercial venture that has succeeded in selling sustainable technologies to "poor people", a distinctive feature of the SELCO business model is customization, which amounts to user-driven innovation in the development, configuration and installation of its products. SELCO has built on this strength by starting "SELCO Labs" in 2009 to further this commitment to the development of innovative products. These are intentionally located in a rural setting, which "gives the lab access to local customers, instant feedback, and visibility into available resources and constraints" (SELCO, 2012).

The Honey Bee Network (HBN) is a strategy to gather, document, share and commercialize grassroots innovation and traditional knowledge. In this process, priority is accorded to recognizing the innovators and sharing profits with them. Through partnerships with India's Council of Scientific and Industrial Research and the Indian Council of Medical Research, the HBN seeks to blend "informal and formal science, technology and innovation systems" (Gupta, 2009: 141). The network now has a database of over 100,000 innovations, many of which have gone on to be developed further, with acknowledgement and credit accorded to the innovator (Gupta, 2009).

The experiences of SELCO and the HBN offer two useful lessons for the green economy discourse. First, local, user-generated or user-informed innovations are widespread and practical, and help transform people from hapless recipients of development to active agents in shaping their livelihoods and well-being. Policies and institutions that complement this dispersed freedom to innovate foster the liberating and emancipatory potential of technology. The present green economy strategy of unevenly focusing on the diffusion of technology from the developed to the developing world fails to grasp the possibilities of grassroots innovation. Additionally, a basic issue such as the relevance of a technology package being diffused to the social milieu receiving it is a perennial challenge that is yet to be adequately resolved.

Second, an important theme underlying the work of SELCO and the HBN is social inclusion. By building on users' innovations or closely interfacing with users (as seen in the SELCO business model, as well as in

SELCO Labs) during the innovation process, these strategies are better suited to addressing problems of relevance, ownership and agency. By agency we mean the ability to actively direct the development of technology in accordance with evolving normative priorities germane to the context. This space for socially reflexive technology innovation is not a trivial accomplishment. It has the additional benefit of being a practical strategy for distributing the ability to *generate* wealth, rather than the conventional approach to development that emphasizes the redistribution of wealth. As noted by Anil Gupta (2009: 138), "one cannot first create exclusion and then hope to do something for those who are left out. The strategies for inclusive development will have to build upon the resources in which poor people are especially rich: their knowledge, values, social networks, and institutions."

Last but not least, these models of innovation are not premised on "material abundance" as an end in itself, but rather emerge from user-defined objectives and values such as frugality, multi-functionality and simultaneity (Gupta, 2009).

The United States

Moving to the context of a highly industrialized or post-industrial context, we highlight an alternative policy direction for the green economy discourse from the state of Delaware in the United States. In 2007, the state devised an innovative policy strategy and passed accompanying legislation to create the first Sustainable Energy Utility (SEU). The SEU exemplifies practical legislative and policy measures for arranging energy–society relations that emphasize reducing energy use and promoting user-sited generation of electricity using renewable energy technologies (SEU, 2007).

> The most important feature of the SEU is that energy users can build a relationship with a single organization whose direct interest is to help residents and businesses *use less energy and generate their own energy cleanly*. Directly put, the SEU becomes the point-of-contact for efficiency and self-generation in the same way that conventional utilities are the point-of-contact for energy supply. (SEU, 2007: 2, emphasis in the original)

The existing green energy discourse builds from the centralized and socially isolated energy infrastructure and seeks merely to substitute oxidizing hydrocarbon molecules with sunlight, blowing wind or flowing water. Although this is a worthwhile strategy as far as it goes, it remains wedded to the unsustainable notion of an abundance of energy and materials as a precondition for human society. The SEU, with its institutional viability contingent on using less energy, is an effort pointing to a more sustainable and equitable direction.

The SEU as a generalized template builds on two concepts, "commonwealth economy" and "community trust" (Byrne et al., 2009), to revive inclusive institutions, norms and practices and shift the political economy of energy towards sustainability and equity.

The idea behind the commonwealth economy is to organize a commons-based or shared institutional structure to capture and pool savings that accrue from using less energy. Such savings, whose viability is endorsed by the widespread energy service company business model, are now effectively a new revenue stream that is used to amortize investments in energy efficiency or user-located renewable energy. It is called a commonwealth because it is a community formed by residences and businesses that join it voluntarily and agree to an arrangement of shared savings. In this manner, capital accumulates within a commons arrangement dedicated to investments for reducing energy use and promoting user-located renewable energy technologies. It is not burdened by the inherent conflict of interest afflicting traditional utilities when they seek to reduce energy consumption.

As noted, the commonwealth economy is built on shared savings. This arrangement has to by necessity be based on trusting that all voluntary members of the community will adhere to principles of efficiency, conservation, renewable energy and sharing. Failure by the community to valorize these principles will result, in the long term, in the failure to build a commonwealth and eventually in the demise of the SEU. For this purpose, community trust is crucial to facilitate dialogue and deliberation through which the "meaning and practice of sustainability and equity are created and continually revised" (Byrne et al., 2009: 89).

Conclusion

The idea of a green economy, although over two decades old, is enjoying a revival and is widely seen as an adequate response to the environmental and economic crises afflicting the world today. In this chapter we have adopted a cautionary tone and observed that the existing green economy discourse is perhaps set up for failure.

We have noted that on three crucial requirements for sustainability – living within the planet's limits; achieving equity in the space of valuable ends such as health, human security and agency; and social inclusiveness – the green economy discourse as presently articulated fails to offer a viable path forward. Its promise of a sustainable and equitable future is premised on more growth and more expert-managed technical fixes.

This is not to imply that appropriate innovations and developments in technology are unimportant, but rather to urge realignment to give greater importance to the normative and institutional aspects of the task at hand.

We outlined two illustrations of practices that are moving towards a truly green economy. Both illustrations, from contexts as dissimilar as India and the United States, acknowledge the planet's limits and promote equity by being more inclusive of both non-experts and experts in managing the energy–society relationship. They point towards ways in which public policy can move towards sustainability and equity. The green economy, as it is presently being promoted, appears to be an end in itself and does not focus on what is really the point of this whole effort of reform and course correction – living within the planet's limits with equality of well-being for all.

Notes

1. It is 50 years since the publication of Rachel Carson's *Silent Spring*, which is widely considered as the harbinger of the modern environmental movement. This duration of time is also a decade shy of two human generations.
2. Addressing the Plenary Session of the 1972 United Nations Conference on the Human Environment in Stockholm, India's then prime minister, Indira Gandhi, rhetorically posed the now famous question: "Are not poverty and want the greatest polluters?" She went on to conclude: "The environment cannot be improved in conditions of poverty. Nor can poverty be eradicated without the use of science and technology" (Gandhi, 1975: 193).
3. The financial basis for valuation can be limited and must be complemented by evaluations that can reflect greater informational richness. To its credit, the TEEB team acknowledges that, "in situations involving multiple ecosystems and services, and/or plurality of ethical or cultural convictions, monetary valuations may be less reliable or unsuitable" (TEEB, 2010: 12).
4. See Byrne and Yun (1999), who further develop and apply this argument to explain the contradictions in liberal democratic societies' responses to climate change.
5. Of course, in engineering terms, efficiency is not even "monochromatic", it is dimensionless, what we might call achromatic.
6. At the end of 2010, solar PV capacity was about 40 GW (REN21, 2011). Although the solar PV installation numbers for 2011 have not been finalized yet, early predictions estimate that over 26 GW were installed in 2011 (Osborne, 2012).
7. Depending on the scenario considered, World Energy Outlook, 2011 (IEA, 2011) projects primary energy demand from fossil fuels of 9,195–14,617 million tonnes of oil equivalent (Mtoe) in 2035. Corresponding numbers for "other renewables" are variously 1,161 and 481 Mtoe. These projections reflect energy intensity reductions of between 44 per cent and 31 per cent. For comparison, in 2009, fossil fuel demand was 9,820 Mtoe and demand for "other renewables" was 99 Mtoe.
8. Of the 40 GW solar PV installed at the end of 2010, about 10 GW was installed as utility-scale facilities, and this is recognized as a growing trend. Utility-scale PV plants are those

above 200 kW (REN21, 2011). There are roughly 6,000 such plants today, the largest of which is about 100 MW (Lenardic, 2011).
9. See SELCO's website: ⟨http://www.selco-india.com/index.html⟩.

REFERENCES

Asia-Pacific Youth Forum (2011) "Asia-Pacific Youth Position Paper Toward Rio+20", presented at the Asia-Pacific Youth Forum on Climate Actions and Mountain Issues, Kathmandu, Nepal, 12 August.
Ban, K.-M. (2011a) "New York, 14 January 2011 – Secretary-General's Remarks to the General Assembly on 2011 Priorities". Available at ⟨http://www.un.org/apps/sg/sgstats.asp?nid=5034#⟩ (accessed 23 January 2012).
Ban, K.-M. (2011b) "Preface", in UNDESA, *World Economic and Social Survey 2011: The Great Green Technological Transformation*. New York: United Nations Department of Economic and Social Affairs.
Byrne, J. and S.-J. Yun (1999) "Efficient Global Warming: Contradictions in Liberal Democratic Responses to Global Environmental Problems", *Bulletin of Science, Technology and Society*, 19(6): 493–500.
Byrne, J., L. Glover and C. Martinez (eds) (2002) *Environmental Justice: Discourses in International Political Economy*, Vol. 8. New Brunswick, NJ: Transaction Publishers.
Byrne, J., N. Toly and L. Glover (eds) (2006) *Transforming Power: Energy, Environment and Society in Conflict*. Energy and Environmental Policy Series, Vol. 9. New Brunswick, NJ: Transaction Publishers.
Byrne, J., C. Martinez and C. Ruggero (2009) "Relocating Energy in the Social Commons: Ideas for a Sustainable Energy Utility", *Bulletin of Science, Technology and Society*, 29(2): 81–94.
Crutzen, P. J. (2002) "Geology of Mankind", *Nature*, 415(3): 23.
Daly, H. E. (1990) "Sustainable Growth: An Impossibility Theorem", *Development*, 3(4): 45–47.
Daly, H. E. (1991) *Steady State Economics*, 2nd edn. Washington, DC, and Covelo, CA: Island Press.
Daly, H. E. (1996) *Beyond Growth: The Economics of Sustainable Development*, 1st edn. Boston: Beacon Press.
Daly, H. E. and J. B. Cobb (1989) *For the Common Good: Redirecting the Economy Toward Community, the Environment, and a Sustainable Future*. Boston: Beacon Press.
Feenberg, A. (1991) *Critical Theory of Technology*. New York: Oxford University Press.
Gandhi, I. (1975) *Indira Gandhi: Speeches and Writings*. New York: Harper & Row.
Gandhi, M. K. ([1909] 1938) *Hind Swaraj or India Home Rule*. Ahmadabad: Navjivan Trust.
Global Footprint Network (2011) "World Footprint: Do We Fit on the Planet?", ⟨http://www.footprintnetwork.org/en/index.php/GFN/page/world_footprint/⟩ (accessed 23 January 2012).

Glover, L. (2006) "From Love-ins to Logos: Charting the Demise of Renewable Energy as a Social Movement", in J. Byrne, N. Toly and L. Glover (eds), *Transforming Power: Energy, Environment and Society in Conflict*. New Brunswick, NJ: Transaction Publishers, pp. 1–32.

Grigsby, M. (2004) *Buying Time and Getting by: The Voluntary Simplicity Movement*. New York: State University of New York Press.

Guha, R. (2006) *How Much Should a Person Consume? Environmentalism in India and the United States*. Berkeley: University of California Press.

Guha, R. and J. Martinez-Alier (1997) *Varieties of Environmentalism: Essays North and South*. London: Earthscan Publications Ltd.

Gupta, A. (2009) "Grassroots Green Innovation for Inclusive, Sustainable Development", in A. Lopez-Carlos (ed.), *The Innovation for Development Report: Strengthening Innovation for the Prosperity of Nations*. New York: Palgrave, pp. 137–146.

Huber, J. (2000) "Towards Industrial Ecology: Sustainable Development as a Concept of Ecological Modernization", *Journal of Environmental Policy & Planning*, 2: 269–285.

Hughes, T. P. (1994) "Technological Momentum", in M. R. Smith and L. Marx (eds), *Does Technology Drive History? The Dilemma of Technological Determinism*. Cambridge, MA: MIT Press, pp. 101–113.

IEA (International Energy Agency) (2011) *World Energy Outlook, 2011*. Paris: IEA. Available at ⟨http://www.worldenergyoutlook.org/⟩ (accessed 23 January 2012).

Jackson, T. (2009) *Prosperity Without Growth? The Transition to a Sustainable Economy*. Sustainable Development Commission. Available at ⟨http://www.sd-commission.org.uk/publications.php?id=914⟩ (accessed 23 January 2012).

Kosambi, D. D. (1960) *Atomic Energy for India*. Pune: Popular Book House.

Lenardic, D. (2011) "Large-Scale Photovoltaic Power Plants: Annual and Cumulative Installed Power Output Capacity 2000–2010". Available at ⟨http://www.pvresources.com/Portals/0/Download/AnnualReview2010.pdf⟩ (accessed 23 January 2012).

Lovins, A. B. (1977) *Soft Energy Paths: Toward a Durable Peace*. San Francisco: HarperCollins.

Maier, C. (1977) "The Politics of Productivity: Foundations of American International Economic Policy after World War II", *International Organization*, 31(4): 607–633.

Martinez-Alier, J. (2002) *The Environmentalism of the Poor: A Study of Ecological Conflicts and Valuation*. Northampton, MA: Edward Elgar.

Martinez-Alier, J., U. Pascual, F-D. Vivien and E. Zaccai (2010) "Sustainable Degrowth: Mapping the Context, Criticisms and Future Prospects of an Emergent Paradigm", *Ecological Economics*, 69: 1741–1747.

Mathai, M. V. (2004) "Exploring Freedom in a Global Ecology: Sen's Capability Approach as a Response to the Environment-Development Crisis", paper presented at the 4th International Conference on the Capability Approach: Enhancing Human Security, University of Pavia, Italy, 5–7 September.

Metz, B., O. R. Davidson, P. R. Bosch, R. Dave and L. A. Meyer (eds) (2007) *Climate Change 2007: Mitigation of Climate Change*. Contribution of Working

Group III to the Fourth Assessment Report of the Intergovernmental Panel on Climate Change, 2007. Cambridge and New York: Cambridge University Press.
Mies, M. and V. Bennholdt-Thomsen (1999) *The Subsistence Perspective: Beyond the Globalized Economy*. London and New York: Zed Books.
Mol, A. P. J. and G. Spaargaren (2000) "Ecological Modernization Theory in Debate: A Review", *Environmental Politics*, 9(1): 17–49.
Mumford, L. (1934) *Technics and Civilization*. New York: Harcourt, Brace and Co.
Mumford, L. (1964) "Authoritarian and Democratic Technics", *Technology and Culture*, 5(1): 1–8.
Osborne, M. (2012) "Global PV Installations for 2011 Could Have Topped 26GW, Say Analysts", *PV TECH*, 10 January. Available at 〈http://www.pv-tech.org/news/global_pv_installations_for_2011_could_have_topped_26gw_say_analysts〉 (accessed 23 January 2012).
Pearce, D., A. Markandya and E. Barbier (1989) *Blueprint for a Green Economy*. London: Earthscan Publications Ltd.
Planning Commission of India (1985) *Seventh Five Year Plan, 1985–90*. New Delhi: Government of India. Available at 〈http://planningcommission.nic.in/plans/planrel/fiveyr/default.html〉 (accessed 23 January 2012).
REN21 (2011) *Renewables 2011 Global Status Report*. Paris: REN21 Secretariat. Available at 〈http://www.ren21.net/Portals/97/documents/GSR/GSR2011_Master18.pdf〉 (accessed 26 January 2012).
Rogoff, K. (2012) "Rethinking the Growth Imperative", Project Syndicate, 2 January. Available at 〈http://www.project-syndicate.org/commentary/rogoff88/English〉 (accessed 23 January 2012).
Rostow, W. W. (1960) *The Stages of Economic Growth: A Non-Communist Manifesto*. New York: Cambridge University Press.
Sen, A. K. (1987) *Commodities and Capabilities*. New Delhi: Oxford University Press.
Sen, A. K. (1992) *Inequality Reexamined*. Cambridge, MA: Harvard University Press.
Sen, A. K. (1999) *Development as Freedom*. New York: Knopf Inc.
SELCO (Solar Electric Light Company) (2012) "SELCO Labs", 〈http://www.selco-india.com/selco_labs.html〉 (accessed 23 January 2012).
SEU (Sustainable Energy Utility) (2007) *The Sustainable Energy Utility: A Delaware First*. A Report to the Delaware State Legislature by the Sustainable Energy Utility Task Force. Available at 〈http://www.seu-de.org/docs/final_report_4-21.pdf〉 (accessed 23 January 2012).
Smith, A. ([1776] 1994) *An Inquiry into the Nature and Causes of the Wealth of Nations*. New York: Random House.
TEEB (The Economics of Ecosystems and Biodiversity) (2010) "The Economics of Ecosystems and Biodiversity. Mainstreaming the Economics of Nature: A Synthesis of the Approach, Conclusions and Recommendations of TEEB". Available at 〈http://www.teebweb.org/TEEBSynthesisReport/tabid/29410/Default.aspx〉 (accessed 23 January 2012).
UNDESA (United Nations Department of Economic and Social Affairs) (2011) *World Economic and Social Survey 2011: The Great Green Technological*

Transformation. New York: UNDESA. Available at ⟨http://www.un.org/en/development/desa/policy/wess/index.shtml⟩ (accessed 23 January 2012).

UNEP (United Nations Environment Programme) (2011) *Towards a Green Economy: Pathways to Sustainable Development and Poverty Eradication*. Available at ⟨http://www.unep.org/greeneconomy/⟩ (accessed 23 January 2012).

Vitousek, M. P., H. Mooney, A. J. Lubchenco and J. M. Melillo (1997) "Human Domination of Earth's Ecosystems", *Science*, 277(5325): 494–499.

WCED (World Commission on Environment and Development) (1987) *Our Common Future*. New York: United Nations.

Weale, A. (1998) "Politics of Ecological Modernization", in J. S. Dryzek and D. Scholsberg (eds), *Debating the Earth: The Environmental Politics Reader*. Oxford: Oxford University Press, pp. 301–318.

Wilhite, H. and J. S. Norgard (2004) "Equating Efficiency with Reduction: A Self-Deception in Energy Policy", *Energy and Environment*, 15(6): 991–1009.

York, R. and E. A. Rosa (2003) "Key Challenges to Ecological Modernization: Institutional Efficacy, Case Study Evidence, Units of Analysis, and the Pace of Eco-Efficiency", *Organization Environment*, 16(3): 273–288.

4

The political economy of green growth: Food, fuel and electricity in southern Africa

Danielle Resnick, Finn Tarp and James Thurlow

Introduction

In recent years, the international community has shifted from promoting "sustainable development" to advancing concepts such as green growth, the green economy and green jobs. The use of the "green" modifier implies that developmental objectives, such as job creation, high economic growth and poverty alleviation, can be easily reconciled with environmental goals. This is the tenor of many recent reports on the topic. For instance, the United Nations Environment Programme (UNEP) defines the green economy as one that "results in improved human well-being and social equity, while significantly reducing environmental risks and ecological scarcities" (UNEP, 2011: 1). Likewise, the Organisation for Economic Co-operation and Development (OECD) notes that "[g]reen growth means fostering economic growth and development while ensuring that natural assets continue to provide the resources and environmental services on which our well-being relies" (OECD, 2011: 9). For the United Nations Economic and Social Commission for Asia and the Pacific (UNESCAP), green growth is a policy of "environmentally sustainable economic progress to foster low-carbon, socially inclusive development" (UNESCAP, 2011).

There are a number of notable cases where green initiatives offer greater stewardship of the environment while simultaneously providing growth opportunities or helping the poor. For example, the World Bank (2010) points to the Mediterranean Solar Plan, which aims to provide 20

Green economy and good governance for sustainable development: Opportunities, promises and concerns, Puppim de Oliveira (ed.),
United Nations University Press, 2012, ISBN 978-92-808-1216-9

gigawatts of solar power by 2020 to reduce reliance on fossil fuels and allow Middle Eastern and North African countries to export power to Europe. UNEP (2011) highlights the case of the Grameen Shakti programme in Bangladesh where microfinance is used to help rural residents afford solar home systems. Yet these and many other promising enterprises often are discussed in isolation from countries' broader development strategies, with little reference to the opportunity costs already forgone by certain investments or the political economy challenges of shifting towards large-scale, green strategies.

This chapter therefore poses the following question: what are the economic implications and the political challenges of a broad green growth strategy for developing countries? We argue that a number of trade-offs are inherent in green growth and, therefore, it is often less win–win than much of the literature suggests. Specifically, at the macro level, such strategies often require countries to deviate from the prescriptions of conventional development theory as well as their current development trajectories, which can be extremely costly and potentially detrimental to the poor in the short term. In addition, like many other past trends promoted by the development community, a green growth agenda often overlooks the domestic political challenges to adopting new development strategies, such as the formation of anti-reform coalitions that might include the poor.

To illustrate these points in greater detail, we focus on the region of southern Africa. This region represents a high level of diversity, ranging from mineral-rich to agricultural-dependent economies and includes both middle-income and extremely poor countries. In particular, we look at three countries within this region: Malawi, Mozambique and South Africa. These cases were chosen because they are currently pursuing development strategies that revolve around fertilizers, biofuels and coal, respectively. Although these strategies generate large costs to the environment, they are being used to address development issues, such as the provision of adequate food, fuel and electricity, that are highly relevant to the broader African context. Moreover, such strategies allow each of these three countries not only to tackle their current development priorities but also to pursue their respective comparative advantage in terms of resource availability.

More specifically, Malawi's comparative advantage lies in its favourable agro-ecological conditions. Yet, given its land scarcity, the sustainability of an agriculture-led development strategy requires a more intense use of the available land. To do this, the government of Malawi has been heavily promoting the use of fertilizer, even though fertilizer can be highly detrimental to water sources and generates high levels of greenhouse gases (GHG). Since fertilizer use has been promoted through a subsidy scheme that is highly popular among poor farmers and therefore an electoral boon to many politicians from the ruling party, shifting towards a more environmentally friendly mode of enhancing soil fertility will be extremely challenging.

In contrast to Malawi, Mozambique's comparative advantage lies in its land abundance as well as possessing ideal agro-ecological conditions for growing biofuels. The country has therefore pursued an agricultural extensification strategy that involves clearing forests in order to grow sugar and jatropha. Even though such deforestation is a major contributor to GHG, the biofuels industry offers the potential to create jobs for the rural poor and offers a diversified export base for Mozambique. A more environmentally friendly strategy for biofuels production would involve a more intensive plantation approach, but this would create fewer employment opportunities. Therefore certain interest groups would be opposed to shifting towards such a strategy.

Finally, an abundance of mineral resources constitutes South Africa's comparative advantage. In a country where electricity demands are high, South Africa has exploited its coal resources for energy production. Shifting to a more environmentally friendly source of electricity, including nuclear and renewable energy, requires South Africa to forgo long-standing and expensive investments in physical capital. Moreover, electricity generated from coal is relatively cheaper than other potential alternatives, which is critical in a country where much of the poor population still lacks any type of reliable and affordable electricity. Deviating from coal production will not be popular for unionized workers in the mining and metals industries, private businesses and poor South Africans who cannot afford higher electricity prices. The government's potential adoption of a carbon tax to reduce energy demand likewise produces powerful anti-reform constituencies.

In order to further illustrate these points, the following section elaborates on the nexus between economic development, green growth and the political economy of reform. Subsequently, each of the three country cases is discussed in greater detail. The final section summarizes the case studies and concludes.

Green growth, economic development and the political economy of reform

Development strategies and green growth

Whereas there is debate over the role of government in promoting economic development, there is greater consensus on the nature of the development process itself, which involves a reallocation of resources away from less productive activities towards more advanced, higher-value-added industries (see Lewis, 1954). The literature examining this structural transformation in developing countries predicts that agriculture's importance will decline with industrialization. However, although the underlying transformation process may be similar, countries' patterns of development have been shown to vary considerably (Chenery and Syrquin, 1975). The debate surrounding the appropriate choice of development strategies for low-income countries thus centres on the primacy of agriculture versus industry in initiating the development process, and, therefore, on the targeting and sequencing of sector-oriented investments and policies (see Diao et al., 2007).

Governments in low-income countries are usually advised to base their development strategies on observed comparative advantages. From this perspective, countries should promote exports that use abundant resources most intensively. For example, countries with favourable agro-ecological conditions or large mineral deposits should adopt strategies that promote agriculture or mining-focused industrialization, respectively. The concept of comparative advantage as a means of identifying growth opportunities is perhaps most applicable during early stages of development, when countries have not accumulated sufficient capital (human, physical, etc.) and must therefore rely on natural resources. As development proceeds, the concept of competitive advantage becomes more relevant (Porter, 1985), which is the idea that more developed countries possess a wider range of higher-value growth opportunities beyond their natural comparative advantage. Development strategies should then focus more on identifying global market opportunities and creating the necessary knowledge and productivity levels to exploit them.

Comparative advantage remains a key consideration when designing development strategies in low-income countries. Countries may, however, possess a number of natural advantages from which to choose. Here the concept of *growth linkages* becomes pertinent. A sector has strong linkages when its growth generates positive spillovers in other sectors, and so these sectors are often favoured over others. For example, agriculture is often promoted as a strategic sector because it supports downstream agro-processing, and thus its growth creates both farm and off-farm jobs and promotes industrialization. Agriculture is therefore a priority sector in many low-income countries' development strategies, including those of Malawi and Mozambique, because it exploits these countries' favourable agro-ecological conditions (that is, comparative advantage) and generates growth linkages that support economy-wide development (Diao et al., 2007). Similarly, South Africa has exploited its mineral resources and established downstream metals and heavy industries, which are still favoured in national policies and constitute the country's main comparative *and* competitive advantages in its current development strategy.

Adopting a green growth strategy means that developing countries may have to deviate from the strategies traditionally promoted based on comparative advantage and growth linkage considerations. Certain natural resources may have to remain unused, such as coal and crude oil. Developing countries may also have to adopt new technologies and therefore abandon past investments in physical and human capital. This could weaken growth linkages, at least in the short run, as new green technologies are often imported until local industries can be established and made sustainable. Finally, many new technologies underpinning green growth are more expensive than existing options. Developing countries will therefore have to adopt more expensive strategies that redirect scarce resources away from other development priorities. Green growth strategies may therefore be at odds with traditional prescriptions and could require countries to adopt strategies that are more expensive and less effective in the short run for achieving development objectives.

Political economy considerations

Any development strategy has distributional consequences and therefore influences the formation of pro- and anti-reform interest groups. Interest group analyses assume that individuals are self-interested and that their preferences for certain policies are determined deductively according to their position within the economy. A large range of political economy literature is based on this presumption (for example, Frieden and Rogowski, 1996; Hiscox, 2001; Milner, 1997), and initiatives such as the World Bank's Poverty and Social Impact Analyses have incorporated interest group analyses to determine whether and who will support pro-poor reforms (World Bank, 2003).

Much of the literature on the political economy of reform focuses on trade, finance or structural adjustment policies. Like these reforms, green growth policies exhibit a strong temporal component because the promised benefits occur in the long term but significant costs can be incurred in the short term, and those who ultimately gain may not be the same as those who sacrificed. There is also a wide range of actors whose interests are at stake, including farmers, consumers, unionized workers, politicians and business.

The interest group approach posits that policy decisions are often the result of the interaction between citizens' and governments' preferences, as well as those of important external actors (see Putnam, 1988). For individual citizens, Nelson (1992) observes that there are at least three main channels through which government policies demonstrate an impact and influence preferences: employment and incomes, prices of goods and services consumed, and the provision of public services. Naturally, individuals' willingness to accept trade-offs across these different channels depends on their socioeconomic position and the availability of alternative coping mechanisms.

Yet individuals possess unequal abilities to convey their preferences. Van de Walle (2001) argues that the mere existence of certain economic preferences among a segment of the population does not guarantee their effective representation within the political system. Certain groups possess greater resources and access to policy-makers, which thereby ensures that their voices are better heard during periods of reform (see Olson, 1965; Srinivasan, 1985).

Indeed, the decision to respond to the interests of individuals will in turn depend on a government's own preferences. In some instances, this might be an ideological commitment to improve national well-being. In others, particularly in democracies, it may be more oriented towards basic political survival. The timing of the electoral cycle can play an important role in this regard because incumbents are rarely inclined to undertake unpopular reforms right before an election (see Haggard and Kaufman, 1992). The promise of financial rewards from important external actors, such as private corporations, may also influence government policy decisions.

Consequently, we expect that governments will pursue green growth policies only when these benefit a sizeable proportion of the electorate or result in alternative sources of support from other important constituencies. In all three of the cases that we discuss below, both the rural and the urban poor remain a highly important electoral constituency owing to their size. Shifting to a green growth development strategy creates short-term disadvantages for the poor, including higher prices for electricity in South Africa, forgone employment opportunities in Mozambique, and reduced access to farm inputs in Malawi. This is particularly true given the added costs for these countries of deviating from their prevailing development strategies. Collectively, this suggests that green growth is no more win–win than many other policy reforms and highlights that a number of additional interventions would be needed from the international community in order to make green growth more financially and politically feasible.

Electricity and coal in South Africa

Though well endowed with mineral resources, South Africa faces tremendous challenges in terms of improving the welfare of its citizens. The country has some of the world's highest inequality, and unemployment, broadly defined, averages around 40 per cent. Since the ending of apartheid, improving service delivery for the poor has been a major objective of the ruling African National Congress (ANC). In fact, Section 24 of the country's Bill of Rights stipulates that all citizens have "the right to an environment that is not harmful to their health or well-being" (see RSA, 1996: Section 24). As a result, water connections increased by 1 million in the five years after the ending of apartheid, and more than 1.5 million households were added to the electricity grid (Pape and McDonald, 2002).

Yet the demand for electricity remains high in both rural areas (see Davis, 1998) and urban ones, which are experiencing industrial expansion and rapid population growth. The inadequacy of the electricity system's capacity was evident in early 2008, when peak period shortages led to nationwide blackouts, the temporary closure of energy-intensive industries and measureable losses in national income (Altman et al., 2008). Electricity supply and mining production were also disrupted in neighbouring countries that rely on imported electricity (Childress, 2008). Addressing South Africa's electricity challenge is therefore of both national and regional concern.

Taking advantage of its natural resources, South Africa's development strategy within the electricity sector has long relied on exploitation of the country's substantial coal deposits, state investment in the energy sector and subsidized electricity prices (Büscher, 2009).[1] One of the reasons South Africa has favoured coal-fired technologies is because coal-fired plants have higher load factors than renewables. A power plant's load factor is a measure of its operational output relative to its maximum capacity, and higher load factors typically imply lower unit costs. In turn, this means that coal is a much cheaper source than renewables of bulk electricity. Currently, coal accounts for 81 per cent of total electricity system capacity but is responsible for 94 per cent of actual electricity supply owing to the low load factors associated with hydropower and other renewable sources (RSA, 2011).

This focus on coal-based energy was renewed in the wake of the 2008 shortages when the state-owned electricity supplier, ESKOM, decided to return decommissioned coal-fired plants to service and to commission the building of new coal-fired generators. The World Bank and the African Development Bank are funding the new generators through sizeable loans equivalent to almost 2 per cent of national income.[2] Various donors to the World Bank objected to the loans on environmental grounds, suggesting that investments should be targeted towards cleaner technologies (Goldenberg, 2010). However, the South African government and its lenders defended the continuation of coal-fired plants, highlighting that they were necessary for avoiding further shortages as well as for safeguarding economic growth and the well-being of poorer households (Goldenberg, 2010). Consequently, South Africa is now locked into coal-fired electricity until at least 2020.

In addition to the loans, the costs of the new investments have been concurrently funded by increasing South Africa's historically low electricity tariffs. ESKOM and state regulators agreed to double tariffs during 2010–2015 (RSA, 2011). This has heightened inflationary pressures, which are felt disproportionately by poorer households, who spend a greater share of their incomes on energy (Arndt et al., 2011a). Higher tariffs may also worsen unemployment if businesses close down or shed workers to curb production costs (Altman et al., 2008). Not surprisingly, tariff increases have therefore met considerable resistance. Labour unions arranged national strikes during 2010 and business organizations lobbied the government for smaller tariff increases (SAPA, 2010). The Congress of South African Trade Unions (COSATU) has also joined civil society organizations in protesting against higher electricity prices (Johwa, 2010). The state regulator has not rescinded the tariff increases, but instead responded by lengthening the period over which the increases will take place (SAPA, 2010). It is thus within this context of growing electricity demand and considerable political pressure to curb tariffs that the government must design its environmental policies.

Indeed, this pursuit of coal-based energy is antithetical to the goals of a green growth agenda. In absolute terms, South Africa was the world's thirteenth-largest GHG-emitting country in 2007, with per capita emissions similar to those of the European Union, despite having three times lower per capita income (World Bank, 2011). The country's dirtiness is almost entirely owing to its dependence on coal-based energy, which accounts for 80 per cent of total emissions (RSA, 2010). It is in South Africa's interest to limit climate change, since many projections predict worsening climatic conditions for the country. By not curbing emissions, South Africa also undermines its position in global forums and faces the threat of retaliatory trade policies from countries that do reduce their emissions (Arndt et al., 2011a).

Recognizing this, the government adopted a climate change resolution at a conference in Polokwane that highlighted its intention to mitigate GHG emissions and adopt a low-carbon growth path (see Tyler, 2009). In particular, the government committed to a 42 per cent reduction in GHG emissions by 2025, from a baseline projection (RSA, 2010). However, meeting these commitments via reductions of GHG in the electricity sector would be extremely costly for the country.

Specifically, Figure 1(a) shows South Africa's *business-as-usual* (coal-intensive) investment plan for the electricity sector. Almost all new in-

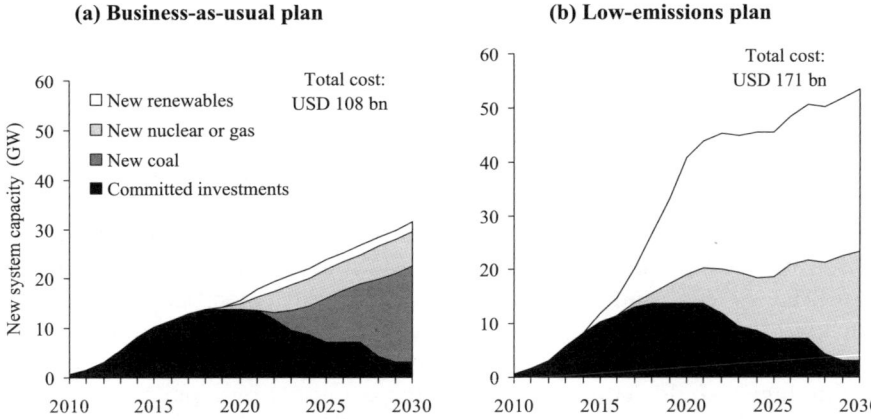

Figure 4.1 Alternative electricity sector investment plans for South Africa.
Source: Authors' calculations using RSA (2011).
Notes: Installed capacity in 2010 was 260 GW. Both scenarios supply the same demand forecast. "Total cost" comprises operational costs and capital investment. Renewables include wind, solar and hydropower.

vestments in infrastructure capacity for the next decade have already been committed, reflecting the long lead times required for investments in electricity generation (decisions must be made well in advance and are difficult and costly to change). The *low-emissions* scenario (Figure 4.1(b)) reflects adjustments in the country's electricity investments to meet its GHG emission targets. The incremental cost of this revised investment strategy is substantial: USD 63 billion, or the equivalent of almost 1 per cent of national income in 2010. This is over and above the USD 108 billion cost of the business-as-usual plan. Costs are higher because renewable technologies are still being developed and because the lower load factors of renewables mean that more installed system capacity is required to achieve the same level of actual electricity supply. Lower load factors also imply higher unit production costs and hence require higher user tariffs. Given past controversy over high tariff prices, the government realized that this low-emissions plan was not politically feasible.

As a result, the government has endorsed a more modest investment strategy that reduces the size of politically unpopular tariff increases (RSA, 2011). The more modest plan includes a substantial shift away from coal towards nuclear and renewables. Under this plan, however, the electricity sector will fail to meet its emissions targets and will instead achieve only an 18 per cent reduction by 2025 (RSA, 2011). Moreover, this will still increase electricity tariffs because higher investment costs will need to be passed on to consumers. It will also make South Africa more dependent on imported technologies. Finally, shifting away from coal means that South Africa will no longer be able to exploit its own natural resources. Proven reserves suggest that there is about 120 years of coal left in South Africa, and so the opportunity cost of not using these resources will be substantial.

A concurrent approach that the government is considering is the introduction of a carbon tax to reduce energy demand. Currently the government has proposed a tax of USD 20 per ton of carbon dioxide (CO_2) (RSA, 2010), which is equivalent to a 5 per cent tax on national income based on current industrial structures and energy use. This tax doubles the price of coal and substantially increases real electricity tariffs. The carbon tax will cause a significant structural transformation of the economy, and the higher cost of investment in new and more energy-efficient technologies could reduce the size of the economy by 2 per cent in 2030, relative to a no-carbon-tax baseline (RSA, 2011).

The effects of the carbon tax will be unevenly distributed across industries and households. Various interest groups have already voiced opposition to this proposed tax. First, business interests, particularly those in mining and heavy industry, are opposed to higher tariffs caused by more expensive electricity generation (Creamer, 2011). Businesses are especially concerned about an erosion of competitiveness in export markets and about heightened competition from imports from countries that do not implement similar environmental policies. Some industries have lobbied for special dispensation (for example, airlines and mines) and for a slower introduction of the carbon tax or for subsidized electricity.

Thus, although the government has demonstrated a willingness to ameliorate its historically high levels of GHG caused by a high dependence on coal-based energy, substantial costs are involved in deviating from its current investment and development strategy. As a result, many important interest groups could be alienated. Poor households and labour unions have already indicated opposition to existing tariffs for electricity and would therefore oppose the even higher tariffs expected in order for the government to meet the GHG emission targets in the modest scenario outlined above. A carbon tax likewise hurts major stakeholders.

Food and fertilizer in Malawi

Malawi differs from the South African case in terms of its much higher levels of poverty and heavy dependence on agricultural production: agriculture accounts for 39 per cent of GDP, compared with 11 per cent for manufacturing (Chirwa et al., 2006); 74 per cent of Malawi's population lives below the USD 1/day poverty line and 80 per cent reside in rural areas, and the country relies heavily on dwindling earnings from tobacco exports (IMF, 2007). Food insecurity remains a perennial threat. In fact, Malawi was seriously affected by droughts in 1991–1992, which affected 5.7 million people and caused a 60 per cent decrease in the production of the country's main staple crop, maize (Babu and Chapasuka, 1997). A decade later, severe flooding reduced maize production by 30 per cent and this, along with a number of institutional and political factors, triggered a famine in 2002 (see Rubin, 2008). During the 2004–2005 growing season, poor weather plunged Malawi into yet another food crisis that resulted in approximately 34 per cent of the population unable to meet its food needs (FAO, 2005).

Nevertheless, owing to Malawi's sub-humid climate, the country possesses a comparative advantage in agro-ecological conditions favourable for maize farm production (Dixon et al., 2001). Land scarcity, however, means that an agricultural intensification approach is unavoidable. Repeated farming on the same land leads to a decline in soil nutrients and to serious land degradation, which has only been exacerbated during periods of flooding (see Phillips, 2007). Most soils in Malawi suffer from poor infiltration and moisture retention, lack key minerals and nutrients such as sulphur, nitrogen and phosphorus, and suffer from high levels of acidity (Munthali, 2007). Pressure from the World Bank in the late 1990s led the government to remove subsidies on fertilizers, seeds and credit. This, combined with liberalization of the parastatal Agricultural Development and Marketing Corporation, left many smallholders without access to affordable inputs (see Dorward and Kydd, 2004; Harrigan, 2003).

In order to address low soil fertility and to avoid further food insecurity, Malawi's President, Bingu wa Mutharika, launched the Agricultural Input Subsidy Program (AISP) in 2005.[3] The main component of the AISP – fertilizer subsidies – had already been a major electoral promise of Mutharika's party, the United Democratic Front (UDF), in the country's 2004 electoral campaign. After defecting from the UDF and forming a new party in 2005, the Democratic Progressive Party (DPP), President Mutharika deviated from the UDF's promise of a universal subsidy and instead announced a more targeted subsidy aimed at resource-constrained maize farmers (see Chinsinga, 2007).

Although donors remained sceptical and the government was forced to fund the entire programme during the 2005–2006 growing season, the fertilizer subsidies quickly demonstrated a notable impact on maize production. Maize production grew from 1.2 million metric tons in 2005 to 3.4 million metric tons by 2007, and Malawi began exporting its surplus to Zimbabwe while also becoming a food aid donor to Lesotho and Swaziland (see Dugger, 2007; Sanchez et al., 2009). Although favourable levels of rainfall were partially responsible for these increases, Denning et al. (2009) note that two-thirds of the increase could be attributed to the subsidies. Even though the cost of the AISP has more recently prompted concern about its impact on Malawi's macro-economy, Dorward and Chirwa (2011) concur that the programme contributed to higher maize yields, higher food availability and declines in poverty. Based on Malawi's success, a number of other African countries, including Ghana, Kenya and Tanzania, began considering the implementation of similar voucher-based fertilizer subsidy schemes (Minot and Benson, 2009).

In many respects, the AISP responded to calls by development practitioners for the creation of an African Green Revolution that revolves around increasing smallholder farmers' access to fertilizers, high-yield seeds and irrigation (see Denning et al., 2009; Sanchez et al., 2009). Indeed, the 2006 Abuja Declaration on Fertilizer for an African Green Revolution advocated an increase from 8 to 50 kg of fertilizer per hectare between 2006 and 2015 (NEPAD, 2011). However, the AISP programme has potentially over-promoted the usage of fertilizer at the expense of other investments, particularly in agricultural research and development.[4]

For a number of reasons, fertilizer use can be detrimental to the environment. First, the manufacture of inorganic fertilizers can lead to high levels of CO_2 emissions and can also stimulate the release of nitrous oxide from the soil, which contributes to GHG. According to the Stern Review (Stern, 2006), fertilizers are the largest single source of GHG emissions created by the agricultural sector, and nitrous oxide possesses a global warming potential that is 300 times greater than that of CO_2. Second, fertilized land needs to be watered more, placing pressure on potentially scarce water resources or requiring irrigation. Third, high levels of fertilizer use can increase toxins in groundwater, with attendant impacts on fishery stocks and human health (Tilman et al., 2002). In India, pollution of waterways and aquifers has been a legacy of that country's Green Revolution (see World Bank, 2010).

As a consequence of these environmental hazards, the AISP approach is contrary to the objectives of green growth. According to the OECD (2011: 126), fertilizer subsidies constitute a "government failure" that not only hinders growth but also creates a number of negative environmental externalities. Alternative approaches include microdosing, which involves the application of only small amounts of fertilizer with the seed at planting time or three to four weeks after the emergence of the crop, and has been used successfully in some parts of Africa (ICRISAT, 2009). In addition, the process of growing two or more crops simultaneously, known as inter-cropping, can result in increases in nutrient- and water-use efficiency (Tilman et al., 2002). Other options include greater use of organic fertilizers and conservation farming techniques that aim to conserve soil and water use by using mulch and minimum tillage to minimize runoff and erosion.

Yet many of these alternatives are not feasible in the short term in Malawi. Specifically, they involve changing the behaviour of farmers on a relatively broad scale. However, Dorward and Chirwa (2011) note that past attempts to promote organic fertilizers have not been widely adopted by Malawian farmers. Moreover, they observe that, although there are efforts to include subsidized legume seeds to encourage inter-cropping, this is far from the major focus of the AISP. Encouraging greater adoption of legumes and other seeds through subsidies would further increase the cost of an already expensive programme.

Most significantly, however, Malawi's fertilizer subsidy programme is both popular among smallholder farmers and politically advantageous to the ruling DPP. Since the DPP is a relatively new party that lacks the same grassroots ties to rural voters as the UDF or the Malawi Congress Party (MCP), President Mutharika used the AISP as a way to consolidate the party's support base in preparation for the May 2009 elections (see Chinsinga, 2009). As Dorward and Chirwa (2011: 16) observe, "[p]olitical pressures to expand the program and to use it for patronage were evident in the run up to the election". Figure 2 illustrates a large increase in costs devoted to the AISP in the year of the 2009 elections.[5] Indeed, the fact that Mutharika overcame ethno-regional voting patterns and won the 2009 elections with 66 per cent of the vote, compared with only about

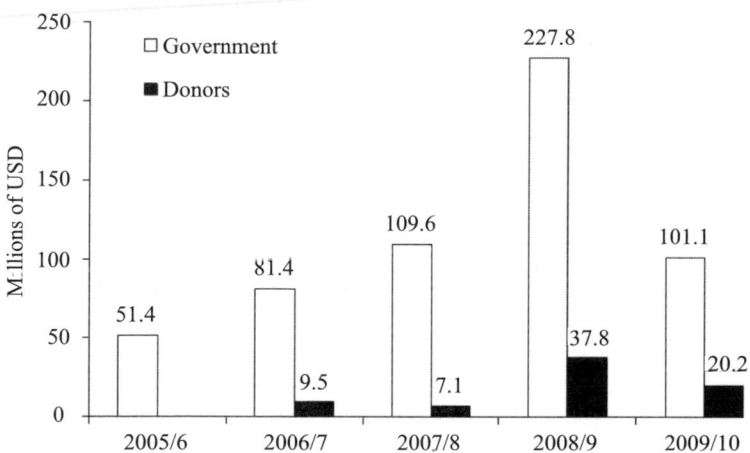

Figure 4.2 Evolution in the financial cost of Malawi's *Agricultural Input Subsidy Program*.
Source: Data from Dorward and Chirwa (2011).

half that vote share five years earlier, illustrates the success of this strategy.

As the 2014 presidential elections loom, Mutharika faces growing discontent over living conditions in urban areas and remains keen to promote his brother as his successor. Thus, the fertilizer input subsidies will remain a useful electoral tool for the DPP to retain support from numerically sizeable rural constituencies. The possible loss of the elections to opposition parties such as the UDF or the MCP would presumably lead to a greater promotion of fertilizer use because both of these parties have long advocated a universal subsidy scheme rather than the targeted one implemented under the DPP (see Smiddy and Young, 2009).

Biofuels in Mozambique

In contrast to Malawi, one of Mozambique's major comparative advantages is land abundance. Specifically, only 12 per cent of Mozambique's 36 million hectares of arable land is under cultivation (GOM, 2006). Much of this land possesses favourable agro-ecological conditions (Diao et al., 2007), although it would have to be cleared in order to be cultivated.

Although there has been some minor success in promoting export crops, such as cashews, Mozambique historically has concentrated on subsistence farming. Recently, poverty reduction has slowed in Mozambique, primarily because of stagnant agricultural production (Arndt et al., 2011b). As a result, the government has been eager to find new opportunities for agricultural growth. This is particularly important given that approximately 70 per cent of the country's population resides in rural areas, and almost half of these rural inhabitants are unable to obtain enough food to meet their daily caloric requirements (Arndt and Simler, 2007).

Consequently, the government has taken advantage of Mozambique's land abundance to promote the production of biofuels. Traditionally, Mozambique has been highly dependent on oil imports. In fact, as of 2007, the government expended 17 per cent of its GDP on fuel and energy (Schut et al., 2010a). Biofuels are therefore viewed as a means of reducing this dependence. Moreover, given the growing global demand for biofuels, especially in the European Union and South Africa, biofuels offer the promise of expanding into more high-value export markets.

Biofuels first appeared on Mozambique's policy agenda during the 2004 election campaign when the country was facing high and volatile oil prices. During this campaign, the government began encouraging farmers to cultivate jatropha, which is used in the production of biodiesel, on marginal lands (Schut et al., 2010a). Subsequently, a Commission on Biofuels was established that recommended producing ethanol from sugar cane, sorghum and cassava, and using jatropha, sunflower, coconut, soya and African palm oil as raw material for biodiesel (Nhantumbo and Salomão, 2010). By 2007, Mozambique's first biofuel project was approved for a company called Procana Ltd, which was offering USD 500 million in investment for 30,000 hectares of sugar cane (Schut et al., 2010b).[6] By mid-2008, the government had requests for the use of almost 12 million hectares of land, most of which were related to biofuels production (Arndt et al., 2010).

By 2009, the government published a National Biofuels Policy and Strategy (NBPS), partly based on an analysis conducted by Econergy. The NBPS stated that the biofuels industry could potentially create 150,000 new jobs (GOM, 2009). Since then, biofuels production has attracted the interest of a number of investors from around the globe, including from Brazil, Canada, China, Italy, Portugal and the United Kingdom (Cuvilas et al., 2010). Currently, there are more than 30 biofuels projects under way in Mozambique, with a total investment of over USD 100 million. If the projects all become operational, it is estimated that the country will save USD 682 million a year by reducing its fuel imports (AIM, 2011). Petromac, the Mozambican oil company, is also projecting the production of 226 million litres of biodiesel via jatropha and the creation of about 800 new jobs (Cuvilas et al., 2010).

Yet, although biofuels promise to reduce oil dependency, increase jobs and generate investment for previously unused land, this fuel alternative also poses a number of threats to the environment. For instance, biofuels can result in land degradation, water pollution, mono-cropping and overuse of water resources (Dufey, 2007). More significant is the threat of increasing deforestation, which globally contributes 14 per cent of GHG emissions each year (World Bank, 2010). Although biofuels produce less CO_2 than traditional fossil fuels, Fargione et al. (2008) find that GHG reductions from using biofuel depend on land use. Clearing new land for biofuels may generate large GHG emissions owing to burning and decomposition of organic matter. According to the Food and Agriculture Organization of the United Nations (FAO, 2011), the amount of forest land in Africa that will be cleared for biofuels production will total 1.3 million hectares by 2030. Since very little land currently is under cultivation in Mozambique, a substantial amount of land clearance will be needed to accommodate current and planned biofuels projects.

A green growth approach would therefore advocate a focus on biofuels production that is less land intensive. This would require concentrating on the production of ethanol rather than biodiesel because jatropha, the source of most biodiesel production in Mozambique, is highly land intensive. By contrast, ethanol production via sugar cane is more capital intensive and based on plantations. Therefore, less land needs to be cleared for production.

Yet this strategy poses important trade-offs. According to Arndt et al. (2010), a biofuels strategy based on jatropha is much more pro-poor owing to its greater use of unskilled labour and to the fact that plantation owners, rather than smallholders, typically accrue land rents for the production of ethanol. In addition, they find that the plantation approach in Mozambique is unlikely to generate many jobs for farm labourers. In other words, whereas sugar cane is more environmentally friendly, jatropha is more pro-poor. Given that the government's original adoption of biofuels was motivated by a desire to create jobs and assist the rural poor, a green growth approach to establishing a biofuels industry would deviate from these objectives.

Conclusions

The three cases presented in this chapter have focused on issues that are highly relevant to Africa's current development needs. The analysis has demonstrated that Malawi, Mozambique and South Africa are all following their comparative advantage by investing in their favourable agro-ecological conditions, land abundance and mineral wealth, respectively. These countries' various development strategies not only adhere to the tenets of prescribed development theory but also benefit the poor by providing affordable electricity in South Africa, employment in Mozambique and food security in Malawi. Consequently, each strategy has generated policy champions among both the poor and other key stakeholders.

Moreover, although we have predominantly focused on these countries in isolation, their current development strategies hold implications for the broader southern African region. South Africa's coal-based electricity is often exported to its neighbours, and the country would provide an important export market for Mozambique, which recently has discovered coal deposits. At the same time, South Africa constitutes a major export market for Mozambique's biofuels industry. Finally, as noted, maize production spurred by Malawi's fertilizer subsidies has been exported to food-scarce countries during periods of drought within the region.

Simultaneously, however, we have shown that each country is pursuing a suboptimal strategy for the environment by focusing on products, such as coal and fertilizers, as well as activities, such as deforestation, that contribute significant shares of GHG. Although shifting to green growth approaches for addressing the development challenges in these countries would provide environmental gains in the long term, they result in economic and political costs in the short term. Therefore, rather than being a win–win alternative, green growth policies are no different from most other types of policy reform, such as structural adjustment. To highlight this, Table 4.1 summarizes the cases and illustrates the short-term costs of shifting to a development strategy more aligned with green growth objectives.

Table 4.1 further emphasizes that, in all three cases, the poor are potential losers as a result of shifting to a green growth strategy. In some cases, powerful actors, including political parties, unions and private sector corporations, also face disadvantages from shifting away from their country's current development strategy. This therefore suggests that a green growth strategy is feasible only when the interests of all of these groups are properly aligned and when the benefits to all constituencies are sizeable.

Employment creation geared towards protecting or restoring environmental quality, otherwise known as *green jobs*, might offer one means of meeting such objectives simultaneously. Such jobs can benefit the poor, constitute new and productive areas of investment for the private sector, and in turn bolster the performance of incumbent governments that are concerned with remaining in office. UNEP (2008) highlights some of these initiatives in the African context, including South Africa's Working for Water programme, which created approximately 25,000 new jobs for the unemployed by involving local communities in the removal of invasive plant species that consume high levels of water. Another initiative is the Kibera Community Youth Programme, which involves Nairobi's unemployed youth in the assembly of small and affordable solar panels that can be used to charge radios and mobile phones in both the slum of Kibera and elsewhere in Kenya.

Such positive examples, however, remain both very micro-oriented and very sparse in Africa, with most initiatives concentrated in industrialized countries. In other words, they are not part of a broader development strategy. Moreover, African governments have faced tremendous challenges in creating large-scale employment for their citizens, let alone jobs that can be considered green. Considerable investment of scarce resources by governments would be needed, as would viable public–private partnerships and a shift in the education system to provide the specific technical skills often required for green jobs.

To confront these costs and the ones associated with the broader green growth agenda, the donor community may need to finance the transfer of technology and technical skills essential for preserving growth linkages and bolstering local job creation. Attention will be needed to both facilitating a transition to new production techniques and reducing resistance

Table 4.1 Summary of case studies

	Current development strategy	Green growth strategy	Short-term costs	Losers
South Africa	Invest in natural resources, particularly coal-fired electricity generation to support heavy industries	Shift to nuclear and renewable energy sources	• Higher electricity prices • Job losses in coal mining with secondary impacts on heavy industry	• Poor consumers • Unionized workers • Corporations in the mining and metals sectors
Malawi	Agricultural intensification based on input subsidies for fertilizers	Shift to conservation farming, organic fertilizers, microdosing, and inter-cropping	• Falling production while smallholders change farming behaviours • Loss of handouts to rural voters	• Current ruling party • Private sector suppliers of fertilizer • Poor smallholders who cannot adapt
Mozambique	Agricultural extensification based on cultivation of feedstock crops for biofuels	Reduce land clearing by either shifting towards plantation-based production or promoting smallholder agricultural intensification	• Fewer rural employment opportunities	• Poor rural farmers

to such transitions among the losers from reform. This, however, may contradict other development objectives, such as reducing the dependence of low-income countries on foreign assistance and technology.

Overall, the green growth agenda undoubtedly has worthy objectives. Stewardship of the environment is essential to the sustainability of economic and social progress in both developed and developing countries alike. Yet its proponents often have neglected to acknowledge the costs, economic and political, inherent in the green growth agenda. The experience of past reform initiatives, such as structural adjustment programmes, cautions against ignoring these trade-offs.

Notes

1. In fact, South Africa's electricity tariffs have, until recently, been amongst the world's lowest (Winkler, 2005).
2. Authors' calculations using World Bank (2011) national income data for 2010.
3. The programme has since been renamed the Fertilizer Input Subsidy Program (FISP).
4. For instance, incremental fertilizer use in Malawi almost doubled between 2005/2006 and 2008/2009, growing from 98,541 to 181,800 metric tons (Dorward and Chirwa, 2011).
5. Although the increase in costs was partially linked to the rise in the price of fertilizer, there was also an increase in the quantity of fertilizer purchased because the government decided to extend the subsidy to other crops, including coffee and tea (see Dorward et al., 2010).
6. The government ultimately cancelled Procana's contract when the company did little with the land it was granted.

REFERENCES

AIM (Agência de Informação de Moçambique) (2011) "Mozambique: Government Confident Biofuels Will Be Ready Next Year", *All Africa*, 5 September. Available at ⟨http://allafrica.com/stories/201109051562.html⟩ (accessed 25 January 2012).

Altman, M., R. Davies, A. Mather, D. Fleming and H. Harris (2008) *The Impact of Electricity Price Increases and Rationing on the South African Economy*. Final Report to the National Electricity Response Team Economic Impact Task Team. Pretoria: Human Sciences Research Council.

Arndt, C. and K. Simler (2007) "Consistent Poverty Comparisons and Inference", *Agricultural Economics*, 37(2–3): 133–143.

Arndt, C., R. Benfica, F. Tarp, J. Thurlow and R. Uaiene (2010) "Biofuels, Poverty, and Growth: A Computable General Equilibrium Analysis of Mozambique", *Environment and Development Economics*, 15(1): 81–105.

Arndt, C., R. Davies, K. Makrelov and J. Thurlow (2011a) "Measuring the Carbon Content of the South African Economy", UNU-WIDER Working Paper 2011-45, Helsinki.

Arndt, C., M. A. Hussain, E. S. Jones, V. Nhate, F. Tarp and J. Thurlow (2011b) "Explaining Poverty Evolution: The Case of Mozambique", UNU-WIDER Working Paper 2011-17, Helsinki.

Babu, S. and E. Chapasuka (1997) "Mitigating the Effects of Drought through Food Security and Nutrition Monitoring: Lessons from Malawi", *Food and Nutrition Bulletin*, 18(1): 71–83.

Büscher, B. (2009) "Connecting Political Economies of Energy in South Africa", *Energy Policy*, 37(10): 3951–3958.

Chenery, H. and M. Syrquin (1975) *Patterns of Development, 1950–1970*. Oxford: Oxford University Press.

Childress, S. (2008) "Power Struggle in Africa, Outages Stifle a Boom", *Wall Street Journal*, 17 April.

Chinsinga, B. (2007) "Reclaiming Policy Space: Lessons from Malawi's 2005/2006 Fertilizer Subsidy Programme", Policy Brief No. 13, Future Agricultures Initiative, Brighton.

Chinsinga, B. (2009) "Malawi's Political Landscape 2004–2009", in M. Ott and F. E. Kanyongolo (eds), *Democracy in Progress: Malawi's 2009 Parliamentary and Presidential Elections*. Zomba: Kachere Books, pp. 115–152.

Chirwa, E., J. Kydd and A. Dorward (2006) "Future Scenarios for Agriculture in Malawi: Challenges and Dilemmas", paper presented at the Future Agricultures Consortium, Institute for Development Studies, University of Sussex, 20–21 March.

Creamer, T. (2011) "SA Moves to Finalise Carbon Tax This Year, Despite Global Loose Ends", *Mining Weekly*, 16 March. Available at ⟨http://www.miningweekly.com/article/sa-moves-to-finalise-carbon-tax-this-year-despite-global-loose-ends-2011-03-16-1⟩ (accessed 25 January 2012).

Cuvilas, C., R. Jirjis and C. Lucas (2010) "Energy Situation in Mozambique: A Review", *Renewable and Sustainable Energy Reviews*, 14: 2139–2146.

Davis, M. (1998) "Rural Household Energy Consumption: The Effects of Access to Electricity – Evidence from South Africa", *Energy Policy*, 26(3): 207–217.

Denning, G., P. Kabambe, P. Sanchez, A. Malik, R. Flor, R. Harawa, P. Nkhoma, C. Zamba, C. Banda, C. Magombo, M. Keating, J. Wangila and J. Sachs (2009) "Input Subsidies to Improve Smallholder Maize Productivity in Malawi: Toward an African Green Revolution", *PLoS Biology*, 7(1): 2–10.

Diao, X., P. Hazell, D. Resnick and J. Thurlow (2007) *The Role of Agriculture in Pro-Poor Growth in Sub-Saharan Africa*. Washington, DC: International Food Policy Research Institute.

Dixon, J., A. Gulliver and D. Gibbon (2001) *Farming Systems and Poverty: Improving Farmers' Livelihoods in a Changing World*. Rome and Washington, DC: Food and Agriculture Organization and the World Bank.

Dorward, A. and E. Chirwa (2011) "The Malawi Agricultural Input Subsidy Programme: 2005–6 to 2008–9", *International Journal of Agricultural Sustainability*, 9(1): 232–247.

Dorward, A. and J. Kydd (2004) "The Malawi 2002 Food Crisis: The Rural Development Challenge", *Journal of Modern African Studies*, 42(3): 343–361.

Dorward, A., E. Chirwa and R. Slater (2010) "Evaluation of the 2008/9 Agricultural Input Subsidy Program, Malawi: Report on Program Implementation", School of Oriental and African Studies, London.
Dufey, A. (2007) "International Trade in Biofuels: Good for Development? And Good for Environment?" IIED Briefing, International Institute for Environment and Development, London.
Dugger, C. W. (2007) "Ending Famine, Simply by Ignoring the Experts", *New York Times*, 2 December. Available at ⟨http://www.nytimes.com/2007/12/02/world/africa/02malawi.html⟩ (accessed 25 January 2012).
FAO (Food and Agriculture Organization) (2005) "Malawi Facing Serious Food Crisis", FAO Newsroom, ⟨http://www.fao.org/newsroom/en/news/2005/107298/index.html⟩ (accessed 25 January 2012).
FAO (Food and Agriculture Organization) (2011) *State of the World's Forests*. Rome: FAO.
Fargione, J., J. Hill, D. Tilman, S. Polasky and P. Hawthorne (2008) "Land Clearing and the Biofuel Carbon Debt", *Science*, 319(5867): 1235–1238.
Frieden, J. and R. Rogowski (1996) "The Impact of the International Economy on National Policies: An Analytical Overview", in R. Keohane and H. Milner (eds), *Internationalization and Domestic Politics*. Cambridge: Cambridge University Press, pp. 25–47.
Goldenberg, S. (2010) "World Bank's $3.75bn Coal Plant Loan Defies Environment Criticism", *The Guardian*, 9 April. Available at ⟨http://www.guardian.co.uk/business/2010/apr/09/world-bank-criticised-over-power-station⟩ (accessed 11 January 2012).
GOM (Government of Mozambique) (2006) *Programa Nacional de Desenvolvimento Agrário (PROAGRI II) 2006–2010*. Maputo: Ministry of Agriculture.
GOM (Government of Mozambique) (2009) *Política e Estratégia de Biocombustíveis*. Maputo: Ministry of Energy.
Haggard, S. and R. Kaufman (1992) "Institutions and Economic Adjustment", in S. Haggard and R. Kaufman (eds), *The Politics of Economic Adjustment*. Princeton, NJ: Princeton University Press, pp. 3–40.
Harrigan, J. (2003) "U-Turns and Full Circles: Two Decades of Agricultural Reform in Malawi 1981–2000", *World Development*, 31(5): 847–863.
Hiscox, M. (2001) "Class versus Industry Cleavages: Inter-Industry Factor Mobility and the Politics of Trade", *International Organization*, 55(1): 1–46.
ICRISAT (International Crops Research Institute for the Semi-Arid Tropics) (2009) "Fertilizer Microdosing: Boosting Production in Unproductive Lands", Hyderabad, India. Available at ⟨http://www.icrisat.org/impacts/impact-stories/icrisat-is-fertilizer-microdosing.pdf⟩ (accessed 25 January 2012).
IMF (International Monetary Fund) (2007) "Malawi Growth and Development Strategy: From Poverty to Prosperity, 2006–2011", IMF Country Report No. 07/55, Washington, DC.
Johwa, W. (2010) "Cosatu Plans to Protest Against Increase in Electricity Prices", *Business Day*, 5 March. Available at ⟨http://www.businessday.co.za/articles/Content.aspx?id=95389⟩ (accessed 25 January 2012).

Lewis, W. A. (1954) "Economic Development with Unlimited Supplies of Labour", *The Manchester School*, 22(2): 139–191.

Milner, H. (1997) *Interests, Institutions, and Information: Domestic Politics and International Relations*. Princeton, NJ: Princeton University Press.

Minot, N. and T. Benson (2009) "Fertilizer Subsidies in Africa: Are Vouchers the Answer?", IFPRI Issue Brief 60, International Food Policy Research Institute, Washington, DC.

Munthali, M. (2007) "Integrated Soil Fertility Management Technologies: A Counteract to Existing Milestone in Obtaining Achievable Economical Crop Yields in Cultivated Lands of Poor Smallholder Farmers in Malawi", in A. Bationo, B. Waswa, J. Kihara and J. Kimetu (eds), *Advances in Integrated Soil Fertility Management in sub-Saharan Africa: Challenges and Opportunities*. Dordrecht: Springer, pp. 531–536.

Nelson, J. (1992) "Poverty, Equity, and the Politics of Adjustment", in S. Haggard and R. Kaufman (eds), *The Politics of Economic Adjustment*. Princeton, NJ: Princeton University Press, pp. 221–269.

NEPAD (New Partnership for Africa's Development) (2011) *The Abuja Declaration on Fertilizers for an African Green Revolution – Status of Implementation at Regional and National Levels*. Johannesburg: NEPAD.

Nhantumbo, I. and A. Salomão (2010) *Biofuels, Land Access, and Rural Livelihoods in Mozambique*. London: International Institute for Environment and Development.

OECD (Organisation for Economic Co-operation and Development) (2011) *Towards Green Growth*. Paris: OECD.

Olson, M. (1965) *The Logic of Collective Action: Public Goods and the Theory of Groups*. Cambridge, MA: Harvard University Press.

Pape, J. and D. McDonald (2002) *Cost Recovery and the Crisis of Service Delivery in South Africa*. Cape Town: Human Sciences Research Council.

Phillips, E. (2007) "The 2002 Malawi Famine", in P. Pinstrup-Andersen and F. Cheng (eds), *Food Policy for Developing Countries: Domestic Policies for Markets, Production, and Environment*. Ithaca, NY: Cornell University Press, pp. 135–148.

Porter, M. (1985) *Competitive Advantage*. New York: Free Press.

Putnam, R. (1988) "Diplomacy and Domestic Politics: The Logic of Two-Level Games", *International Organization*, 42(3): 427–460.

RSA (Republic of South Africa) (1996) *Constitution of South Africa, Chapter 2: Bill of Rights*. Pretoria: Government of the Republic of South Africa.

RSA (Republic of South Africa) (2010) *Reducing Greenhouse Gas Emissions: The Carbon Tax Option*. Pretoria: National Treasury, Government of the Republic of South Africa.

RSA (Republic of South Africa) (2011) *Integrated Resource Plan for Electricity: 2010–2030 (Revision 2 Final Report)*. Pretoria: Department of Energy, Government of the Republic of South Africa.

Rubin, O. (2008) "The Malawi 2002 Famine – Destitution, Democracy, and Donors", *Nordic Journal of African Studies*, 17(1): 47–65.

Sanchez, P., G. Denning and G. Nziguheba (2009) "The African Green Revolution Moves Forward", *Food Security*, 1(1): 37–44.
SAPA (South African Press Association) (2010) "Electricity Price Hikes Slammed", *Mail & Guardian*, 24 February. Available at ⟨http://mg.co.za/article/2010-02-24-electricity-hikes-slammed⟩ (accessed 25 January 2012).
Schut, M., M. Slingerland and A. Locke (2010) "Biofuel Developments in Mozambique: Update and Analysis of Policy, Potential and Reality", *Energy Policy*, 38(9): 5151–5165.
Schut, M., S. Bos, L. Machuama and M. Slingerland (2010) "Working Towards Sustainability: Learning Experiences for Sustainable Biofuel Strategies in Mozambique", Wageningen University and Research Centre, Wageningen.
Smiddy, K. and D. Young (2009) "Presidential and Parliamentary Elections in Malawi, May 2009", *Electoral Studies*, 28(4): 642–673.
Srinivasan, T. N. (1985) "Neoclassical Political Economy, the State, and Economic Development", *Asian Development Review*, 3(2): 38–58.
Stern, N. (2006) *Stern Review on the Economics of Climate Change*. Cambridge: Cambridge University Press.
Tilman, D., K. Cassman, P. Matson, R. Naylor and S. Polasky (2002) "Agricultural Sustainability and Intensive Production Practices", *Nature*, 418(6898): 671–677.
Tyler, E. (2009) *Aligning South African Energy and Climate Change Mitigation Policy*. Cape Town: Energy Research Centre.
UNEP (United Nations Environment Programme) (2008) *Green Jobs: Towards Decent Work in a Sustainable, Low-Carbon World*. Nairobi: UNEP.
UNEP (United Nations Environment Programme) (2011) *Towards a Green Economy: Pathways to Sustainable Development and Poverty Eradication – A Synthesis for Policymakers*. Nairobi: UNEP.
UNESCAP (United Nations Economic and Social Commission for Asia and the Pacific) (2011) *What Is Green Growth?* Bangkok: UNESCAP.
Van de Walle, N. (2001) *African Economies and the Politics of Permanent Crisis, 1979–1999*. New York: Cambridge University Press.
Winkler, H. (2005) "Renewable Energy Policy in South Africa: Policy Options for Renewable Electricity", *Energy Policy*, 33(1): 27–38.
World Bank (2003) *A User's Guide to Poverty and Social Impact Analysis*. Washington, DC: World Bank.
World Bank (2010) *World Development Report: Development and Climate Change*. Washington, DC: World Bank.
World Bank (2011) *World Development Indicators*. Washington, DC: World Bank.

5

Learning for a green society: Towards sustainable consumption and production

Zinaida Fadeeva, Abel Barasa Atiti, Unnikrishnan Payyappallimana, Aurea Tanaka, Mario Tabucanon, Sachiko Yasuda and Kazuhiko Takemoto

Introduction

Agenda 21, the programme of action from the United Nations Conference on Environment and Development (UNCED) held in Rio de Janeiro, Brazil, in 1992, identifies untenable patterns of production and consumption as the major cause of the continued deterioration of the global environment (UNCED, 1992). Fostering a green economy within an Education for Sustainable Development (ESD) framework, as argued in this chapter, has the potential of accelerating the shift towards sustainable consumption and production systems in society.

The concepts of green growth and a green economy present a simple and compelling reason for urgent transformations because contemporary production technologies, modes of operation and dominant assumptions do not permit a degree of efficiency in using natural resources sustainably and in securing societal well-being. In this chapter, green growth is viewed as a set of policies related to the relations between the economy and the environment and creating conducive conditions for sustainable consumption and production systems. It is interpreted not only as a path towards the development of global markets in less environmentally damaging products but as a system that attends more closely to the questions of local sustainability and quality of life.

In order to achieve a green economy, modern patterns of growth, technological pathways and consumer behaviour defining consumption and production systems today have to be radically changed at the global and

Green economy and good governance for sustainable development: Opportunities, promises and concerns, Puppim de Oliveira (ed.),
United Nations University Press, 2012, ISBN 978-92-808-1216-9

local levels. The required change concerns transformation at the individual, organizational, institutional and societal levels through formal and non-formal education.

Development of sustainable systems of consumption and production is a long-term project that involves the formulation of policy frameworks (the main focus of the green growth discourse), working on technical and non-technical innovations, the development of new markets, and changes in lifestyles. It also involves piloting emerging innovations for a green economy and sustainable consumption and production systems and ensuring a degree of flexibility from policy- and decision-makers as well as representatives of the production sector, civil society organizations and the public at large. Differences in context of various regions make the task of institutionalizing green economy innovations impossible without adequate engagement by different regional stakeholders.

Changing consumption and production patterns as an overarching strategy for a green economy as examined in this chapter requires fostering transformative learning processes towards increased resource-use efficiency by the production and service sectors within and across borders, and a change in the way governments manage national resources. Such processes need to be augmented with advocacy and public awareness on product and service selection, creating a mechanism to support green product and service marketing, and integrating the sustainable consumption concept into formal and informal education at all levels.

Consumption and production in a risk society: Challenges of transformation

> "We are all trapped in a shared global space of threats – without exit." (Beck, 2009)

An important thesis on the social conditions of the late twentieth century is the concept, proposed by Beck (1992), that we are living in what he calls a *risk society*. The concept provides a useful framework for demonstrating the appropriateness and necessity of ESD in enhancing more sustainable systems of consumption and production. Becoming a risk society has brought into focus several implications. Although industrial development has produced an enormous amount of goods and a society of material affluence, it has also produced new risks and new dangers. These modern risks are the unwanted by-product of modern consumption and production systems. Beck's central thesis is that "the gain in power from techno-economic *progress* is being increasingly overshadowed by the production of risks" (Beck, 1992: 13). Radioactivity, environmental degradation and destruction, global warming and increased amounts of toxins and pollutants in our daily environment are but a few of the risks facing the citizens of all modern (developed and developing) societies. Such risks, together with de-localization, "incalculableness" and non-compensatability (Beck, 2008), are a certainty irrespective of our geographical location, our position in society and the value system to which we belong. As a result, in terms of learning, what we *do not know* (non-knowledge and not-knowing) becomes of equal significance to the issues and concepts that we do know, and consequently commands serious attention. It has become imperative to define risks and develop collaborative actions to address them through continuous learning structured around ESD principles. In this regard, the role of ESD in the context of the risk society is central to addressing the new global challenges associated with unsustainable systems of consumption and production.

What does it mean for global attempts to develop an economy and production–consumption systems that sustain life? The scope of this chapter does not allow us to present any sort of comprehensive picture. We limit ourselves to highlighting some critical characteristics (from our viewpoint) that have implications for post-modern learning.

With knowledge, predictability, stability, security and control losing their meaning, many decisions – from the design of a policy package supporting a particular consumption–production system to investment in a technology or setting up a new form of enterprise – do not have fully predictable consequences. In other words, the element of non-knowing becomes a permanent fixture of any decision, big or small.

Some other complex and cosmopolitan natures of risks are manifested in dramatic conflicts. For example, driven by the climate argument, the production of biofuels is in many cases proving to threaten food production in the most vulnerable regions. Although biofuel production accounts for only 1 per cent of farmland globally, climate change, population growth, changing dietary and consumption patterns and increases in biofuel demand are expected to further worsen the situation by 2020. In addition, such changes are expected to have a negative impact on biodiversity and ecosystems in terms of threats to the diversity of local cultivars and reducing the resilience of agricultural systems, leading to drought and a reduction in arable land (Stromberg et al., 2009). This exemplifies the differences in perception and development priorities as well as impending conflicts at the different ends of the production chains.

The global or, in the words of Beck, cosmopolitan nature of risks makes the local–global perspective an inextricable part of reality. Although experience of such risks and pressures might not take place simultaneously in different regions, understanding the interconnections of risks – through, among other things, consideration of justice – is critical to shaping decisions. Across the supply chains of various products, issues of human rights, the environment, health and safety, bribery and corruption, and forced and child labour gain the attention of multiple stakeholders. The (extended) producer responsibility concepts and practices generate new important forms of sustainable consumption and production (SCP) actions addressing the externalities of production–consumption systems, however the majority of the power decisions affecting thousands are made on the bases of predominantly economic considerations.

In the face of uncertainty, the traditional "knowledge holders" – experts from inside and outside academia – lose the basis of their knowledge authority (but still retain decision-making power). At the same time, different epistemic communities, often with contradictory and conflicting positions, become concerned about global and local sustainability issues and wish to enter the arena of defining risks and planning actions. An interesting example of redefining roles in the global market is the recent drive of the private sector to engage with the "bottom of pyramid" (Prahalad, 2004) or the "base of the pyramid" (Hart, 2005) – the 4 billion poor who, until recently, have had a limited role as global consumers and were not at all seen, from the perspective of the global economy, as *producers*. Empowering them, often simultaneously, as consumers, co-developers and co-producers in the systems of production and consumption, while securing their access to livelihood opportunities, requires values and approaches that are not traditionally present in the dominant business practices. Developing not only green, low-carbon but also *inclusive* economies calls for learning from and with those whose views were for a long time counted as unimportant for local and global markets (WBCSD, 2010) (see also Chapter 6).

At the same time, there is an increasing need to promote grassroots innovations based on traditional knowledge and resources through private sector and community partnerships, which could meet the socioeconomic needs of local communities grounded on the principles of self-reliance. In the absence of a clear image of the contours of the new green economy and the risks of the global market systems, multiple local innovations in the consumption–production sphere are critical. Research institutions and institutions of higher learning have a challenge ahead to build a knowledge network and promote value addition for local innovations in order to achieve market integration (Gupta et al., 2003).

The turbulence of modern times also means that there is no ultimate "right decision"; new stages of development call for new approaches. Social enterprises could lift a community out of extreme poverty but might have a limited impact once a certain level of prosperity has been reached. For example, in an economic recession, producers of organic cotton and coffee could lose their (often global) customers. This calls into question the sustainability of the SCP system, which is highly dependent on international (rather than local) trade.

Monitoring the unfolding risks and responding rapidly and creatively serve as a guarantee of the continuation of activities and, as a result, the development of a system without catastrophic (small or large) consequences. With the prominence of the not-known (and the consequent limited influence of subject experts), stakeholders' engagement as well as a reflexive learning approach become critical. Some, mainly larger, companies are adopting such practices within the domain of corporate social responsibility, but they are still a minority.

Addressing transformative learning through ESD lenses

ESD underlines the evolving nature of sustainable development processes, as in educating for a green economy. As societies develop, so does knowledge of the issues accompanying this development, leading to the need for new skills, knowledge, attitudes and values appropriate to the emerging challenges. The constantly and rapidly unfolding realities put extraordinary pressure on the institutions of learning to consider the identified societal problems as well as to address them. To deal with the requirements of the long-term perspective, flexibility, uncertainty, innovativeness, diversity and cross-sector engagement in transformation towards a green economy are crucial. The dominant knowledge and learning systems supporting this transformation would also need to undergo radical change. ESD, with its focus on holism, contextuality, life-long learning processes, community engagement and value orientation, is central to enabling change towards a globalized green society.

ESD means creating the space for transformative learning processes (Wals and Corcoran, 2006). Moving towards a globalized green economy as a transformative learning process requires creating the space for challenging dominant assumptions and values in relation to unsustainable consumption and production patterns. Based on the literature (for example, Atiti, 2008; Mezirow, 2009; Taylor, 2009), a transformative approach to educating for SCP and consequently a globalized green economy is based on a number of core elements. These elements, which reflect ESD principles, are outlined in the rest of this section.

Value orientation

If education is to become a transformative force, adhering to value orientation provides a firm moral foundation for questioning and reinventing modern development through greater inclusivity and justice. Value considerations are particularly significant because, for all its importance, the green growth agenda focuses predominantly on issues related to resource and energy efficiency, technology transfer and the development of new growth models. This leaves the critical elements of the transformation of human thinking and discussion of the value base for actions underemphasized.

Education has to go beyond addressing the question of how to improve the individual's quality of life but also of how to reflect upon values and how they manifest themselves in relation to oneself, the community and the world. Value orientation permits the questioning of moral positions and motivations in development at different levels, empowering the learners (within and outside educational institutions) to make choices that avoid what Mahatma Gandhi called the main sins of our time – politics without principle, wealth without work, pleasure without conscience, knowledge without character, commerce without morality, worship without sacrifice, and science and technology without humanity.

Values are of critical importance in the risk society because, in a situation in which uncertainties permeate all aspects of reality and the links between decisions and their consequences are broken, they become the only foundation for the integrity of people, organizations and communities. Ongoing change, while inspiring creativity and experimentation, might significantly limit courses of action. Organizational and personal identities, based on a set of values linked to the vision of solidarity, equality and environmental sustainability, are critical for the formation of governance and informed decision-making.

All the ESD principles are important, but value orientation remains fundamental. It defines the foundation of the organizational vision of reality and the challenges associated with it, and it consequently defines the roles that organization plays in society. Other ESD categories enable coherent long-term translation of the vision into organizational practices.

Awareness of context

Developing an awareness of context involves a deeper appreciation and understanding of the sociocultural factors that influence the attainment of a green economy. Resistance to embracing green economy innovations can be explained from a contextual perspective. It is therefore important for educators to consider the learning contexts of learners when educating for a green economy (Hanks, 1991). The context is important for three reasons: first, the production and consumption patterns manifest themselves differently in different contexts and countries; secondly, innovations for a green economy consist of various interrelated variables that are contextual; finally, there are few universal solutions to address this complexity and hence they have to be addressed appropriately.

The long-standing criticism of the dominant system of education is its tendency to universalization and unification as well as having economic development as a major measure of success. ESD, in contrast, recognizes the importance of *understanding the different cultures and appreciating their contributions to education and development*. For educational institutions, engagement with the society through research and educational processes must respect the cultures and practices of the various stakeholders and communities.

The call to engage with traditional learning and knowledge systems is prominent in many regions of the world. The identification and documentation of sociocultural knowledge traditions, validating them through multi-stakeholder processes and integrating them into educational and research processes represent a critical challenge for education. It is also vital to recognize and realize local communities as co-developers and co-producers in the systems of production and consumption, while at the same time promoting grassroots innovations based on local resources and knowledge. Again, a combination of research and learning processes is critical for adequately addressing the complexity of the task.

Promoting dialogue and creative ideas

Dialogue is the essential medium through which transformation for a globalized green economy can be promoted and developed. It is central to the questioning of flawed consumption and production patterns.

Through dialogue, individuals and organizations are able to reflect on their practices, question their assumptions and beliefs, and ultimately transform their consumption habits and production models. Theorists of deliberative democracy such as Chambers (2003) argue that, under the right conditions, dialogue may expand perspectives, promote tolerance and foster understanding between actors in the context of enabling transformative learning. These conditions include openness, reciprocity, publicness and authenticity. Through dialogue, various communities can come together and creatively understand the implications of addressing the challenges in consumption and production patterns in their contexts.

Fostering dialogue within social spaces has been known to facilitate collective learning and innovations with regard to enabling sustainability (Rist et al., 2007). Individual experiences – of consumers, producers, non-governmental organizations (NGOs) and government representatives – are the primary medium of transformative learning processes for SCP. Individual experiences of SCP provide a pool of ideas to draw upon to create a green globalized economy. Experience is what ESD educators stimulate and create through learning activities and what actors reflect on as they learn new consumption patterns and aspects in a more green society.

Fostering critical reflection and reflexivity

Building on the importance of dialogue as a core element of transformative learning is the fostering of critical reflection among actors. Critical reflection is essential for actors to come to know and understand themselves with regard to any issue. Knowing ourselves is vital to creating new ideas and social relations that may lead to the emergence of a globalized green economy. Furthermore, fostering critical reflection creates the freedom for actors to consider their potential to promote sustainable systems of consumption. Reflection is a process in which actors consider the assumptions and values that influence their actions in order to understand contextual issues related to SCP. Although reflection is often viewed as an individual act, the outcomes are enhanced when it is done collectively. Reflection involves critical questioning and the exploration of new ideas, values and relations to enable SCP patterns. These new ideas, relations and values are useful in modifying existing ones in the direction of a globalized green economy. Providing opportunities for critical reflection when educating for SCP is a good strategy for enabling transformative learning.

Systematic, critical and creative thinking and reflection are emphasized by ESD (UNECE, 2009) as prerequisites for action at all levels. Education is expected to promote reflexivity and the future orientation of knowing and learning how to make the transition towards a society with a better quality of life, solidarity and environmental sustainability.

To develop knowledge and actions it is necessary to understand the historical, cultural, technical and economic causes of particular situations, to acknowledge the importance of vision, strategies and tactics to the required social transformation, and to appreciate the various types, levels and risks of this transformation. The challenge, however, is to go beyond addressing the immediate problems (tactical planning) towards more long-term visioning (strategic thinking and planning) and from critical thinking to creativity.

Adopting a holistic and systemic orientation

To achieve more sustainable ways of producing and consuming, a whole variety of measures has to be implemented. Finding new technologies, testing production models and identifying new funding and distribution mechanisms are only one part of a large puzzle. Questions of governance, social systems and education to support the new more sustainable consumption and production have to be closely and constantly examined and, often, reinvented. A holistic approach to a diversity of development is urgently called for.

Systemic thinking refers to a mode of thinking that keeps actors in touch with the wholeness of their existence in the context of enabling a globalized green economy. This is an essential component of fostering transformative learning processes for SCP. Such an orientation encourages engagement with other ways of knowing, for example indigenous innovations for a green economy, and also understanding the complexity of the transition to sustainability. This is because the web of social reality in communities of practice is composed of too many variables to be considered and addressed comprehensively. These variables become evident when sustainability issues are understood as unsustainable consumption and production patterns in a specific context. Actors therefore need systemic thinking skills in order to understand the complex social reality of fostering sustainable systems of consumption and production and the emergence of a green economy.

Appreciation of the complexity of society's problems and understanding the critical importance of tacit knowledge lead to long-standing recognition of educational engagement with other stakeholders. Business and government were the first partners to have been considered important for economically viable innovation, employment growth and national competitiveness. Recognition of sociocultural and neglected ("orphaned") problems leads to engagement with stakeholders who speak on behalf of these issues. Local communities, NGOs, media organizations and organizations representing both formal and informal sectors of education have been recognized as important partners in knowledge development processes.

Translating the global ESD agenda into regional actions: SCP innovations in multi-stakeholder initiatives

Apart from access to basic, quality education, reorienting learning of various forms and at various levels to integrate sustainability principles has been part of the global sustainability vision since the 1990s. This includes fundamental changes in worldviews; specific approaches, capacities and innovative technologies and tools to deal with social, economic, environmental and cultural challenges; an approach to development oriented to participatory action; and behavioural as well as lifestyle changes. Education for sustainability has attracted political attention since the Earth

Summit in 1992, following calls by the international community, civil society organizations and academics for moves towards transforming education.

Agenda 21 called for a reorientation of various forms and levels of education towards sustainable development, and education was mentioned in many subsequent international and national declarations and resolutions as a key element in advancing towards more sustainable development, however this did not receive adequate attention until the 2002 World Summit on Sustainable Development (WSSD). WSSD also acknowledged the role of partnerships in pursuing the challenges of sustainable development and called for collaboration in supporting the practical implementation of Agenda 21.

The development of partnerships has become the strategy of the United Nations University (UNU) in addressing the priorities of the United Nations Decade of Education for Sustainable Development (UN DESD), which commenced in 2005 following the decision of the 57th session of United Nations General Assembly (see Box 5.1). The UNU Education for Sustainable Development programme was designed to build new perspectives and conceptual clarity as well as to support field-level implementation of projects. The major objectives included networking and collaboration among various stakeholders, higher quality in teaching and learning, supporting the Millennium Development Goals and reforming education at the national level. The programme focused on vision-building and advocacy, consultation and ownership, partnerships and networks, capacity-building and training, research and innovation, information and communication technologies, and monitoring and evaluation.

A major programme within the UNU's DESD initiatives is the Regional Centres of Expertise (RCE) network, which is designed to

Box 5.1 The United Nations Decade of Education for Sustainable Development

> DESD (2005–2014) was launched subsequent to the decision of the 57th Session of United Nations General Assembly. UNESCO became the lead agency for the programme and developed the international implementation scheme.
>
> The educators were given a strong voice and ESD received a much-needed impetus for fostering leaning for sustainable development. Some of the main goals of the DESD have been to strengthen collaboration and partnerships among multi-stakeholders and sectors, to achieve better integration of new knowledge and technologies in sustainable development and to enhance cooperation between various forms and levels of learning process.

translate the broad objectives of DESD, and the network for the Promotion of Sustainability in Postgraduate Education and Research (ProSPER.Net). Both networks contribute to the formation of a global learning space for sustainable development and the transformation of knowledge and learning towards sustainable development (see Box 5.2).

Action learning and research: Facilitating more sustainable systems of consumption and production

The success of RCEs, ProSPER.Net and other programmes of UNU-IAS in addressing the challenges of consumption and production systems has demonstrated the potential of ESD to provide methodological and pedagogical approaches for the required innovations. These approaches allowed the engagement of critical stakeholders in action research addressing the challenges of the regions (value orientation and contextuality). For example, Universiti Sains Malaysia (University of Science, Malaysia) – the facilitator of RCE Penang – developed a partnership with village farmers. In the course of the collaboration, the partners developed affordable technologies for soil enrichment that are simple to apply. These have been successfully implemented and led to increases in agricultural yields (see the description of the cases below). RCE Cebu in the Philippines developed new productive activities for the community living off the only remaining forest on the island. The forest, which faced extinction owing to slash and burn practices, was studied by researchers at the University of Cebu and members of the local community, who identified ecosystem services capable of providing alternative employment related to tourism and education (learning within the local context and value orientation).

ESD communities have demonstrated an ability to open up neutral spaces that enable positions to be taken that might otherwise be perceived as too politically sensitive and, therefore, not possible. In response to a call by the provincial government of Saskatchewan, Canada, for public feedback on a proposed plan for developing nuclear power in the province, faculty members of the higher education partners of RCE Saskatchewan offered an alternative perspective that sought to extend the discussion to include other sustainable energy alternatives. After in-depth discussion, this view was accepted and broader hearings took place. In this significant case, the RCE provided a neutral platform for members of all higher education partners to offer input that was potentially politically sensitive. The collective exploration of more sustainable options led to a learning process that included long-term energy alternatives for the region in addition to advancing trust and respect among the partners.

Box 5.2 UNU's Cross-Sectoral Multi-Stakeholder Initiatives on ESD

A Regional Centre of Expertise (RCE) is a global learning space for sustainable development. It is a partnership of formal, informal and non-formal educational organizations working with local and regional communities. RCE at the local level is not a single organization but a network of existing institutions, which may include schools, public authorities, higher education and research institutions, civil society organizations, businesses, and media with collective strategies and shared responsibilities for ESD based on contextual realities. Apart from strong governance principles, a coordination plan for collaborative action, innovation, research and development and transformative education are central to an RCE. With 100 RCEs around the world (as of March 2012) linked through geographical, thematic and operational partnerships, as well as with a good peer review mechanism, the network as a multi-stakeholder initiative has gone a long way towards linking local and global contexts and processes on sustainable development.

The network for the Promotion of Sustainability in Postgraduate Education and Research (ProSPER.Net) reinforces the role of higher education institutions in order to develop specific capacities, and innovative technologies for sustainable development have been the thrust areas of this programme. Launched in 2008 in the Asia Pacific region, it currently has 21 members and serves as a space for collaboration regionally and globally through transdisciplinary, cross-sectoral and inter-generational learning. Modules for various professionals, reorientation of business school curriculums, e-learning programmes for public policy, alternative approaches to university appraisal based on sustainability principles have been key among the programmes undertaken by the various partners.

Strong horizontal and vertical linkages are also built between the RCE, ProSPER.Net and other regional networks emphasizing university and community collaboration. Such partnerships exist with a European Network on Higher Education for Sustainable Development that has also taken up innovative teaching and life-long learning approaches in the European region. Mainstreaming Environment and Sustainability into African Universities is yet another regional initiative striving to make universities more relevant to local communities, civil society and businesses in the Africa region. Contact with these various networks are also being linked and strengthened through cross-regional higher education collaboration.

Regional ESD initiatives have offered a suitable strategy for reorienting consumption–production systems that are contextually situated. The region of Malmo in Sweden is famous, among other qualities, for its agricultural production. Bearing in mind these characteristics, the schools of Malmo decided to contribute to reshaping the regional food systems, giving priority to organic local producers. The ambitious goal of eventually reaching 100 per cent organic school meals required the collaboration of schools, universities, the municipality and the families of school children. A combination of research, publications, education and network-building supports this ongoing transition facilitated by RCE Skane.

These examples highlight the importance of establishing authentic relationships with actors when educating for a green economy is an essential factor in a transformative experience. Authentic relationships are known to allow actors to share information openly and achieve greater mutual understanding on the issues of a green economy. Striving for a more authentic ESD practice is central to integrating all the core elements of transformative learning as examined here. the strategies adopted by UNU-IAS in implementing ESD aim at achieving this.

Learning across science and society – RCE Penang (Malaysia)

RCE Penang, through Universiti Sains Malaysia (USM) as the leading actor and driver, has contributed to SCP in the region in considerable ways. One of the initiatives of the RCE has been research and extension in close collaboration with agricultural communities in the Penang region. These links have yielded cost-effective and environmentally friendly technologies and approaches. One such improved technology is Worm-Fert, an innovative smart organic fertilizer cum soil conditioner that is rich in beneficial microbes and macro and micro nutrients. This product is formulated from a unique earthworm diet and developed from a special harvesting process that ensures exceptionally high levels of soil-enriching agents. It is used as a soil conditioner/plant additive, fertilizer and natural pesticide.

The collective goal of USM and the villages was defined by the needs of the region to improve the livelihood opportunities of the poorer rural communities (value orientation). Learning across science–development boundaries brought measurable results and strengthened authentic relationships between academia and villages, paving the way for future SCP innovations.

Action research for environmental preservation and livelihood improvement – RCE Cebu (Philippines)

Resource and Poverty Response Mapping Management (REPORMA) is one of the key initiatives of RCE Cebu. The major focus of the programme has been collaborating with forest communities in the CAMP 7 region to reclaim their rights to resources and improved livelihoods. Important components of this successful programme include: mobilizing multiple stakeholders through participatory research on poverty levels among the communities and an inventory of natural resources; the creation of effective and innovative knowledge-sharing systems, including community baseline maps, inventory data on resources and resource management, poverty indicators and poverty responses, and good practices; and participatory planning and the implementation of forest conservation, natural resource management and poverty alleviation activities (job creation), especially through eco-tourism.

Learning within the REPORMA project has been characterized by strong action research and innovation components where development of new inclusive long-term livelihood options followed community learning about local ecosystems (value orientation). The project, based on strong reflection and reflexivity dimensions, demonstrated success in addressing the complexity of modern development problems through a blend of research, education and development.

As in the example of the RCE Penang project, REPORMA emphasized the relevance of life-long learning skills for all partners in society, particularly those who are in a vulnerable state owing to economic, social or environmental conditions.

Learning across the supply chain – RCE Skane (Sweden)

Skåne, a region in southern Sweden, contributes considerably to the agricultural and food production of the country. Sustainable food systems is a flagship project of RCE Skane. In Sweden, municipalities have free meal programmes for all school children. In Malmo city, one of the areas served by RCE Skane, 35,000 meals are served daily by the school restaurants. Targeted at communities in Malmo municipality, the project focuses on increasing organic food in school meals. The programme involves five steps: targeting schools to change to organic food; the preparation of learning materials on food and sustainability targeted towards households; in-service teacher training on food, climate and ESD; fair-trade certification; and collaboration with regional business partners to make the programme sustainable. Malmo being certified as a fair-trade city facilitates multilevel actions and programmes.

The case demonstrates the strong future-oriented thinking and learning in the region. In this programme, a new supply chain is created by building links between organic farmers and schools. While utilizing the leveraging power of the public sector in reorienting business practices, the initiatives allowed a different choice for consumers in the area. The programme was based on multi-step, multi-stakeholder community learning

Table 5.1 Case studies and ESD principles

Case	SCP outcomes (sustainable development value added)	ESD principles observed
Penang	Livelihood improvement	• Value orientation (poverty eradication drive) • Community engagement (link between science and society) • Life-long learning (learning by communities and farmers) • Contextualization (addressing issues relevant to the communities)
Cebu	Protection of ecosystems, livelihood improvement	• Value orientation (protection of the last island forest, poverty eradication drive) • Community engagement (through action research and community learning) • Life-long learning (learning by communities) • Contextualization (addressing issues of livelihood relevant to the local community and protection of natural ecosystems important also for the wider society)
Skane	Greening of the supply chain and bringing different consumer choices	• Value orientation (minimizing impact of consumption and promotion of local production) • Community engagement (link between public sector – schools, society – families and municipality, government, etc.) • Life-long learning (learning by different sectors – from education to NGOs, families, etc.) • Contextualization (addressing issues of health, local resilience and sustainability relevant to the communities) • Future-oriented thinking (reliance on local suppliers and organic choices)
Saskatchewan	Clean, diverse and safe energy solutions	• Value orientation (new energy alternatives) • Community engagement (link between science and society) • Life-long learning (learning by academia, government) • Contextualization (addressing issues relevant to the community and the nation) • Future-oriented thinking (alternative to nuclear power)

PRAM project	Poverty reduction and livelihood improvement	• Value orientation (developing learning systems bringing sustainable development outcomes), • Community engagement (link between science, development and communities) • Life-long learning (learning by government, i.e. extension officers, and the communities) • Contextualization (addressing issues relevant to the community and the region) • Future-oriented thinking (modelling new learning systems within institutions of higher education)
Reorientation of business schools	Poverty reduction and pro-poor development	• Value orientation (fostering corporate social responsibility practices towards sustainable development outcomes) • Community engagement (link between knowledge production, transfer for communities' development, improved livelihoods, self-reliance and well-being) • Life-long learning (private sector and communities' learning and empowerment) • Contextualization (addressing issues relevant to the community and the region) • Future-oriented thinking (development of methods and pedagogies for sustainable practices in higher education)

and innovation and was implemented through workshops and teacher-training on food and SCP perspectives. The remarkable design of the programme addressed various elements in the consumption–production system by working with multiple stakeholders as well as linking it to local, regional and global dimensions (system action and learning).

Developing a sustainable energy supply – RCE Saskatchewan (Canada)

In response to the call by the regional authorities for public feedback on the proposed plan for developing a nuclear power station, the higher education institutions of RCE Saskatchewan offered an alternative that, after deep discussion, has been accepted. In this significant case, the RCE provided a neutral platform for all higher education partners to propose potentially politically sensitive innovation. The collective exploration of more sustainable options led to a learning process about the long-term energy alternatives for the region and the nation as well as contributing to the development of trust and respect among the partners.

Innovative pedagogies in poverty reduction

In 2010, ProSPER.Net members, led by the Asian Institute of Technology (AIT), developed a project to identify innovative mechanisms for postgraduate curriculum improvement and to guide changes in educational practices based on programmes tailored to develop skills and competences according to local communities' challenges and needs and that have an impact on poverty levels.

The project focused on the successful implementation of the Poverty Reduction and Agricultural Management (PRAM) initiative, a collaborative activity undertaken by AIT in partnership with the Wetlands Alliance Programme and the Lao PDR government. PRAM was designed to target Lao government officers who work in local communities and lacked the practical and technical training to implement poverty reduction policies. For this purpose, a unique programme was created, using pedagogic approaches such as problem- and project-based learning and assessment based on poverty reduction indicators. The curriculum offers a basic orientation course, with a requirement to continue taking core and elective courses, and, overall, it is composed of mainly practical learning activities related to training people to solve specific local problems related to poverty reduction. For the elective courses, students are requested to undertake projects and in order to complete a course, it is necessary to demonstrate that their interventions had an impact on poverty levels in the communities they are working with.

Aiming to carry out an analysis of PRAM and how its lessons can be abstracted and transferred to other countries in other contexts, AIT, the University of the Philippines, Universitas Gadjah Mada (Indonesia) and Universiti Sains Malaysia conducted interviews and field visits. Through these they were able to identify important elements of curriculum design and implementation, such as a degree of flexibility to incorporate poor communities' needs and provide students with a specific set of skills needed to address these challenges, as well as constant evaluation of this process, to ensure quality on the one hand and a meaningful programme offering that has a significant impact on reducing poverty levels.

Also identified were positive outcomes that reflect the effectiveness of the fit-for-purpose approach used in the programme, which serves the needs of both students (government officers) and the local community. For example, it was possible to list an improvement in people's livelihoods, stronger and closer ties with the local community, the use of local and inexpensive solutions to improve local production activities, a multiplying effect in terms of creating alternative solutions, and the establishment of local networks, which provide useful information and foster information-sharing and awareness of simple measures to secure food and a better livelihood.

Learning with future leaders: The integration of sustainability in business schools

Recognizing the important role that the private sector plays in fostering innovation and sustainable practices in the daily management of business and production, as well as the need to provide future professionals in this sector with the skills to be socially responsible about the impacts of their activities in their communities and on the environment, AIT proposed a project to integrate sustainability issues into the curriculums, teaching and learning of business schools. The project was jointly carried out with Universiti Sains Malaysia, Universitas Gadjah Mada (Indonesia) and Yonsei University (South Korea).

In a first phase, the project partners developed a series of activities ranging from a research project to appraise how sustainable development is being embedded in Southeast Asian business schools' curriculums, to the incorporation of sustainability-related themes in the various courses, to developing case studies on corporate social responsibility and social business and the design of new MBA programmes based on the sustainability paradigm. Further developing these activities, the partners sought in a second phase to focus on curriculum development initiatives by producing educational materials on social business and social entrepreneurship in the context of poverty alleviation and training materials based on the principles of the United Nations Global Compact.

The outcomes of this project include a collection of case studies and teaching notes on the setting up and operation of social business, including elements of experiential learning. This helps students to develop specific skills through customized tools for business in the context of poverty alleviation and pro-poor development. Also, the case studies documented the development of social enterprises in various countries in the region – China, Indonesia, Laos, Malaysia, Pakistan, the Philippines and Thailand – that address specific and local challenges in a variety of fields such as water and energy supply, agribusiness, handicrafts and e-commerce, as well as providing training in management skills, including information and communication technologies, thus empowering small business owners to consolidate and eventually expand their activities.

The way forward: Cultivating global networks for green economy innovations

The potential of ESD for a green society: Upscaling and mainstreaming innovative practices

The value added of ESD

The experience of learning for a green economy based on ESD principles delivered in global networks has the potential to:
- foster the values, behaviours and lifestyles required for SCP;
- put in place a process of transformative learning towards a deeper understanding of how the three pillars of ESD (social, economic and environmental) give shape and content to SCP patterns in society;
- increase the capacity of communities to transform their visions of society into reality and become agents of SCP;
- inspire the belief that communities within a specific context have the power and responsibility to facilitate a green economy on a local and global scale.

Despite the significance of individual stories of learning and innovation for sustainability, the crucial challenge remains of progressing from individual good practices to multiple manifestations of new ways of doing things. Even with large networks such as RCE and PRoSPER.Net, some strategic efforts to mainstream and upscale successes are required.

Systematic engagement with global sustainability processes

The growth of experience in local communities and continuous international collaboration enable large networks with growth potential, such as RCEs and ProSPER.Net, to engage with global sustainability-related processes. Such engagement would not only allow the translation of the global discourses into terms appropriate for local realities but also, and most importantly, provide an avenue for feedback on global (and regional) policies. For example, some materials and capacity development processes developed by UN or developmental agencies could be tested by the RCEs in various regions. Learning from these processes could go back to the facilitators for further development. ESD networks could also assist in identifying regional SCP needs and participate in discussions of the policy portfolios.

Such concerted action, feeding on local innovation and contributing to global efforts for change, would need to be based on some essential principles, including constantly revisiting the developmental direction of the world and the communities of practice within local communities of practice, research and capacity development.

Exploring research and capacity development opportunities for SCP

There is a need to explore opportunities for further research on SCP and public policy. ESD practitioners need to link up with consumer behaviour researchers, analysts of operational practices or organizations, theorists of community innovation and other relevant topics. If learning for a greener society is to be different, one of the critical questions is the availability of research and pedagogical skills to satisfy requests for new ways of learning. Understanding such needs is not a trivial matter in societies where the power to ask questions (and more specifically to define research questions) often resides with recognized experts and expert organizations (Beck, 2008). ESD insists that the answer is to engage the local regions/communities in defining educational/capacity development needs and for the funders/developers to accept local inputs.

Communities of practice: Framework for analysing learning for a green society

Conceptualizing global networks as communities of practice (CoPs) for transformative learning provides a useful analytical framework for examining the emergence of a globalized green economy. CoPs provide contexts in which actors can interact to identify and deliberate on sustainability issues related to SCP. Although CoPs occur in various forms, they share a basic structure that consists of the following three essential elements (Wenger et al., 2002):
1. A *domain* of knowledge that creates common ground and a sense of common identity for members in communities of practice.
2. A *community* of people who care about their common ground and a sense of identity, for example, contributing to sustainable systems of consumption and production and a globalized green economy.

3. The *practices* in the form of frameworks, ideas, tools, information, language and documents that community members share. Sharing such practices through dialogue can sustain transformative learning processes aimed at addressing unsustainable consumption and production patterns.

Seely Brown and Duguid (1991) consider CoPs as suitable sites for innovation. They view learning and innovating as closely related forms of human activity. In order to foster innovations for green economy, nations need to conceive of themselves as CoPs. They also need to redesign themselves as reflexive social learning systems with the capability to participate in broader CoPs (Wenger, 2000). Innovation necessitates a deep understanding of contextual factors that constrain transformative learning processes. Engaging actors in deliberating and acting on such factors has the potential of developing their capabilities to innovate for SCP systems. It also has the potential of transforming dominant assumptions and values in relation to unsustainable consumption and production patterns in a CoP.

Fostering a globalized green economy through CoPs (for example, RCEs) has the potential of realizing the "triple bottom line" of sustainability – that is, achieving economic, environmental and societal objectives (Elkington, 1999) as envisaged in the three pillars of ESD. CoPs can be designed and developed as sites of transformative learning and the application of practical knowledge for a green economy in three steps. The first step is to identify potential CoPs within a region. Practical knowledge about the sustainable systems of consumption and production required by communities usually exists in some form. The second step is to provide infrastructure and support to the evolving community of practice. Although informal CoPs may be self-sustaining, they lack legitimacy and the budgetary resources of an established organization. Countries may appreciate them, promote them and use them for their sustainability initiatives, or they may hinder them. The third and last step is to use non-traditional methods to measure, value and adapt reward systems for evaluation. This entails documenting and sharing the "good practices" of communities of practice on a wider scale. UNU-IAS follows a similar process in recruiting and coordinating members of the global RCE community.

Through supported communities of practice (for example, RCEs) actors can deliberate on and collectively address unsustainable practices. They can envision themselves and their communities as a sustainable society with a view to exploring innovations for a green economy. The relative autonomy of CoPs is central in allowing the creative reshaping of contextual sustainable consumption and production practices through participation and mutual engagement.

REFERENCES

Atiti, A. B. (2008) "Critical Action Research: Exploring Organisational Learning and Sustainability in a Kenyan Context", PhD thesis, Macquarie University.
Beck, U. (1992) *Risk Society – Towards a New Modernity*. London: Sage.
Beck, U. (2008) "Risk Society's 'Cosmopolitan Moment'", Lecture at Harvard University, 12 November.
Beck, U. (2009) *World at Risk*. Cambridge: Polity Press.
Chambers, S. (2003) "Deliberative Democratic Theory", *Annual Review of Political Science*, 6: 307–326.
Elkington, J. (1999) *Cannibals with Forks: The Triple Bottom Line of the 21st Century Business*. Oxford: Capstone.
Gupta, A. K., R. Sinha, D. Koradia, R. Patel, M. Parmar, P. Rohit, H. Patel, K. Patel, V. S. Chand, T. J. James, A. Chandan, M. Patel, T. N. Prakash and P. Vivekanandan (2003) "Mobilizing Grassroots' Technological Innovations and Traditional Knowledge, Values and Institutions: Articulating Social and Ethical Capital", *Futures*, 35: 975–987.
Hanks, W. (1991) "Foreword", in J. Lave and E. Wenger (eds), *Situated Learning: Legitimate Peripheral Participation*. Cambridge: Cambridge University Press, pp. 13–24.
Hart, S. L. (2005) *Capitalism at the Crossroads: The Unlimited Business Opportunities in Solving the World's Most Difficult Problems*. Upper Saddle River, NJ: Wharton School.
Mezirow, J. (2009) "Transformative Learning Theory", in J. Mezirow and E. Taylor (eds), *Transformative Learning in Practice: Insights from Community, Workplace, and Higher Education*. San Francisco: Jossey-Bass, pp. 18–31.
Prahalad, C. K. (2004) *The Fortune at the Bottom of the Pyramid*. Philadelphia: University of Pennsylvania, Wharton School Publishing.
Rist, S., F. Delgado and U. Wiesman (2007) "Social Learning Processes and Sustainable Development: The Emergence of Transformation of an Indigenous Landuse System in the Andes of Bolivia", in A. E. J. Wals (ed.), *Social Learning Towards a Sustainable World: Principles, Perspectives and Praxis*. Wageningen, The Netherlands: Wageningen Academic Publishers.
Seely Brown, J. and P. Duguid (1991) "Organizational Learning and Communities-of Practice: Toward a Unified View of Working, Learning and Innovation", *Organization Science*, 2(1): 40–57.
Stromberg, P., M. Esteban and D. Thompson-Pomeroy (2009) "Interlinkages in Climate Change: Vulnerability of a Mitigation Strategy?", UNU-IAS Report, Yokohama, Japan.
Taylor, E. (2009) "Fostering Transformative Learning", in J. Mezirow and E. Taylor (eds), *Transformative Learning in Practice: Insights from Community, Workplace, and Higher Education*. San Francisco: Jossey-Bass, pp. 3–17.
UNCED (United Nations Conference on Environment and Development) (1992) *Agenda 21: Earth Summit – The United Nations Programme of Action from Rio*. Available at ⟨http://www.un.org/esa/dsd/agenda21/res_agenda21_00.shtml⟩ (accessed 4 February 2012).

UNECE (United Nations Economic Commission for Europe) (2009) *Learning from Each Other: The UNECE Strategy for Education for Sustainable Development*. New York and Geneva: United Nations Economic Commission for Europe.

Wals, A. and P. B. Corcoran (2006) "Sustainability as an Outcome of Transformative Learning", in J. Holmberg and B. Samuelsson (eds), *Drivers and Barriers for Implementing Sustainable Development in Higher Education*. Paris: UNESCO.

WBCSD (World Business Council for Sustainable Development) (2010) "Business and Development: Challenges and Opportunities in a Rapidly Changing World", Geneva. Available at ⟨http://www.wbcsd.org/web/development/business_and_development.pdf⟩ (accessed 25 January, 2012).

Wenger, E. (2000) "Communities of Practice and Social Learning Systems", *Organization*, 7(2): 224–246.

Wenger, E., R. McDermott and W. Snyder (2002) *Cultivating Communities of Practice: A Guide to Managing Knowledge*. Boston: Harvard Business School Press.

6

Revitalizing socio-ecological production landscapes through greening the economy

Kaoru Ichikawa, Robert Blasiak and Aya Takatsuki

Introduction

The Millennium Ecosystem Assessment (2005) revealed that human use of ecosystem services is expanding at the expense of considerable modification to the Earth's ecosystems. With the global population expected to rise to 9.3 billion by 2050 (UNDESA, Population Division, 2011), pressure on the world's ecosystems will continue to be severe and the conditions of ecosystem services will worsen unless society takes action to combat these adverse trends (Millennium Ecosystem Assessment, 2005). Actually, many global issues we are facing today, such as poverty, food insecurity and freshwater scarcity, are linked to environmental degradation. Although having a healthy environment is essential to the well-being of current and future generations, economic growth and environmental conservation have been seen as mutually exclusive "trade-offs" (UNEP, 2011). However, when considering the green economy and the sustainable development that it can potentially serve as a mechanism to achieve, it should be noted that many people around the world are directly dependent on natural resources for their survival, namely through agriculture, forestry or fishery. Degradation of the environment negatively affects such production activities and thus the livelihoods of the people. Likewise, how such people manage natural resources affects the ecosystems supporting their production activities. It is particularly important to draw attention to the types of sustainable production system that have developed in many areas around the world. Such landscapes are

Green economy and good governance for sustainable development: Opportunities, promises and concerns, Puppim de Oliveira (ed.),
United Nations University Press, 2012, ISBN 978-92-808-1216-9

characterized by very close linkages between nature and people, resulting in sustainable systems rather than a variety of "trade-offs". Thus, it can be asserted that, if the interactions between humans and nature are properly maintained, the result would be landscapes that sustain healthier ecosystems and biodiversity while at the same time benefitting humans by positively affecting their livelihoods.

Such practices and systems should serve as important clues for efforts aimed at the establishment of sustainable societies built on green economies. This chapter first introduces the diversity of sustainable production systems that have been developed based on close linkages between humans and nature, and also discusses why and how economic aspects need to be incorporated into the efforts to sustain ecosystems and the activities of people in such landscapes. We continue by providing an analysis of how international efforts can play a key role in promoting a green economy. An example is provided in the form of the *Satoyama* Initiative, which is a global effort started through a joint collaboration between the Ministry of the Environment of Japan (MOEJ) and the United Nations University Institute of Advanced Studies (UNU-IAS) in 2009 to sustain such landscapes (see Box 6.1).

Socio-ecological production landscapes where humans interact with nature

Humans have always depended on the surrounding environment for food, clothing, shelter, medicine and so forth. Ways to effectively utilize and manage such natural resources have been explored and adopted in many different regions across generations of such interactions between humans and nature. Such time-tested systems for natural resources management are often recognized as sustainable. Some of the characteristics common to traditional sustainable landscapes include extensive use of locally available and renewable resources, recycling of nutrients, spatial and temporal diversity, reliance on local crop varieties, and building on the knowledge and culture of local inhabitants (Gliessman, 2007). Use of land by rotating through appropriate cycles and combining crops/ livestock with fallow periods contributes to sustaining productivity by ensuring the recovery of soil fertility and the growth of vegetation. A well-known example is provided by the practice of shifting cultivation, which has a long history of being practised throughout the world (Finegan and Nasi, 2004). Transhumance systems in mountainous areas have adapted to the variation in conditions across different elevations and seasons (Ono and Sadakane, 1986), while nomadic systems were developed in arid and

Box 6.1 The *Satoyama* Initiative and Its International Partnership

The *Satoyama* Initiative was created within the context of biodiversity and ecosystem conservation. Since 2009, a series of workshops and meetings have been held in Malaysia, France, Brazil and Japan, led by the Ministry of the Environment of Japan and the United Nations University Institute of Advanced Studies. The objective has been to share experiences with socio-ecological production landscapes (SEPLs) drawn from the perspectives of each region and area of speciality, and to develop the concept of the *Satoyama* Initiative and the partnership's framework. Participants have included members of the Bureaus of the CBD Conference of the Parties (COP) and the Subsidiary Body on Scientific, Technical and Technological Advice (SBSTTA), biodiversity and community development experts from intergovernmental and governmental agencies, academic institutions and non-governmental organizations, in particular those working closely with indigenous and local communities.

As indicated by its vision of realizing "societies in harmony with nature", the *Satoyama* Initiative targets areas formed through human–nature interactions. Such areas were shaped by agriculture, forestry and fishery activities carried out in a manner aligned with the natural processes of each region. These areas cover large parts of the globe and have a significant impact on the world's ecosystems and biodiversity, while providing people with a variety of different benefits. Among other things, the *Satoyama* Initiative addresses issues confronting these areas in a changing world marked by population increase, growing reliance on technology and an increasingly globalized economy. To achieve its vision, the *Satoyama* Initiative follows a holistic approach, which is evident in its Conceptual Framework (see Figure 6.1).

During the Tenth meeting of the Conference of the Parties to the Convention on Biological Diversity (CBD-COP10) in October 2010 in Nagoya, Aichi Prefecture, Japan, a decision was adopted on the "Sustainable Use of Biodiversity" (Decision X/32), which specifically recognizes the *Satoyama* Initiative as a potentially useful tool to better understand and support human-influenced natural environments for the benefit of biodiversity and human well-being (UNEP/CBD/COP/DEC/X/32; see COP, 2010).

The International Partnership for the *Satoyama* Initiative (IPSI) was officially launched at the CBD-COP10 as a partnership consisting of 51 founding organizations. It has grown to include 105 organizations from across six different continents (as of November 2011). The members also constitute a broad range of organizational types. These

Box 6.1 (cont.)

include national governmental organizations, local governmental organizations, non-governmental and civil society organizations (NGOs/CSOs), indigenous or local community organizations, academic/educational/research institutes, industry/private-sector organizations and other UN and intergovernmental organizations.

IPSI promotes diverse activities in order to enhance understanding and raise awareness of the importance of SEPLs, while also supporting and expanding such landscapes. These activities are divided into five clusters: (1) knowledge facilitation, (2) policy research, (3) research for indicators, (4) capacity-building and (5) on-the-ground activities. Projects that fall within one or more clusters and are carried out cooperatively by multiple member organizations are promoted as IPSI Collaborative Activities. As of November 2011, there were 15 Collaborative Activities.

semi-arid areas to adapt to irregularity in terms of the spatiotemporal variability of rainfall (Niamir-Fuller, 1998).

The home garden, which is characterized by an "intimate, multistory combination of various trees and crops, sometimes in association with domestic animals, around the homestead" (Kumar and Nair, 2004: 135), also has a long history of being practised in the tropics and other regions. This system has been identified as contributing to sustainability through efficient nutrient cycling resulting from the multi-species composition and many other environmental and socioeconomic functions, including, among others, conservation of biodiversity, risk avoidance through product diversification, and the opportunity for gender equality in managing these systems. Such multiple land-use systems can be seen in other parts of the world. Agro-sylvo-pastoral systems in Europe, such as the Dehesa systems in Spain, which utilize shifting cultivation of cereals and pulses, were practised in sparse wood pasture where animals are being grazed and also serve as an example of integrated land use (Vicente and Alés, 2006). *Satoyama* landscapes in Japan are characterized by a mosaic feature of both terrestrial and aquatic systems comprising different ecosystems such as woodland, grassland, paddy field, farmland, irrigation ponds and canals that have been maintained in an integrated manner (JSSA, 2010). There has been growing understanding of the sustainability and multiple benefits in the landscapes that entail such systems as people have increasingly recognized the fact that modern economic development has been achieved through the extensive use of fossil fuels and at the cost of ecosystem degradation.

Over generations of close interactions between humans and nature, vast quantities of traditional knowledge have been accumulated, which have helped to sustain ecosystems and biodiversity in each landscape over the years. Full use was made of knowledge regarding the management of natural resources as well as the sharing of benefits and burdens, and rules and norms within the communities were reinforced, which led to a further strengthening of the mechanisms for the sustainable management of natural resources. Pastoral groups in Sahelian Africa manage the environmental variability of arid and semi-arid ecosystems with nested resource tenure and institutional mechanisms guided by flexible rules and customs regarding herd relocation, which have been fine-tuned through continuous monitoring and information exchange among different groups (Niamir-Fuller, 1998). Institutional systems are often deeply rooted in or influenced by cultural values – for example, Andean *ayni*, reciprocity (Augment and Wong, 2010) and religious beliefs such as sacred groves in India (Ormsby and Bhagwat, 2010) and elsewhere in the world (Bhagwat and Rutte, 2006).

Building on such knowledge and practices, land-use systems and institutional systems have co-evolved according to changes in natural and socioeconomic conditions, forming unique landscapes in each region. Within these areas, it is therefore impossible to consider the ecological, social and economic aspects of the landscapes independently of one another. In the discussion presented within the Japan Satoyama Satoumi Assessment (JSSA), use is made of the framework of the Millennium Ecosystem Assessment to assess *satoyama* and *satoumi* landscapes, focusing on the links between ecosystems and human well-being. The JSSA recognized the benefits of having such multifaceted nature in *satoyama* and *satoumi* landscapes, which it defines as "a dynamic mosaic of managed socio-ecological systems producing a bundle of ecosystem services for human well-being" (JSSA, 2010). The term "socio-ecological production landscape" does a good job of effectively describing the nature of landscapes such as those mentioned above and is now used by the *Satoyama* Initiative to describe its target areas.

The green economy in socio-ecological production landscapes

Traditional systems in socio-ecological production landscapes (SEPLs) have developed within the context of a subsistence economy in which production was undertaken on a relatively small scale to meet local needs. These systems, however, have been undergoing a major transformation. The pressures of population growth have increasingly generated a push towards intensification of food production. In the case of shifting

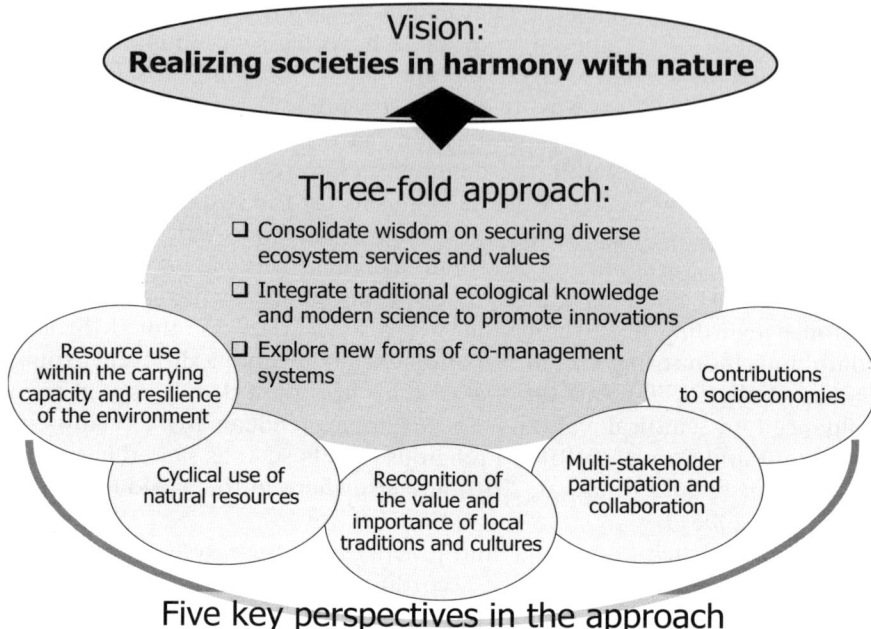

Figure 6.1 Conceptual framework of the *Satoyama* Initiative.

cultivation, if the current production cycle does not meet increasing demand, the result is a decrease in the length of the fallow period, which would not allow full recovery of soil fertility levels or sufficient levels of vegetal growth. Owing to the commercialization of agriculture, cultivation systems are becoming more specialized. Diversified land uses are being converted to monoculture production, which is highly dependent on agrochemicals. In such modern production systems, traditional knowledge accumulated in each environmental and sociocultural setting is either neglected or under-appreciated, and methods and techniques built on scientific knowledge are ubiquitously applied. Although such methods may prove effective in some places, they sometimes result in ecosystem degradation. Today, over half of the world's population lives in urban areas (UNDESA, Population Division, 2010). This also has meant that there is a decreasing and ageing population in rural areas and a lack of successors in primary production activities, which often results in insufficient management or the abandonment of farmland.

Considering the global trends underlying many of the issues presented above, such as population increase, urbanization and globalization, the respective solutions will require innovative approaches that could revitalize and advance such systems and not just restore and preserve traditional styles (Takeuchi, 2010). In this context, the green economy approach is expected to be particularly important in achieving both conservation of ecosystems and biodiversity and improvement of people's livelihoods.

Conserving protected areas with local communities

As shown in the previous section, SEPLs can be observed in many parts of the world. These include protected areas, where the concept of perceiving humans and nature as separate entities often underpins conservation activities, with a resulting exclusion of human influences from their boundaries. However, with the understanding of the role of indigenous and local communities in forming their landscapes, there is growing understanding of the essential nature of including such communities in nature conservation in order to successfully maintain biodiversity and ecosystems (Van Oudenhoven et al., 2010). In addition, important areas in respect to biodiversity often overlap with the places where many people live (Cincotta et al., 2000). Therefore it is inescapable that the livelihoods of local communities must be incorporated into conservation projects. In Western Siem Pang in Cambodia, the landscape is thought to have been shaped by dry season burning activities of generations of native people. It includes seasonal pools called *trapaengs* with fresh grasses, which provide water and dry season forage resources for wild animals as well as a habitat for endangered bird species (Box 6.2). Conservation activities are engaged in by local communities with the aim of developing a protocol for *trapaeng* management in order to meet the needs of the community while ensuring the essential ecological functions of the *trapaengs*. Furthermore, in return for monitoring the nesting sites of the target bird species, villagers are offered small financial incentives.

Improving livelihoods by greening production

The development of production activities in agriculture, forestry and fisheries in the latter half of twentieth century aimed to maximize productivity and profit and they built on practices such as monoculture, the application of agrochemicals and genetic manipulation of domesticated plants and animals. This tended to compromise future productivity in favour of immediate gains in productivity in the present, and had a range of effects resulting in ecosystem degradation, including soil erosion, scarcity of water, loss of genetic diversity and environmental pollution, the by-products of modern consumption and production systems (see also Chapter 5).

Box 6.2 Natural Resource Management in Western Siem Pang, Cambodia (Costello and Vorsak, 2011)

> Since 2006, the Cambodia programme of BirdLife International has focused on improving natural resource management and supporting livelihood activities among local communities in Western Siem Pang (WSP). The landscape is thought to have been shaped by dry season burning activities of generations of native people and includes seasonal pools called *trapaengs*, which provide a habitat for several of the world's most endangered large bird species. Poverty and expanding populations have put further stress on these ecosystems, and BirdLife International has worked with local communities to identify local land-use practices, food security levels and the economic status of residents. The organization has developed ways for local communities to engage in the sustainable harvesting and protection of local forests, and has established community-based "Site Support Groups" (SSGs). These SSGs bring together people with a shared interest in conservation, many of whom volunteer for a variety of economic, cultural and religious reasons. SSGs have assisted BirdLife International in an information campaign aimed at introducing new sustainable natural resource management concepts to local communities. There is also collaboration with researchers from the University of East Anglia in the United Kingdom and with local communities on measures to protect the critically endangered White-shouldered Ibis (WSI). This has resulted in a nest reward scheme, which provides local communities with financial incentives for finding and protecting WSI nesting sites.

Apart from such negative impacts on the environment, it is also important to recognize that farmers are faced with significant expense when employing conventional practices with a high dependence on external inputs such as agrochemicals, non-renewable energies to run farm machinery or irrigation pumps, and newly developed species. Thus practices that are beneficial to the surrounding environment, such as utilizing renewable energies and organic fertilizers, are also beneficial in terms of the reduction in production costs. Farmers therefore also potentially stand to gain economic benefits (Mendoza, 2002).

Some aspects of traditional farming have also been reported to have economic merit. Diverse products available year-round derived from multi-layered systems comprising trees, shrubs and herbs from home gardens have contributed to food security in local communities (Christanty, 1990). Moreover, when compared with temporal fluctuations throughout the annual cultivation cycle in monoculture cropping, home gardens require a relatively even amount of labour input throughout the year, leading to the generation of employment opportunities throughout the seasons (Karyono, 1990).

Growing awareness among consumers of the safety and quality of products may provide support for greening production activities related to the management of natural resources. The market share of organic food and global sales of fair-trade products are showing upward trends and there is a large demand for food produced in a sustainable manner (UNEP, 2011). In Japan, for example, using certain fauna species such as the Oriental Stork (*Ciconia boyciana*) and the Japanese Medaka fish (*Oryzias latipes*) as symbols of products (often in product names) is becoming increasingly popular. These symbols indicate that the products are generated using environmentally friendly practices, such as reducing or eliminating the use of pesticides or chemical fertilizers and flooding paddies during the wintertime. The latter practice aims to restore the bio-diverse environment that is key to the survival of certain species. At least 39 such brands of specially marked rice are being sold at relatively higher prices in Japan (PRIMAFF, 2010). Such trends are expected to help to boost local economies and revitalize *satoyama* landscapes.

The beautiful and unique landscapes shaped across numerous generations of communities interacting with nature are attractive to many people and have become good tourism resources. These can, in turn, contribute to the local economy, for example through the hiring of locals to work as guides (Allali, 2006). Such landscapes are also being registered as national parks and UNESCO World Heritage sites (for example, Marchese et al., 2010).

With increases or fluctuations in the price of fossil fuels as well as climate change, the use of locally produced biomass as a source of energy is expected to reduce carbon emissions and promote the circulation of resources at a local scale. For example, timber production in Japan has been in decline owing to the availability of cheap imported wood since the 1960s, and large tracts of timber forests were left unmanaged. Efforts have been initiated by a private company in collaboration with the local government and forestry cooperative in order to utilize such unused bio-resources in biomass power generation. This will also lead to the creation of new job opportunities (Box 6.3).

Utilizing new markets and policies for the internalization of environmental benefits

Many practices that have been developed locally in SEPLs should be recognized as the basis for sustainable societies in these areas. Within the

Box 6.3 Biomass Power Generation in Gokase River Watershed, Nobeoka, Japan (Asahi Kasei Corporation and Gokase River Satoyama Project, 2011)

> Asahi Kasei Chemicals Corporation, a private company in Japan, is currently preparing to start biomass power generation operations in the summer of 2012 in Nobeoka City, Miyazaki Prefecture. Following the initial stage, during which other types of biomass will also be used, Asahi Kasei plans to make use solely of wood derived from the thinning of local planted forests in the Gokase River watershed dominated by Japanese Cedar (*Cryptomeria japonica*) and Japanese Cypress (*Chamaecyparis obtusa*), where timber production has been in decline owing to the availability of cheap imported wood. About 100,000 tons of woody biomass are planned to be used annually. It is expected that the utilization of local woody materials will boost the local economy by providing job opportunities, and proper forest management practices can have a positive impact on local biodiversity. The gap between the buying and selling prices of thinned wood is an issue that must be resolved in order to ensure the success of this project. Asahi Kasei is cooperating with local governments and forestry associations to establish a system for ensuring the sustainable use of forests, while contributing to the economy and biodiversity conservation.

context of globalization and economic growth, efforts should be made to incorporate approaches that utilize new market mechanisms as well as policies that internalize environmental benefits/costs.

There are increasing efforts to capture the value of biodiversity and ecosystem services. One such example is provided by The Economics of Ecosystems and Biodiversity (TEEB, 2009). This will eventually lead to environmental costs being internalized within the price system and other decision-making processes. For example, rough estimates by Eliasch (2008) point to forest conservation generating annual savings of USD 3.7 trillion in reduced greenhouse gas emissions and to pollinators, a key indicator of healthy ecosystems and species biodiversity, annually providing USD 190 billion in benefits to the agricultural sector.

Ankeniheny-Zahamena Corridor (CAZ) in Madagascar's largest remaining rainforest area contains high levels of biodiversity across a range of different zones and land designations, but it faces pressures such as slash-and-burn agriculture and mining. Conservation International (CI) is carrying out on-the-ground activities in CAZ and has estimated that the rainforest serves to protect river flows that feed local agriculture and directly provide around 325,000 residents with water (Box 6.4). A pilot REDD+ (Reducing Emissions from Deforestation and Forest Degrada-

Box 6.4 Ankeniheny-Zahamena Corridor, Madagascar (Raik, 2011)

> Conservation International (CI), an international NGO carrying out on-the-ground activities in Madagascar's Ankeniheny-Zahamena Corridor (CAZ), has intentionally been making more of an attempt to incorporate economic aspects into its activities. CI employs a set of measures to meet the current and future needs of communities by securing ecosystem services provided by natural systems. Spanning 381,000 hectares of one of Madagascar's largest remaining rainforest areas, CAZ contains high levels of biodiversity across a range of different zones and land designations, but it faces pressures such as slash-and-burn agriculture and mining. Among other things, CI has worked to develop innovative mechanisms for measuring the economic value of the forest and distributing this value in an equitable fashion, something CI itself refers to as the "green economy approach". Recent estimates by CI underscore the tremendous value of the ecosystem services provided by rainforests. Analysis of a pilot REDD+ initiative at CAZ, for example, shows not only that the rainforest plays a crucial role in protecting water flows that support agriculture and over 325,000 local residents, but that deforestation in CAZ releases vast quantities of carbon dioxide, estimated at 270 tons per hectare. In other steps towards promoting income-generating activities, CI has begun providing small grants to community-level associations, worked to develop the sustainable tourism sector, and created conservation agreements with local communities so that they benefit directly from conservation management tasks. Since its inception, the project has brought together a comprehensive set of stakeholders and partners at various levels, including regional government authorities, local NGOs and community associations. During stakeholder meetings and discussions, the decision was made to adopt a co-management governance type emphasizing "community-level participation and empowerment" and composed of two main parts, namely a strategic orientation component and a management component.

tion) initiative is also under way at CAZ, and CI has estimated that 1 hectare of deforestation in CAZ releases an average of 270 tons of carbon dioxide into the atmosphere.

Efforts at the policy level to internalize environmental impacts into the cost of development activities are also under way. For example, Aichi Prefecture in Japan is preparing for the implementation of compensatory mitigation, which takes into account the damage done to natural landscapes by unavoidable development activities and provides the responsible parties with the opportunity to compensate for associated biodiversity

Box 6.5 Compensatory Mitigation in Aichi Prefecture, Japan (Aichi Prefectural Government, Natural Environment Division, 2011)

> Although characterized by an active business sector and an enthusiasm for regional development, Aichi Prefecture, Japan, has also stated that conservation and the sustainable use of biodiversity are major objectives. In order to achieve these objectives, it has started projects centred around the concepts of ecosystem networking and compensatory mitigation. Human activity often results in the fragmenting of natural landscapes, and ecosystem networking aims to reconnect these land-based and aquatic areas in order to allow for the free movement of animals. To facilitate this concept, the Aichi Prefectural Government drafted Japan's first ever map of potential habitats based on 16 biodiversity indicator species. The second concept, namely compensatory mitigation, takes into account the damage done to natural landscapes by unavoidable development activities and provides the responsible parties with the opportunity to compensate for associated biodiversity loss by implementing activities on public land to benefit these ecosystems. These activities are to be implemented in accordance with the ideals of ecosystem networking and include the preparation of biotopes on public land, including schools and parks. Activities should be carried out as close to the damaged area as possible and can be used, for example, to connect two previously isolated forest areas with a green corridor. Using compensatory mitigation to promote ecosystem networking has been referred to as the "Aichi Method".

loss by implementing activities on public land to benefit these ecosystems (Box 6.5).

The form in which traditional practices were developed in subsistence economies may not be customizable to stable large-scale production with high levels of productivity generating high revenues. However, considering the large impact of the fluctuations in prices of products generated through monoculture production, the role of traditional production systems should be recognized, for example home gardens, which enhance food security through the cultivation of diverse products throughout the year. Such benefits of traditional practices should first be recognized and enhanced in order to facilitate a greening of production.

As shown above, there are many possibilities for enhancing economic benefits in both direct and indirect ways, which would contribute to revitalizing and advancing SEPLs to match the changing conditions and needs of the world. Such benefits include a reduced cost burden owing to the reduction or elimination of agrochemicals, cash income from sustainable production, and employment opportunities generated by work related to conservation projects or tourism. There are also new markets and policies relevant to SEPLs, which can aid in internalizing environmental costs.

Considering the socioeconomic and ecological diversity of SEPLs, it is inevitable that the effectiveness of employing specific approaches and the extent of this application are entirely dependent on the local context. Local communities possess extensive knowledge of the areas in which they live, which has been accumulated through generations of interactions with the environment. The rationality and usefulness of such knowledge should be examined and properly understood. It should then be incorporated and taken into account during all critical decision-making processes, because local people are the ones who stand to directly benefit or suffer from the impacts of such activities. At the same time, the involvement of local stakeholders provides opportunities for understanding the linkage between local practices and activities and some global concerns. The involvement of multiple stakeholders, including local communities, and mutual learning and cooperation among these stakeholders are therefore essential, as can be seen in many of the examples described in this chapter and in Chapter 5. This involvement will also guarantee that lessons learned can be immediately implemented at a local level. Therefore, it can be stated that a bottom-up approach may be particularly well suited to promoting the green economy in SEPLs.

Global initiative at the local scale – the green economy's missing piece

As described earlier, although each of the SEPLs spread around the world has characteristics specific to its location, many of the challenges that they currently face have a common background: a changing world marked by population increase, growing reliance on technology and an increasingly globalized economy. In such situations, it is reasonable and effective to tackle these issues together.

It is from within this context that the *Satoyama* Initiative, a global effort initiated in Japan, emerged, aiming to support SEPLs in achieving its vision of realizing societies in harmony with nature (Box 6.1). The initiative was developed within the framework of biodiversity and ecosystem conservation, as indicated by its presence at the Tenth Meeting of the Conference of the Parties to the Convention on Biological Diversity (CBD-COP10) in October 2010, where the *Satoyama* Initiative was recognized as "a potentially useful tool to better understand and support human-influenced natural environments for the benefit of biodiversity and human well-being" (COP, 2010: 3). This provided it with a sufficient level of recognition, which is essential to incorporating social and economic aspects into such efforts. The International Partnership for the

Satoyama Initiative (IPSI), which was also established at the CBD-COP10, provides a platform for the promotion of sharing and discussing experiences, good practices and lessons learned in activities related to SEPLs. It is expected that synergies and complementarities among the activities of member organizations will be ensured, and there is also the expectation that human, financial and other resources will be maximized, thereby strengthening such activities.

IPSI is open to all organizations (governments, NGOs, indigenous and local communities, academic institutes, international organizations, private sector organizations), but the importance of on-the-ground efforts is very much recognized. Aspects of the *Satoyama* Initiative have focused on production activities at the local scale, where high levels of biodiversity have resulted from long-term interactions between humans and nature, that have the potential to fill a key gap in the green economy concept.

Although the green economy has the potential for providing an alternative development model (Kim, 2011), considerable risks have been pointed out in that it has the potential to be watered down to encompass solely environmental technologies and energy production (Simon and Dröge, 2011). Major gatherings of key decision-makers and heads of state provide the opportunity to address key barriers such as perverse subsidies and counterproductive investments. However, referring to the United Nations Environment Programme's definition of a green economy as one that results in human well-being and social equity while significantly reducing environmental risks and ecological scarcities, it is clear that a substantial contribution can and must be made by local communities within the global architecture for green growth (UNEP, 2011).

In order to ensure that action is taken towards achieving a green economy and sustainable development, it therefore seems risky to rely on governments alone, despite excellent examples being set by a number of countries around the world (Young, 2011). Furthermore, government support for a green economy has thus far seemed largely limited to major infrastructure projects. Therefore, IPSI, which is unique in offering a platform for collaboration among a broad range of entities and organizations, plays an important role by placing an emphasis on local-scale efforts and it has the potential to further promote the greening of the economy and the realization of sustainable societies.

Promoting the green economy through IPSI

By offering a platform for organizations spanning a range of institutional types and geographical locations, IPSI enables its members to share and learn from each other's experiences and lessons learned in activities related to SEPLs. As one of the mechanisms for facilitating such information-sharing, IPSI requires that each member submit at least one case study on its experiences with SEPLs. It is expected that such a highly diverse group of members with different specialities and strengths will yield an equally diverse selection of case studies dealing with SEPLs. Using IPSI as a mechanism for sharing these experiences and this knowledge among IPSI members, as well as policy-makers and a wider audience, will ensure the promotion not only of the *Satoyama* Initiative but also of the green economy. Plans are under way to fully utilize these collected case studies by extracting knowledge and lessons learned in SEPLs from around the world as an IPSI Collaborative Activity (see Box 6.1). This knowledge facilitation will make it possible to contribute to capacity-building, replication and upscaling of good practices.

Another activity implemented within the IPSI framework involves community development following the spirit of the *Satoyama* Initiative. This collaborative activity, Community Development and Knowledge Management for the *Satoyama* Initiative (COMDEKS), is being implemented by the United Nations Development Programme (UNDP), MOEJ, the CBD Secretariat and UNU. It serves as an excellent example of how to draw maximum benefit from the strengths of each IPSI member, because it fully utilizes existing small grants delivery mechanisms, which have been implemented by UNDP. It will leverage existing resources and networks for sustainable human development to the long-term benefit of local communities and ecosystems. The project also codifies and manages outputs, including replicable and upscalable practices from the community development component based on the concept of the *Satoyama* Initiative. In the initial phase of the programme, 11 countries – Cambodia, India, Nepal, Fiji, Ethiopia, Ghana, Malawi, Slovakia, Turkey, Brazil and Grenada – will participate in knowledge-sharing and communities in these countries will be eligible for small grants. The practices developed over the span of many generations will be revitalized in the rural communities of these countries, new techniques will be learned and knowledge will be shared regarding traditional farming systems and the conservation of biodiversity and natural resources.

Conclusion

The green economy concept of incorporating environmental and social aspects into economic systems has been embodied in many of the traditional practices in socio-ecological production landscapes. In these landscapes, there has been a co-evolution of production activities conducted within the capacities of each ecosystem and social system that was directly linked to natural resource management by norms and rules. Many of the mechanisms that are beneficial to the well-being of communities following such traditional systems should be thoroughly evaluated and incorporated into modern approaches. Although no universally effective approach exists for all of the SEPLs currently facing challenges around the world, there are a number of approaches that should be employed depending on the local context. These should be implemented and developed through the active participation of local communities in order to promote economic growth and the well-being of the people in these communities and to contribute to solving global issues including biodiversity degradation, poverty and food insecurity.

The global movement towards a green economy could be further strengthened by taking into account an important element that has thus far received insufficient attention, namely the existing local-scale efforts by people who are directly dealing with natural resources in SEPLs. Global initiatives such as the *Satoyama* Initiative, which involves the concept of a green economy and recognizes the importance of efforts at a local scale, can also make a substantial contribution to achieving a green economy and building sustainable societies through enhancing understanding of the importance of all the socio-ecological and production aspects of landscapes as well as mutual learning and collaboration among diverse organizations.

Acknowledgements

We are grateful to colleagues at UNU-IAS who assisted in preparing this chapter, including Fumiko Nakao, Akane Minohara, Ayumi Takahashi, Kazuhiko Takemoto, Abel Barasa Atiti and Jose Puppim de Oliveira. Thanks are also due to Kurtis Nakamura, a graduate student at the University of California, San Diego, and an intern at UNU-IAS, who provided a great deal of assistance.

REFERENCES

Aichi Prefectural Government, Natural Environment Division (2011) "Working for Improved Harmony With Nature – Aichi's Environmental Initiatives Based on the Aichi Environment Conservation Strategy", in *Summary Report: First Global Conference of International Partnership for the Satoyama Initiative (IPSI)*. Yokohama: Secretariat of the International Partnership for the

Satoyama Initiative, pp. 10–11. Available at ⟨http://satoyama-initiative.org/file/Draft-Summary-Report-of-the-First-Global-Conference-of-IPSI_final.pdf⟩ (accessed 26 January 2012).

Allali, K. (2006) *Agricultural Landscape Externalities, Agro-tourism and Rural Poverty Reduction in Morocco*. Rome: ESA/FAO. Available at ⟨ftp://ftp.fao.org/es/ESA/Roa/pdf/oct05_env_morocco.pdf⟩ (accessed 26 January 2012).

Asahi Kasei Corporation and Gokase River Satoyama Project (2011) "Conserving Biodiversity by Utilising Wood Thinned from Forests as Biomass Fuel for Power Generation", in *Summary Report: First Global Conference of International Partnership for the Satoyama Initiative (IPSI)*. Yokohama: Secretariat of the International Partnership for the *Satoyama* Initiative, pp. 47–48. Available at ⟨http://satoyama-initiative.org/file/Draft-Summary-Report-of-the-First-Global-Conference-of-IPSI_final.pdf⟩ (accessed 26 January 2012).

Augment, A. and B. Y. L. Wong (2010) "The *Ayllu* System of the Potato Park (Peru)", in C. Bélair, K. Ichikawa, B. Y. L. Wong and K. J. Mulongoy (eds), *Sustainable Use of Biological Diversity in Socio-ecological Production Landscapes. Background to the "Satoyama Initiative for the Benefit of Biodiversity and Human Well-being"*, CBD Technical Series no. 52. Montreal: Secretariat of the Convention on Biological Diversity, pp. 84–90.

Bhagwat, S. A. and C. Rutte (2006) "Sacred Groves: Potential for Biodiversity Management", *Frontiers in Ecology and the Environment*, 4(10): 519–524.

Christanty, L. (1990) "Home Gardens in Tropical Asia, with Special Reference to Indonesia", in K. Landaue and M. Brazil (eds), *Tropical Home Gardens*. Tokyo: United Nations University Press.

Cincotta, R. P., J. Wisnewski and R. Engelman (2000) "Human Population in the Biodiversity Hotspots", *Nature*, 404(6781): 990–992.

COP (Conference of the Parties to the Convention on Biological Diversity) (2010) "Decision X/32: Sustainable Use of Biodiversity", Secretariat of the Convention on Biological Diversity, Montreal. Available at ⟨http://www.cbd.int/doc/decisions/cop-10/cop-10-dec-32-en.pdf⟩ (accessed 26 January 2012).

Costello, L. and B. Vorsak (2011) "Natural Resource Management in the Critical Habitat of Western Siem Pang (BirdLife International)", Secretariat of the Partnership for the *Satoyama* Initiative, Yokohama. Available at ⟨http://satoyama-initiative.org/en/case_studies-2/area_asia-2/natural-resource-management-in-the-critical-habitat-of-western-siem-pang-birdlife-international/⟩ (accessed 26 January 2012).

Eliasch, J. (2008) *Climate Change: Financing Global Forests. The Eliasch Review*. London: HMSO. Available at ⟨http://www.official-documents.gov.uk/document/other/9780108507632/9780108507632.pdf⟩ (accessed 26 January 2012).

Finegan, B. and R. Nasi (2004) "The Biodiversity and Conservation Potential of Shifting Cultivation Landscapes", in G. Schroth, G. A. B. Fonseca, C. A. Harvey, C. Gascon, H. L. Vasconcelos and A. M. N. Izac (eds), *Agroforestry and Biodiversity Conservation in Tropical Landscapes*. Washington, DC: Island Press, pp. 151–197.

Gliessman, S. R. (2007) *Agroecology: The Ecology of Sustainable Food Systems*, 2nd edn. Boca Raton: CRC Press.

JSSA (Japan Satoyama Satoumi Assessment) (2010) *Satoyama-Satoumi Ecosystems and Human Well-being: Socio-ecological Production Landscapes of Japan – Summary for Decision Makers*. Tokyo: United Nations University.

Karyono (1990) "Home gardens in Java: Their Structure and Function", in K. Landauer and M. Brazil (eds), *Tropical Home Gardens*. Tokyo: United Nations University Press, pp. 138–146.

Kim, S. (2011) "Statement by H.E. Ambassador Kim Sook for the Retreat for Permanent Representatives on UNCSD (Rio+20)", 30 September. Available at ⟨http://www.fes-globalization.org/new_york/wp-content/uploads/2011/10/HEAmbKIMSook_speech.pdf⟩ (accessed 26 January 2012).

Kumar, B. M. and P. K. R. Nair (2004) "The Enigma of Tropical Homegardens", *Agroforestry Systems*, 61: 135–152.

Marchese, F., C. Gardi and L. Montanarella (2010) "Cinque Terre National Park: Where Farmland Meets the Sea", in C. Bélair, K. Ichikawa, B. Y. L. Wong and K. J. Mulongoy (eds), *Sustainable Use of Biological Diversity in Socio-ecological Production Landscapes. Background to the "Satoyama Initiative for the Benefit of Biodiversity and Human Well-being"*, CBD Technical Series no. 52). Montreal: Secretariat of the Convention on Biological Diversity, pp. 152–156.

Mendoza, T. C. (2002) "Comparative Productivity, Profitability and Energy Use in Organic, LEISA and Conventional Rice Production in the Philippines", *Livestock Research for Rural Development*, 14(6): 93–115. Available at ⟨http://www.lrrd.org/lrrd14/6/mend146.htm⟩ (accessed 26 January 2012).

Millennium Ecosystem Assessment (2005) *Ecosystems and Human Well-being: Synthesis*. Washington, DC: Island Press.

Niamir-Fuller, M. (1998) "The Resilience of Pastoral Herding in Sahelian Africa", in F. Berkes and C. Folke (eds), *Linking Social and Ecological Systems*. New York: Cambridge University Press, pp. 250–284.

Ono, Y. and A. Sadakane (1986) "Natural Background of the Yak Transhumance in the Langtang Valley, Nepal Himalaya", *Geographical Reports of Tokyo Metropolitan University*, 21: 95–109.

Ormsby, A. A. and S. A. Bhagwat (2010) "Sacred Forests of India: A Strong Tradition of Community-based Natural Resource Management", *Environmental Conservation*, 37(3): 320–326.

PRIMAFF (Policy Research Institute, Ministry of Agriculture, Forestry and Fisheries) (2010) *Environmental Project Research Material, 2: Seibutsu tayosei hozen ni hairyo shita nogyoseisan no eikyohyoka to sono shokushin hosaku [Impact Evaluation and Promotion of Agricultural Production in Consideration of Biodiversity Conservation]*. Tokyo: PRIMAFF. Available at ⟨http://www.maff.go.jp/primaff/koho/seika/project/pdf/kanky02.pdf⟩ (accessed on 9 January 2012).

Raik, D. (2011) "Ankeniheny-Zahamena Corridor, A Field Demonstration Model (Conservation International, Madagascar)", ⟨http://satoyama-initiative.org/en/case_studies-2/area_africa-2/ankeniheny-zahamena-corridor-a-field-demonstration-model-conservation-international-madagascar/⟩ (accessed 26 January 2012).

Simon, N. and S. Dröge (2011) "Green Economy: Connecting the Dots", SWP Comment, German Institute for International and Security Affairs. Available at ⟨http://www.swp-berlin.org/fileadmin/contents/products/comments/2011C29_dge_sin_ks.pdf⟩ (accessed 26 January 2012).

Takeuchi, K. (2010) "Rebuilding the Relationship between People and Nature: The Satoyama Initiative", *Ecological Research*, 25(5): 891–897.

TEEB (The Economics of Ecosystems and Biodiversity) (2009) *TEEB – The Economics of Ecosystems and Biodiversity for National and International Policy Makers – Summary: Responding to the Value of Nature*. Geneva: TEEB. Available at ⟨http://www.teebweb.org/LinkClick.aspx?fileticket=I4Y2nqqIiCg%3d&tabid=1019&language=en-US⟩ (accessed 26 January 2012).

UNDESA (United Nations, Department of Economic and Social Affairs), Population Division (2010) *World Urbanization Prospects: The 2009 Revision*. New York: United Nations. Available at ⟨http://esa.un.org/wup2009/unup⟩ (accessed 26 January 2012).

UNDESA (United Nations, Department of Economic and Social Affairs), Population Division (2011) *World Population Prospects: The 2010 Revision*. New York: United Nations. Available at ⟨http://esa.un.org/unpd/wpp/index.htm⟩ (accessed 26 January 2012).

UNEP (United Nations Environment Programme) (2011) *Towards a Green Economy, Pathways to Sustainable Development and Poverty Eradication*. Nairobi: United Nations Environment Programme. Available at ⟨http://www.unep.org/greeneconomy/GreenEconomyReport/tabid/29846/Default.aspx⟩ (accessed 26 January 2012).

Van Oudenhoven, F. J. W., D. Mijatović and P. B. Eyzaguirre (2010) "Bridging Managed and Natural Landscapes: The Role of Traditional (Agri)culture in Maintaining the Diversity and Resilience of Social-ecological Systems", in C. Bélair, K. Ichikawa, B. Y. L. Wong and K. J. Mulongoy (eds), *Sustainable Use of Biological Diversity in Socio-ecological Production Landscapes: Background to the 'Satoyama Initiative for the Benefit of Biodiversity and Human Well-being*, CBD Technical Series no. 52. Montreal: Secretariat of the Convention on Biological Diversity, pp. 8–21.

Vicente, Á. and R. Alés (2006) "Long term Persistence of Dehesas. Evidences from History", *Agroforestry Systems*, 67(1): 19–28.

Young, S. (2011) "Green Growth as a New Paradigm for Sustainable Development and Climate Change Cooperation: A Korean Perspective", Keynote Speech at the Retreat for Permanent Representatives on the UN Conference on Sustainable Development (Rio+20), 30 September. Available at ⟨http://www.fes-globalization.org/new_york/wp-content/uploads/2011/10/Dr_Young_SpeechRio+20Retreat.pdf⟩ (accessed 26 January 2012).

7

Governance challenges for promoting the green economy in Africa

Timothy Afful-Koomson

Introduction

The two core themes expected to define the scope for the Rio+20 conference negotiations in June 2012 are (1) the green economy in the context of sustainable development and poverty eradication and (2) an institutional framework for sustainable development. These core themes shape the focus of this chapter – the governance of the green economy in Africa. Institutions and actors are the basic elements of governance and it is essential to explore the appropriate governance framework that may be useful for promoting the green economy in Africa.

The fact is that the landscape of multilateral environmental diplomacy that underlies governance for sustainable development has been more dynamic and flexible than the institutions, policies and instruments that emerged from the related negotiated agreements. This has rendered some of the institutions, policies and instruments for sustainable development governance obsolete and irrelevant to the current context and challenges. Some of these institutions, policies and instruments are also posing severe obstacles to the implementation of agreements and decisions that are meant to facilitate the realization of sustainable development. The challenge, therefore, is to make the key institutions, policies and instruments for sustainable development governance contextually relevant to help promote sustainable development, particularly at the national and local levels. This challenge is not unique to African countries but faces other regions as well. It is currently under intense discussion at the global

Green economy and good governance for sustainable development: Opportunities, promises and concerns, Puppim de Oliveira (ed.),
United Nations University Press, 2012, ISBN 978-92-808-1216-9

level and will continue to feature prominently in global discourse on sustainable development even after Rio+20.

The major objective of this chapter is to explore the necessary elements of institutional arrangements that may be vital for addressing critical governance challenges for the green economy in Africa. To do this, I will analyse the institutional set-up of most African countries for sustainable development programmes vis-à-vis the changing dynamics of multilateral diplomacy for global sustainable development governance. I will also provide the theoretical framework of governance and the institutional imperatives for effective representation, participation and contribution from all stakeholders for collaborative governance of the green economy in Africa. I will then make recommendations on how these institutional imperatives for good governance should be taken into consideration in crafting the governance structures and mechanisms for the green economy at the regional, national and local levels in Africa. This chapter complements the knowledge needs management and capacity development of National Councils for Sustainable Development (NCSD) by the United Nations University Institute for Natural Resources in Africa (UNU-INRA) in 10 African countries to support and provide value-added services to African governments so that they can improve their national formulation and implementation of Rio+20 green economy programmes.

Background to the institutionalization of sustainable development in Africa

This section provides a brief historical and analytical review of the major events that characterized the multilateral negotiations for global sustainable development governance and the nature of the institutions that emerged from them. This information is intended to aid understanding of the nature of the institutionalization of sustainable development councils and related entities in Africa. The diagnosis of the NCSDs and related entities will draw extensively from national reports submitted by national coordinating institutions for sustainable development to the United Nations Economic Commission for Africa (ECA).

Multilateral diplomacy and global governance institutions for sustainable development

In June 1972, the United Nations General Assembly (UNGA) agreed to convene an international conference on the human environment, partly as a result of a report submitted by the Economic and Social Council

(ECOSOC) in July 1968. This report echoed the concerns raised largely by non-governmental organizations (NGOs), scientists and conservationists about the deteriorating global environment (ECOSOC, 1968). The conference, which came to be known as the United Nations Conference on the Human Environment, was held in Stockholm, Sweden, as a result of significant initiative and support demonstrated by the Swedish government. In terms of institutionalization, the Stockholm Conference led to the establishment of the following: (1) a 54-member Governing Council for the United Nations Environment Programme (GCUNEP), which reports to the UNGA through the ECOSOC, (2) the Environment Fund to help finance UN environmental initiatives, and (3) the United Nations Environment Programme (UNEP), to provide support and to report to the GCUNEP (United Nations, 1972).

Thus UNEP, which was the first major institution that came out of the first international conference on the environment, was yoked with the bureaucratic weight of reporting to the General Assembly through the intergovernmental GCUNEP, which reports to the ECOSOC, which reports to the UNGA. Moreover, although the 1968 ECOSOC report that provided the impetus for the Stockholm Conference was largely initiated by concerns raised by non-governmental actors such as conservationists and scientists, there was no NGO representation on the GCUNEP. Besides, even though information from Rachel Carson's epic book *Silent Spring* (Carson, 1962) – which implicated the chemical industry and raised the alarm on the impacts of pesticide use on human health, wildlife and ecosystems – featured prominently in the environmental discourse even before the Stockholm Conference, no consideration was given to bringing industry representatives onto the GCUNEP, even as co-opted members.

The Rio Earth Summit (the United Nations Conference on Environment and Development) was convened 20 years after the Stockholm Conference. In terms of institutionalization, the Rio Earth Summit led to the establishment of the United Nations Commission on Sustainable Development (UNCSD), which is currently one of the key institutions for global sustainable development governance. The UNCSD was to be a coordinating entity for sustainable development under the ECOSOC and, like its predecessor, UNEP, reports to the UNGA through ECOSOC (United Nations, 1992).

The communication channels for both UNEP and UNCSD constrain their direct access and reporting to the UNGA and have huge potential for screening and toning down the urgency of recommendations for critical action on environmental and sustainable development issues. These forerunner institutions were also not autonomous and did not have much latitude to set their own agenda and to prioritize the implementation of specific focal programmes to safeguard the environment and promote sustainable development. UNEP is a subsidiary programme of the UNGA, with a mandate and activities focused primarily on environment-related issues. Although the UNCSD has a much broader mandate than UNEP, it is also a coordinating organ for UNGA sustainable development programmes through ECOSOC.

Multilateral diplomacy and governance institutions for sustainable development in Africa

Many African countries responded to the Rio Earth Summit provision encouraging governments to establish national coordinating institutions for sustainable development or similar entities (see ECA, 2005). As noted above, the global institutions that emerged from the earlier multilateral processes were intergovernmental in nature – national representation on the board or committee was appointed, supported or endorsed by the home government. They also lacked broad-based representation from all stakeholders and were not autonomous. These characteristics were mirrored by most of the NCSDs in Africa and, as may be obvious later in the diagnosis below, the multilateral processes in the international spatial context influenced the type and structure of most of the sustainable development institutions that emerged in Africa.

Regional governance institutions for sustainable development

At the regional level, UNEP established the Regional Office for Africa (ROA) to facilitate better coherence and coordination in the effective delivery of environmental capacity-building and technical support at all levels in response to country needs and priorities (UNEP, 2011a). ECA also established the sub-programme on Food Security and Sustainable Development (FSSD) to strengthen the capacity of member states to design institutional arrangements and to implement national policies and programmes that reinforce the linkages within the nexus of food security, population, environment and human settlements. These initiatives are promoted in order to contribute to building the capacity of African countries to utilize science and technology in achieving sustainable development (ECA, 2011a). The African Union Commission (AUC), through the New Partnership for Africa's Development, has programmes to promote regional and national initiatives on, in particular, climate change, natural resources management, agriculture and food security (NEPAD, 2011). The African Development Bank Group (AfDB) has also programmes for mainstreaming environment and sustainable development issues in development investments.

However, most of the regional initiatives are characterized by the excessive influence of state actors and low participation from private actors.

Moreover, these regional initiatives are usually fragmented, with overlapping mandates and weak linkages, and have low coordination, synergies and mutual reinforcement of regional-level programmes (ECA, 2011b). It is encouraging to see some recent regional activities such as the preparatory process for Rio+20 engaging all the major regional institutions to collaborate and leverage each institution's resources and capabilities to ensure a more coordinated and effective regional process.

National governance institutions for sustainable development

The institutions established at the national level largely mirrored the characteristics of the global and regional institutions. For example, all the countries surveyed by ECA studies indicated that their NCSDs and other related coordinating institutions were located within government administrative structures.[1] Several of the NCSDs were chaired by the prime minister, president or vice president or were located under their office. Furthermore, some of the NCSDs located within government ministries and agencies were chaired by a prime minister, a president or a vice president. Although, the multilateral processes in the international arena may have influenced this situation, it might also be the result of the political system of excessive government control of decision-making mechanisms in Africa. It is, however, worth noting that some reasonable arguments were given for locating the NCSDs within government administrative structures. Some of the reasons for those located under the office of the president or the prime minister are that "high level positioning ensures effective coordination of policies and plans" and, for NCSDs located within ministries, they were meant to "ensure continuity and effective collaboration with other sectoral ministries" (ECA, 2005: xiv). Another reason could be the demonstration of political commitment if the location of the institution is at the highest political level.

Despite these legitimate reasons, locating such institutions under the highest political office has great potential to limit the representation and participation of equally legitimate non-state actors. Moreover, sustainable development programmes become entangled in hierarchical and highly centralized bureaucratic systems. Only 36 per cent of the surveyed countries have NCSDs or closely related bodies that are multi-stakeholder entities. None of the surveyed countries has all of the nine major groups – children and youth, women, indigenous people, NGOs, local authorities, workers and trade unions, business and industry, science and technology communities, and farmers – identified as key stakeholders of sustainable development represented in the NCSDs. Only Botswana has six to eight groups represented, and approximately 52 per cent have only two to three groups represented. Most of the NCSDs do not have any representation from the private sector or from academia. Considering the enormous financial and technical resources that the private sector could bring on board to support sustainable development, this lack of representation from the private sector in the NCSDs could be rather unfortunate. The same goes for the lack of representation from research institutions and academia, considering the importance of science, technology and innovation for sustainable development.

Just like UNEP, there is also a predominance of environment-related mandates and activities despite the fact that the NCSDs are meant to be patterned after the UNCSD. Only about 9 per cent of the surveyed countries have NCSDs with a broad mandate and corresponding broad-based activities that address all three pillars of sustainable development. About 23 per cent have a sustainable development mandate but execute environment-related activities. About 32 per cent have an environment-related mandate and execute environment-related activities, although 62 per cent of the surveyed countries ensure that their NCSDs have representation from government institutions or ministries in the social, economic and environment sectors.

The NCSDs of the countries surveyed do not have adequate decentralized institutional structures. Only 23 per cent indicated that they have NCSDs with actual decentralization; and this is mostly decentralization implicit in having subnational bodies within the local government structure without any reference to representation and participation at the local level of all key stakeholders. Some also imply decentralization in terms of the representation of local-level focal persons in national bodies. Arguably, when decentralization is implied in terms of local representation of government ministries at the district and local levels without broad-based participation by all stakeholders, it actually becomes the conduit for extending national bureaucratic influence and operations to the local level. This is unlikely to achieve the desired impacts of decentralization for sustainable development.

The NCSDs of the countries surveyed are also burdened with inadequate institutional, technical and financial capacity to support their national sustainable development agenda. About 94 per cent of the NCSDs indicated that their major obstacle to implementing sustainable development activities is inadequate human, financial and institutional capacity. Most of the countries surveyed "have not established financing mechanisms to generate additional funds, but continue to depend on government budgetary allocations and donor funds" (ECA, 2005: xvi). It was also noted by ECA analyses of the survey data that, although there are several international financing mechanisms and non-formal agreements such as Type II partnership agreements, most of the survey countries are "either not aware of these initiatives, or have not fully internalized their benefits" (ECA, 2005: xvi).

As indicated in this brief diagnosis of the NCSDs, the institutions created in Africa to coordinate the sustainable development agenda in Africa largely mimic the global institutions that emerged from, in particular, early multilateral environmental diplomacy. They are controlled largely by government actors, lack autonomy and broad-based representation and participation by all stakeholders, do not have adequate decentralized structures, and lack the capacity to support the implementation of the activities under their mandate. UNEP and UNCSD are currently undergoing intense criticism and analysis. The discourse is directed largely towards their transformation or restructuring to improve the global governance of sustainable development and the green economy. African countries may be better served if they listen in to these discourses at the international level and use these events as an opportunity to put their NCSDs and related institutions under the microscope so that they can create or transform their institutions to aid green economy governance in their respective countries. The next section will explore a theoretical framework that may help guide African countries in their choice of institutional structures, processes and mechanisms for green economy governance.

A theoretical framework of governance

The current institutional arrangements for sustainable development governance in most African countries are deficient. Such institutions may not serve as the appropriate structures and mechanisms for green economy governance. This section will therefore explore a theoretical framework to guide the choice of institutional set-up for green economy governance in Africa. I shall briefly review some definitions and conceptualizations of governance not only to provide the normative frame of governance but also to underscore the importance of developing the appropriate structures and mechanisms for green economy governance in Africa. These conceptual building blocks, though largely normative, may provide some guidance to African governments in crafting regional and national governance mechanisms to address both the changing dynamics of multilateral diplomacy and the integrated and pragmatic nature of the green economy.

Diverse usage of the term "governance"

Most scholars use "sustainable development governance" and "environmental governance" interchangeably, although the latter term has a much more restricted scope than the former. Despite several scholarly works on sustainable development governance, this field of study is still relatively underdeveloped. There is currently no conceptually comprehensive theory of sustainable development governance. Moreover, the discourse and the theoretical framing of sustainable development governance have focused largely on governance at the global level, to the unfortunate neglect of a theory of sustainable development governance at the regional, national and local levels. I therefore seek to contribute to the development of a theoretical framework at the national and local levels.

According to Krahmann (2003), definitions and uses of governance are as varied as the issues and levels of analysis to which the concept is applied. Governance has been used to describe many political processes, institutions, decision-making and management entities. Governance has been used to imply the minimal state, corporate governance, new public management, good governance, the socio-cybernetic system, self-organizing networks, policy-making in the absence of an overarching political authority, withdrawal of the European welfare state, and even public sector reforms in Africa (Krahmann, 2003; Rhodes, 1996). Although governance as a term has been used to describe several political structures and processes dating back to when humans established systems of government, its popularity as a concept is associated with the emergence of neo-liberalism and new public management, particularly in Europe (Bevir and Rhodes, 2003; Leach et al., 2007). The World Bank is credited with introducing the term into general discourse through its 1989 report *Sub-Saharan Africa: From Crisis to Sustainable Growth* (World Bank, 1989; see also Leach et al., 2007).

Some definitions of governance

There are different types of governance. For example, we can talk of social governance, political governance, corporate governance and environmental governance. Although the diverse usage of the term gives it a broader range of usefulness, it also constrains the development of a conceptually coherent theory of governance. The diverse usage of the term has also produced several definitions of governance. Most of these definitions have limited usage and may be comprehensible only when applied in the discipline of the original author credited with that definition. The few definitions selected for this chapter do not imply their superiority in terms of comprehensiveness, but they are intended to serve as epistemic panels to help construct a fairly lucid theoretical framework here.

According to Leach et al. (2007), governance could be defined in a broader sense as political processes and institutions. This definition underscores the two key components of governance: political processes and institutions. Through these political processes and institutions, governance "shapes how scientific and technological processes are directed, how environmental and health issues are defined and addressed, and how social consequences [are] distributed. They shape – and are shaped by – the interactions between people, technology and environment, and how these dynamics unfold over time" (Leach et al., 2007: 1). Thus institutions form the fundamental structures for decision-making on a wide range of development issues. They are also the mechanisms for the allocation of power, which usually determines who gets what of the national goods and services. The competition for control over resource allocation and distribution underpins the transformation of governance as decision-making processes into political processes where the divergent interests, positions, demands and expectations of the different institutions clash.

As O'Toole (2000: 276) notes, governance involves a "multi-layered structural context of rule-governed understanding, along with the role of multiple social actors in arrays of negotiation, implementation and service delivery. Addressing governance requires attending to social patterns and ideas about how to concert action among them." Realizing the outcome of concerted action for policy- and decision-making involves arrays of negotiations, positioning, bargaining, trade-offs and other exchanges between the key actors. The interactions and exchanges are likely to produce consensus and broad ownership of negotiated agreements when the relationships between the actors are symmetrical and there is more flexibility and gestures of compromise between actors on a fairly level playing field. When the relationship is asymmetrical and power is concentrated in the hands of one or a few actors with the clout to dominate and impose their interests and demands on the other equally legitimate actors, the furtherance of concerted action becomes very remote.

This is one reason some scholars may prefer to view governance as theoretically and analytically different from government. Though both are characterized by institutions and political processes, the "governance without government" school of thought has the perspective that, where the influence of state actors dominates or where state actors are the key players in the policy- and decision-making processes, then that is theoretically government and not governance (Peters, 1993; Rhodes, 1997; Stoker, 2000). Interestingly, one of the theoretical leanings of the governance without government school renders old-fashioned the traditional concept that regards government as a controlling and regulating organization for society (Bekke et al., 1995; Peters and Pierre, 1998). Implicit in their argument is that "government is out of vogue and governance is the new fad". Regarding how governance came to be in vogue, Krahmann (2003) notes that a consensus emerged among advanced industrialized nations in the 1980s that existing government policy-making structures were unsatisfactory and needed to be replaced. "The blueprint for an alternative, namely governance, was provided by neoliberal and new-right ideologies" (Krahmann, 2003: 327). There is also an argument that the dominant pattern of management for most advanced industrial democracies such as the United Kingdom and the United States is governance without government (Peters and Pierre, 1998; Rhodes, 1997).

Theoretical building blocks of governance

Although currently there is no coherent and comprehensive theory of governance, owing to the diverse usage of the term with different meanings by different disciplines, an understanding of what governance is could be enhanced by putting together the major conceptual blocks of governance.

Governance involves hollowing-out of the state of its legitimate powers

It is argued that the traditional concepts of the state as possessing the monopoly over the legitimate use of decision-making authority and of government as the sole entity that controls the distribution of power and resources of a nation are outmoded (Bekke et al., 1995; Peters and Pierre, 1998). This argument may have some conceptual traction considering the current age of globalization where the territorial range of authority that defines the classical state is more diffused. Governance involves hollowing out of the state by distributing power to other key actors (Peters, 1993; Rhodes, 1997). Some of the noted examples for hollowing out the legitimate power of the state include public activities that are delegated to non-state agencies at the national and local levels, or when the state relinquishes to multilateral institutions its sovereign jurisdiction over national issues or resources with global or transboundary dimensions (Leach et al., 2007; Rhodes, 1997). It could also be envisaged when, within the frame of contractual agreements, a state gives multinational companies control over the exploitation, allocation and distribution of national goods and services. Although hollowing-out may be viewed by some scholars as tantamount to a decline in state powers (Peters, 1993; Rhodes, 1997; Stoker, 1998) and in the centrality of the state (Leach et al., 2007), the state could strategically hollow out its decision-making and policy implementation authority to competent non-state actors to leverage their expertise, resources and capacities to complement the usual scarce resources, low capacity and limited expertise of the state. When hollowing-out is strategically initiated by the state in order not to entrench the locus and scope of its traditional bureaucratic and political authority but to tap into the competencies of other stakeholders, it may expand its development capacities and improve the efficiency of delivery of goods and services. Moreover, when the state strategically hollows out its powers to competent stakeholders, it explicitly recognizes and legitimizes their values for collaboration. This strategic and concerted alliance may transform the image of the state from being authoritarian to being a catalyst, facilitator, adviser and coordinator for national sustainable development.

Governance involves making state officials and organizations effective and efficient

This conceptual building block of governance draws largely from analytical models of the new public management (NPM) movement. Some scholars argue that, although NPM and emerging forms of governance have many similar features, there are fundamental differences between the two models, particularly at the theoretical level (Peters, 1996; Peters and Pierre, 1998). Some scholars also consider the boundaries between the two models to be so blurred that they use the term interchangeably (Hood, 1991). Despite the subtle differences that may exist between the two models, their conceptual bases in terms of making state officials and organizations effective and efficient are to a large extent similar.

According to Peters and Pierre (1998), governance and NPM have a common feature in terms of their changing views of the roles of elected officials. The classic Weberian view of political officers as the elites wielding the power of domination, legitimization and authority is undervalued by both NPM and governance models. Both recognize that the traditional roles that should be reserved for political officers are those needed for defining and setting the goals and priorities of the public sector. The governance model advocates that elected officials be political entrepreneurs in facilitating the development of networks and in pooling public and private resources (Peters and Pierre, 1998).

For public organizations, it is argued that their highly centralized and hierarchical structure makes them inefficient and ineffective in the delivery of public goods and services (Peters and Pierre, 1998; Rhodes, 1997; Stoker, 1998; Terry, 1998). One strand of the argument advocates pruning the Weberian bureaucratic structure grounded on the rational-legal authority of all unnecessary power appendages and branches to make them more lean, diversified, integrated and efficient (Peters and Pierre, 1998). Another strand of the argument advocates the introduction of corporate mechanisms such as competitive tendering, internal auditing, performance indicators and incentives to make public organizations more efficient (Krahmann, 2003; Peters and Pierre, 1998). As Peters and Pierre (1998) note, the notion of using competition as a means to increase public efficiency is a good example of corporate ideals penetrating the public sector. Some of the advantages may be the availability of corporate decision-making tools to help public organizations estimate the actual costs of initiatives more accurately and consequently guide the selection of cost-effective options. Competition within the public sector may also provide benchmarks and other meaningful bases for comparison and improve customer service and accountability.

Governance involves the active participation of private actors in policy-making and implementation

Governance has been distinguished from government "in order to describe the emergence of policy making arrangements that in addition to government, increasingly involve private actors – such as nongovernmental agencies, firms, associations and interest groups – in the provision of public services and in social and economic regulation" (Krahmann, 2003: 326). According to Stoker (2000: 17), "governance refers to the development of governing styles in which the boundaries between and within public and private sectors have become blurred. The essence of governance is its focus on mechanisms that do not rest on recourse to the authority and sanctions of government." Governance facilitates the involvement of private actors by providing the potential for contracting, franchising and instituting new forms of regulation (Stoker, 2000) and by providing the avenue of participation in the provision of public services through privatization, outsourcing, co-production and public–private partnerships (Krahmann, 2003). By providing the avenue for constructive participation by private actors, governance could endow public organizations with diverse multiple instruments for policy-making and implementation. According to Peters and Pierre (1998), when a government enters into a public–private partnership for policy, it indicates its willingness to operate within the governance framework to develop alternative means of making and implementing policy. Providing the avenue for active participation by private actors demonstrates a government's flexibility and willingness to innovate in the selection of policy instruments. Governance may therefore imply the use of a wider repertoire of instruments than might be used by a more traditional public sector (Peters and Pierre, 1998) and may also imply coordinated efforts and interactions between diverse actors, institutions and artefacts (Leach et al., 2007).

Governance involves the mutual reinforcement of the potential of public policy and markets

A related ideology of improving the efficiency of public organizations and of promoting private actors' participation in policy-making as conceptual building blocks of governance is the relationship between public policy and markets within a neo-Keynesian economic framework. Market-driven administrative reforms, particularly in the West European countries in the 1980s and 1990s, resulted in the greater use of markets, quasi-markets and networks in the delivery of public services (Bevir and Rhodes, 2003; Leach et al., 2007) and helped to transform many of the traditional features and outcomes of public bureaucracies such as higher taxes and public regulations that constrain the efficient allocation of resources and trade (Derlien, 1993; Pierre, 1993; Rouban, 1993).

Leach et al. (2007), drawing from Scharpf (1997), reiterate that the emergence of governance perspectives does not signal the demise of public institutions or of markets. Governance rather provides the frame for blurring the respective potentials of these two long-established institutions (Leach et al., 2007; Rhodes, 1997). The operation of internal markets is critical for competition within public organizations (Peters and Pierre, 1998). It may also ensure cost-effectiveness, comparative performance analysis and benchmarking and improve customer service, accountability and efficiency.

However, it is worth noting that, despite their instrumentality in ensuring efficiency, markets could also constrain the range of choice available to a nation, they could serve as potential sources of resource waste and they may induce organizations to over-supply services (March and Olsen, 1989; Peters and Pierre, 1998; Whitley and Kristensen, 1997). The deregulation of credit and housing markets, especially in the United States, and the inability of market forces to accurately price mortgage-related financial products, which contributed to the global financial crises in 2007, may also signal the deficiencies of markets. One possible antidote that may be prescribed, particularly by neo-Keynesian economists, to address these potential defects of markets would be the intervention of public policy. By providing the nesting bed for such interesting theoretical symbiosis between public policy and markets, governance endorses neo-Keynesian economic concepts that not only recognize the interplay between the two institutions but also advocate increasing the role of politics and public policy in governing or regulating market forces. The current global financial crises may therefore give some credibility and broader acceptance to neo-Keynesian economics and, by implication, to governance as a theoretical framework.

Governance involves the use of networks and partnerships for collective action

"Perhaps the dominant feature of the governance model is the argument that networks have come to dominate public policy. The assertion is that these amorphous collections of actors – not formal policy-making institutions in government – control policy" (Peters and Pierre, 1998: 225). Although usually considered as unstructured, the flexibility, dynamism and transient nature of networks provide them with sufficient resilience and capacity for self-organization (Marsh and Rhodes, 1992; Peters and

Pierre, 1998) and have made them emerge as preferred modes of steering and coordination in the realization of policy objectives (Leach et al., 2007; Stoker, 1998). Networks and partnerships are also increasing in importance as an alternative to the hierarchical and centralized system of government because their structure is more horizontally integrated and there is no single member in the network or partnership that has monopoly over the use of decision-making authority. Government institutions participate in the networks as equals and they are mutually dependent on the other non-state actors to the same extent as the other actors are dependent on them. This, however, does not make the state totally impotent; rather, its role and capacity evolve from direct control to influence and the state now has to bargain with the other stakeholders in the network as relative equals rather than resorting to unilateral use of power if the decisions and outcomes are not favourable (Peters and Pierre, 1998).

The use of networks facilitates the blending of public sector and private sector resources and, when done within formal partnership agreements, this may permit public and private partners to have access to resources and capacities that might not be at their disposal outside the realm of the partnership. Citing Rhodes (1988), Peter and Pierre (1998) note that this mutual resource dependency was previously associated largely with the relationship between central governments and subnational government institutions but has been extended in the current context to cover the "gamut of relationships" between central government and the other organizations with which it interacts.

The complex and diversified nature of global issues such as sustainable development requires an alliance of stakeholders not only with common and collective interests but also with diverse resources and capabilities for collective action. As discussed below, this is one of the reasons networks and partnerships are becoming increasingly favoured as the alternative to the classic hegemonic regime-building that characterized the early years of multilateral diplomacy and global sustainable development governance. The cooperation between stakeholders in the network, alliance or partnership is premised on a relationship of equals and the achievement of collective action that does not rest on recourse to the authority of the state (Richards and Smith, 2002; Stoker, 2000). There are intricate interdependencies within stakeholders of the network and their pursuit of collective actions enhances the synergies between them.

Some scholars are of the opinion that the significance of knowledge in the conceptualization of society–nature interactions should make it an important dimension of governance and an important component in contemporary mainstream thinking and practice in governance (Fischer, 2003; Leach et al., 2007). Citing (Melucci, 1995), Leach et al. (2007)

acknowledge that the politics of knowledge is envisaged by some scholars as part of national and regional networks and that shared problem framings are increasingly central to binding movement in networks and solidarities among people and institutions across globally interconnected spaces. When knowledge is conceptualized in this context, it could be perceived as part of the resources and capacities that are brought into the network or partnership by some of the network stakeholders. This conceptualization is particularly useful for sustainable development governance for the following reasons. Knowledge is power, and recognizing the importance of the non-formal indigenous knowledge of local communities, as well as the science-based knowledge of the formal epistemic communities, will legitimize the significance of their membership in the network. We can now talk about different dimensions of power in complementary relationships in a network setting – political power, knowledge power, investment power and technological power.

In summary, governance is about institutions, actors, networks and the political processes that define policy- and decision-making to advance a particular development path. It involves hollowing out or distributing power from the state to other competent private stakeholders to enable them to participate actively in policy-making and implementation; making state officials and organizations effective and efficient; encouraging the active participation of private actors in policy-making and implementation; providing the setting for the mutual reinforcement of the potentials of public policy and markets; and using networks and partnerships for collective action.

The opportunities and challenges of green economy governance in Africa

To understand why having the appropriate governance framework will be critical for realizing the potential of the green economy in Africa it will be useful to look briefly at the opportunities and challenges of promoting a green economy in Africa. It will also be useful to put governance and the vital elements of a green economy into perspective.

Three of the major reasons for the increasing poverty and the continued deterioration of the environment in Africa are (1) the extremely high dependence on natural resources for livelihood activities such as agriculture and forest-based enterprises; (2) low resource efficiency (even in the mining, oil and gas sectors where exports are mainly in the form of raw materials); and (3) the low diversification of economies that lock a greater percentage of the rural population into subsistence farming, underemployment, unemployment and poverty. Although these factors are currently posing great challenges, they could actually be viewed as opportunities to chart a sustainable development path without much investment in reversing past unsustainable development pathways as pertain in some advanced countries (such as funding the incremental costs of retrofitting fossil-fuel-based power plants). Africa's endowments of rich natural resources offer great opportunities for a development model in which sustainable biological processes replace resource-intensive and environmentally harmful processes and for decoupling economic growth from environmental degradation. The green economy has the potential to direct such a development model.

The green economy framework offers great opportunities for addressing the three major factors of poverty and environmental degradation specified above. The green economy framework is buttressed on three major pillars: (1) low-carbon technology, (2) resource-use efficiency, and (3) socially inclusive growth (UNEP, 2011b). These three pillars have great relevance for sustainable development, poverty eradication and inclusive growth in Africa.

There are four major reasons why the current institutional framework for sustainable development particularly in most African countries may not work for green economy governance.

1. Unlike Agenda 21 in particular, which advocates the need to incorporate environmental sustainability into economic policies without providing guidance on "how" (UNESCAP, 2011), the green economy framework operationalizes sustainable development into its three major pillars and forges greater convergence between the three pillars of sustainable development: economic sustainability, environmental sustainability and sociopolitical sustainability. The current situation, in which NCSDs in some African countries have their mandates limited to environment-related issues and undertaking exclusively environment-related activities, may not work for green economy governance. For these institutions to be relevant to current governance challenges for a green economy, they should be given broader mandates and should be provided with adequate resources and capacities to forge greater convergence and coordination between activities covering the three pillars of sustainable development.

2. The integrated and decentralized nature of the green economy may require broader stakeholders for collective action. The current situation, in which state actors dominate most NCSDs with no or minimal representation from non-state actors, may not work for green economy governance. Besides, the green economy is more results focused in terms of increasing innovation for exploring and developing new technologies for low-carbon production, increasing productivity from the efficient use of resources, recycling, reuse and reducing waste, and increasing the potential for employment from "green" jobs, alternative income and socially inclusive growth. This may require stakeholders to

come together with diverse resources and capabilities (investment, technologies, capital assets, knowledge, etc.) for collective action. For the NCSDs and related institutions to be relevant, their representation and participation structure should be broadened to cover competent private actors. The investment power, knowledge power and technological power of these private actors should legitimize their membership in the NCSDs.
3. The green economy framework seeks to integrate other mechanisms, such as Agenda 21. This could be a welcome improvement considering the current proliferation of mechanisms, some of which overlap or duplicate the objectives and activities of other mechanisms. For example, the green economy touches on the socioeconomic development, conservation and environmental management of Agenda 21 as well as the environmental management, low-carbon technology and renewable energy of the Clean Development Mechanism of the Kyoto Protocol. It also embraces the low technology, renewable energy, resource efficiency and sustainable lifestyles, cities and societies of the Sustainable Consumption and Production (SCP) initiative. Will the NCSDs have adequate capacity to coordinate and integrate these diverse mechanisms? This may require networks and partnerships with different stakeholders for more integrated and collective action to use the green economy as an integrated framework to meet the objectives of other mechanisms.
4. The changing dynamics of the multilateral diplomacy and governance of sustainable development have undervalued the structure, composition and mandates of the NCSDs and related state institutions in Africa. The Johannesburg World Summit on Sustainable Development (Rio+10 Earth Summit) changed the traditional meaning of summitry as a centralized, Type I (or track one) form of multilateral regime-building when the Summit became dominated by agreements on about 300 partnership initiatives that required participation and resources from non-governmental actors. The Rio+10 Earth Summit saw active participation from both government and non-governmental actors and introduced informal Type II partnership mechanisms for achieving Agenda 21 and the Millennium Development Goals. Networks and partnerships for environmental governance and sustainable development have come to stay and they are likely to feature prominently in the Rio+20 negotiations and in green economy governance even after the negotiations.

One of such networks and partnerships that emerged from the Rio+10 conference and that may be relevant for green economy governance in Africa is what has come to be known as the Marrakech Process to support the implementation of projects and strategies on SCP. This is a global and informal multi-stakeholder process in response to the call by Chapter III of the Johannesburg Plan of Implementation (JPOI) to develop a 10 Year Framework of Programmes (10YFP) on SCP covering the period 2011–2021, based on Agenda 21, the Rio Declaration and the JPOI (UNEP, 2010). Africa was the first region to develop its 10YFP on SCP, with financial support from the German Federal Ministry for the Environment, Nature Conservation and Nuclear Safety (BMU) through the Marrakech Task Force on Cooperation with Africa, and facilitated by UNEP and the United Nations Department of Economic and Social Affairs. The Africa 10YFP was approved in March 2005 by the African Ministerial Conference on the Environment at the Second Partnership Conference on the Implementation of the Environment Action Plan of the New Partnership for Africa's Development, in Dakar, Senegal. There are currently 13 African countries with national cleaner production centres (NCPCs). These NCPCs have played key roles in mainstreaming SCP policies in their nations and replicating best practices for SCP across the continent. They have also developed a continent-wide and cross-sectoral eco-labelling programme called the Eco Mark Africa and have played an instrumental role in creating a regional network of NCPCs through the Africa Roundtable for SCP.

Although these NCPCs are multi-stakeholder networks and in some countries have not yet received political support and commitment from their national governments, the processes they have initiated for the past seven years to mainstream SCP policies and to encourage the development of low-carbon and resource-efficient technologies could serve as a solid foundation for national initiatives to establish networks and partnerships for green economy governance. Their involvement in any national institutional arrangements for green economy governance cannot be overemphasized.

A framework for green economy governance in Africa

As noted above, and as illustrated in Figure 7.1, governance involves institutions, individual actors and networks with sometimes collective interests and coming together to leverage their diverse resources and capabilities for policy-making and collective action. The collaborative, integrated and decentralized nature of green economy instruments reinforces the need to restructure the current institutional framework for sustainable development in most African countries.

As Figure 7.1 shows, the transition to a green economy in Africa may require national commitments to promote science, technology and innovation. This brings to the fore the necessity to bring on board not only

Figure 7.1 A theoretical framework of green economy governance in Africa.

the formal epistemic community but also local actors with indigenous knowledge in, for example, traditional low-carbon technologies. This will make decentralization of green economy governance key. It may also involve a network of scientists that transcends national boundaries to tap into the pool of knowledge outside the locus of traditional national jurisdictions. Appropriate governance structures may be vital to direct the pace and direction of science, technology and innovation for a green economy. As the review of the theoretical building blocks of governance indicates, the knowledge of indigenous and formal epistemic communities should legitimize their value and make their active participation in any green economy governance structure imperative.

The need for low-carbon and resource-efficient production will require substantial investment and infrastructure, and this should make partnerships between national governments and the private sector imperative. Because governance embraces policy-making and implementation arrangements that increasingly involve private actors, African nations will stand to benefit if they create the governance structures to leverage the financial resources, technology and management capabilities of the private sector. The need for low-carbon and resource-efficient production also emphasizes the relevance of the interaction between public policy and markets. The governance structure adopted by African countries should provide the setting to mutually reinforce the potentials of public policy and the operation of market forces.

Figure 7.1 also shows that governance underpins regulation, policy mainstreaming and implementation for a particular development path and could define who gets what of the benefits from this development path. This policy dimension of governance and its related impacts on especially the poor have been given detailed analysis by Resnick, Tarp and Thurlow in Chapter 4 of this book. For equity and fairness in resource allocation, governments should institute policies that will not just ensure that benefits trickle down from the wealthy elites and politicians to the poor but rather provide the poor with the capacity and the infrastructure to participate viably in national productive activities to enjoy economic profits. As the review of the theoretical building blocks of governance shows, his may require the state to hollow out its powers and provide the resources to legitimize and delegate to local communities the authority and capacity to pursue socioeconomic activities that promote, for example, employment, rural entrepreneurship and inclusive growth. It may also entail recognizing key local institutions as valued partners and members of the green economy governance networks and making state officials and organizations that work with local stakeholders and vulnerable communities less bureaucratic and more efficient. This is not unattainable in Africa. With the appropriate governance structure and the right policies such a development pathway could be achieved. There are several examples in Asian countries where pro-poor development strategies such as land reform and microeconomic reforms have provided the impetus for low-carbon, labour-intensive sectors to thrive and create employment with consequent unprecedented improvements in the living standards of the rural poor (Van Arkadie, 2005; Van Arkadie and Mallon, 2003).

Conclusion

The green economy framework may offer African countries tremendous opportunities to pursue low-carbon and resource-efficient production to decouple economic growth from social inequalities and environmental degradation. It may also provide African countries with the opportunity to bypass the inefficient, resource-intensive and environmentally harmful development pathways of most developed countries and leapfrog into sustainable and efficient development pathways. To do this, African countries should establish appropriate governance structures that are relevant to the current context and to the vital elements of a green economy. Without these appropriate governance structures, Africa may enter Rio+40 with the same moderate results in terms of sustainable development, and the paradox of Africa having enormous wealth in natural resources and yet being the poorest continent with worsening environmental degradation will still be valid 20 years from today.

Arguably, one of the reasons for such moderate results in terms of sustainable development on the continent is the highly deficient institutional structure for sustainable development governance in most African countries. This chapter has explored the necessary elements of governance that should support the institutional arrangements for green economy governance in Africa. It has provided the theoretical framework of governance based on the major conceptual building blocks of governance. Green economy governance in Africa should involve national governments "hollowing out" power to other competent private stakeholders to enable them to participate actively in policy-making and the implementation of green economy initiatives. It may also entail making state officials and organizations effective and efficient and providing the setting for the mutual reinforcement of the potentials of public policy and markets. The ability to level the playing field to provide the incentives for non-state stakeholders to bring their resources, expertise and capabilities into partnerships and development networks for collective action will be a great asset for any national government to have. Finally, the chapter has made recommendations for the institutional imperatives that should represent the appropriate framework for green economy governance. It is hoped that African governments will take into consideration these institutional imperatives in crafting the governance structures and mechanisms for green economy governance at the regional, national and local levels.

Note

1. UNECA distributed a survey questionnaire to all 53 member countries of Africa. This had a 43 per cent response rate, so references to sample distributions of the "survey countries" are based on the 23 countries that completed and returned the questionnaire.

REFERENCES

Bekke, H. A. G. M., W. J. M. Kickert and J. Kooiman (1995) "Public Management and Governance", in W. J. M. Kickert and F. A. Van Vught (eds), *Public Policy and Administrative Sciences in the Netherlands*. London: Harvester-Wheatsheaf, pp. 199–216.

Bevir, M. and R. Rhodes (2003) *Interpreting British Governance*. London: Routledge.

Carson, R. (1962) *Silent Spring*. Boston: Houghton Mifflin.

Derlien, H. U. (1993) "German Unification and Bureaucratic Transformation", *International Political Science Review*, 14: 319–334.

ECA (Economic Commission for Africa) (2005) *National Councils for Sustainable Development in Africa: A Review of Institutions and their Functioning*. Addis Ababa: Economic Commission for Africa. Available at ⟨http://www.uneca.org/sdd/documents/ncsd_book.pdf⟩ (accessed 27 January 2012).

ECA (Economic Commission for Africa) (2011a) "Programme Overview of Food Security and Sustainable Development", ⟨http://www.uneca.org/fssdd/default.htm⟩ (accessed 2 February 2012).

ECA (Economic Commission for Africa) (2011b) *Africa Report on Institutional and Strategic Frameworks for Sustainable Development: Summary for Policy Makers*. Seventh Session of the Committee on Food Security and Sustainable Development (CFSSD-7) and the African Regional Preparatory Conference for the United Nations Conference on Sustainable Development (Rio+20), 20–25 October. Addis Ababa: Economic Commission for Africa.

ECOSOC (United Nations Economic and Social Council) (1968) "Resolution 1346 (XLV): Question of Convening an International Conference on the Problems of Human Environment", 30 July. New York: United Nations Economic and Social Council.

Fischer, F. (2003) *Reframing Public Policy: Discursive Politics and Deliberative Practices*. Oxford: Oxford University Press.

Hood, C. (1991) "A Public Management for All Seasons", *Public Administration*, 69: 3–19.

Krahmann, E. (2003) "National, Regional and Global Governance: One Phenomenon or Many?", *Global Governance* 9(3): 323–346.

Leach, M., G. Bloom, A. Ely, P. Nightingale, I. Scoones, E. Shah and A. Smith (2007) "Understanding Governance: Pathways to Sustainability", STEPS Working Paper 2, STEPS Centre, Brighton.

March, J. G. and J. P. Olsen (1989) *Rediscovering Institutions*. New York: Free Press.

Marsh, D. and R. W. Rhodes (1992) *Policy Networks in British Government*. Oxford: Clarendon Press.

Melucci, A. (1995) "The New Social Movements Revisited: Reflections on a Sociological Misunderstanding", in L. Malhue (ed.), *Social Movements and Social Classes: The Future of Collective Action*. London: Sage, pp. 107–119.

NEPAD (New Partnership for Africa's Development) (2011) "About NEPAD", ⟨http://www.nepad.org/about⟩ (accessed 30 January 2012).

O'Toole, L. J., Jr (2000) "Research on Policy Implementation: Assessment and Prospects", *Journal of Policy Administration and Theory*, 10(2): 263–288.

Peters, B. G. (1993) "Managing the Hollow State", in K. Elliassen and J. Kooiman (eds), *Managing Public Organizations*. London: Sage, pp. 46–57.

Peters, B. G. (1996) *The Future of Governing: Four Emerging Models*. Kansas: Lawrence University Press.

Peters, B. G. and J. Pierre (1998) "Governance Without Government? Rethinking Public Administration", *Journal of Public Administration Research and Theory*, 8(2): 223–243.

Pierre, J. (1993) "Legitimacy, Institutional Change and the Politics of Public Administration in Sweden", *International Political Science Review*, 14: 387–401.

Rhodes, R. W. (1988) *Beyond Westminster and Whitehall*. London: Unwin Hyman.

Rhodes, R. W. (1996) "The New Governance: Governing without Government", *Political Studies*, 44: 652–657.

Rhodes, R. W. (1997) *Understanding Governance*. Buckingham: Open University Press.

Richards, D. and M. J. Smith (2002) *Governance and Public Policy in the United Kingdom*. Oxford: Oxford University Press.

Rouban, L. (1993) "France in Search of a New Administrative Order", *International Political Science Review*, 14: 403–418.

Scharpf, F. W. (1997) "Introduction: The Problem-solving Capacity of Multi-level Governance", *Journal of European Public Policy*, 4(4): 520–538.

Stoker, G. (1998) "Governance as Theory: Five Prepositions", *International Social Science Journal*, 50(1): 17–28.

Stoker, G. (2000) *The New Politics of British Local Governance*. London: Macmillan.

Terry, L. (1998) "Administrative Leadership, Neo-Managerialism, and the Public Management Movement", *Public Administration Review*, 58(3): 194–200.

UNEP (United Nations Environment Programme) (2010) *ABC of SCP: Clarifying Concepts on Sustainable Consumption and Production*. Nairobi, Kenya: UNEP.

UNEP (United Nations Environment Programme) (2011a) "About Regional Office for Africa", Nairobi, Kenya. Available at ⟨http://www.unep.org/roa/AboutROA/tabid/7000/Default.aspx⟩ (accessed 30 January 2012).

UNEP (United Nations Environment Programme) (2011b) *Towards a Green Economy: Pathways to Sustainable Development and Poverty Eradication – A Synthesis for Policy Makers*. Nairobi, Kenya: UNEP.

UNESCAP (United Nations Economic and Social Commission for Asia and the Pacific) (2011) "Conceptual Framework for Green Economy / Green Growth", Bangkok. Available at ⟨http://www.greengrowth.org/capacity_building/National-Seminar/2011/Thailand/Documents/GENERAL/GG-CONCEPT.pdf⟩ (accessed 30 January 2012).

United Nations (1972) "Resolution 2997 (XXVII): Institutional and Financial Arrangements for International Environment Cooperation", 26 September. New York: United Nations General Assembly.

United Nations (1992) "Resolution 47/197: International Cooperation for the Eradication of Poverty in Developing Countries", 22 December. New York: United Nations General Assembly.

Van Arkadie, B. (2005) "Economic Reform in Vietnam and Tanzania: A Comparative Commentary", in M. Tribe, J. Thoburn and R. Palmer-Jones (eds), *Development Economics and Social Justice: Essays in Honour of Ian Livingstone*. London: Ashgate, pp. 121–140.

Van Arkadie, B. and R. Mallon (2003) *Vietnam: A Transition Tiger?* Canberra: Asia Pacific Press at the Australian National University.

Whitley, R. and P. H. Kristensen (1997) *Governance at Work: The Social Regulation of Economic Relations*. Oxford: Oxford University Press.

World Bank (1989) *Sub-Saharan Africa: From Crisis to Sustainable Growth*. Washington, DC: World Bank.

8
Geothermal energy and the Millennium Development Goals

Ingvar B. Fridleifsson

Energy and the Millennium Development Goals

At the United Nations Millennium Summit in September 2000, the largest gathering of world leaders in history, the Millennium Declaration was adopted from which the Millennium Development Goals (MDGs) were later extracted. Most of these goals and targets were set to be achieved by the year 2015 on the basis of the global situation during the 1990s. The MDGs provide countries around the world with a framework for development and time-bound targets by which progress can be measured (United Nations, 2006).

In 2002, government leaders, heads of industry, civil society and representatives of United Nations organizations met in Johannesburg at the World Summit on Sustainable Development (WSSD). This conference brought energy and environmental issues to the centre of the global debate.

A key paper on energy and the MDGs is a report entitled *Energy Services for the Millennium Development Goals*, prepared by experts from Columbia University, the Energy Sector Management Assistance Program (ESMAP), the United Nations Development Program (UNDP) and the World Bank (Modi et al., 2006). Energy services refer to the services that energy and energy appliances provide. Such services include lighting, fuel for cooking and space heating, power for transport, water pumping and grinding, and numerous other services that fuel electricity and make mechanical power possible. The core message of the report is that energy

Green economy and good governance for sustainable development: Opportunities, promises and concerns, Puppim de Oliveira (ed.),
United Nations University Press, 2012, ISBN 978-92-808-1216-9

services are essential to both social and economic development and that much wider and greater access to energy services is critical in achieving all of the MDGs.

Even though no MDG refers to energy explicitly, improved energy services – including modern cooking fuels, improved cook stoves, increased sustainable biomass production and expanded access to electricity and mechanical power – are necessary for meeting the goals (Modi et al., 2006). From the point of view of the user, what matters is the energy service, not the sources. Whether in business, home or community life, what matters is the reliability, affordability and accessibility of the energy services. It is therefore essential to have a clear understanding of which energy services are needed to support the MDGs and to examine the role that different energy carriers can play in providing these services in the most practical and affordable fashion to support human development at large (Modi et al., 2006). This chapter does not go into the specific roles of the different energy carriers.

World energy situation and population

Among the top priorities for the majority of the world's population is access to sufficient and affordable energy. There is a very limited equity in energy use in the different parts of the world. Some 70 per cent of the world's population have per capita energy consumption levels that are one-quarter of that of Western Europe and one-sixth of that of the United States. Over 2 billion people, one-third of the world's population, have no access to modern energy services. A key issue in improving the standard of living of the poor is to make clean energy available to them at prices they can cope with. World population is expected to double by the end of the twenty-first century. To provide sufficient commercial energy (not to mention clean energy) to the people of all continents is an enormous task.

Population growth is, of course, a central issue in studies of how to meet the energy requirements of the world. Figure 8.1 shows historical developments from 1850 to 1990 and the World Bank projection to 2100 (Bos et al., 1992), by rural–urban distribution and by macro-region. As stated by Nakićenović et al. (1998), the good news in the 1992 World Bank and other global projections is that population growth is slowing down. The next doubling of the world's population is expected to take much longer than the last one, which took only 40 years. The population is expected to rise from the present 7 billion to approximately 10.4 billion by 2100, according to the 1996 long-range projection by the International Institute for Applied Systems Analysis (IIASA). Virtually all of the

(a) Urban–rural distribution

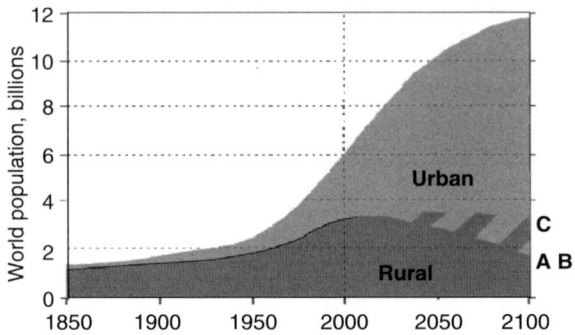

(b) Population by macro-region

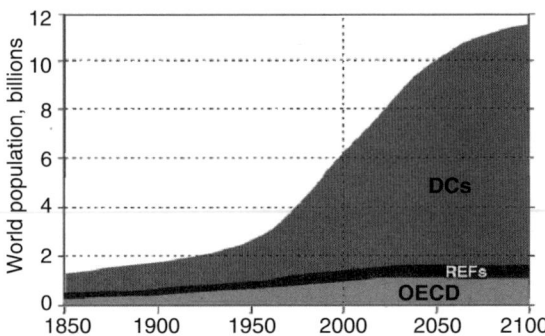

Figure 8.1 World population showing historical developments, 1850–1990, and the World Bank projection to 2100: (a) by rural–urban distribution and (b) by macro-region.
Source: Nakicenovic et al. (1998).
Notes: A, B and C display different population growth scenarios from a projection by the World Bank in 1992 (Bos et al., 1992). Urbanization trends are based on United Nations (1994) and Berry (1990). REFs = Eastern Europe and the former Soviet Union; DCs = developing countries.

population growth is expected in the South. By 2100, the population of the United States, Canada and the whole of Europe combined will drop to less than 10 per cent of the world total, according to studies by the World Bank, the IIASA and the United Nations.

By the year 2100, according to the World Energy Council (WEC), the presently categorised developing countries can be expected to account for about 80 per cent of the global energy demand (WEC, 1993). Even then, energy per capita availability in the developing countries is likely to be far less than in the rest of the world – perhaps only 50–60 per cent of that in the OECD (Organisation for Economic Co-operation and Development) area by then. The WEC (1993) study suggests that by the end of the twenty-first century close to three-quarters of the world's population is likely to be urbanized and the interim pressures on housing, sanitation, air and water quality, health care and congestion are likely to be intense. Energy systems geared towards providing the comforts, motive power and mobility that people seek from energy may have lead to some profound changes. The challenge to city transportation systems over that time frame is likely to have called forth some imaginative responses (WEC, 1993).

World energy sources

The scarcity of energy resources forecasted in the 1970s did not occur. With technological and economic development, estimates of the ultimately available energy resource base continue to increase. Economic development over the next century will apparently not be constrained by geological resources. Environmental concerns and financing and technological constraints appear more likely sources of future limits (Fridleifsson, 2002).

In all of the WEC's scenarios, the peak of the fossil fuel era has already passed (Nakićenović et al., 1998). Oil and gas are expected to continue to be important sources of energy in all cases, but the role of renewable energy sources and nuclear energy and the level to which these energy sources replace coal vary a great deal in the scenarios. In all of the scenarios, renewables are expected to become very significant contributors to global primary energy consumption, providing 20–40 per cent of primary energy in 2050 and 30–80 per cent in 2100. It is anticipated that renewables will cover a large part of the increase in energy consumption and will replace coal.

It is legitimate to ask whether these scenarios are realistic. Table 8.1 shows the technical potential – the yearly availability – of renewable energy resources (IPCC, 2011). There is no question that the technical potential is sufficiently large to meet future world energy requirements. The question is, however, how large a part of the technical potential can be harnessed in an economically, environmentally and socially acceptable way. This will probably vary between the energy sources. It is worth noting, however, that the present annual consumption of primary energy in the world is about 510 exajoules (EJ) (IEA, 2011).

World primary energy consumption in 2009 (IEA, 2011) was as follows: fossil fuels provided 81 per cent of the total, with oil (33 per cent) in first

Table 8.1 Ranges of technical potential of renewable energy sources

Source	EJ per year
Hydropower	50–52
Biomass	50–500
Solar energy	1,575–49,837
Wind energy	85–580
Geothermal energy	128–1421
Total	1,888–52,390

Source: IPCC (2011: Figure TS.1.7).
Note: EJ = exajoules.

place, followed by coal (27 per cent) and natural gas (21 per cent). Renewables collectively provided 13 per cent of the primary energy, mostly in the form of bioenergy (10 per cent) and much less by hydropower (2 per cent) and the "new renewables" (biomass, geothermal, wind, solar and tidal energy) (1 per cent). Nuclear energy provided 6 per cent of the world's primary energy.

If we look only at electricity production, the role of hydropower becomes much more significant. World electricity production was about 20,000 terawatt hours (TWh) in 1999, compared with 6,000 TWh in 1973 (IEA, 2011). Most of the electricity was produced by coal (41 per cent), followed by hydro (16 per cent), nuclear (13 per cent), natural gas (21 per cent) and oil (5 per cent). Only 3 per cent of the electricity was provided by the "new renewables".

Table 8.2 shows the installed capacity and electricity production in 2009 for renewable energy sources (hydropower, bioenergy, and wind, geothermal and solar energy). The table clearly reflects the variable capacity factors of power stations using renewable sources. The capacity factor of 72 per cent for geothermal is by far the highest. Geothermal energy

Table 8.2 Electricity from renewable energy resources in 2009

Source	Installed capacity		Production per year		Capacity factor (per cent)
	GWe	Per cent	TWh/year	Per cent	
Hydropower	926.0	78.9	3,551.0	83.8	44.0
Bioenergy	55.0	4.7	267.0	6.3	55.0
Wind energy	160.0	13.6	325.0	7.7	23.0
Geothermal energy	10.7	0.9	67.2	1.6	72.0
Solar energy	22.0	1.9	26.0	0.6	13.0
Total	1173.7	100.0	4,236.2	100.0	41.0

Source: Compiled from IPCC (2011).
Notes: GWe = gigawatt electrical; TWh = terawatt hours.

is independent of weather conditions, in contrast to solar, wind or hydro applications. It has an inherent storage capability and can be used for both base load and peak power plants. The relatively high share of geothermal energy in electricity production in relation to its installed capacity (1.6 per cent of electricity production compared with only 0.9 per cent of the installed capacity) reflects the reliability of geothermal plants, which can be (and are in a few countries) operated at capacity factors in excess of 90 per cent.

It should be stressed that Table 8.2 is not intended to diminish the importance of wind or solar energy. On the contrary, it serves to demonstrate that renewable energy sources can contribute significantly more to the mitigation of climate change by cooperating than by competing. The table shows that geothermal energy is available day and night, every day of the year, and can thus serve as a supplement to energy sources that are available only intermittently. It is most economical for geothermal power stations to serve as a base load throughout the year, but they can also, at a cost, be operated to meet seasonal variations and as peak power.

Geothermal energy utilization

Geothermal resources have been identified in some 90 countries and there are quantified records of geothermal utilization in 79 countries. Electricity is produced by geothermal sources in 24 countries. Nine of these countries obtain 5–26 per cent of their national electricity from geothermal. The worldwide use of geothermal energy was reported in 2010 to be about 67 TWh/year of electricity (Bertani, 2010) and 122 TWh/year for direct use (Lund et al., 2010). Figure 8.2 shows the installed capacity and the energy produced by geothermal on the different continents.

Electricity production increased by 21 per cent between 2005 and 2010, an annual growth rate of 3.8 per cent (Bertani, 2010). Direct use increased by 60 per cent between 2004 and 2009, an annual growth rate of 9.9 per cent (Lund et al., 2010). Only a small fraction of the geothermal potential has been developed so far, and there is ample space for an accelerated use of geothermal energy both for direct applications and for electricity generation. Table 8.3 lists the top 16 countries in the world in geothermal electricity production and in direct use of geothermal energy (in gigawatt hours per year) as reported in 2010.

Every year, the World Bank publishes tables of selected world development indicators in the *World Development Report*. The tables classify all World Bank member economies and all other economies with populations of more than 30,000. Economies (countries) are divided into income groups according to their 2009 gross national income per capita per year.

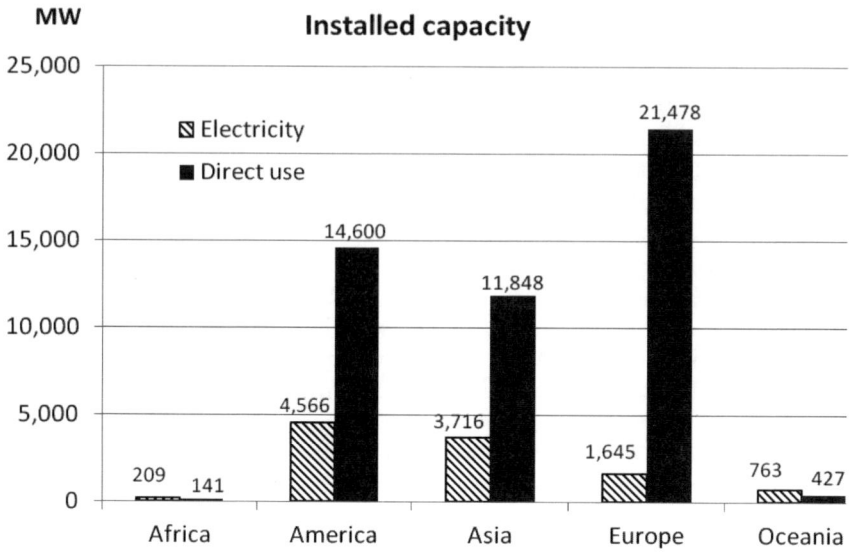

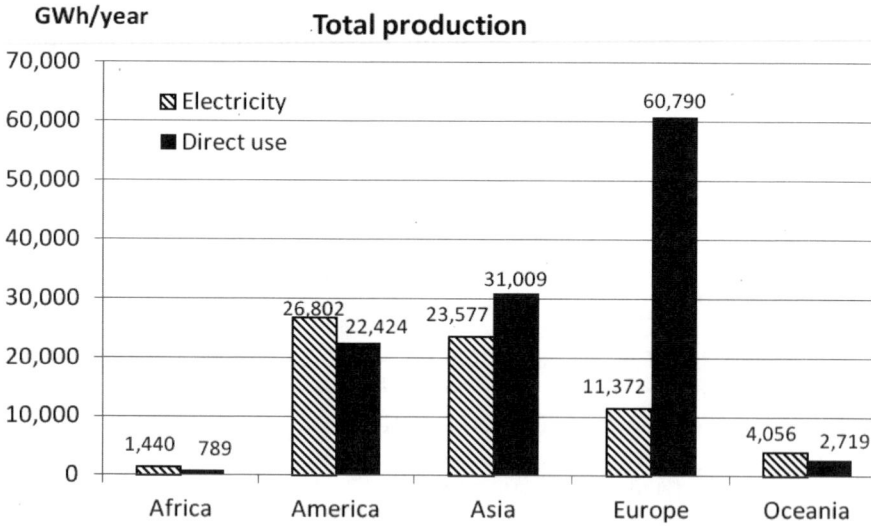

Figure 8.2 Installed geothermal capacity (megawatts) and production (gigawatt hours per year) for electricity generation and direct use, by continent.
Sources: Data from Bertani (2012) and Lund et al. (2011).
Notes: MW = megawatts; GWh/year = gigawatt hours per year.

Table 8.3 Top 16 countries utilizing geothermal energy

Geothermal electricity production, 2010		Geothermal direct use, 2009	
	GWh/year		GWh/year
United States	16,603	China	20,932
Philippines	10,311	United States	15,710
Indonesia	9,600	Sweden	12,585
Mexico	7,047	Turkey	10,247
Italy	5,520	Japan	7,139
Iceland	4,597	Norway	7,001
New Zealand	4,055	Iceland	6,768
Japan	3,064	France	3,592
Kenya	1,430	Germany	3,546
El Salvador	1,422	Netherlands	2,972
Costa Rica	1,131	Italy	2,762
Turkey	490	Hungary	2,713
Papua New Guinea	450	New Zealand	2,654
Russia	441	Canada	2,465
Nicaragua	310	Finland	2,325
Guatemala	289	Switzerland	2,143

Sources: Data on electricity from Bertani (2010) and on direct use from Lund et al. (2010).
Notes: GWh/year = gigawatt hours per year.

The groups are low-income countries (LIC), with USD 995 or less; lower-middle-income countries (LMC), with USD 996–3,945; upper-middle-income countries (UMC), with USD 3,946–12,195; and high-income countries, with USD 12,196 and above. The high-income countries are further divided into OECD and non-OECD countries.

Table 8.4 shows how many of the 79 countries with quantified records of geothermal utilization fall within each of the World Bank categories.

Table 8.4 Number of countries in different economic categories using geothermal for electricity production and direct use, 2010

Economic category[a]	Number of countries	Top 16 countries utilizing geothermal	
		Electricity production	Direct use
High-income OECD	29	5	14
High-income none-OECD	3	–	–
UMC	22	4	1
LMC	21	6	–
LIC	4	1	1

[a]As defined by the World Bank (2011).

The table also compares the number of countries in each category that are among the top 16 countries using geothermal for electricity production and direct use, respectively. Among the top 16 countries in electricity production with geothermal in 2009, there are 6 LMCs, 5 high-income OECD countries, 4 UMCs and only 1 LIC (Kenya). Among the top 16 countries making direct use of geothermal, there are 14 high-income OECD countries, 1 UMC (Turkey) and 1 LIC (China), which is actually at the top of the list in terms of direct use of geothermal.

Electricity generation

In the electricity sector, the geographical distribution of suitable geothermal fields is restricted and mainly confined to countries or regions on active plate boundaries or with active volcanoes (see Table 8.3 above).

Figure 8.3 shows the top 14 countries with the highest percentage share of geothermal in their national electricity production. Special attention is drawn to the fact that El Salvador, Costa Rica and Nicaragua are among the top seven countries in Figure 8.3, and that Guatemala is in tenth place. Central America is one of the world's richest regions in terms of geothermal resources. Geothermal power stations provide about 12 per cent of the total electricity generation of the four countries Costa Rica,

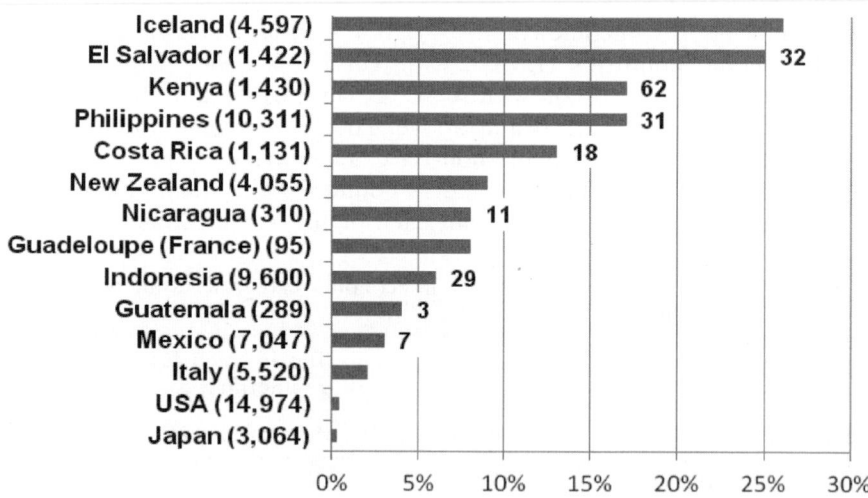

Figure 8.3 The 14 countries with the highest percentage share of geothermal energy in their national electricity production.
Notes: Numbers in parentheses give annual geothermal electricity production in GWh in 2010 (data from Bertani, 2010). The number of UNU-GTP graduates from each country is shown to the right of the columns.

El Salvador, Guatemala and Nicaragua, according to data provided by the countries (CEPAL, 2010). The electricity generated in the geothermal fields is in all cases replacing electricity generated by imported oil. Hydro stations provide 46 per cent of electricity for the four countries, and wind energy 2 per cent. With an interconnected grid, it would be relatively easy to provide all the electricity for the four countries by renewable energy (Fridleifsson and Haraldsson, 2011).

The geothermal potential for electricity generation in Central America has been estimated at some 4,000 megawatts electrical (MWe) (Lippmann, 2002), and less than 500 MWe have been harnessed so far. With the large untapped geothermal resources and the significant experience in geothermal as well as hydro development in the region, Central America may become an international example of how to reduce overall emissions of greenhouse gases in a large region. Similar developments can be foreseen in the East African Rift Valley, as well as in several other countries and regions rich in high-temperature geothermal resources. This clearly demonstrates how significant geothermal energy can be in the electricity production of countries and regions rich in high-temperature fields, which are associated with volcanic activity. There are examples from many developing countries of rural electrification and the provision of safe drinking water, schools and medical centres in connection with the development of geothermal resources. Such projects are in line with the MDGs.

Kenya was the first country in Africa to utilize its rich geothermal resources and in the foreseeable future will be able to produce most of its electricity with hydropower and geothermal energy. Geothermal energy is also expected to play an important role in meeting the MDGs in undeveloped parts of eastern Baringo, Kenya, where less than 1 per cent of the population have access to electricity (Ogola et al., 2011a). Ethiopia and several other countries in the East African Rift Valley could follow suit. Indonesia is probably the world's richest country in geothermal resources and could in the future replace a considerable part of its fossil-fuelled electricity by geothermal.

Direct utilization

The main types of direct use of geothermal energy are: space heating, 63 per cent (of which 49 per cent is accounted for by heat pumps); bathing and swimming (including balneology), 25 per cent; horticulture (greenhouses and soil heating), 5 per cent; industry, 3 per cent; fish farming, 3 per cent; snow melting and other uses, 1 per cent (Lund et al., 2010). The main growth in the direct use sector during the past decade has been in geothermal (ground source) heat pumps (GHPs). This is owing, in part, to the ability of GHPs to utilize groundwater or ground-coupled temperatures anywhere in the world for heating and/or cooling.

In many developing and transitional countries, the main use of geothermal has been for washing and bathing, greenhouses and fish ponds (aquaculture). These activities significantly improve people's quality of life. In addition, tourism is often a significant source of income at geothermal locations.

The largest potential in the direct use sector is space heating and water heating, because these constitute a significant part of the energy budget in large parts of the world. In industrialized countries, 35–40 per cent of total primary energy consumption is used in buildings. In Europe, 30 per cent of energy use is for space and water heating alone, representing 75 per cent of total building energy use (Fridleifsson et al., 2008). The largest potential for direct use of geothermal is in China. Owing to geological conditions, there are widespread low-temperature geothermal resources in most provinces of China, which are already widely used for space heating, balneology, fish farming and greenhouses during the cold winter months and for hot tap water also in the summer.

Until recently, most GHP installations have been in North America and Europe, increasing from 26 countries in 2000, to 33 countries in 2005 and to 43 countries in 2010 (Lund et al., 2010). China is, however, the most significant newcomer in the application of heat pumps for space heating. The government of China has in recent years made significant efforts to save energy and reduce carbon dioxide (CO_2) emissions. Since the Renewable Energy Law came into effect in 2006, the development of geothermal energy, and of other renewable energy sources, was encouraged. Under the market economy, investors are willing to invest in geothermal development. In direct use applications in China, geothermal space heating has continued a steady increase of about 10 per cent annually. The annual increase has been 20–23 million m^2 of heating area (with partial cooling). The GHP installed capacity grew from 383 megawatts thermal (MWt) to 5,210 MWt in 2009 (Zheng, 2010). Many large projects gained financial support from the Ministry of Construction and the Ministry of Finance. GHP systems were installed in many games halls and stadiums for the 2008 Beijing Olympic Games. Renewable energy accounted for about 26 per cent of the total heating and cooling requirements of the Olympic venues in Beijing and served as a good demonstration of the use of these forms of energy. The total geothermal district heating area in China exceeded 30.2 million m^2 in 2010 (Zheng et al., 2010).

China is blessed with low-temperature geothermal resources in most provinces of the country. These have been used through the centuries for bathing, washing, fish farming, horticulture (greenhouses), etc. In the future, these resources will be used on a large scale for space heating as well as space cooling with the application of heat pumps. GHPs driven by fossil-fuelled electricity reduce CO_2 emissions by at least 50 per cent compared with fossil fuel fired boilers (Fridleifsson et al., 2008).

In Kenya, the main commercial application of geothermal energy for direct use is a flower farm near the Olkaria geothermal power station, where some of the greenhouses are heated during the night and thus kept dry by geothermal heat (Simiyu, 2010). Some 30,000 people work on flower farms in the region (only a few use geothermal as yet), and it is estimated that tens of thousands of people earn their livelihood from this. The flower companies, which export cut flowers (mainly roses) by air to Europe, provide the staff and their families with good housing, water, electricity, schools and medical centres. All the MDGs of the United Nations are basically met. The Kenya Flower Council indicates that the flower farming industry employs 500,000 people indirectly through formal and informal industries such as transport, packaging, business suppliers, fertilizers, irrigation engineers, chemicals, consultants and auditors (350,000 indirect jobs are associated with the Lake Naivasha flower industry) throughout the product chain (Kenya Flower Council, 2009; Ogola et al., 2012). About 75 per cent of the labour force in horticulture and the flower industries is female.

Another interesting (and unusual) example of the benefits of geothermal development in Africa is in Tunisia, where greenhouses replace cooling towers to cool irrigation water from 2–3 km deep wells in the Sahara desert (Mohamed, 2010). Owing to the Earth's thermal gradient, the temperature of the water from the wells is up to 75 degrees Celsius and needs to be cooled to 40 degrees Celsius to be used for irrigation. Some 194 hectares of greenhouses have been built in the oasis. The main products are tomatoes and melons, which are exported to Europe. This has created a lot of jobs for both men and women. Here the geothermal energy development is a by-product of the irrigation project. It is planned to have 315 hectares of greenhouses in 2016.

The cost of geothermal

Geothermal projects typically have high upfront investment costs because of the need to drill wells and construct power plants, transmission lines (for electricity) and/or insulated pipelines (for district heating systems). But the geothermal projects have relatively low operating costs. Operating costs vary depending on plant capacity, make-up and/or injection well requirements and the chemical composition of the geothermal fluids. Without fuel costs, operating costs for geothermal plants are predictable in comparison with combustion-based power plants, which are subject to market fluctuations in fuel prices (IPCC, 2011).

Table 8.5 Levellized cost of renewable energy sources with commercially available technologies for electricity and direct use

	Electricity (UScent$_{2005}$/KWh)	Direct use (USD$_{2005}$/GJ)
Biomass	2–36	1–82
Geothermal	2.5–17.5	7–78
Hydropower	1–15	
Ocean	12.5–32	
Solar	7.5–87	1.5–200
Wind	2.7–23	

Source: Compiled from IPCC (2011: Figure SPM.5).

Table 8.5 shows the levelized cost of renewable energy sources with commercially available technologies for electricity (UScent$_{2005}$/kWh) and direct use (USD$_{2005}$/GJ). For geothermal energy, the lowest unit prices are commonly obtained with co-generation of electricity and direct use (for example, hot water for space heating, swimming, greenhouses, fish farming, etc.). In such cases, the high-enthalpy steam is used for electricity production and the low-enthalpy water is used for heating and subsequently re-injected into the geothermal reservoir. In such cases very little energy goes to waste.

Climate mitigation

One of the major concerns today is the ever-increasing emission of greenhouse gases into the atmosphere and the threat of global warming. It is internationally accepted that a continuation of the present way of producing most of our energy by burning fossil fuels will bring significant climate change, global warming, rises in sea level, floods, droughts, deforestation and extreme weather conditions. The sad fact is that the poorest people in the world, who have done nothing to bring about the changes, will suffer most. One of the key solutions to avoid these difficulties is to reduce the use of fossil fuels and increase the sustainable use of renewable energy sources. Geothermal energy, as well as other renewable energy sources, can play an important role in this aspect in many parts of the world.

As mentioned previously, it is of interest to compare Table 8.3 (the top 16 countries utilizing geothermal energy for electricity production and direct use) with Table 8.4 (the countries in the different economic categories). Among the top 16 countries in electricity production with geothermal in 2009, there are 6 LMCs, 5 high-income OECD countries, 4 UMCs and 1 LIC (Kenya). Electricity production with geothermal is thus relatively evenly spread between countries in the different economic categories. This is in considerable contrast to the list of the top 16 countries making direct use of geothermal, where there are 14 high-income OECD countries, 1 UMC (Turkey) and 1 LMC (China), which is actually at the top of the list of direct use of geothermal.

In the geothermal direct use sector, the potential is very large because space heating and water heating are significant parts of the energy budget in large parts of the world. In industrialized countries, 35–40 per cent of total primary energy consumption is used in buildings. More and more countries are seriously considering how they can use their indigenous renewable energy resources. The decision of the Commission of the European Union to reduce greenhouse gas emissions in the member countries by 20 per cent by 2020 compared with 1990 has resulted in a significant acceleration in the use of renewable energy resources. Most of the EU countries already have some geothermal installations. The same applies to the United States and Canada, where the use of GHPs is widespread for both space heating and cooling. Apart from China, the developing countries have as yet shown very limited interest in the installation of heat pumps for space heating/cooling. With their limited economic resources, climate mitigation through a reduction of CO_2 emissions is not among the top priorities.

Industrialized countries can, however, make significant contributions by assisting developing countries in this field, in the form of both technology transfer and financial support for energy projects. The global response to climate change began with the adoption of the United Nations Framework Convention on Climate Change (UNFCCC) in 1992, which was not legally binding, and subsequently the Kyoto Protocol in 1997, a legally binding instrument. One of the flexible market-based mechanisms introduced was the Clean Development Mechanism (CDM).

The CDM is currently playing a critical role in delivering renewable energy to developing countries, with geothermal energy being one of the contributors to the carbon credit market. The importance of geothermal energy in climate change and MDGs is that it provides energy services from a clean source, it is secure and it is free from fuel price fluctuations, thus increasing the amount of financial resources available for economic development and the attainment of the MDGs. The potential for combining mitigation and adaptation strategies in geothermal projects also has greater co-benefits in emissions reduction and improving coping mechanisms through direct and indirect utilization (Ogola et al., 2011b).

The potential of carbon finance has attracted several geothermal projects to be registered under the CDM. As of January 2012, 12 geothermal projects (Table 8.6) had been registered and were eligible to receive carbon credit revenues (UNFCCC, 2012). All of these are electricity

Table 8.6 Registered geothermal CDM projects as of January 2012

Country	Project	Average annual emissions reduction (tCO$_2$eq/year)	Crediting period	Total emissions reduction (tCO$_2$eq)
El Salvador	Berlin binary cycle power plant (11.56 MWe)	44,141	7 years (2007–2014)	308,984
El Salvador	LaGeo S.A. de C.V., Berlin geothermal project phase 2 (44 MWe)	176,543	6 years (2007–2013)	1,235,798
Guatemala	Amatitlan geothermal project (25.2 MWe)	82,978	7 years (2008–2015)	580,849
Indonesia	Darajat Unit III geothermal project (110 MWe)	717,391	7 years (2007–2014)	5,021,734
Indonesia	Lahendong II 20 MWe geothermal project	66,713	7 years (2009–2016)	466,990
Indonesia	Wayang Windu phase 2 geothermal power project (117 MWe)	794,832	7 years (2010–2017)	5,563,824
Indonesia	Kamojang geothermal (63 MWe)	402,780	7 years (2010–2017)	2,819,461
Kenya	Olkaria III Phase 2 geothermal expansion project in Kenya (35 MWe)	177,600	7 years (2010–2017)	1,243,198
Kenya	Olkaria II geothermal expansion project (35 MWe)	149,632	7 years (2010–2017)	1,047,423
Nicaragua	San Jacinto Tizate geothermal project (66 MWe)	280,703	7 years (2005–2012)	1,964,919
Papua New Guinea	Lihir geothermal power project (55 MWe)	278,904	10 years (2006–2016)	2,789,037
Philippines	Nasulo geothermal project (20 MWe)	74,975	7 years (2008–2015)	524,825

Source: UNFCCC (2012).
Notes: tCO$_2$eq = tonnes of carbon dioxide equivalent; MWe = megawatt electrical.

projects. Two direct use projects are presently under evaluation for eligibility. Both are geothermal district heating projects, one in China and one in South Korea.

The importance of capacity-building

Renewable energy sources are expected to provide 20–40 per cent of the world's primary energy in 2050, depending on the scenario. The technology has been developed for the main renewable energy sources. There is already significant professional experience in the exploration, construction and operation of renewable energy power stations, but the experience is mainly confined to the industrialized countries.

A key element in the mitigation of climate change is capacity-building in renewable energy technologies in the developing countries, where the main growth in energy use is expected. An innovative training programme for geothermal energy professionals developed in Iceland is an example of how this can be done effectively (Fridleifsson, 2010). The mandate of the United Nations University Geothermal Training Programme (UNU-GTP) is to assist developing countries with significant geothermal potential to establish groups of specialists through six months of specialized training for professionals already employed in geothermal research and/or development.[1] The hallmark is to give university graduates engaged in geothermal work intensive on-the-job training in their chosen fields of specialization.[2] The trainees work side by side with geothermal professionals in Iceland – the majority with the Iceland GeoSurvey (ISOR).[3] Specialized training is offered in geological exploration, borehole geology, geophysical exploration, borehole geophysics, reservoir engineering, then chemistry of thermal fluids, environmental studies, geothermal utilization and drilling technology. Between 1979 and 2011, 482 scientists/engineers from 50 developing countries completed the sixmonth courses. In many countries in Africa, Asia, Central America and Eastern Europe, UNU-GTP Fellows are among the leading geothermal specialists. The UNU-GTP also organizes workshops and short courses on geothermal development (Georgsson, 2010) in Africa (started in 2005), Central America (started in 2006) and Asia (started in 2008). This is a contribution of the government of Iceland towards the MDGs. The courses and workshops are set up in cooperation with the energy and earth science institutions responsible for the exploration, development and operation of geothermal energy utilities in the respective countries/regions. Part of the objective is to increase cooperation between specialists in neighbouring countries in the field of the sustainable use of geothermal resources. The courses may in the future develop into sustainable regional geothermal training centres. This is well under way in Kenya for the benefit of African countries and in El Salvador for Latin American countries.

One way to measure the overall impact of the accomplishments of UNU Fellows is to look at their participation in the international arena, such as at the World Geothermal Congress (WGC), which is organized every five years by the International Geothermal Association (IGA). The WGC 2010 was held in Bali in Indonesia. There were over 2,000 participants from over 100 countries. Of the 1,034 refereed papers accepted by the Technical Committee and published in the proceedings, 199 papers (19 per cent) were authored or co-authored by 139 former UNU Fellows from 31 developing and transitional countries. The level of activity of the UNU Fellows in the international geothermal community is well reflected in the fact that one-third of the 424 graduates of the UNU-GTP between 1979 and 2009 were authors of refereed papers at the WGC 2010.[4] At the WGC 2005 in Turkey there were over 1,300 participants from 80 countries, and the conference proceedings included 705 refereed papers, 141 of which (20 per cent of all papers) were authored or co-authored by 104 former UNU Fellows (out of 318) from 26 developing and transitional countries.

The key to the success of the UNU-GTP is the selection of the UNU Fellows. Candidates for the specialized training must have a university degree in science or engineering, have a minimum of one year's practical experience in geothermal work, speak English fluently, be under 40 years of age and have a permanent position dealing with geothermal at an energy company/utility/research institution/university in their home country. Site visits are conducted by UNU-GTP representatives to countries requesting training. The potential role of geothermal in the energy plans of the particular country is assessed and an evaluation is made of its institutional capacities in the field of geothermal research and utilization. Based on this, the training needs of the country are assessed and recipient institutions selected. All qualified candidates are interviewed personally.

Capacity-building and the transfer of technology are key issues in the sustainable development of renewable energy resources. Many industrialized and developing countries have significant experience in the development and operation of renewable energy installations for direct use and/ or electricity production. It is important that they open their doors to newcomers in the field. We need strong international cooperation on the transfer of technology and the financing of renewable energy development in order to meet the MDGs and combat the threats of global warming.

Conclusion

Renewable energy sources are expected to provide 20–40 per cent of the world's primary energy in 2050, depending on the scenario. A key element in the mitigation of climate change is capacity-building in renewable energy technologies in the developing countries, where the main growth in energy use is expected. Geothermal already contributes significantly to electricity production in several countries in Central America, Asia and Africa. Many of the key geothermal professionals in these countries are graduates of the UNU-GTP six-month specialized training in Iceland.

The direct use of geothermal can replace fossil fuels in densely populated areas where space heating and/or cooling is needed. The potential is very large because space heating/cooling and water heating are significant parts of the energy budget in large parts of the world. In industrialized countries, 35–40 per cent of total primary energy consumption is used in buildings. Most of the EU countries already have some geothermal installations. The same applies to the United States and Canada, where the use of GHPs is widespread for both space heating and cooling. Apart from China, the developing countries have as yet shown very limited interest in the installation of heat pumps for space heating/cooling.

The CDM has the potential of playing a critical role in delivering renewable energy to developing countries, with geothermal energy being one of the contributors to the carbon credit market. The importance of geothermal energy in climate change and MDGs is that it provides energy services from a clean source, it is secure and it is free from fuel price fluctuations, thus increasing the amount of financial resources available for economic development and the attainment of the MDGs. The potential for combining mitigation and adaptation strategies in geothermal projects also has significant co-benefits in emissions reduction and in improving coping mechanisms through direct and indirect utilization. As of January 2012, 12 geothermal projects to produce electricity had been registered and were eligible to receive carbon credit revenues (UNFCCC, 2012), and two direct use projects were under evaluation for eligibility. Both are geothermal district heating projects, one in China and one in South Korea. This is a good sign for the future.

Acknowledgements

Many thanks are due to Arni Ragnarsson, Ingimar G. Haraldsson and Malfridur Omarsdottir for their assistance in preparing this chapter. This chapter is partly based on previous papers by the author (Fridleifsson, 2002, 2007, 2010; Fridleifsson et al., 2008).

Notes

1. See the UNU-GTP website at ⟨http://www.unugtp.is⟩ (accessed 31 January 2012).
2. See ⟨http://www.unugtp.is⟩ (accessed 31 January 2012).
3. See the ISOR website at ⟨http://www.isor.is⟩ (accessed 31 January 2012).
4. The papers are accessible at ⟨http://www.unugtp.is⟩ (accessed 31 January 2012).

REFERENCES

Berry, B. J. L. (1990) "Urbanization", in B. Turner II, W. C. Clark, R. W. Kates, J. F. Richards, J. T. Mathews and W. B. Meyers (eds), *The Earth as Transformed by Human Action: Global and Regional Changes in the Biosphere over the Past 300 Years*. Cambridge: Cambridge University Press, pp. 103–119.

Bertani, R. (2010) "Geothermal Power Generation in the World, 2005–2010 Update Report", *Proceedings World Geothermal Congress 2010*, Bali, Indonesia, 25–29 April.

Bertani, R. (2012) "Geothermal Power Generation in the World: 2005–2010 Update Report", *Geothermics*, 41: 1–29.

Bos, E., M. T. Vu, A. Leven and R. A. Bulatao (1992) *World Population Projections 1992–1993*. Baltimore, MD: Johns Hopkins University Press.

CEPAL (Comisión Económica para América Latina y el Caribe) (2010) *Centro-América: Estadísticas del subsector electric, 2009*. United Nations, Comisión Económica para América Latina y el Caribe, Sede Subregional en México.

Fridleifsson, I. B. (2002) "Energy Requirements for the New Millennium", in H. van Ginkel, B. Barrett, J. Court and J. Velasquez (eds), *Human Development and the Environment: Challenges for the United Nations in the New Millennium*. Tokyo: United Nations University Press, pp. 220–233.

Fridleifsson, I. B. (2007) "Geothermal Energy and the Millennium Development Goals of the United Nations", *Proceedings of the European Geothermal Congress 2007*, Unterhaching, Germany, 30 May–1 June.

Fridleifsson, I. B. (2010) "Capacity Building in Renewable Energy Technologies in Developing Countries", *Proceedings of the World Energy Congress 2010*, Montreal, Canada, 12–16 September.

Fridleifsson, I. B. and I. G. Haraldsson (2011) "Geothermal Energy in the World with Special Reference to Central America", *Proceedings of Short Course on Geothermal Drilling, Resource Development, and Power Plants*, El Salvador, 16–22 January. Available at ⟨http://www.unugtp.is⟩ (accessed 31 January 2012).

Fridleifsson, I. B., R. Bertani, E. Huenges, J. W. Lund, A. Ragnarsson and L. Rybach (2008) "The Possible Role and Contribution of Geothermal Energy to the Mitigation of Climate Change", in O. Hohmeyer and T. Trittin (eds), *Pro-

ceedings of the IPCC Scoping Meeting on Renewable Energy Sources. Luebeck, Germany: Intergovernmental Panel on Climate Change, Working Group III, pp. 59–80.

Georgsson, L. S. (2010) "UNU Geothermal Training Programme – Taking the Training to the Developing Countries", *Proceedings World Geothermal Congress 2010*, Bali, Indonesia, 25–29 April.

IEA (International Energy Agency) (2011) *Key World Energy Statistics*. Paris: International Energy Agency. Available at ⟨http://www.iea.org/publications/⟩ (accessed 31 January 2012).

IIASA (International Institute for Applied Systems Analysis) (1996) *The Future Population of the World: What Can We Assume Today*, revised edn, ed. W. Lutz. London: Earthscan Publications. Available at ⟨http://www.iiasa.ac.at/Admin/PUB/Documents/XB-96-003.pdf⟩ (accessed 3 February 2012).

IPCC (Intergovernmental Panel on Climate Change) (2011) "Renewable Energy Sources and Climate Change Mitigation", in O. Edenhofer, R. Pichs-Madruga, Y. Sokona, K. Seyboth, P. Matschoss, S. Kadner, T. Zwickel, P. Eickemeier, G. Hansen, S. Schlömer and C. von Stechow (eds), *Special Report of the Intergovernmental Panel on Climate Change*. Cambridge: Cambridge University Press.

Kenya Flower Council (2009) "The Flower Industry in Kenya and Market Data", ⟨http://www.kenyaflowercouncil.org/floricultureinkenya.php⟩ (accessed 31 January 2012).

Lippmann, M. J. (2002) "Geothermal and the Electricity Market in Central America", *Geothermal Resources Council Transactions*, 26: 37–42.

Lund, J. W., D. H. Freeston and T. L. Boyd (2010) "Direct Utilization of Geothermal Energy 2010 Worldwide Review", *Proceedings World Geothermal Congress 2010*, Bali, Indonesia, 25–29 April.

Lund, J. W., D. H. Freeston and T. L. Boyd, (2011) "Direct Utilization of Geothermal Energy 2010 Worldwide Review", *Geothermics*, 40: 159–180.

Modi, V., S. McDade, D. Lallement and J. Saghir (2006) *Energy and the Millennium Development Goals*. New York: Energy Sector Management Assistance Program, United Nations Development Programme, UN Millennium Project, and World Bank. Available at ⟨http://www.unmillenniumproject.org/documents/MP_Energy_Low_Res.pdf⟩ (accessed 31 January 2012).

Mohamed, M. B. (2010) "Geothermal Direct Application and Its Development in Tunisia", *Proceedings World Geothermal Congress 2010*, Bali, Indonesia, 25–29 April.

Nakićenović, N., A. Grübler and A. McDonald (eds) (1998) *Global Energy Perspectives*. Cambridge: Cambridge University Press.

Ogola, F. P. A., B. Davidsdottir and I. B. Fridleifsson (2011a) "Lighting Villages at the End of the Line with Geothermal Energy in Eastern Baringo Lowlands, Kenya – Steps towards Reaching the Millennium Development Goals (MDGs)", *Renewable and Sustainable Energy Reviews*, 15(8): 4067–4079.

Ogola, F. P. A., B. Davidsdottir and I. B. Fridleifsson (2011b) "Opportunities for Adaptation-Mitigation Synergies in Geothermal Energy Utilization – Initial Conceptual Frameworks", *Mitigation and Adaptation Strategies for Global Change*, DOI 10.1007/s11027-011-9339-1 (in press).

Ogola, F. P. A., B. Davidsdottir and I. B. Fridleifsson (2012) "Contribution of Geothermal Energy Projects to Infrastructural and Welfare Development in Kenya: Comparing and Contrasting Naivasha to Undeveloped East Pokot with Possible Benefit Transfer" (under review).

Simiyu, S. M. (2010) "Status of Geothermal Exploration in Kenya and Future Plans for Its Development", *Proceedings World Geothermal Congress 2010*, Bali, Indonesia, 25–29 April.

UNFCCC (United Nations Framework Convention on Climate Change) (2012) "Project Search", ⟨http://cdm.unfccc.int/Projects/projsearch.html⟩ (accessed 3 February 2012).

United Nations (1994) *World Urbanization Prospects: The 1992 Revision*. New York: United Nations.

United Nations (2006) *United Nations Development Goals Report*. New York: United Nations.

WEC (World Energy Council) (1993) *Energy for Tomorrow's World*. New York: St Martin's Press.

World Bank (2011) *World Development Report 2011*. Washington, DC: World Bank, pp. 341–363.

Zheng, K. (2010) "Growth of the Use of Geothermal Heat Pumps in China", *Proceedings World Geothermal Congress 2010*, Bali, Indonesia, 25–29 April.

Zheng, K., Z. Han and Z. Zhang (2010) "Steady Industrialized Development of Geothermal Energy in China. Country Update Report 2005–2009", *Proceedings World Geothermal Congress 2010*, Bali, Indonesia, 25–29 April.

9

Enabling green economic transitions through biodiversity conservation: Potential and challenges

M. S. Suneetha and Alexandros Gasparatos

Biological diversity and human well-being

Human societies have benefited from biodiversity and ecosystems throughout time, but a more mainstream recognition of nature's role in human well-being has been achieved relatively recently (Mooney and Ehrlich, 1997).[1] In the past few decades a significant body of literature has emphasized why and how biological diversity is important for ecosystem functioning and the provision of ecosystem goods and services that are important to human well-being (MA, 2005a). A simplified schematic representation of the links between biodiversity and human well-being is highlighted below (Naeem et al., 2009):[2]

Biodiversity → Ecosystem Functioning/Processes → Ecosystem Services → Human Well-being

The Millennium Ecosystem Assessment (MA) was the most important initiative of recent decades aiming to elucidate the contribution of ecosystem services to human well-being (MA, 2005a). The MA started from the understanding that ecosystems provide a number of services and goods that are important for human well-being and divided these services into provisioning services (for example food, timber, fibre), regulating services (for example water purification, climate change regulation), supporting services (for example nutrient cycling) and cultural services (for example recreation). Since then, several other classifications of ecosystem

Green economy and good governance for sustainable development: Opportunities, promises and concerns, Puppim de Oliveira (ed.),
United Nations University Press, 2012, ISBN 978-92-808-1216-9

services have been proposed depending on the context of the analysis and the valuation mechanisms adopted (see, for example, Boyd and Banzhaf, 2007; Fisher et al., 2009; TEEB, 2010; UK NEA, 2011). In all these frameworks biodiversity is not an ecosystem service per se but "the foundation of ecosystem services to which human well-being is intimately linked" (MA, 2005b: 18).

Some of these goods and services, such as food, timber and fibre, are consumed directly by humans (MA, 2005b) with humans being now the largest appropriators of net primary production (Haberl et al., 2007; Imhoff et al., 2004). In addition, within the major species used for food and fibre, humans have developed over time a diverse range of commercial varieties and breeds that contain a high level of genetic diversity (MA, 2005a). Furthermore, urban and rural populations in most developing countries are still highly dependent on food and biomass from natural ecosystems, for example for high-value timber logging, biomass energy and wild food consumption such as bush meat, wild tubers and fruits (Ahrends et al., 2010; Davies and Brown, 2007). Biodiversity also directly provides genetic resources to several other industries (for example, the pharmaceutical and cosmetics industries[3]) and inspiration for creating novel technologies, as is the case with biomimicry (MA, 2005a).

Highly biodiverse ecosystems can also contribute to the regulation of climate, diseases and the quality of air and water. In some cases, biodiverse ecosystems manage to achieve this in a more cost-effective manner than technologies developed by humans. One such example is the Catskill Watershed, which was restored for the filtration of the water consumed in New York City because it was shown that this was more cost-effective than building a water filtration plant (NRC, 2004). Some highly biodiverse ecosystems (for example, primary forests) contain larger carbon stocks than plantations (Diaz et al., 2009) and others have the capacity to sequester higher quantities of atmospheric carbon than similar biodiverse-poor ecosystems (Reich et al., 2001). Considering the potentially high economic costs associated with climate change (Stern, 2006), maintaining and fostering highly biodiverse ecosystems would be a significantly cost-effective way to mitigate climate change and curb its impacts on human well-being (Diaz et al., 2009). There is also evidence to suggest that biodiversity protects organisms, including humans, from the transmission of infectious diseases (Keesing et al., 2010).

Biodiversity-rich areas are also centres of cultural diversity. It has been shown that the regions with the highest cultural diversity coincide with regions of high biological diversity (Oviedo et al., 2000). In fact, specific management practices have evolved over centuries to manage landscapes and resources in accordance with prevailing sociocultural contexts (Bélair et al., 2010). However, it is these regions that are under the highest threat of losing their biological and cultural diversity (Maffi, 2007). This is a consequence of several interrelated factors such as urbanization, cultural homogenization and the relatively meagre monetary benefits from conserving low-value biological resources (MA 2005b; Roe, 2010).

Biodiversity conservation institutions

This growing realization that biodiversity and human well-being are inextricably linked exerted significant pressure for the adoption of a sufficiently broad international policy framework that could coordinate biodiversity conservation efforts globally. The culmination of this process was the Convention on Biological Diversity (CBD), which was opened for signature at the 1992 Earth Summit in Rio de Janeiro and came into effect in December 1993. The main goals of the CBD (CBD, 1992) are to promote:
1. The conservation of biological diversity
2. The sustainable use of its components
3. The fair and equitable sharing of the benefits arising out of the utilization of genetic resources

The CBD has been instrumental in promoting the notion that natural resources are not infinite and that a precautionary approach should be adopted when conserving biological diversity. In fact, the CBD tries to link seemingly disparate issues such as environmental integrity, development, markets and equity within a common legal (and therefore regulatory) framework. It seeks to achieve these objectives through several instruments, including guidelines for best practices, assessments of the status of biodiversity and measures required to enhance the implementation of the Convention, as well as various capacity-building and awareness-raising measures. It has been increasingly emphatic about drawing the links between healthy ecosystems and biodiversity and the achievement of various development goals at multiple scales – international, national and subnational – in both urban and rural contexts. A notable milestone of the Convention was the acceptance of the 2010 biodiversity targets, which were adopted during the Sixth Meeting of the Conference of the Parties (COP6) in 2002. COP6 Decision VI/26 further acknowledged the strong links between biodiversity and human well-being and emphatically stated the need "to achieve by 2010 a significant reduction of the current rate of biodiversity loss at the global, regional and national level as a contribution to poverty alleviation and to the benefit of all life on earth" (CBD, 2002). Despite it being headline policy, it allowed the member countries to undertake more focused action to conserve biodiversity. In 2010, a new strategic plan with more realistic biodiversity targets and indicators was adopted during COP10, with better expectations for the realization of the stated goals.

Various other intergovernmental bodies also promote biodiversity conservation through specific mandates ranging from the regulation (and monitoring) of trade in endangered species (Convention on International Trade in Endangered Species) to the conservation of migratory species (Convention on Migratory Species), the conservation of wetland ecosystems and resources (Ramsar Convention) and the conservation and use of agricultural biodiversity (International Treaty on Plant Genetic Resources for Food and Agriculture). All of these initiatives also have an inherent focus on development issues because they relate to ensuring the sustained availability of the resources to meet various human needs.

Incentives for conservation: Enabling and benefiting from green economy transitions in developing nations

Lately, the preservation of ecosystem services and halting biodiversity loss have emerged as key pillars of the concept of green economy (UNEP, 2011), thus reaffirming their significant role in the Rio+20 process.

Considering that biodiversity can be an important component of economic sectors as diverse as agriculture, forestry, tourism and public utilities, biodiversity conservation could potentially be an important agent of poverty alleviation and the transition to a green economy. This is particularly true in developing countries where there are significant overlaps between highly biodiverse areas (biodiversity hotspots) and deep and multifaceted poverty (Fisher and Christopher, 2007).

However, it remains unclear whether biodiversity exploitation or biodiversity conservation (with an associated transition to a green economy) would be a better strategy for poverty alleviation in developing nations. On the one hand, it is well documented that biodiversity exploitation and subsequent degradation can spur local and regional economic growth. On the other hand, it is also acknowledged that in some cases the initial human welfare benefits from biodiversity overexploitation are nullified in the long term (Braimoh et al., 2010; MA, 2005b; Rodrigues et al., 2009;) and that those most negatively affected are communities whose daily livelihood depends the most on biological resources and ecosystems (MA, 2005b; Roe, 2010).

A recent comprehensive review has concluded that biodiversity conservation can sometimes be an agent of poverty alleviation and of a transition to regional green economies, but this depends greatly on the local context and the conservation mechanism applied (Roe, 2010). For example, conservation mechanisms such as community timber enterprises, nature-based tourism, fish spillover, protected area jobs, agroforestry and agrobiodiversity conservation have contributed to poverty alleviation in some geographical contexts (Roe, 2010). Other conservation mechanisms, such as non-timber forest products, payments for environmental services, mangrove restoration and grassland management, did not manage to eradicate poverty in the studied areas but did contribute to some extent to poverty reduction or provided a safety-net in times of need (Roe, 2010). It can be said that the success of biodiversity conservation in spurring green economic transitions depends on the recognition that poverty can be a major constraint on conservation initiatives (Fisher and Christopher, 2007).

The above suggests that biodiversity conservation can in some cases indeed alleviate poverty and be an agent of green economic transition in developing countries. However, much care and effort would be required to choose the most appropriate policy and conservation mechanisms according to the contextual realities of the targeted areas.

We argue here that it is possible to enable and enhance such green economic transitions from biodiversity conservation initiatives through the innovative implementation of strategies that are participatory in nature and involve stakeholders on the ground.[4] There are two key elements that can ensure the successful implementation of conservation strategies in local communities.

First of all, in several cases local communities have been shown to play a stewardship role in environmental management (Berkes, 2008; Valderrama and Arico, 2010). For example, there is evidence that the state of forest ecosystems and the welfare of communities improved when a policy of joint forest management was adopted between communities and the state (or community forestry) in Nepal and India (Mukherjee, 2003; Pokharel and Suvedi, 2007). This inclusive and participatory management approach led to fewer conflicts between the stakeholders, an understanding of roles and responsibilities and better capture of economic and other benefits.

The second element relates to the thinking that led to the adoption in 2010 by the member nations of the CBD of the Nagoya Protocol on Access to Genetic Resources and the Fair and Equitable Sharing of Benefits Arising from Their Utilization. This is an attempt to ensure that all stakeholders comply with standards of ethical and equitable practice when they seek to access and utilize biological resources (CBD, 2010b). In many ways this is an effort to ensure a fair redistribution of the benefits derivable from biodiversity and ecosystem use among all those involved in the trade, research and development of biological resources and can act as an incentive for successfully implementing conservation strategies.

For example, a comparative study conducted by the United Nations University Institute of Advanced Studies (UNU-IAS) and the United Nations Environment Programme (UNEP) in communities across the tropics that are partners in UNEP's Equator Initiative, observed that several local communities are utilizing the power of cooperative action to build small and medium-sized enterprises based on biological resources. These range from agricultural products to herbal medicinal products, fishery products, crafts and services such as ecotourism. In each case, communities combine their in-depth knowledge of their ecosystem and use biodiverse components for economic gain. They operate within the parameters of the legal system and strive to increase their well-being by securing tangible and intangible assets using their skills and capabilities and by adopting new ideas from external systems. Analysing how these activities contribute to their well-being beyond economic gains, it was observed that several parameters such as the sustainable use of biological resources, the equity of transactions among members of a community and increasing intangible strengths such as skills of negotiation, education and innovation were being actively fostered in the communities to varying degrees (Subramanian et al., 2010; Suneetha and Pisupati, 2009).

Extending this argument further, it is obvious that the broad-based development achievements seen in such communities fit right into the broader policy objectives articulated by the green economy. This implies that policies that aim to promote green economic transitions through biodiversity conservation would need to be flexible to enable these local communities to perceive the relevance of global biodiversity targets to their well-being and to provide incentives for biodiversity conservation that can be developed endogenously. Policies could range from better access to biological resources, encouraging economic opportunities from conservation actions (for example, ecotourism), the sustainable use of resources (better resource prices and benefits from the trading of resources for enterprise activity), the provision of relevant social, cultural and political services, and the involvement of local communities as co-partners in the management and use of biological resources.

Challenges

There are several challenges that need to be overcome if biodiversity conservation is to become an agent of the green economy in developing nations. These challenges result from the incomplete understanding of how coupled social and ecological systems operate and the inefficient design of institutions that aim to tackle biodiversity conservation and poverty alleviation simultaneously. Some of the key challenges are: poverty traps; conservation beyond protected areas; the development of adequate biodiversity targets; institutional fragmentation and regulatory compliance.

Poverty traps

As mentioned in the previous section, conserving biodiversity does not automatically entail green economic transitions or improvements in human well-being. It has been shown that, on some occasions, conservation goals might conflict with poverty alleviation concerns. This phenomenon is most commonly manifested in areas surrounding protected areas, particularly in developing countries, giving rise to "poverty traps" (Adams and Hutton, 2007; Cernea and Schmidt-Soltau, 2006), which can be a result of numerous interconnected factors (see, for example, Barrett et al., 2011). In some cases, preliminary findings might indicate that a protected area can be a poverty trap, but a closer look might refute these initial observations (Ferraro et al., 2011; McNally et al., 2011; Naughton-Treves et al., 2011). Understanding potential causalities between conservation projects and poverty traps becomes even more pertinent when considering the significant overlap of biodiversity hotspots and multifaceted poverty (Fisher and Christopher, 2007). Significant research that takes into account local contexts and local knowledge needs to be conducted in order to understand the mechanisms through which such poverty traps might emerge and to prevent their emergence when conservation efforts are undertaken as a means of encouraging a green economic transition in developing countries.

Conservation beyond protected areas

Currently only a small fraction of terrestrial ecosystems (and an even smaller fraction of marine ecosystems) lies within protected areas.[5] Given that most of the world's population resides outside protected areas and that non-protected (or semi-protected) areas host significant biodiversity (Butchart et al., 2010), achieving green economic transitions will increasingly require efforts to conserve biodiversity beyond protected areas A series of different mechanisms, ranging from ecological restoration to biodiversity-friendly farming techniques, schemes for reducing emissions from deforestation and forest degradation (REDD+), green procurement and other measures that aim to reduce urban consumption, can be pursued in order to reduce human pressure on non-protected ecosystems. The effectiveness of such measures should be assessed within different environmental and socioeconomics contexts with the aim of scaling up the successful approaches (Rands et al., 2010).

The development of adequate biodiversity targets

The CBD's new Strategic Plan has defined several target indicators for achieving the objectives of biological conservation, the sustainable use of biological resources and equitable transactions between stakeholders (CBD, 2010b). If followed in both letter and spirit, the plan should be able to achieve both conservation of biodiversity and improvements in human well-being. However, despite the alignment of these targets with the ecosystem approach, the fact remains that the 2010 biodiversity targets are unable to capture (a) functional diversity, (b) environmental uncertainty, (c) interaction between targets and (d) trade-offs between targets (Perrings et al., 2011a). Furthermore, given that these targets were set before the concept of the green economy had gained prominence among policy-makers, it is doubtful that they can be meaningfully used at the interface of biodiversity and the green economy.

There is thus a need to develop biodiversity targets that clearly articulate how biodiversity should be preserved in order to spur green economic transitions and thus improve human well-being locally and globally. These targets need to reflect the real interests that people have in the benefits provided by biodiversity, to be able to stimulate constructive action, to be easily monitored using unambiguous metrics, to reflect priorities relevant to the health and well-being of people, and to be sensitive to the fact that biodiversity change involves both costs and benefits (Mace et al., 2010; Perrings et al., 2011a). Moreover, these indicators should produce results that are robust enough to be integrated into future biodiversity scenarios (Pereira et al., 2010). The development of this new generation of relevant biodiversity indicators could be addressed within the mandate of the Intergovernmental Science-Policy Platform on Biodiversity and Ecosystem Services (Perrings et al., 2011b).

Institutional fragmentation and regulatory compliance

Sometimes seemingly well-thought-out institutions and compliance mechanisms do not deliver the desired conservation and poverty alleviation outcomes, especially in local contexts. Ongoing research at the United Nations University indicates that the design of institutions and tools used to monitor compliance often does not match local realities (Suneetha and Pisupati, 2009). This leads to problems of either multiple compliance efforts through various independent institutions or, at the other extreme, a failure to address of key issues because it is difficult to know which institution's jurisdiction they fall under. This institutional fragmentation and its potential toll on green economic transition through biodiversity conservation can be illustrated with an example.

Medicinal plants are an ecosystem good that is directly provided by biodiversity. In several developing countries, medicinal plants are important sources of income for particular segments of the society and as a result they can have a significant green economic potential. In India, the harvesting of medicinal plants (primarily from the wild) comes under the jurisdiction of agencies within the Ministry of Environment and Forests, whereas issues related to traditional medicine and medical practices fall under relevant agencies of the Ministry of Health and Family Welfare. Other medicinal plants are also edible crops that can be cultivated, and issues related to nutrition, food quality and the cultivation and marketing of crops come within the ambit of the Ministry of Agriculture and, to some extent, the Ministry of Health and Family Welfare). As a result, it is not always clear which administrative department is responsible for medicinal plant issues. Decisions taken by one administrative body could impinge on the functioning of another. Each of these ministries has various schemes to promote different aspects related to the resources within the purview of their mandates, and it might be feasible to explore joint implementation in areas that overlap. This would help the pooling of limited resources to enhance the effectiveness of programme implementation, but this is easier said than done. Such institutional interplays and their implications for the management of biodiversity-related components with a green economic potential need to be identified.

Conclusions

The evidence discussed in this chapter makes clear that biodiversity contributes significantly and in many ways to human well-being. As a result, biodiversity conservation is situated well within the broader principles of sustainable development and could become a key component of green economies. However, despite biodiversity's value in terms of both pecuniary benefits and in sustaining natural cycles and systems, calls from various stakeholders and the adoption of a slew of multilateral and national policy instruments, the rate of biodiversity loss is still alarming (Barnosky et al., 2011; Butchart et al., 2010; CBD, 2010a). This to a large extent reflects the ineffective design and implementation of related policies and laws.

The stewardship role that local communities could play in environmental management, combined with the incentives provided by the adoption of the Nagoya Protocol, could help achieve win–win solutions at the interface of biodiversity conservation, poverty alleviation and the green economy. However, a number of factors – such as the potential emergence of poverty traps around conservation areas, the need to conserve biodiversity beyond protected areas, institutional fragmentation and the lack of appropriate biodiversity targets at the interface of biodiversity conservation and the green economy – pose significant challenges to the achievement of such win–win solutions.

Concerted efforts between policy-makers, practitioners and academics are required to overcome these challenges. The recent resolution passed by the United Nations General Assembly to foster harmony in human–nature interactions is a clear call to action by all relevant stakeholders to uphold principles of environmental stewardship (see United Nations, 2011). Research and policy reports also strongly point out that it is possible to be prosperous without the need for continuous growth (Jackson, 2009; Stiglitz et al., 2009). Although the evolution of practices tends to outpace policy development, the impacts of policies in defining actions cannot be overemphasized. Implementable rules with sufficient incentives that allow contextual flexibility in enforcement can go a long way in meeting the goals and objectives at the interface of biodiversity conservation and the green economy. It remains to be seen if we can muster the political will and the conviction to act on promoting practices and policies that can take this mission forward to ensure global well-being.

Acknowledgements

Alexandros Gasparatos acknowledges the support of the Oxford Martin School through a James Martin Research Fellowship.

Notes

1. According to the Convention on Biological Diversity, biodiversity is "the variability among living organisms from all sources including, inter alia, terrestrial, marine and other aquatic ecosystems and the ecological complexes of which they are part: this includes diversity within species, between species and of ecosystems" (CBD, 1992: 3).
2. The links between biodiversity, ecosystem functioning, ecosystem services and human well-being can be complex, involving feedbacks. Significant further effort is required to unravel these links. Nevertheless, there is a clear consensus that humans can either enhance or destroy these interactions. This indicates that human activity is a major component of the integrity of these systems (Mooney et al., 2009).
3. Hundreds of different drugs are derived from natural products (Li and Vederas, 2009; Newman and Cragg, 2007; Zhu et al., 2011). In addition, several communities around the world rely significantly on medicinal plants directly collected from adjacent ecosystems (McDade et al., 2007; Suneetha and Chandrakanth, 2006).
4. Particularly those local communities and primary producers of bio-products that continue to be highly dependent on biological resources for their livelihoods and sustenance.
5. Roughly 12 per cent of the land surface, 5.9 per cent of territorial seas and 0.5 per cent of oceans are currently protected (Rands et al., 2010).

REFERENCES

Adams W. and J. Hutton (2007) "People, Parks and Poverty: Political Ecology and Biodiversity Conservation", *Conservation and Society*, 5: 147–183.
Ahrends A., N. D. Burgess, S. A. H. Milledge, M. T. Bulling, B. Fisher, J. C. R. Smart, G. P. Clarke, B. E. Mhoro and S. L. Lewis (2010) "Predictable Waves of Sequential Forest Degradation and Biodiversity Loss Spreading from an African City", *Proceedings of the National Academy of Sciences of the United States of America*, 107: 14556–14561.
Barnosky A. D., N. Matzke, S. Tomiya, G. O. U. Wogan, B. Swartz, T. B. Quentall, C. Marshall, J. L. McGuire, E. L. Lindsey, K. C. Maguire, B. Mersey and E. A. Ferrer (2011) "Has Earth's Sixth Mass Extinction Already Arrived?", *Nature*, 471: 51–57.
Barrett, C. B., A. J. Travis and P. Dasgupta (2011) "On Biodiversity Conservation and Poverty Traps", *Proceedings of the National Academy of Sciences of the United States of America*, 108: 13907–13912.
Bélair C., K. Ichikawa, B. Y. L. Wong and K. J. Mulongoy (eds) (2010) *Sustainable Use of Biological Diversity in Socio-ecological Production Landscapes. Background to the "Satoyama Initiative for the Benefit of Biodiversity and Human Well-being"*. Technical Series No. 52, Secretariat of the Convention on Biological Diversity, Montreal.
Berkes, F. (2008) *Sacred Ecology*, 2nd edn. New York and London: Routledge.
Boyd, J. and S. Banzhaf (2007) "What Are Ecosystem Services? The Need for Standardized Environmental Accounting Units", *Ecological Economics*, 63: 616–626.
Braimoh, A. K., S. M. Subramanian, W. Elliott and A. Gasparatos (2010) "Climate and Human Related Drivers of Biodiversity Decline in Southeast Asia", UNU-IAS Policy Report, Yokohama.
Butchart, S. H. M., M. Walpole, B. Collen, A. Van Strien, J. P. W. Scharlemann, R. E. A. Almond, J. E. M. Baillie, B. Bomhard, C. Brown, J. Bruno, K. E. Carpenter, G. M. Carr, J. Chanson, A. M. Chenery, J. Csirke, N. C. Davidson, F. Dentener, M. Foster, A. Galli, J. N. Galloway, P. Genovesi, R. D. Gregory, M. Hockings, V. Kapos, J. F. Lamarque, F. Leverington, J. Loh, M. A. McGeoch, L. McRae, A. Minasyan, M. H. Morcillo, T. E. E. Oldfield, D. Pauly, S. Quader, C. Revenga, J. R. Sauer, B. Skolnik, D. Spear, D. Stanwell-Smith, S. N. Stuart, A. Symes, M. Tierney, T. D. Tyrrell, J. C. Vié and R. Watson (2010) "Global Biodiversity: Indicators of Recent Declines", *Science*, 328: 1164–1168.
CBD (Convention on Biological Diversity) (1992) "Text of the Convention on Biological Diversity", ⟨http://www.cbd.int/convention/text/⟩ (accessed 1 February 2012).
CBD (Convention on Biological Diversity) (2002) "COP 6 Decision VI/26: Strategic Plan for the Convention on Biological Diversity", ⟨http://www.cbd.int/decision/cop/?id=7200⟩ (accessed 1 February 2012).
CBD (Convention on Biological Diversity) (2010a) *Global Biodiversity Outlook 3*. Montreal, Canada: Secretariat of the Convention on Biological Diversity.

CBD (Convention on Biological Diversity) (2010b) "COP 10 Decision X/2: Strategic Plan for Biodiversity 2011–2020 and the Aichi Biodiversity Targets", ⟨http://www.cbd.int/decision/cop/?id=12268⟩ (accessed 1 February 2012).

Cernea, M. and K. Schmidt-Soltau (2006) "Poverty Risks and National Parks: Policy Issues in Conservation and Resettlement", *World Development*, 34: 1808–1830.

Davies, G. and D. Brown (eds) (2007) *Bushmeat and Livelihoods: Wildlife Management and Poverty Reduction*. Oxford: Wiley-Blackwell.

Diaz, S., D. A. Wardle and A. Hector (2009) "Incorporating Biodiversity in Climate Change Mitigation Initiatives", in S. Naeem, D. E. Bunker, A. Hector, M. Loreau and C. Perrings (eds), *Biodiversity, Ecosystem Functioning, and Human Wellbeing: An Ecological and Economic Perspective*. Oxford: Oxford University Press, pp. 149–166.

Ferraro, P. J., M. M. Hanauer and K. R. E. Sims (2011) "Conditions Associated with Protected Area Success in Conservation and Poverty Reduction", *Proceedings of the National Academy of Sciences of the United States of America*, 108: 13913–13918.

Fisher, B. and T. Christopher (2007) "Poverty and Biodiversity: Measuring the Overlap of Human Poverty and the Biodiversity Hotspots", *Ecological Economics*, 62: 93–101.

Fisher, B., R. K. Turner and P. Morling (2009) "Defining and Classifying Ecosystem Services for Decision Making", *Ecological Economics*, 68: 643–653.

Haberl, H., K. H. Erb, F. Krausmann, V. Gaube, A. Bondeau, C. Plutzar, S. Gingrich, W. Lucht and M. Fischer-Kowalski (2007) "Quantifying and Mapping the Human Appropriation of Net Primary Production in Earth's Terrestrial Ecosystems", *Proceedings of the National Academy of Sciences of the United States of America*, 104: 12942–12947.

Imhoff, M. L., L. Bounoua, T. Ricketts, C. Loucks, R. Harriss and W. T. Lawrence (2004) "Global Patterns in Human Consumption of Net Primary Production", *Nature*, 429: 870–873.

Jackson, T. (2009) *Prosperity without Growth? The Transition to a Sustainable Economy*. London: Sustainable Development Commission.

Keesing, F., L. L. Belden, P. Dazdak, A. Dobson, C. D. Harvell, R. D. Holt, P. Hudson, A. Jolles, K. E. Jones, C. E. Mitchell, S. S. Myers, T. Bogich and R. S. Ostfeld (2010) "Impacts of Biodiversity on the Emergence and Transmission of Infectious Diseases", *Nature*, 468: 647–652.

Li J.W. and J. C. Vederas (2009) "Drug Discovery and Natural Products: End of an Era or an Endless Frontier?", *Science*, 325: 161–165.

MA (Millennium Ecosystem Assessment) (2005a) *Ecosystems and Human Well-Being. Volume 1: Current State and Trends*. Millennium Ecosystem Assessment Series. Washington, DC: Island Press. Available at ⟨http://www.millenniumassessment.org/en/Condition.aspx⟩ (accessed 1 February 2012).

MA (Millennium Ecosystem Assessment) (2005b) *Ecosystems and Human Wellbeing: Biodiversity Synthesis*. Washington, DC: World Resources Institute.

Available at ⟨http://www.maweb.org/documents/document.354.aspx.pdf⟩ (accessed 1 February 2012).

McDade, T. W., V. Reyes-Garcia, P. Blackinton, S. Tanner, T. Huancaand W. R. Leonard (2007) "Ethnobotanical Knowledge Is Associated with Indices of Child Health in the Bolivian Amazon", *Proceedings of the National Academy of Sciences of the United States of America*, 104: 6134–6139.

Mace, G. M., W. Cramer, S. Diaz, D. P. Faith, A. Larigauderie, P. Le Prestre, M. P. Palmer, C. Perrings, R. J. Scholes, M. Walpole, B. A. Walther, J. E. M. Watson and H. A. Mooney (2010) "Biodiversity Targets after 2010", *Current Opinion in Environmental Sustainability*, 2: 3–8.

McNally, C. J., E. Uchida and A. J. Gold (2011) "The Effect of a Protected Area on the Tradeoffs between Short-run and Long-run Benefits from Mangrove Ecosystems", *Proceedings of the National Academy of Sciences of the United States of America*, 108: 13945–13950.

Maffi, L. (2007) "Biocultural Diversity and Sustainability", in J. Pretty, A. Ball, T. Benton, J. Guivant, D. R. Lee, D. Orr, M. Pfeffer and H. Ward (eds), *The SAGE Handbook of Environment and Society*. London: Sage Publications, pp. 267–277.

Mooney, H. A. and P. R. Ehrlich (1997) "Ecosystem Services: A Fragmentary History", in G. C. Daily (ed.), *Nature's Services: Societal Dependence on Natural Ecosystems*. Washington, DC: Island Press, pp. 11–19.

Mooney, H., A. Larigauderie, M. Cesario, T. Elmquist, O. Hoegh-Guldberg, S. Lavorel, G. M. Mace, M. Palmer, R. Scholes and T. Yahara (2009) "Biodiversity, Climate Change, and Ecosystem Services", *Current Opinion in Environmental Sustainability*, 1: 46–54.

Mukherjee, P. (2003) "Community Forest Management in India: The Van Panchayats of Uttranchal", paper presented at the XII World Forestry Congress, Quebec, Canada. Available at ⟨http://www.fao.org/DOCREP/ARTICLE/WFC/XII/0108-C1.HTM⟩ (accessed 1 February 2012).

Naeem, S., D. E. Bunker, A. Hector, M. Loreau and C. Perrings (eds) (2009) *Biodiversity, Ecosystem Functioning, and Human Wellbeing: An Ecological and Economic Perspective*. Oxford: Oxford University Press.

Naughton-Treves, L., J. Alix-Garcia and C. A. Chapman (2011) "Lessons about Parks and Poverty from a Decade of Forest Loss and Economic Growth around Kibale National Park, Uganda", *Proceedings of the National Academy of Sciences of the United States of America*, 108: 13919–13924.

Newman, D. J. and G. M. Cragg (2007) "Natural Products as Sources of New Drugs over the Last 25 Years", *Journal of Natural Products*, 70: 461–477.

NRC (National Research Council) (2004) *Valuing Ecosystem Services: Toward Better Environmental Decision-Making*. Washington, DC: The National Academies Press. Available at ⟨https://download.nap.edu/catalog.php?record_id=11139#toc⟩ (accessed 1 February 2012).

Oviedo, G., L. Maffi and P. B. Larsen (2000) *Indigenous and Traditional Peoples of the World and Ecoregion Conservation: An Integrated Approach to Conserving the World's Biological and Cultural Diversity*. Gland, Switzerland:

WWF-International and Terralingua. Available at ⟨http://www.terralingua.org/publications/Sharing/EGinG200rep.pdf⟩ (accessed 1 February 2012).

Pereira, H. M., P. W. Leadley, V. Proença, R. Alkemade, J. P. W. Scharlemann, J. F. F. Fernandez-Manjarrés, M. B. Araújo, P. Balvanera, P. Biggs, W. W. L. Cheung, L. Chini, H. D. Cooper, E. L. Gilman, S. Guénette, G. C. Hurtt, H. P. Huntington, G. M. Mace, T. Oberdorff, C. Revenga, P. Rodrigues, R. J. Scholes, U. R. Sumaila and M. Walpole (2010) "Scenarios for Global Biodiversity in the 21st Century", *Science*, 330: 1496–1501.

Perrings, C., S. Naeem, F. Ahrestani, D. E. Bunker, P. Burkill, G. Canziani, T. Elmqvist, R. Ferrati, J. Fuhrman, F. Jaksic, J. Kawabata, A. Kinzig, G. M. Mace, F. Milano, H. Mooney, A. H. Prieur-Richard, J. Tschirhart and W. Weisser (2011a) "Ecosystem Services for 2020", *Science*, 330: 323–324.

Perrings, C., A. Duraiappah, A. Larigauderieand and H. Mooney (2011b) "The Biodiversity and Ecosystem Services Science-Policy Interface", *Science*, 331: 1139–1140.

Pokharel, R. K. and M. Suvedi (2007) "Indicators for Measuring the Success of Nepal's Community Forestry Program: A Local Perspective", *Human Ecology Review*, 14(1): 68–75.

Rands, M. R. W., M. M. Adams, L. Bennun, S. H. M. Butchart, A. Clements, D. Coomes, A. Entwistle, I. Hodge, V. Kapos, P. W. Schalerman, W. J. Sutherland and B. Vira (2010) "Biodiversity Conservation: Challenges beyond 2010", *Science*, 329: 1298–1303.

Reich, P. B., J. Knops, D. Tilman, J. Craine, D. Ellsworth, M. Tjoelker, T. Lee, D. Wedin, S. Naeem, D. Bahauddin, G. Hendrey, S. Jose, K. Wrage, J. Goth and W. Bengston (2001) "Plant Diversity Enhances Ecosystem Responses to Elevated CO_2 and Nitrogen Deposition", *Nature*, 410: 809–810.

Rodrigues, A. S. L., R. M. Ewers, L. Parry, C. Souza Jr, A. Veríssimo and A. Balmford (2009) "Boom-and-Bust Development Patterns across the Amazon Deforestation Frontier", *Science*, 324: 1435–1437.

Roe, D. (2010) *Linking Biodiversity Conservation and Poverty Alleviation: A State of Knowledge Review*. CBD Technical Series No. 55. Montreal, Canada: Secretariat of the Convention on Biological Diversity. Available at ⟨http://povertyandconservation.info/docs/20101108-CBD-ts-55.pdf⟩ (accessed 1 February 2012).

Stern, N. (2006) *Stern Review on the Economics of Climate Change*. London: HM Treasury. Available at ⟨http://webarchive.nationalarchives.gov.uk/+/http://www.hm-treasury.gov.uk/sternreview_index.htm⟩ (accessed 1 February 2012).

Stiglitz, J. E., A. Sen and J.-P. Fitoussi (2009) *Report by the Commission on the Measurement of Economic Performance and Social Progress*. Available at ⟨http://www.stiglitz-sen-fitoussi.fr/documents/rapport_anglais.pdf⟩ (accessed 1 February 2012).

Subramanian, S. M., W. Hiemstra and B. Verschuuren (2010) "Bio-enterprises, Endogenous Development and Well-being", Policy Brief, COMPAS, Equator Initiative, UNEP and UNU-IAS.

Suneetha, M. S. and B. Pisupati (2009) *Learning from the Practitioners: Benefit Sharing Perspectives from Enterprising Communities*. UNU-IAS and UNEP.

Suneetha, M. S. and M. G. Chandrakanth (2006) "Establishing a Multi-stakeholder Value Index in Medicinal Plants: An Economic Study on Selected Plants in Kerala and Tamilnadu States of India", *Ecological Economics*, 60: 36–48.

TEEB (The Economics of Ecosystems and Biodiversity) (2010) *The Economics of Ecosystems and Biodiversity: Ecological and Economic Foundations*. London: Earthscan.

UK NEA (UK National Ecosystem Assessment) (2011) *The UK National Ecosystem Assessment Technical Report*. Cambridge: UNEP-WCMC.

UNEP (United Nations Environment Programme) (2011) *Towards a Green Economy: Pathways to Sustainable Development and Poverty Eradication*. Nairobi, Kenya: United Nations Environment Programme. Available at ⟨http://www.unep.org/GreenEconomy/Portals/93/documents/Full_GER_screen.pdf⟩ (accessed 1 February 2012).

United Nations (2011) "Harmony with Nature: Report of the Secretary-General", A/65/314, 19 August.

Valderrama, G. C. and S. Arico (2010) "Traditional Knowledge: From Environmental Management to Territorial Development", in S. M. Subramanian and B. Pisupati (eds), *Traditional Knowledge in Policy and Practice: Approaches to Development and Human Wellbeing*. Tokyo: United Nations University Press, pp. 208–225.

Zhu, F., C. Qin, L. Tao, X. Liu, Z. Shi, X. Ma, J. Jia, Y. Tan, C. Cui, J. Lin, C. Tan, Y. Jiang and Y. Chen (2011) "Clustered Patterns of Species Origins of Nature-derived Drugs and Clues for Future Bioprospecting", *Proceedings of the National Academy of Sciences of the United States of America*, 108: 12943–12948.

Part II
Governance

10
Visioning transformative sustainable development governance

Norichika Kanie

Introduction

The limitations of the bureaucratic structures responsible for the environment were identified some time ago in debates about environmental governance at the international level (Ansell and Weber, 1999; Charnovitz, 2002; Haas et al., 2004). Since 1972, the international environmental regime has tried to treat the symptoms each time a problem arises but, with its available finances, staffing and authority, the United Nations Environment Programme (UNEP) – though charged with a coordination function within the United Nations (UN) system – has been unable to coordinate affairs with the comprehensiveness needed for environmental policies, compared with international economic and social organizations. Currently, coordination is not being done adequately even *within* the environmental category. Coordination among the more than 200 multilateral environmental agreements is inadequate.

To deal with these issues, two major topics are being proposed for the United Nations Conference on Sustainable Development (Rio+20) in 2012: an institutional framework for sustainable development, and the green economy in the context of sustainable development and poverty eradication. Discussions in the UN context about sustainable development are generally based on three pillars – the environment, sustainable social development and sustainable economic development. In my view, there are actually only two, not three, pillars. The environment provides the foundations (constraints) for the two pillars and, if the foundation is

---

Green economy and good governance for sustainable development: Opportunities, promises and concerns, Puppim de Oliveira (ed.),
United Nations University Press, 2012, ISBN 978-92-808-1216-9

not sound, the pillars will not stand solidly. At any rate, the environment is another crucial factor in the structure of sustainable development, and institutional frameworks relating to the environment are one of the important topics at the Rio+20 conference.

A number of proposals have been discussed to date in the process leading up to Rio+20. However, the discussions so far do not show any indication of convergence regarding the expectations of all states. Instead, many recent practices of global negotiation, such as the fifteenth session of the Conference of the Parties (COP15) to the United Nations Framework Convention on Climate Change (UNFCCC) or the nineteenth Commission on Sustainable Development session (CSD19), have faced difficulties in getting deals concluded. We may need a transformative reform of environmental governance rather than an incremental one. Transformative reform of environmental governance also requires transformative reform of sustainable development governance, not only because the issues are deeply intertwined but also because of the governance architecture. For example, environmental problems have emerged as a result of economic activities; therefore, transformative reform may not be realized unless the economic pillar of sustainable development is addressed. The same is true of organizational issues: duplication of activities between UNEP and the Commission on Sustainable Development (CSD) cannot be resolved fully unless both of them are reformed. Therefore, even though my primary concern is with environmental governance, we need to deal with governance for sustainable development in order to deal with the issues in their entirety.

In the sections that follow, I first review the discussion on the institutional framework for sustainable development (IFSD) in the context of Rio+20 and clarify the stalled state of discussions, which are making little progress in reaching a consensus. This leads to the necessity for innovative ideas that would stimulate the transformative governance architecture in the context of the twenty-first century. An attempt has been made by the International Environmental Governance Architecture Research Group and the International Human Dimensions Programme on Global Environmental Change (IHDP) Earth System Governance Project to host a series of activities in this regard. The first was a "World Café" style of conversation to identify the strengths and weaknesses of the current architecture of international governance and the key issues in transforming the architecture in international environmental governance. Following the World Café and the assessment of the state of sustainable development governance by leading experts on the issue, a workshop was organized. This workshop also applied, in part, a World Café format and identified issues that require more serious attention in relation to the fundamental transformation of the institutional framework for sustainability. The chapter concludes with the ideas identified as a result of the series of activities that call for a transformative change of the architecture of sustainable development governance in the twenty-first century.

The debate on the institutional framework for sustainable development

Reform of international environmental and sustainable development governance has already been demanded and has for a long time been debated both politically and in academia. Some countries, such as Germany and France, call for the creation of a World Environment Organization to enhance coordination mechanisms and mainstream environmental issues in other related issues, with universal membership and an enhanced and secured budget (Biermann, 2005; Charnovitz, 2005). Other reform proposals include: upgrading UNEP to a specialized agency of the United Nations on a par with the World Health Organization (WHO) or the United Nations Food and Agriculture Organization; the creation of a world environment court (Pauwelyn, 2005); and reforming the UN Trusteeship Council to become a UN Environment Trusteeship Council (Redgwell, 2005). According to Bradnee Chambers (2005), the issue has repeatedly gained political attention when discussed at large-scale global summits on sustainable development, such as in Rio in 1992 and Johannesburg in 2002, but opportunities for reform were missed.

Still, the need and demand for institutional reform have continued to attract interest. The World Summit Outcome Document in 2005 recognizes "the need for more efficient environmental activities in the United Nations system, with enhanced coordination, improved policy advice and guidance, strengthened scientific knowledge, assessment and cooperation, better treaty compliance, while respecting the legal autonomy of the treaties, and better integration of environmental activities in the broader sustainable development framework at the operational level, including through capacity-building" (United Nations, 2005: para. 169). It was also agreed to "explore the possibility of a more coherent institutional framework to address this need, including a more integrated structure, building on existing institutions and internationally agreed instruments, as well as the treaty bodies and the specialized agencies." This agreement resulted in an informal consultation process in the UN General Assembly on the institutional framework for United Nations environment work, led by the ambassadors of Mexico and Switzerland. A consensus was reported in the initial report to the President of the General Assembly in June 2006 (United Nations, 2006) that the system needed strengthening to improve coordination and coherence, and a number of options were presented to delegates in the following year. This process was followed throughout 2008 by a series of discussion processes on a draft resolution. Although a consensus continues to exist on the need for the international environmental governance system to be strengthened in order to improve coordination and coherence, no consensus was reached about how this could be achieved. In mid-February 2009, the co-chairs decided to stop negotiations on the resolution, because progress had been so slow that they felt that no consensus on real content could be reached. In their report dated 10 February 2009, they expressed hope that ministers of the environment would "find a political compromise and entrust their delegations in New York with pragmatic, creative and constructive proposals, which allow improving the current system" (United Nations, 2009: 7). The recommendation was followed by Decision 25/4 of the twenty-fifth session of UNEP's Governing Council / Global Ministerial Environment Forum (GC/GMEF) (Governing Council of UNEP, 2009), which established a Consultative Group of Ministers or High-level Representatives on International Environmental Governance.

The group met on 27 and 28 June 2009 in Belgrade and 28 and 29 October 2009 in Rome, attended by 39 and 43 governments, respectively. Two co-chairs were selected, one from a developing country (Kenya) and one from a developed country (Italy). The discussions were reflected in a co-chairs' summary called "Belgrade Process: Moving forward with developing a set of options on international environmental governance" (Consultative Group of Ministers or High-level Representatives, 2009a), which was presented at the GC/GMEF's eleventh special session in February 2010. The options identified include the following five objectives and corresponding functions for international environmental governance within the UN system (Consultative Group of Ministers or High-level Representatives, 2009b):

a) Creating a strong, credible and accessible science base and policy interface
  i. Acquisition, compilation, analysis and interpretation of data and information.
  ii. Information exchange.
  iii. Environmental assessment and early warning.
  iv. Scientific advice.
  v. Science–policy interface.
b) Developing a global authoritative and responsive voice for environmental sustainability.
  vi. Global agenda setting and policy guidance and advice.
  vii. Mainstreaming environment into other relevant policy areas.
  viii. Promotion of rule making, standard setting and universal principles.
  ix. Monitoring, compliance and accountability for agreed commitments and building related capacity.
  x. Dispute avoidance and settlement.

c) Achieving effectiveness, efficiency and coherence within the United Nations system.
  xi. Coordination of policies and programmes.
  xii. Efficient and effective administration and implementation of Multilateral Environmental Agreements (MEAs).
  xiii. Facilitating interagency cooperation on the environment.
d) Securing sufficient, predictable and coherent funding.
  xiv. Mobilizing and accessing funds for the global environment
  xv. Developing innovative financing mechanisms to compliment [sic] official funding sources.
  xvi. Utilising funding effectively and efficiently in accordance with agreed priorities.
e) Ensuring a responsive and cohesive approach to meeting country needs.
  xvii. Human and institutional capacity building.
  xviii. Technology transfer and financial support.
  xix. Mainstreaming environment into development processes.
  xx. Facilitating South-South, North-South and triangular cooperation.

They further identified the following forms of broader institutional reform:

i. enhancing UNEP;
ii. a new umbrella organization for sustainable development;
iii. a specialized agency such as a World Environment Organization;
iv. possible reforms to ECOSOC and the Commission on Sustainable Development; and
v. enhanced institutional reforms and streamlining of present structures.

GC/GMEF established a Second Consultative Group of Ministers or High-level Representatives on International Environmental Governance in its Decision SS.XI/1 of 26 February 2010. The group was requested to "consider the broader reform of the international environmental governance system, building on the set of options but remaining open to new ideas" (Governing Council of UNEP, 2010). The group has two co-chairs, one from a developing country (Kenya) and one from a developed country (Finland), and consists of between four and six governments to represent each of the United Nations regions, while remaining open to participation by other interested governments. The group met first on 7–9 July 2010 in Nairobi, attended by representatives of 58 countries, and the second time on 21–23 November 2010 in Espoo, Finland, attended by representatives of 44 countries. The outcome of the Consultative Group, the *Nairobi–Helsinki Outcome* (Consultative Group of Ministers or High-level Representatives, 2010), was presented to the twenty-sixth session of GC/GMEF in February 2011. The Nairobi–Helsinki Outcome was built upon the bases of the Belgrade Process; its function-based proposals are in line with the options presented in the report of the Belgrade

Process, and the form-related aspects of its broader reform proposal are the same as the options put forward in the report of the Belgrade Process. Although it states that the proposals are open to new ideas, the Nairobi–Helsinki Outcome further reduced the number of form-based reform options to three by eliminating options for "establishing a new umbrella organization for sustainable development" and "reforming the United Nations Economic and Social Council and the United Nations Commission on Sustainable Development" because these would best be addressed in the wider sustainable development context rather than in the environmental context.

In its Decision 26/1 in February 2011, GC/GMEF invited the President of the Governing Council to "transmit the Nairobi-Helsinki Outcome to the Preparatory Committee for the United Nations Conference on Sustainable Development at its second session and to the General Assembly at its sixty-sixth session" (Governing Council of UNEP, 2011). It also invited the "Preparatory Committee for the United Nations Conference on Sustainable Development at its second session to initiate a full analysis of the financial, structural, and legal implications and comparative advantages of the options identified in the Nairobi-Helsinki Outcome". This is to say that the outcome is transmitted from the UNEP process to the Rio+20 preparation process.

According to negotiators involved in the Rio+20 preparatory process and officials working closely in the process, the situations, positions and level of knowledge around the negotiations on IFSD reform are yet to produce an emerging consensus. The political situation on consensus on the issue has not changed much since 2008 and 2009, when the informal consultation process in the UN General Assembly on the institutional framework for UN environmental work stopped. There is no sign of a consensus emerging on "how" to conduct the innovative reform ideas and a creative vision will be needed if the IFSD is to offer transformative governance to solve problems in the twenty-first century. According to many practitioners engaged in the international process on institutional reform, incremental solutions are necessary but not sufficient. Given the difficulties in decision-making at the international level – for example, CSD19 and UNFCCC COP15 concluded without finding effective solutions to the problems – transformative change is necessary. The issues and political dynamics in the twenty-first century are different from those in 1945 when the institutions of the United Nations were established. Today's problems are characterized by temporal, spatial and sectoral interdependencies, as well as by complexity and uncertainty. Although incremental changes have enabled some progress towards sustainability, the current system governing sustainable development is no longer sufficient, given the number, impact, interdependence and complexity of the problems associated with global change. Governance for sustainability requires transformative reforms and a clear vision to guide such reforms.

Identifying issues for transformative governance

The first World Café in Colorado

As noted above, there is a shared recognition that more efficient environmental activities are necessary and that institutional reform is needed, but a gap exists in "how" to conduct reform. One way to break the stalemate is to start with a shared vision and then narrow it down to concrete behaviours to realize the vision. Unless the underlying institutions and behavioural patterns that are governed by the institutions are discussed, debate over institutional forms will just end up with political conflict (Young, 2008). Institutional forms inevitably have financial implications for member states, which then inevitably lead to disputes about political control over the decision-making process. An evaluation of the functioning of existing institutions is a prerequisite to clarifying the necessary vision and blueprint for the future.

In order to proceed with such a process of problem identification and drawing the necessary vision and blueprint for transformative governance for sustainable development in the twenty-first century, it was decided to undertake a series of initiatives. Some existing research has done various evaluations of the current institutions on issues related to environment and sustainable development, but not enough has been done yet for mutual learning and shaping the results in terms of moving towards transformative ideas. What we need now, therefore, is not yet another evaluation of the state of international institutions and more proposals, but efforts to reshape existing studies and ideas through mutual learning.

The methodology we employed here is called a "World Café". The World Café design enables participants in the café to "participate together in evolving rounds of dialogue with three or four others while at the same time remaining part of a single, larger, connected conversation. Small, intimate conversations link and build on each other as people move between groups, cross-pollinate ideas, and discover new insights into questions or issues that really matter" (Brown, 2005: 4). As a result, knowledge-sharing grows as "the network of new connections increases" and "a sense of the whole becomes increasingly strong. The collective wisdom of the group becomes more accessible, and innovative possibilities for action emerge" (2005: 4). The World Café is "designed on the assumption that people already have within them the wisdom and creativity to confront even the most difficult challenges" (2005: 4).

The World Café process invites stakeholders to converse about questions that matter in a small group format. Five key features of the World Café in general are as follows (Brown, 2005):

Setting: Create a "special" environment, most often modelled after a café, i.e. small, round tables with checked tablecloths, easel paper, coloured pens, a vase of flowers and an optional "talking stick" item. There should be four chairs at each table.

Welcome and introduction: The host begins with a warm welcome and an introduction to the World Café process, setting the context and putting participants at ease.

Small group rounds: The process begins with the first of three or more 20-minute rounds of conversation for the small group seated around a table. At the end of the 20 minutes, each member of the group moves to a new table. They may or may not choose to leave one person as the "table host" for the next round, who welcomes the next group and briefly fills them in on what happened in the previous round.

Questions: Each round is prefaced with a question designed for the specific context and desired purpose of the session. The same questions can be used for more than one round, or they can be built upon to focus the conversation or guide its direction.

Harvest: After the small groups (and/or in between rounds, as desired), individuals are invited to share insights or other results from their conversations with the rest of the large group. These results are reflected visually in a variety of ways, most often using graphic recorders at the front of the room.

The first World Café on the institutional framework for sustainable development was held on the occasion of the Colorado Conference on Earth System Governance (on 19 May 2011, at Colorado State University, United States). The café was attended by approximately 50 people, many of whom were researchers involved in the Earth System Governance Project network,[1] but some policy-makers at local, national and global levels also participated. This session applied the World Café process to address the following questions:

1. What are the strengths and weaknesses of the current architecture of international governance?
2. What are key issues in transforming the architecture of international environmental governance?

The strengths and weaknesses of the current architecture of international governance

On the first question, the participants pointed to the following strengths and weaknesses. The existing framework is viewed as both a strength and weakness: the current institutions could be a foundation for future development but could also be an obstacle to fundamental reform because interests are embedded in an established institutional framework. There is also a view that the existing structure causes a lack of attention to the drivers of global environmental change; the current multilateral regime formation does not question the fundamental drivers of environmental decline.

Many participants argued that the existing multilateral treaty system provides an important venue for ongoing discussions and dialogue. Although the treaties themselves may not provide a foundation for transformative change, the ongoing process is important for keeping issues of global environmental change in the spotlight and developing shared understandings of the problems. The process also normalizes the global environment as a problem that needs to be addressed together. In particular, framework conventions are viewed as a forum for face-to-face dialogue on the particular issue and to carry out implementation, and where a variety of robust discussions take place. On the other hand, the fragmentation of actors, efforts, incentives and events is regarded as a weakness by many, leading to bad bureaucracy. Some also saw fragmentation as separating environment from other meaningful governance sectors.

At the same time, some have pointed out that there is innovative action outside the intergovernmental arena and that the intergovernmental system has the potential to mobilize resources to support these initiatives. In this regard, linkage between public and private actors and activities and partnerships between them are potentially an important device.

In contrast, a lack of democratic legitimacy in the ongoing process is also pointed out as a weakness. This can be found in the global process itself, or a lack of legitimate government hinders legitimacy in some areas. In the short term, the current powerful actors in the current power distribution have a larger role to play.

There were also mixed views on participation. Some saw the diverse representation and universal participation of the UN system as strengths, whereas others saw them as insufficient. Fragmentation and bureaucracy are considered to be one of the weakest parts of the current system, as many studies also suggest.

Key issues in transforming the architecture of international environmental governance

The World Café then moved on to two rounds of conversation on the question: "What are the key issues in transforming the architecture in international environmental governance?" The ideas presented can be divided into seven broad groupings.
1. *The re-articulation of values and new ways of thinking.* Many ideas were expressed about the necessity to reframe environmental issues.

Although there is a view that sustainable development and not just the environment should frame the issue, many still see the importance of mainstreaming the "environment" at global and local levels by internalizing environmental and other externalities into the decisions that structure human activity (for example, the World Trade Organization, local scales). These two views are, however, not mutually exclusive. Articulating and institutionalizing environmental values can contribute to big-picture thinking and to promoting creative solutions in the name of incrementalism. Some even argued for moving beyond incrementalism by introducing ideas more in line with transformation, recognizing that it is a billion-dollar challenge. For such transformative change, it is necessary to facilitate a shift in priorities.

2. *Consolidation.* International environmental governance needs to simplify the system by bringing together the most similar experiences. Reducing waste (of time, labour, etc.) within international environmental governance can be achieved by consolidating regimes across all issues, both environmental and others such as trade.

3. *The need for learning and reflexivity.* A flexible governance architecture was called for by many participants. Transformative architecture must be flexible, and the nature of the architecture required to maintain flexibility needs to be rethought. In fact, expectations of governance can be seen as an evolving process that has to include learning, and not a fixed known path. In order for the process to be reflexive, it is important to align short- and long-term goals, to align the process with the goals and to learn how to learn. It is necessary to look at connections within and between systems to create opportunities for experimentation and learning, and to move from a blueprint architecture to a vernacular, fluid architecture.

4. *Participation and voice.* The inclusion of key stakeholders and decision-makers is seen as important for transformative change, but it is currently lacking. It is necessary to transform the game and the players and include direct citizen representation. It is also pointed out that it is necessary to maintain and enhance the volume of soft voices (little-heard stakeholders) and groups that are often invisible in environmental governance. Public consultation and the use of existing participatory instruments are one way to do this. The public needs to take responsibility in participation mechanisms as well as individually to put pressure on governments/policy-makers and to express their opinion. In this way, political will that does not come just from politicians can be better delivered.

5. *Work at multiple levels.* Linking global institution-building to deal with problems on the ground is important because the real problems are on the ground. Hierarchical goal structures that allow for flexibility at

the lower operational levels and compliance at middle to upper operational levels would work better. It is worth acknowledging where there is consistency at mid-operational level. Such change would facilitate a shift in priorities at many levels.
6. *Leadership.* Strong facilitation and leadership with authority (delegated by the group) are integral parts of transformative change.
7. *Reform the global economic system.* There is a fundamental questioning of the system of production and consumption, and there is a need for fundamental system innovation. Such transformative thinking about a new economic environment, based on environmental policy integration, needs to be introduced and permeate the international environmental governance architecture. This could include the United Nations introducing a global carbon tax and mobilizing other financial resources to spur innovation. For this, visionary leadership is also considered to be important.

In sum, transformational change will require a re-articulation of values and new ways of thinking to put environmental issues in a different framework. This will also require reform of the global economic system and environmental issues being considered within a wider framework of sustainable development. Transformative change requires resilient and flexible governance structures that promote learning and reflexivity and are capable of working at multiple levels. This seems to be where public–private networks and partnerships, including wider representation and participation in decision-making and implementation processes, have an advantage. These new forms of governance are not a panacea and they must be designed with careful consideration of what kind of actors (or combination of actors) would work effectively on different governance components and on issues of equity, accountability and effectiveness on the ground.

Expert assessment on the state of the institutional framework for sustainable development

In the wake of the Colorado Conference, a policy assessment on the state of the IFSD was conducted by the Earth System Governance Project in preparation for Rio+20. The assessment outlines core areas where urgent action is required, based on the state of knowledge in the social sciences in this field. The policy brief was compiled by members of the lead faculty, scientific steering committee, and other affiliates of the Earth System Governance Project. The policy brief, entitled "Transforming Governance and Institutions for a Planet under Pressure. Revitalizing the Institutional Framework for Global Sustainability: Key Insights from Social Science

Research", identified 10 key points, many of which share the ideas identified at the World Café as described above, but they highlight the issues in a more systemic manner (Earth System Governance, 2011a: 2).

- Strengthen international environmental treaties: Governments must engage in structural reforms in how international environmental negotiations are conducted and treaties designed. Present and future treaties must rely more on systems of qualified majority voting in specified areas.
- Manage conflicts among multilateral agreements: International economic institutions must advance transitions to a sustainable economy, including by multilaterally harmonized systems that allow for discriminating between products on the basis of production processes, based on multilateral agreement. Global trade and investment regimes must be embedded in a normative context of social, developmental and environmental values.
- Fill regulatory gaps in international sustainability governance: New or strengthened international regulatory frameworks are needed in several areas, including on emerging technologies, water, food and energy.
- Upgrade UNEP: Governments need to engage in negotiations for the upgrading of UNEP to a specialized UN agency, along the lines of the World Health Organization or the International Labour Organization.
- Better integrate sustainable development policies within the UN system: Governments need to support overall integrative mechanisms within the UN system that better align the social, economic and environmental pillars of sustainable development.
- Strengthen national governance: New policy instruments are a promising complement to regulation if carefully designed. But they are not panaceas.
- Streamline and strengthen public–private governance networks and partnerships: The CSD and other bodies need a stronger mandate and better methodologies for the verification and monitoring of partnerships. Despite the growing role of non-state actors, there is still a strong need for effective and decisive governmental action.
- Strengthen accountability and legitimacy: Novel accountability mechanisms are needed, including mandatory disclosure of accessible, comprehensible and comparable data about government and corporate sustainability performance. Stronger consultative rights for civil society representatives in intergovernmental institutions should be introduced.
- Address equity concerns within and among countries: Equity concerns must be at the heart of the institutional framework for sustainable development. High consumption levels in industrialized countries and in some parts of the emerging economies require special and urgent action. Financial transfers from richer to poorer countries are inevitable, either through direct support payments for mitigation and adaptation programmes or through international market mechanisms, for example global emissions markets.
- Prepare global governance for a warmer world: Global adaptation programmes need to become a core concern of the UN system and governments.

Visioning for IFSD in the twenty-first century

The World Café at the Colorado Conference on Earth System Governance and the policy brief "Transforming Governance and Institutions for a Planet under Pressure" identified key issues for transformative governance for sustainable development. The two assessments used different methodology yet arrived at similar results. Based on these assessments, there was a move to look at the problems and issues in more depth and to identify a vision and blueprint for transformative reform. For this purpose, the "Hakone Vision Factory on Earth System Governance: Bridging the Science–Policy Boundary" was held in Hakone, Japan, 27–29 September 2011. The workshop brought together about 20 experts from the Earth System Governance scientific community and policy-makers from local, national and global levels. Participants at the workshop already had the wisdom and creativity to confront the challenges of sustainable development from their respective experiences, and what was required was interactive learning to further develop the idea and the vision. Learning from the successful results from Colorado, the workshop employed the World Café methodology.

In order to foster creativity, only one question was prepared in advance for the café; the rest of the questions were identified as the conversation developed. In this way, it was possible to further deepen the insights. Time was also secured for further discussion after each "harvest" regarding the views identified in the World Café session, by which collective thought and learning could also be deepened. The questions addressed, including the first one, were as follows:

- What distinguishes the problems we are now facing (or will be facing) from those our institutions were designed to respond to? This question was chosen as the kick-off question of the workshop, because both evaluations identified the changing character of the problems of the twenty-first century from 1945 when the UN institutional design was established, and this is the point of departure.
- What kind of governance architecture can ensure the simultaneous achievement of the three pillars of sustainable development?
- Who should be heard? What values and criteria should be used?
- What kind of body should be used? What kind of decision-making mechanism/structure should be used?

Each session was divided into two sets of conversations (each person, except for one person staying at the table, moving to a different table for the next round), each lasting around 25 minutes.

The World Café sessions were followed by discussion among participants to shape the ideas towards producing a vision and blueprint for a governance architecture for sustainability in the twenty-first century. Noting that the issues and political dynamics in the twenty-first century are different from those in 1945, when the institutions of the United Nations were founded, the ideas for visions for transformative governance were clustered around three interrelated issues: aspirations, actors and architecture (Earth System Governance, 2011b).[2]

Aspirations

> We are living in a highly dynamic, human-dominated Earth system in which non-linear, abrupt, and irreversible changes are not only possible but also probable. Governance for sustainability in the "anthropocene" era requires that objectives, underlying values and norms, as well as knowledge and uncertainty, be refined and operationalized.

Planetary boundaries illustrate the finiteness of natural resources and resource use and define the safe operating space for humans. Governance for integrative economic, social and environmental sustainability must respect these boundaries, and other limits to human, intellectual and natural resources, and simultaneously ensure just and equitable development and stewardship. Governance for sustainability must be capable of governing legitimate and effective policy responses to potential changes to natural systems that could result from crossing planetary boundaries and potentially triggering tipping points in the Earth system. Similarly, policy responses to natural disasters that are likely to occur more frequently and with larger magnitude owing to global change require new, effective governance mechanisms at the global level to complement, coordinate and improve existing disaster reduction and management policies at national and local levels.

- Governance goals have changed from those in 1945 when the post-WWII institutions were established. This requires changes in governance systems. The international community should discuss the priorities, pathways and qualitative and normative goals of sustainability.
- The emerging discussion on the Sustainable Development Goals (SDG) in line with and complementing the Millennium Development Goals (MDG), could become an important political target, providing momentum and attention to sustainable development. Careful consideration is required to determine how the SDG's can be positioned alongside the successful MDG's, which continue to be of high relevance and importance.
- Approaches to sustainability governance based on economic values are insufficient – and partly the cause of unsustainable development. There is a clear need to go beyond GDP and market-value in measuring development. Human well-being and the quality of life are important additional values, as

are considerations of ecosystem services and the non-anthropocentric values of other living beings.
- Alternative metrics to GDP have been developed, such as the Human Development Index. Further development of the goals of sustainable development and methodologies could result in a sustainable development indicator, combining variables from the three pillars of sustainable development, or a small suite of indices that have to be pursued simultaneously and without tradeoffs. This is considered to have potential as a useful and policy relevant tool, but only when institutional and financial underpinnings are provided.

The economic, social and environmental pillars of sustainable development are strongly interrelated. Horizontal harmonization is therefore crucial to ensure that actions are mutually reinforcing and to realize the governance goals for sustainability. Vertical integration is needed within each pillar to achieve improved implementation of sustainable development.

Actors

> Governance for sustainability demands the broadening of meaningful and accountable participation and solutions from people for people.

Governance for sustainability should be as inclusive as possible for all groups in society. Inclusiveness requires governance systems to listen to all voices and to have transparent mechanisms to moderate, synthesize and prioritize them to allow for inclusive, representative and effective decision-making. The level of inclusiveness, the type of inclusion and the mechanisms to ensure this could be tailored differently for each distinct step in the policy cycle, noting that there is a distinction between listening and decision-making. Deciding whose voices shall be heard and whose views should help determine decision-making outcomes is a highly normative and extremely sensitive process that needs further research and deliberation, as well as a system of checks and balances. Initially, meeting basic human needs could be the core criterion for making these choices.

- Information technologies, including social media, have the potential to support governance for sustainability by giving voice to those groups and individuals that have been marginalized in the decision making process, and stimulating and facilitating trans-boundary communication and deliberation. However, contentious issues remain regarding the legitimacy and accountability of decentralized participation (e.g. referenda), in particular because these technologies are not universally available and affordable.

- The evolving nature of governance and the problems of global change have engaged a wide variety and large number of non-state actors. Mechanisms to include non-state actors in the intergovernmental UN system (for example, through Major Groups in the CSD) are laudable but insufficient and not truly inclusive, often leading to misrepresentation.
- One way to improve representation in the current intergovernmental system would be to add a mechanism of checks and balances (between governments and non-state actors) that could be inspired by the example of the EU Parliament in relation to the EU Council. In designing such a mechanism, attention should also be paid to the risk of paralysis.
- Mechanisms to enable meaningful involvement of other actors, including persons or organisations of high respect, cities, communities, and social movements in governance for sustainability, are needed.
- The emergence of new actors requires a governance system with a larger range of instruments. While states are the central actors, non-state actors are necessary for accountable and effective governance for sustainability. Options include improved private governance (such as the Forest Stewardship Council or Marine Stewardship Council) and public-private partnerships. Safeguards need to be in place to ensure the accountability and legitimacy of non-state actors.

Architecture

- The architecture for sustainability governance needs to be re-built to include better integration, as well as improved institutions and decision-making mechanisms.
- Proposals for the required transformative changes in the architecture of governance for sustainability need to be assessed based on a set of criteria, including:
  1. Membership: Meaningful participatory approaches that are inclusive and account for power differentials between nation states, non-state actors, and other groups in society.
  2. Funding: Appropriate and stable levels of funding.
  3. Authority/Mandate: Appropriate authority and efficiency.
  4. Compliance and Implementation: Appropriate capacity to address compliance and implementation.
  5. Adaptability: Effective adaptive approaches that could include sunset clauses and scheduled re-chartering moments in agreements, dynamic criteria to all selection and decision-making mechanisms to reflect changes in natural and social systems, and network approaches.
  6. Accountability: Strong accountability and transparency safeguards.
- The absence of suitable arrangements on one or more of these criteria will jeopardize prospects for transformative change.

Governance for sustainability concerns governance at all levels, from global to local. Efficient and legitimate governance mechanisms at the global level are important to support efforts at other levels. Likewise, governance mechanisms at other levels can support governance initiatives at the global level.

Effective management of the global commons[3] is in each country's interest, because global problems increasingly have local impacts, and local problems have transboundary consequences. Responsible decisions are needed that respect the transboundary nature of the causes and consequences of global change, as well as of the appropriate policy responses. Here, the UN system plays a key role in the current and future architectures for sustainability governance. Transformative change will require stronger links between the institutions and organizations working within the UN system and those of the Bretton Woods system and other sustainable development activities taking place outside the UN system. Accountability, legitimacy and authority within the UN system need improvement, and mechanisms need to be newly developed for global efforts towards sustainable development outside the United Nations.

Consideration of a UN Sustainable Development Council

Drawing on the discussion of *Aspirations*, *Actors*, and *Architecture*, the Hakone Vision Factory discussed and evaluated many of the proposals for a restructured institutional framework for sustainable development that would improve governance and determined that proposals for a Sustainable Development Council deserve more serious consideration.

- The process towards the establishment of the Sustainable Development Council needs to be carefully balanced with other governance reforms for sustainable development and with consideration to the oversight of the process, and the positioning and configuration of the Council in the constellation of the institutional framework for sustainable development, including but not limited to the UN system. The six requirements for the architecture of the governance for sustainability, as mentioned above, should be applied when assessing institutional framework for sustainable development.
- The mandate of the Sustainable Development Council needs to result from further research and a deliberative process that could be set in motion at the 2012 United Nations Conference on Sustainable Development. Amongst others, the mandate and charter of such a Council could include mechanisms and authority for governance of crisis, for example along the lines of the WHO.
- Membership of the Sustainable Development Council could include the following set of members, whereby different responsibilities could be assigned to different member groups. The optimal number of members for each member group needs further exploration.
  1. Primary member states. Countries with high capacity to contribute to the implementation of sustainable development through various forms of capital. These same countries also have a high capacity to contribute to the

problem of unsustainable development if their actions are not changed in significant ways. Selected based on a set of criteria (of which GDP could initially be an important part until adequate alternative metrics are common and accepted, for example also including scores of countries on the SDG's). At set points in time (not too frequent), membership will be reassessed based on changed scores on criteria.
2. Rotating member states. Countries most affected by specific issues of sustainable development and thus called into the group depending on the issue on the table.
3. Non-state actors. Selected through a mechanism that reflects the criteria for architecture of governance for sustainability.

- The total number of members should be kept sufficiently small to allow decisions to be made reasonably efficiently.
- Taking into account the evolving nature of governance, gradually, and over the medium to long-term, the Council could create a dual-chamber system, consisting of governments on one side and issue specific representatives from non-state actors on the other.
- Generally, qualified majority voting is a promising way to improve the quality and decisiveness of decision making in governance for sustainable development. Given the high level of the Council, careful development of decision-making procedures, whether based on the common one-state one-vote unanimous decision making procedures, re-definition of consensus, or on other innovative models, is needed.
- The academic and political considerations and development of a Sustainable Development Council should not exclude the required strengthening of the environmental pillar (such as upgrading UNEP) of sustainable development; and should take place with meaningful involvement and strengthening of integration with economic governance. But such reform directions suggest a review on the role and future of the CSD.

Conclusion

Reform of the institutional framework for sustainable development has been discussed for decades, both in scholarly and political terms, but the process has not yet shown a convergence of expectations. A reason for this is a growing gap between the UN institutions, and in particular institutions for the environment and sustainable development, and the political reality on sustainable development issues. Tackling this requires a transformative reform of sustainable development governance. This is why the Hakone Vision Factory has added to the existing knowledge and taken the initiative to further investigate the state of the IFSD and provide appropriate visions for a required reform, drawing upon the state of knowledge in the social sciences in the field. Without the right vision, reform cannot achieve what is needed, but so far the vision has been missing in the discussion.

Based on a World Café in Colorado and the policy brief "Transforming Governance and Institutions for a Planet under Pressure", the Hakone Vision Factory on Earth System Governance further evaluated the state of the IFSD and identified key issues for transformative reform, thereby clarifying the visions for transformative reform. These are identified by aims, actors and architecture.

Aims: Approaches to sustainable governance based on economic values are insufficient and there is a clear need to go beyond GDP and market value in measuring development. In this connection, strong voices are calling for support for the development of SDGs in line with and complementing the MDGs.

Actors: The emergence of a wide variety and large number of non-state actors is recognized. Mechanisms to include non-state actors in the intergovernmental UN system (for example, through Major Groups in the CSD) are laudable but insufficient and not truly inclusive (misrepresentation). A way to overcome this may be by adding checks and balances (between governments and non-state actors) that could be inspired by the example of the EU Parliament. The emergence of new actors requires a governance system with a larger range of instruments. Although states have been, and will be for some time to come, the central actors, non-state actors are necessary for accountable and effective governance for sustainability.

Architecture: There is wide recognition of the need for better integration and for improved institutions and decision-making mechanisms. Therefore, proposals need to be assessed based on a set of principles for the architecture of governance for sustainability. These principles include the following:
- Meaningful participatory approaches and the inclusion of non-state actors
- Appropriate and stable levels of funding
- Appropriate authority and capacity to address issues of compliance
- Adaptive approaches (sunset clauses, scheduled re-chartering, dynamic criteria for all selection and decision mechanisms to reflect changes in natural systems and in social systems – wealth, power, vulnerability)
- Strong accountability safeguards

The UN system has a key role. However, it is recognized that transformative change could place more emphasis on governance outside the United Nations. Although accountability, legitimacy and authority within the United Nations need improvement, solutions outside the United Nations also need to be newly developed.

Given the changing nature of the pressing issues, most sustainable development issues are related to security nowadays. This increases the necessity of establishing a Sustainable Development Council, following the model of the Security Council, but it needs to be modified to fit the character of the issues and the nature of governance in the twenty-first century.

Fundamental improvements in the economic system are necessary, in addition to improved governance for sustainability. The green economy should be linked with IFSD in this regard. Ultimately, such reform may involve amending the UN Charter to better reflect the challenges of the twenty-first century. In this sense, the vision provided in this chapter is leading us towards a Charter moment.

Acknowledgements

This chapter is based on the outcome of a research project conducted by International Environmental Governance Architecture Research Group, which is funded by the Japan Foundation Center for Global Partnership (CGP). Among the members of the group, I would like to thank Professor Michele Betsill, Colorado State University, and Mr Ruben Zondervan, Earth System Governance Project and Lund University, for their comments and inputs to an earlier version of this chapter.

Notes

1. This Project is a 10-year research initiative under the auspices of the International Human Dimensions Programme on Global Environmental Change, which is sponsored by the International Council for Science, the International Council for Social Science and the United Nations University. The project has evolved into the largest social science network in its field, involving about 1,700 colleagues along with a core network of 12 institutions in the Global Alliance of Earth System Governance Research Centres.
2. The Hakone Vision, whose main contents are presented in this section, was prepared by Ruben Zondervan.
3. By global commons, we include global resources such as the climate system and the stratospheric ozone layer in addition to the traditional concept of the areas outside the scope of the jurisdiction of nation-states, such as the high seas.

REFERENCES

Ansell, C. K. and S. Weber (1999). "Organizing International Politics: Sovereignty and Open Systems", *International Political Science Review*, 20(1): 73–93.

Biermann, F. (2005) "The Rationale for a World Environment Organization", in F. Biermann and S. Bauer (eds), *A World Environment Organization: Solution or Threat for International Environmental Governance?* Aldershot: Ashgate, pp. 117–144.

Brown, J., with D. Isaacs and the World Café Community (2005) *The World Café: Shaping Our Futures Through Conversations That Matter*. San Francisco: Barrett-Koehler Publishers.

Chambers, W. B. (2005) "From Environmental to Sustainable Development Governance: Thirty Years of Coordination within the United Nations", in W. B. Chambers and J. F. Green (eds), *Reforming International Environmental Governance: From Institutional Limits to Innovative Reforms*. Tokyo: United Nations University Press, pp. 13–39.

Charnovitz, S. (2002) "A World Environment Organization", in W.B. Chambers and J. F. Green (eds), *Reforming International Environmental Governance: From Institutional Limits to Innovative Reforms*. Tokyo: United Nations University Press, pp. 93–123.

Charnovitz, S. (2005) "Toward a World Environment Organization: Reflections upon a Vital Debate", in F. Biermann and S. Bauer (eds) *A World Environment Organization: Solution or Threat for International Environmental Governance?* Aldershot: Ashgate, pp. 87–115.

Consultative Group of Ministers or High-level Representatives (2009a) "Belgrade Process: Moving Forward with Developing a Set of Options on International Environmental Governance". Co-Chairs' Summary of the first meeting of the Consultative Group of Ministers or High-level Representatives on International Environmental Governance, Belgrade, 27–28 June 2009. Available at ⟨http://www.unep.org/environmentalgovernance/IEGReform/tabid/2227/Default.aspx⟩ (accessed 14 February 2012).

Consultative Group of Ministers or High-level Representatives (2009b) "Set of Options for Improving International Environmental Governance", Second meeting of the Consultative Group of Ministers or High-level Representatives on International Environmental Governance, Rome, 28–29 October 2009.

Consultative Group of Ministers or High-level Representatives (2010) "Nairobi-Helsinki Outcome", Second meeting of the Consultative Group of Ministers or High-level Representatives on International Environmental Governance, Espoo, Finland, 21–23 November 2010.

Earth System Governance (2011a) "Transforming Governance and Institutions for a Planet under Pressure. Revitalizing the Institutional Framework for Global Sustainability: Key Insights from Social Science Research", Planet Under Pressure Policy Brief, 3.

Earth System Governance (2011b) "Towards a Charter Moment: Hakone Vision on Governance for Sustainability in the 21st Century", International Environmental Governance Architecture Research Group, Tokyo. Available at ⟨http://www.earthsystemgovernance.org/news/2011-10-25-hakone-vision-governance-sustainability-21st-century⟩ (accessed 2 February 2012).

Governing Council of UNEP (2009) *Proceedings of the Governing Council/Global Ministerial Environment Forum at Its Twenty-Fifth Session*, Nairobi, 16–20 February. UNEP/GC.25/17, 26 February.

Governing Council of UNEP (2010) *Proceedings of the Governing Council/Global Ministerial Environment Forum at Its Eleventh Special Session*, Bali, Indonesia, 24–26 February. UNEP/GCSS.XI/11, 3 March.

Governing Council of UNEP (2011) *Proceedings of the Governing Council/ Global Ministerial Environment Forum at Its Twenty-Sixth Session*, Nairobi, 21–24 February. UNEP/GC.26/19, 24 February.

Haas, P. M., N. Kanie and C. N. Murphy (2004) "Conclusion: Institutional Design and Institutional Reform for Sustainable Development", in N. Kanie and P. M. Haas (eds), *Emerging Forces in Environmental Governance*. Tokyo: United Nations University Press, pp. 263–281.

Pauwelyn, J. (2005) "Judicial Mechanisms: Is There a Need for a World Environment Court?", in W. B. Chambers and J. F. Green (eds), *Reforming International Environmental Governance: From Institutional Limits to Innovative Reforms*. Tokyo: United Nations University Press, pp. 150–177.

Redgwell, C. (2005) "Reforming the United Nations Trusteeship Council", in W. B. Chambers and J. F. Green (eds), *Reforming International Environmental Governance: From Institutional Limits to Innovative Reforms*. Tokyo: United Nations University Press, pp. 178–203.

United Nations (2005) *2005 World Summit Outcome*. Resolution Adopted by the General Assembly, A/RES/60/1, 24 October.

United Nations (2006) "Co-Chairs' Summary of the Informal Consultative Process on the Institutional Framework for the UN's Environmental Activities", New York, 27 June, ⟨http://www.un.org/ga/president/61/follow-up/environment/Letter-Summary-Co-Chairs.pdf⟩ (accessed 14 February 2012).

United Nations (2009) "Informal Consultations of the General Assembly on the Institutional Framework for the United Nations' Environment Work: Report", 10 February, ⟨http://www.un.org/ga/president/63/PDFs/ReportIEG100209.pdf⟩ (accessed 14 February 2012).

Young, O. R. (2008) "The Architecture of Global Environmental Governance: Bringing Science to Bear on Policy", *Global Environmental Politics*, 8(1): 14–32.

11

Oceans and sustainability: The governance of marine areas beyond national jurisdiction

Marjo Vierros, Anne McDonald and Salvatore Arico

Introduction

In 2002, the World Summit on Sustainable Development adopted the Johannesburg Plan of Implementation (JPOI), which contained a set of strong targets on oceans, coastal areas and islands. The JPOI (United Nations, 2002) included targets related to topics such as application of the ecosystem approach by 2010 (para. 30(d)); maintenance and restoration of fish stocks no later than 2015 (para. 31(a)); and the use of diverse approaches and tools for promoting the conservation and sustainable use of resources, including representative networks of marine protected areas by 2012 (para. 32(c)). The adoption of these targets represented a commitment by governments to undertake urgent action towards the conservation and sustainable use of ocean resources and biodiversity.

Ten years later, it has become evident that the targets will likely not be reached on a global scale by their specified timelines. Nationally and regionally, though, they have catalysed activities towards improved management of ocean resources and biodiversity. Most countries have undertaken at least some actions within their national waters to put in place ecosystem-based management of marine resources, improve fisheries management and implement marine protected areas and networks (CBD, 2010a). Although these actions are not collectively sufficient to reduce biodiversity loss in the face of increasing pressures (CBD, 2010a; Vierros et al., 2011), they represent a step in the right direction. The failure to reach the targets also highlights the difficulties of prioritizing

Green economy and good governance for sustainable development: Opportunities, promises and concerns, Puppim de Oliveira (ed.),
United Nations University Press, 2012, ISBN 978-92-808-1216-9

environmental protection in the midst of economic uncertainty; the complex nature of the connections between human development, population growth and biodiversity loss; and the need to develop and test additional and creative solutions to combat biodiversity loss (Mora and Sale, 2011).

The actions undertaken in response to the targets in the JPOI have almost universally been in areas under national jurisdiction. This leaves the majority, or 64 per cent of the surface of the ocean and nearly 95 per cent of its volume, severely under-protected. These deep seabed[1] and open ocean[2] areas hold enormous biodiversity and provide goods and services of importance to humankind, as is described later in this chapter. Biodiversity in deep sea habitats and open ocean waters (both within and beyond national jurisdiction) faces serious threats from resource exploitation and the impacts of climate change and ocean acidification, but its holistic and comprehensive management in areas beyond national jurisdiction has been difficult to achieve owing to the status of those areas as the global commons. The lack of equitable access to genetic resources in the deep seabed beyond national jurisdiction, as well as the lack of benefit-sharing, has created a divide between some developed and developing countries that needs to be bridged for meaningful conservation and management to be achieved. Lessons from coastal management and the management of exclusive economic zones may be applied to marine areas beyond the limits of national jurisdiction to ensure that modern conservation principles and tools are utilized and that conservation and sustainable use go hand-in-hand with concerns related to equity.

The United Nations Conference on Environment and Development to be held in 2012 (Rio+20) provides an opportunity for countries to address and provide meaningful leadership in the management and conservation of marine areas beyond national jurisdiction, as well as equity in the use of marine genetic resources. With the momentum gained on these issues at recent meetings at the United Nations, the time is right to make progress on providing for the sustainable use of this unique and diverse portion of our planet and the resources therein, and to enhance our ability to reach targets adopted by the World Summit on Sustainable Development in 2002.

The importance of biodiversity in deep and open oceans

The deep seabed and open oceans of the world that lie beyond the jurisdiction of individual countries were long considered remote, hostile and biologically barren. Although these areas have captured the imagination of explorers both past and present, the vast majority of the world's population has not given them much thought, and their management and conservation have taken a back seat to more pressing day-to-day concerns. Hence, these areas were viewed as a source of fish proteins and as routes for transporting commodities, cruise-ship tourism, military activities or the laying of underwater cables, all with practically no strings attached. In fact, these and other human activities in the deep and open oceans,[3] including oil and mineral exploration and marine scientific research, were conducted with little attention to possible adverse impacts on the marine environment. Yet, recent research has shown that open oceans and deep seas not only are incredibly diverse biologically also are vital for our survival on Earth (Koslow, 2007). Our economies, be they global or local, and our livelihoods and well-being are directly tied to the food resources, climate regulation and potential for scientific and technological innovation that are provided by the oceans. Without them, life as we know it would not be possible. Similarly, sustainable development will not be achievable without their improved management.

Recent scientific studies have shown that biodiversity in the oceans provides numerous benefits to people, which include food resources, regulation of the Earth's climate and cancer-curing medicines. Life in the deep sea has been found to play a fundamental role in global biogeochemical cycles, including nutrient regeneration and production of oxygen, as well as the maintenance of the Earth's climate through the global carbon cycle (Armstrong et al., 2010; Riser and Johnson, 2008; Smith et al., 2009). An estimated 50 per cent of the carbon in the atmosphere that becomes bound or "sequestered" in natural systems is cycled into the seas and oceans. Not only do oceans represent the largest long-term sink for carbon but they also store and redistribute carbon dioxide (CO_2). Some 93 per cent of the Earth's CO_2 is stored and cycled through the oceans (Armstrong et al., 2010).

The value of fisheries to humankind has been well documented. According to the Food and Agriculture Organization of the United Nations, fish provides more than 1.5 billion people globally with almost 20 per cent of their average per capita intake of animal protein. The number doubles to 3 billion for those whom fish provides 15 per cent of their animal protein intake. In 2007, total animal protein from fish was 18.3 per cent in developing countries and 20.1 per cent in low-income food-deficit countries (FAO, 2010). Fishing fleets have shifted to fishing further offshore and in deeper waters to meet global demand since the 1960s (Cochonat et al., 2007; Morato et al., 2006). The deep sea is a source of several important and lucrative commercial species, which include the orange roughy, roundnose grenadier, redfish, oreos and blue ling, as well as shellfish, such as crab and shrimp. A third of shark and ray species spend most of their life in the deep sea (Morato et al., 2006). Important deep sea habitats, including cold water coral reefs and seamounts, are believed to be crucial in supporting fish populations (Armstrong et al., 2010).

The value of the enormous biodiversity found in the deep seas is not yet well understood owing to our limited knowledge about the full range of species that inhabit this remote part of the planet and the functioning of ecosystems there. Current estimates of species diversity range from 500,000 to 10 million species (Census of Marine Life, 2010; Koslow, 2007), with new species being continuously discovered. This potential for discovery of new species, genes and adaptations is of great interest to biotechnology. Many deep sea organisms have adapted to life under extreme conditions (so-called "extremophiles"), and thus have unusual molecular and metabolic adaptations. This is particularly true of bacteria found on and around hydrothermal vents, where toxic, high temperature conditions prevail, but also of bacteria found in the deep seabed, the water column and polar environments (Turley, 2000). Not surprisingly, the deep seas are considered to represent the largest reservoir of genetic resources, including some of major interest for commercial and industrial applications. A recent study (Yooseph et al., 2007) reports the discovery of thousands of new genes and proteins in just a few litres of water, promising many potential new functions.

Investigations of the unusual characteristics of deep sea and polar organisms have already resulted in a number of patents and products covering a diverse range of functions, from the development of enzymes for industrial processes to pharmaceuticals and skin care products (Leary et al., 2009). For example, an enzyme extracted from a microbe from the Mid-Atlantic Ridge is currently used in the development of biofuels. Antarctic and deep water sponges are sources of potential pharmaceuticals, including a cancer drug now undergoing testing. Some fish and other organisms from polar areas have yielded anti-freeze proteins used for the control of cold-induced damage in medical, food and cosmetic products (Arico and Salpin, 2005; Leary et al., 2009; UNU-IAS, 2012).

It has recently become evident that high biodiversity has values beyond its potential for innovation, and that these values relate directly to ecosystem functioning and the provision of services. In coastal seas, biodiversity has been found to be a major contributor to ecosystem resilience to change and a provider of valuable goods and services (Hughes et al., 2005). For example, the value of coral reefs to humankind has been estimated to be between USD 130,000 and USD 1.2 million per hectare, per year, and "some 30 million people in coastal and island communities are totally reliant on reef-based resources as their primary means of food production, income and livelihood" (TEEB, 2010: 8). Because the deep seas are now known to be home to a major part of the world's biodiversity, it is likely that they also provide services related to resilience and functioning. This theory is supported by recent research, which shows that ecosystem functioning is positively and exponentially related to biodiversity in all deep sea regions investigated, and thus a reduction in biodiversity would have profound impacts on ecosystem functioning (Danovaro et al., 2008).

The case for improved management

Despite their high biodiversity, the deep and open oceans beyond national jurisdiction are some of the least protected areas on Earth. This may have to do with their status as a "global commons", where their ownership is shared by all countries and their citizens, and thus their conservation is not a specific responsibility of any one country or group. For a long time, the resources in the oceans were thought to be endless, and their use was primarily guided by the concept of "freedom of the seas" (Rayfuse, 2010). *Mare Liberum* or freedom of the seas was a principle coined by the Dutch jurist and philosopher Hugo Grotius in 1609. According to this principle, the sea was considered to be international territory, and all nations were free to use it for seafaring trade.

The United Nations Convention on the Law of the Sea (UNCLOS), adopted in 1982 and entered into force in 1994 and often considered to be the "constitution for the oceans",[4] similarly provides that the high seas are open to all states in accordance with the freedom of the high seas, which includes navigation, overflight, fishing, scientific research, laying of submarine cables and pipelines, and construction of artificial islands and other installations permitted under international law (United Nations, 1982). These freedoms are to be exercised by all states with due regard for the interests of other states in their exercise of the freedom of the high seas, and also with due regard for the rights under UNCLOS with respect to activities in the "Area".[5] These freedoms also come with obligations, and the freedom of the high seas must be exercised under the conditions laid down by UNCLOS and other rules of international law (UNCLOS, Article 87). These conditions include those laid down in Section 2 of Part VII on the conservation and management of the marine living resources of the high seas, Part VI on the continental shelf and Part XIII on marine scientific research. This also includes the general obligation to preserve the marine environment (Kimball, 2005).

The text of UNCLOS, which balances freedom with responsibility, may be viewed as an emerging understanding that the mounting pressures on oceans, which include fishing, shipping, pollution, ocean dumping, and oil, gas and mineral exploration could result in a "tragedy of the commons". In the 1980s, modern technology such as faster ships and refrigeration enabled the exploitation of deeper and more distant areas, resulting in loss of biodiversity and depletion of fish stocks (Pauly et al., 2002), a trend that continues today. In addition, climate change and ocean acidification increasingly threaten oceans and the life within them. As a result, even the deepest oceans are no longer pristine and untouched, and pressures on ecosystems and species in these areas are increasing (van den Hove and Moreau, 2008).

These pressures are now relatively well documented by recent global marine and environmental assessments (for example, the Millennium Ecosystem Assessment, the Global International Waters Assessment, the Global Environment Outlook, the Global Biodiversity Outlook and the Assessment of Assessments) and a body of published scientific research. All have found serious declines in marine living resources, losses of habitats, elevated pollution levels, poor water quality in many areas, and overall deterioration of the marine environment exacerbated by the effects of climate change and, in the future, ocean acidification. Economies on both local and global scales are adversely affected by such trends, which put the capacity of the marine environment beyond its sustainable limit.

For example, the biological resources of seamounts have been targets of intensive exploitation, resulting in over-fishing and major crashes in stocks on some seamounts (Clark and Koslow, 2007), along with large impacts on the benthic communities of many studied seamounts caused mainly by bottom fishing (Collie et al., 2000; Koslow et al., 2000; Watling et al., 2007; Watson and Morato, 2004). Most cold water coral reefs that have been studied thus far show physical damage from trawling activities (Hourigan et al., 2008). Overall, 80 per cent of the world's fish stocks for which assessment information is available are reported as fully exploited or overexploited and are in particular need of effective and precautionary management (FAO, 2008); and exploitation of fish and other biodiversity in the deep sea has increased worldwide, especially over the last 20 years (Sissenwine and Mace, 2007). Stocks assessed since 1977 have experienced an 11 per cent decline in total biomass globally, with considerable regional variation, and the average maximum size has declined by 22 per cent since 1959 globally (Worm et al., 2009).

The environmental impacts of shipping include the spread of invasive alien species, pollution and oil spills. With 90 per cent of world trade carried by sea, the global network of merchant ships provides one of the most important modes of transportation for the spread of invasive species through discharged ballast water and hull fouling. Invasive species have caused species extinctions and damage to ecosystems, livelihoods, health and economies in coastal areas throughout the world (Kaluza et al., 2010). In the United States alone, the financial loss related to biological invasions is estimated at USD 120 billion per year (Pimental et al.,

2005). Other shipping impacts include the release of oil through accidental or illegal discharge and air pollution. The growing Arctic ship traffic will also bring with it air pollution that has the potential to accelerate climate change, increasing warming by approximately 17–78 per cent (Corbett et al., 2010).

Mining of polymetallic sulphide deposits associated with hydrothermal vent systems poses a future threat, which is moving closer to becoming a reality as the first applications for mining in the seabed beyond the limits of national jurisdiction have been filed with the International Seabed Authority. Because most invertebrate diversity at hydrothermal vents consists of rare species, habitat destruction by mining could be devastating to local and regional populations (CBD, 2008). The environmental impacts of such mining are unknown, but would involve disturbance to benthic ecosystems and communities (Koslow, 2007; van Dover, 2010).

Other threats include those resulting from a burgeoning carbon economy, which provides incentives for commercial experimentation with ocean fertilization and deep sea carbon sequestration. Both of these techniques come with possible environmental impacts, including the potential to exacerbate chemical changes to the oceans, with potentially serious consequences for biodiversity (CBD, 2009).

These human pressures will combine with the impacts of climate change, which will become more severe in the future. Ocean acidity has increased by 30 per cent since pre-industrial times owing to the uptake of anthropogenic CO_2. It is projected to rise by another 100 per cent by 2100 if CO_2 emissions continue at current rates, resulting in conditions corrosive for calcareous organisms in polar oceans as early as 2050 (Orr et al., 2005). Cold water corals and calcareous plankton at the basis of the polar food webs will probably be affected. There is little doubt that ocean warming and acidification, as well as other climate-induced changes, will have an impact on life in the deep ocean, but the manner in which this will happen is nearly impossible to predict because of our limited understanding of the functioning of deep sea ecosystems (Koslow, 2007).

Accelerated resource depletion, environmental degradation and increased pressures on the oceans in the absence of improved management could contribute to increased economic losses. For example, it is estimated that USD 50 billion is lost annually from global marine fisheries as a result of overexploitation of commercially valued fish stocks owing to inflated subsidies, inadequate regulation and lack of enforcement of existing rules; from 1974 to 2008 the estimated cumulative loss was USD 2.2 trillion (IBRD/World Bank, 2009). "[T]he failure to account for the full economic values of ecosystems and biodiversity has been a significant factor in their continuing loss and degradation" (TEEB, 2010: 9; CBD,

2010b). Economic valuation of deep and open seas could contribute to sustainable management and net economic benefits as opposed to depletion, degradation and global economic losses. Potentially, too, sustainable management of the oceans could contribute to equity and an improvement in the income security of a larger percentage of global citizens.

The growing body of scientific research documenting resource depletion, the nearing of ecological limits and the worsening state of the ocean environment indicates that the era of the freedom of the seas is over. In fact, the oceans are already being increasingly regulated through a landscape of international and regional agreements (Rayfuse, 2010). Chief amongst these agreements is UNCLOS, which provides the overarching framework for ocean uses by all states. In addition, other international agreements, such as the Convention on Biological Diversity (CBD), various fisheries agreements and agreements relating to marine pollution regulate specific activities and provide for conservation measures. Regional agreements, where they exist, complete the web of regulation and provide increasingly specific rules on the use and conservation of shared regional resources. Some of these, such as the Antarctic Treaty System, are sophisticated agreements that have pioneered new approaches for the implementation of the ecosystem and precautionary approaches. Others are focused on regulating the harvest of a single species, with no ecosystem considerations and no ability to regulate anything else (Gjerde et al., 2008). Additionally, how well each of these instruments is implemented by member states varies broadly.

Although there is more that could be done to improve the implementation of existing instruments, there has also been much international debate recently about whether the international legal regime, in all its complexity, is sufficient to regulate all human uses and activities in the oceans, and thus provide protection for biodiversity. A systematic analysis of both geographical and substantive coverage of existing legal instruments related to the oceans (Gjerde et al., 2008) shows clearly that, when viewed together, the existing agreements do not yet adequately address all uses of ocean space and resources. The geographical coverage of the regional agreements does not span all oceans, and there are a number of activities, including biological prospecting and new and emerging activities such as climate change mitigation techniques, that do not have detailed international rules and standards. Modern conservation principles such as the ecosystem approach and the precautionary approach are not consistently incorporated, and it is not possible to apply area-based management tools, such as marine protected areas (MPAs), consistently across all oceans. Also lacking are environmental impact assessment (EIA) and strategic environmental assessment (SEA) tools (Gjerde et al., 2008). The latter of these would allow for the assessment of cumulative impacts over time and across different sectors. In short, we lack a toolbox for the conservation and management of the oceans, and the existing legal instruments are complex, fragmented and often sectorally rather than holistically oriented.

Given these deficiencies, it is not surprising that the world's oceans as a whole are poorly managed. Overall, only approximately 1.17 per cent of the oceans receive some level of protection inside MPAs. However, this figure is deceiving. Areas closer to shore are generally better managed and protected, with 4.32 per cent of continental shelves covered by protected areas. Deep seabed and open ocean areas beyond national jurisdiction receive very little protection of any kind, compromising the sustainable management of resources found there. It should also be noted that these figures apply only to MPAs and that other area-based management measures also exist, though there is no current estimate of their coverage (Toropova et al., 2010). In general, most of those management measures are employed within national jurisdiction.

Although these figures paint a grim picture of ocean protection beyond national jurisdiction, there are some bright spots of recent conservation success. For example, the Convention for the Protection of the Marine Environment of the North-East Atlantic (the OSPAR Convention) has made substantial progress in identifying potential MPAs beyond national jurisdiction. In 2010, the OSPAR Ministerial Meeting took the significant step of adopting decisions establishing six MPAs in areas beyond national jurisdiction and adopted recommendations on their initial management (OSPAR, 2010). Several Regional Fisheries Management Organisations (RFMOs) have closed off vulnerable marine ecosystems to fisheries. For example, the Northwest Atlantic Fisheries Organization adopted bottom fishing closures on five seamounts. The North East Atlantic Fisheries Commission prohibited bottom trawling and fishing with static gear on four seamounts and a section of the Mid-Atlantic Ridge in 2004, with additional closures in 2007 and 2008. In 2006, the South East Atlantic Fisheries Organisation identified 13 vulnerable areas (mostly seamounts) and closed 10 of them to all bottom fishing for an interim period. These initiatives demonstrate that it is possible to make immediate progress in conserving biodiversity beyond national jurisdiction using existing legal instruments (CBD, 2010a).

Given the increasing threats to biodiversity in the oceans and the gaps in the existing legal regime, marine areas beyond the limits of national jurisdiction present a particularly urgent challenge that can be resolved only collectively by the global community. Access to resources beyond national jurisdiction is open to everyone, with the consequence that there is generally a drive to maximize individual profit and there are limited incentives to conserve and sustainably manage resources. With an ongoing intensification of existing and new uses in these areas, a number of governments are now increasingly focused on finding the most effective way to regulate uses and realize responsibilities for conservation and sustainable use. As will be seen in the following sections, there have been calls to undertake this through the development of a new multilateral agreement under UNCLOS.

The need for equity

The case for the conservation and sustainable use of biodiversity in marine areas beyond national jurisdiction is a compelling one, but it cannot be achieved without concurrently addressing equity between ocean users, including states. The basic reason for this lies in the nature of the deep seas, which are remote and difficult to access; to reach them requires a very significant input of financial resources and, often, sophisticated technology. Only developed countries with substantial financial resources are able to mount scientific expeditions with the sophisticated research vessels, instrumentation, submersibles and remotely operated vehicles that are required to explore these areas (Zewers, 2008). Countries that are able to explore and sample deep sea environments are also able to benefit from the resulting discoveries. As was discussed in the previous section, deep sea organisms have been the source of a number of important patents and products ranging from pharmaceuticals to enzymes used in industrial processes, as well as other beneficial and potentially lucrative innovations (Arico and Salpin, 2005; Leary et al., 2009). Because so much of the deep sea is still unexplored, and because it contains high biodiversity and hosts organisms that have adapted to extremes of temperature and pressure, the potential for discovery is enormous. In addition, the development of new molecular and high-speed genetic sequencing techniques has facilitated faster sequencing and investigation of previously obscure micro-organisms. For example, recent research expeditions in the Sargasso Sea found 1,800 new species of microbes, including 150 new species of bacteria, and over 1.2 million new genes (Venter et al., 2004).

And therein lies the problem. A survey of patents associated with marine genes shows that they originate from only 31 of the 194 countries in the world, and 10 countries own 90 per cent of all the patents related to marine genetic resources. These countries represent only about 20 per cent of the world's coastline but are able to benefit from access to advanced technologies to explore the oceans (Arnaud-Haond et al., 2011). Because these countries benefit from any resulting financial rewards associated with the patents, they are also able to invest more resources into exploring the deep sea and making further discoveries. Thus, both the capacity and income gaps are likely to widen further with time, unless there is a serious investment in capacity-building and technology transfer.

The capacity imbalance and the increasing privatization of what is seen as a common resource have resulted in many developing countries seeking to address the issue within the United Nations. In particular, there are two processes mandated by the UN General Assembly to consider issues related to oceans: the Ad Hoc Open-ended Informal Working Group to study issues relating to the conservation and sustainable use of marine biological diversity beyond areas of national jurisdiction (the Working Group) and the Open-ended Informal Consultative Process on Oceans and the Law of the Sea (the Consultative Process).

This debate is particularly complicated because international law is not clear as regards the status of genetic resources in the seabed and ocean floor beyond the limits of national jurisdiction. UNCLOS was drafted before the exploitation of genetic resources in the deep seabed was foreseen, and thus it deals explicitly only with the exploitation of mineral resources (Kimball, 2005) and fisheries. UNCLOS divides marine space into a number of zones, both within and beyond the limits of national jurisdiction. The areas beyond national jurisdiction are divided into two zones: (i) all parts of the sea that are not included in the exclusive economic zone, in the territorial sea or in the internal waters of a state, or in the archipelagic waters of an archipelagic State (Article 86); and (ii) "the seabed and ocean floor and subsoil thereof, beyond the limits of national jurisdiction", designated as "the Area" (Article 1, para. 1). The Area and its resources are, according to UNCLOS, the common heritage of mankind, and their exploration and exploitation shall be carried out for the benefit of mankind as a whole (UNCLOS, Articles 136 and 140). The resources are defined as all solid, liquid or gaseous mineral resources in situ in the Area at or beneath the seabed, including polymetallic nodules (Article 133), but living or genetic resources are not explicitly mentioned. The high seas, on the other hand, are free for all states to use with due regard for other states' interests (see above).

Because UNCLOS is not explicit with regard to marine genetic resources to be found in areas beyond national jurisdiction, there has been considerable debate within the United Nations about whether marine genetic resources are subject to the "common heritage of mankind" regime in the same way that seabed mineral resources are, or to "freedom of the high seas". The implication is that, if they are covered by the common heritage of mankind principle, then some form of benefit-sharing should take place between those countries that are collecting and commercializing genetic resources from the Area and those that do not have the means to do so.

Most developing countries, particularly the G-77 and China, support the common heritage principle. According to a statement made by the G-77 and China at the UN Working Group in May/June 2011:

> [T]the exclusive exploitation by a few [has] serious global economic and social implications. We would like to stress how inconsistent this manner of exploitation is with general principles of international law, in particular those on equity; principles that are also enshrined in UNCLOS, as the Area and its resources are to be explored and exploited for the benefit of mankind as a whole. (Group of 77, 2011)

Many developed countries do not support this viewpoint, arguing that the products derived from marine genetic resources, such as pharmaceuticals, already benefit all countries.

The debate on this issue remained deadlocked for many years, until the UN Working Group in 2011 made progress by recommending that a process be initiated by the General Assembly with a view to ensuring that the legal framework for the conservation and sustainable use of marine biodiversity in areas beyond national jurisdiction effectively addresses those issues by identifying gaps and ways forward, including through the implementation of existing instruments and the possible development of a multilateral agreement under UNCLOS. The process would consider marine genetic resources, including questions on the sharing of benefits, measures such as area-based management tools, including MPAs and EIAs, capacity-building and the transfer of marine technology. The UN General Assembly, in Resolution A/RES/66/231, agreed to initiate the process as described above.

The dialogue on benefit-sharing received a boost from the 2010 adoption of the Nagoya Protocol on Access to Genetic Resources and the Fair and Equitable Sharing of Benefits Arising from their Utilization to the Convention on Biological Diversity (Nagoya Protocol). The Nagoya Protocol is an international agreement that aims at sharing the benefits arising from the utilization of genetic resources in a fair and equitable way, including by appropriate access to genetic resources and by appropriate transfer of relevant technologies, taking into account all rights over those resources and to technologies, and by appropriate funding, thereby contributing to the conservation of biological diversity and the sustainable use of its components. It was adopted by the Conference of the Parties to the CBD at its tenth meeting on 29 October 2010 in Nagoya, Japan (CBD, 2011). The Nagoya Protocol is open for signature by Parties to the Convention from 2 February 2011 until 1 February 2012 at the United Nations Headquarters in New York.[6]

There was considerable debate during the many years of negotiation leading up to the Protocol about whether it should apply to genetic resources in areas beyond national jurisdiction. In the end, the Protocol as adopted applies only to genetic resources falling within the scope of Article 15 of the Convention, which is to say within national jurisdiction. However, Article 10 of the Protocol provides a possible pathway for developing a global multilateral benefit-sharing mechanism. The article states that:

> Parties shall consider the need for and modalities of a global multilateral benefit-sharing mechanism to address the fair and equitable sharing of benefits derived from the utilization of genetic resources and traditional knowledge associated with genetic resources that occur in transboundary situations or for which it is not possible to grant or obtain prior informed consent. The benefits shared by users of genetic resources and traditional knowledge associated with genetic resources through this mechanism shall be used to support the conservation of biological diversity and the sustainable use of its components globally. (CBD, 2011: Article 10)

Article 10 thus provides for an enabling cause that could be used towards future negotiation of a benefit-sharing mechanism for marine areas beyond the limits of national jurisdiction, as well as other global commons, such as Antarctica.

It seems clear that, whatever future negotiations will be undertaken, the process will be a long and difficult one. For the results to be viable, they would need to consider equitable access to, and benefit-sharing of, marine genetic resources in areas beyond national jurisdiction, as well as their conservation and sustainable use. As Article 10 of the Nagoya Protocol indicates, these components are directly linked and the benefits generated from the commercialization of genetic resources should contribute to financing conservation and sustainable use. The mechanism of how this might happen is unclear, but there have been proposals relating to the generation of conservation trusts in which a certain percentage of profits would be held (for example, Leary et al., 2009). While this debate remains unresolved, there is, overall, a need for forms of regulation and governance that foster equity and limit adverse environmental impacts. There may also be a need for evaluating successful strategies for management and benefit-sharing from coastal areas to see how and whether they might apply to oceans beyond national jurisdiction.

Regardless of how future negotiations on this topic unfold, it is clear that capacity-building and technology transfer will need to be part of the solution to address the capacity gap in marine scientific research. This may include the participation of developing country scientists in deep sea expeditions and training and technology transfer on new molecular biology and DNA sequencing techniques.

Lessons from coastal area management that can be applied further offshore

As efforts to better manage and protect biodiversity and resources in marine areas beyond the limits of national jurisdiction gain international momentum, there are some lessons that could be learned from the many decades of experience that countries have in applying integrated marine and coastal area management in their national waters (for example, AIDEnvironment et al., 2004; CBD, 2006; Cicin-Sain and Knecht, 1998; Kay and Alder, 1999; Ramsar Convention Secretariat, 2007; Sorensen, 2002; Thia-Eng, 1993, 1998). Coastal environments and exclusive economic zones should, admittedly, be easier to govern in that they fall under national laws and policies and have in place institutions and mechanisms for management and enforcement. Regardless, coastal managers are confronted with the need to work with multiple stakeholders and levels of government from local to national. They need to take into account the concerns and priorities of sectoral entities ranging from coastal development to fisheries, tourism and shipping, as well as provide for equity and access and benefit-sharing arrangements. Many environmental problems call for the coordinated efforts of neighbouring countries or regions sharing common ecosystems, resources or routes of migratory species, thus requiring processes and institutions for regional collaboration. The difference in managing areas beyond and within national jurisdiction is one of ownership, rights and responsibility, in that beyond national jurisdiction no one owns the ocean and its resources but everyone has a right to utilize them, and thus no one is directly responsible for their conservation in spite of the general obligation to protect and preserve the marine environment.

Although these fundamental differences of ownership and rights exist, some lessons learned from coastal management could apply for marine areas beyond national jurisdiction, and can be condensed from publications addressing integrated and ecosystem-based management both within and beyond national jurisdiction (CBD, 2006; Freestone, 2008; Toropova et al., 2010; Vierros et al., 2006, 2011). Amongst these are the following:
- All management is place based and is centred on an ecosystem or area of concern. This may be a seamount or a group of seamounts threatened by unsustainable fishing, an upwelling system or confluence of

currents that is particularly productive, or a set of habitats that are important for migratory species. Regardless of the specific case, the most effective management approach is an *ecosystem approach* that takes into account not only the species in question but also their interactions with other species, their environment (biological, physical and chemical) and the humans who are users of the ecosystem.
- There is never enough scientific information to create absolute certainty in management decisions. This is true both in relatively data-rich coastal areas and even more so in deep and open oceans where there is a paucity of scientific data. Experience has shown that the most effective way to deal with uncertainty is to manage using the *precautionary approach*. Thus, by nature, exploitation of resources should be conservative and have built-in safety limits.
- The well-being of an ecosystem or species needs to be a common concern of all stakeholders, and thus everyone will need to have a voice in decisions related to conservation and management. Ownership is built through participation, and those coastal management efforts that have been built upon genuine *stakeholder participation* have generally been most successful.
- The costs and benefits of conservation and management need to be equitably shared. This includes both the costs of activities, such as putting in place and managing MPAs, as well as the benefits derived from the protection and exploitation of resources. Thus *equity* is an important principle of successful management, and examples of access and benefit-sharing arrangements in coastal areas, although fundamentally different, may offer some guidance for implementing agreements beyond national jurisdiction.
- Management should be underpinned and supported by the *best available science*, which in some cases may be local or traditional knowledge. The availability of timely and management-relevant scientific research is a vital component of successful management and should encompass monitoring for the purposes of *adaptive management*.

In addition to these general principles, there exists a large body of experience from many countries and regions of the world about the use of modern conservation tools, such as MPAs, EIAs and SEAs (Toropova et al., 2010). In some cases, these tools have been applied in deep water systems that resemble those that are found beyond national jurisdiction. This experience provides valuable insight into the management and governance of all of the world's oceans (Freestone, 2008).

One practical example of how experience gained in coastal areas has been used to facilitate protection of marine areas beyond national jurisdiction comes from the CBD, and relates to the identification of ecologically and biologically significant areas (EBSAs). EBSAs are areas of the ocean that meet certain criteria that will make them high priorities for management or protection. The criteria for this purpose were adopted by the Conference of the Parties to the CBD in 2006 after a long process that included a review of national criteria and two expert group meetings. The identification of an EBSA is a scientific first step in a longer process that will eventually lead to the consideration of an appropriate management regime for the area (CBD, 2009). At the present time, the CBD Secretariat is coordinating a set of regional workshops that will start the scientific process of identification of such EBSAs. The declaration and management of identified EBSAs in areas beyond national jurisdiction cannot be done under the CBD, however, and some other process, regional or global, will need to be found to perform this vital step.

A similar process of identifying vulnerable marine ecosystems (VMEs) is being undertaken by many RFMOs. The criteria for identifying VMEs are similar to the CBD EBSA criteria (Gjerde, 2010), with the distinction that VMEs are put in place primarily to protect vulnerable areas from the impacts of bottom fishing practices and can be directly designated by the RFMO in question (FAO, 2009).

Both the EBSA and the VME processes are examples of how the lessons of area-based protection and management learned in coastal areas can be transferred further offshore and into marine areas beyond national jurisdiction. Both processes are only now starting, and no doubt there will be further experience gained as their application progresses. It is also hoped that the concurrent work on EBSAs and VMEs results in much-needed collaboration between conservation and fisheries sectors (Gjerde, 2010). There is already some evidence that this may be the case, as the OSPAR Commission and the North East Atlantic Fisheries Commission prepared to hold a joint workshop in late 2011 to identify EBSAs in the North Atlantic. Further such joint workshops between fisheries and conservation agencies to identify areas for protection and management are likely to result in increased cooperation and coherence in policy-making (Gjerde, 2010).

Similarly, EIAs and SEAs have long been required by many national authorities around the world prior to some types of coastal development (Freestone, 2008; Toropova et al., 2010). Although guidelines for EIAs and SEAs exist, none are specific to marine environments beyond national jurisdiction. Of the global and regional legal instruments that apply to marine areas, only the Antarctic Treaty System, and specifically its Madrid Protocol, has in place stringent EIA provisions, although the OSPAR Convention has recently adopted them. The CBD Secretariat is currently facilitating the development of voluntary guidelines for the consideration of biodiversity in EIAs and SEAs in marine and coastal areas, which would be particularly applicable to activities that are currently unregulated and have no process for assessing impacts. These voluntary guidelines could provide a useful basis for developing regulations relating to EIAs and SEAs for marine areas beyond the limits of national jurisdiction in the future, and could facilitate further sectoral cooperation and mainstreaming of biodiversity concerns into the work of sectoral and development agencies (Gjerde, 2010).

As is evident from the progress already made, regional initiatives might be key in applying lessons learned from coastal management in local areas to the global level. The Regional Seas Programme of the United Nations Environment Programme could be developed to better link activities among the 13 regional partner programmes focusing first on integrated action plans among the five partner programmes for the Antarctic, Arctic, North-East Atlantic, Baltic Sea and Caspian Sea regions. Other regional initiatives such as Partnerships in Environmental Management for the Seas of East Asia, OSPAR and the Joint Baltic Research Programme, as well as RFMOs that strive to facilitate the implementation of ecosystem-based management and provide interdisciplinary research to guide managers and other stakeholders, could act as facilitators for better governance and sustainable resource use in open oceans and the deep seabed, both within and beyond national jurisdiction.

Options for governance and the way forward in the context of Rio+20

It is evident that biodiversity in the oceans, including in areas beyond national jurisdiction, continues to face multiple and increasing pressures. Unless these pressures are adequately managed or reduced, marine resources and biodiversity will continue to decline, to the detriment of economies and human well-being locally and globally. The targets relating to oceans and coasts adopted by the World Summit on Sustainable Development in 2002 will also probably not be reached under the current conditions, because the oceans as a whole are still relatively underprotected and poorly managed. Because marine areas beyond national jurisdiction are considered to be global commons, resources in these areas have, in many cases, been unsustainably exploited. The future will bring a number of unforeseen challenges, including a warming climate and acidification and its impacts. Related to this is the emergence of new technologies (ocean fertilization, carbon sequestration, floating wind farms) that are not yet fully addressed by existing legal regimes.

The current international legal regime covering marine areas beyond national jurisdiction is complex and fractured. Many of the older agreements are reflections of their time and do not fully consider the impacts of human activities on ecosystems and non-target species. Modern conservation principles such as the ecosystem and precautionary approaches, and tools such as MPAs and EIAs, are not comprehensively incorporated. There also remain geographical gaps in the regional regime, which leave large parts of the global commons without a regional agreement. Additionally, none of the agreements address the important issue of equity and the specifics of access and benefit-sharing beyond national jurisdiction as far as marine genetic resources are concerned (Gjerde et al., 2008).

Nonetheless, progress can be made through the implementation of existing instruments, and many important efforts towards area-based management are already under way. These efforts will no doubt help improve the state of biodiversity in selected areas in the short term. There also exist further possibilities for collaboration and cooperation between institutions and international agreements and for voluntary activities that can be undertaken by countries and regions. Although all such efforts are valuable, they are unlikely to be sufficient to reverse biodiversity loss in the oceans as a whole. Nor will they provide for comprehensive and coordinated management of all human activities in the oceans, while also addressing equity concerns related to marine genetic resources beyond national jurisdiction.

The Rio+20 Conference has, therefore, an important and valuable opportunity to consider the future conservation and management of marine areas beyond national jurisdiction. This includes ways and means for improved implementation of existing instruments, but also – following the consensus recommendations adopted by the UN Working Group on marine biodiversity beyond national jurisdiction in June 2011, and Resolution A/RES/66/231 of the UN General Assembly – the possible development of a multilateral agreement under UNCLOS. In accordance with recommendations of the Working Group, the agreement should address the conservation and sustainable use of marine biodiversity in areas beyond national jurisdiction, including through modern conservation measures (for example, area-based management tools such as MPAs and EIAs), together with marine genetic resources and modalities for benefit-sharing. It is important that all these issues be considered together and that they also include capacity-building and the transfer of marine technology. Improving the governance of marine areas beyond national jurisdiction will not only provide benefits for biodiversity but also help create more sustainable and equitable economies that can better withstand future environmental change.

Notes

1. Deep seabed is a non-legal term commonly understood by scientists to refer to the seafloor below 200–300 metres. In other words, it is non-shelf area.
2. Open ocean is a non-legal term commonly understood by scientists to refer to the water column beyond the continental shelf, in other words, non-coastal. Open ocean may occur in areas within national jurisdiction in states with a narrow continental shelf.
3. The terms "deep and open oceans" and "deep seas and open ocean" are non-legal terms encompassing the deep seabed and open ocean as described in notes 1 and 2.
4. See remarks by Tommy T. B. Koh of Singapore, President of the Third United Nations Conference on the Law of the Sea, at ⟨http://www.un.org/depts/los/convention_agreements/texts/koh_english.pdf⟩ (accessed 3 February 2012).
5. The "Area" is defined in UNCLOS as "the seabed and ocean floor and subsoil thereof, beyond the limits of national jurisdiction".
6. See ⟨http://www.cbd.int/abs/⟩ (accessed 8 February 2012).

REFERENCES

AIDEnvironment, National Institute for Coastal and Marine Management/ Rijksinstituut voor Kust en Zee (RIKZ), Coastal Zone Management Centre, The Netherlands (2004) *Integrated Marine and Coastal Area Management (IMCAM) Approaches for Implementing the Convention on Biological Diversity*, CBD Technical Series No. 14. Montreal, Canada: Secretariat of the Convention on Biological Diversity.

Arico S. and C. Salpin (2005) *Bioprospecting of Genetic Resources in the Deep Seabed: Scientific, Legal and Policy Aspects*. UNU-IAS Report. Tokyo, Japan: United Nations University Institute of Advanced Studies.

Armstrong, C. W., N. Foley, R. Tinch and S. van den Hove (2010) *Ecosystem Goods and Services of the Deep Sea*. HERMIONE Project. Available at ⟨http://median-web.eu/IMG/pdf/ecosystem_goods_and_services.pdf⟩ (accessed 3 February 2012).

Arnaud-Haond, S., J. M. Arrieta and C. M. Duarte (20100) "Marine Biodiversity and Gene Patents", *Science*, 331(6024): 1521–1522.

CBD (Convention on Biological Diversity) (2006) *Report of the Ad Hoc Technical Expert Group on Implementation of Integrated Marine and Coastal Area Management (IMCAM)*. UNEP/CBD/COP/8/INF/23, 12 February. Available at ⟨http://www.cbd.int/doc/meetings/cop/cop-08/information/cop-08-inf-23-en.pdf⟩ (accessed 3 February 2012).

CBD (Convention on Biological Diversity) (2008) *Synthesis and Review of the Best Available Scientific Studies on Priority Areas for Biodiversity Conservation in Marine Areas beyond the Limits of National Jurisdiction*, Technical Series No. 37. Montreal, Canada: Secretariat of the Convention on Biological Diversity.

CBD (Convention on Biological Diversity) (2009) "Azores Scientific Criteria and Guidance for Identifying Ecologically and Biologically Significant Marine Areas and Designing Representative Networks of Marine Protected Areas in

Open Ocean Waters and Deep Sea Habitats". Secretariat of the Convention on Biological Diversity, Montreal, Canada. Available at ⟨http://www.cbd.int/marine/doc/azores-brochure-en.pdf⟩ (accessed 3 February 2012).

CBD (Convention on Biological Diversity) (2010a) *Report on Implementation of the Programme of Work on Marine and Coastal Biological Diversity*. UNEP/CBD/SBSTTA/14/INF/2, 14 April. Available at ⟨http://www.cbd.int/doc/meetings/sbstta/sbstta-14/information/sbstta-14-inf-02-en.pdf⟩ (accessed 3 February 2012).

CBD (Convention on Biological Diversity) (2010b) *Global Biodiversity Outlook 3*. Montreal: Secretariat of the Convention on Biological Diversity. Available at ⟨http://www.cbd.int/doc/publications/gbo/gbo3-final-en.pdf⟩ (accessed 3 February 2012).

CBD (Convention on Biological Diversity) (2011) *Nagoya Protocol on Access to Genetic Resources and the Fair and Equitable Sharing of Benefits Arising from their Utilization to the Convention on Biological Diversity: Text and Annex*. Montreal: Secretariat of the Convention on Biological Diversity. Available at ⟨http://www.cbd.int/abs/⟩ (accessed 3 February 2012).

Census of Marine Life (2010) *First Census of Marine Life 2010: Highlights of a Decade of Discovery*. Washington DC: Census of Marine Life International Secretariat. Available at ⟨http://www.coml.org/pressreleases/census2010/PDF/Highlights-2010-Report-Low-Res.pdf⟩ (accessed 3 February 2012).

Cicin-Sain, B. and R. Knecht (1998) *Integrated Coastal and Ocean Management: Concepts and Practices*. Washington, DC: Island Press.

Clark, M. R. and J. A. Koslow (2007) "Impacts of Fisheries in Seamounts", in T. J. Pitcher, T. Morato, P. J. B. Hart, M. R. Clark, N. Haggan and R. E. Santos (eds), *Seamounts: Ecology, Fisheries and Conservation*. Oxford: Blackwell Publishing, pp. 413–441.

Cochonat, P., S. Durr, V. Gunn, P. Herzig, C. Mevel, J. Mienert, R. Schneider, P. Weaver and A. Winkler (2007) *The Deep-Sea Frontier: Science Challenges for a Sustainable Future*. Luxembourg: Office for Official Publications of the European Communities.

Collie, J. S., G. A. Escanero and P. C. Valentine (2000) "Photographic Evaluation of the Impacts of Bottom Fishing on Benthic Epifauna", *ICES Journal of Marine Science*, 57: 987–1001.

Corbett, J. J., D. A. Lack, J. J. Winebrake, S. Harder, J. A. Silberman and M. Gold (2010) "Arctic Shipping Emissions Inventories and Future Scenarios", *Atmospheric Chemistry and Physics*, 10(19): 9689.

Danovaro, R., C. Gambi, A. Dell'Anno, C. Corinaldesi, S. Fraschetti, A. Vanreusel, M. Vincx and A. J. Gooday (2008) "Exponential Decline of Deep-Sea Ecosystem Functioning Linked to Benthic Biodiversity Loss", *Current Biology*, 18: 1–8.

FAO (Food and Agriculture Organization of the United Nations) (2008) *State of the World Fisheries and Aquaculture 2008*. Rome: FAO.

FAO (Food and Agriculture Organization of the United Nations) (2009) *International Guidelines for the Management of Deep-Sea Fisheries in the High Seas*. Rome: FAO. Available at ⟨http://www.fao.org/docrep/011/i0816t/i0816t00.htm⟩ (accessed 3 February 2012).

FAO (Food and Agriculture Organization of the United Nations) (2010) *State of the World Fisheries and Aquaculture 2010*. Rome: FAO.

Freestone, D. (2008) "Principles Applicable to Modern Oceans Governance", *International Journal of Marine and Coastal Law*, 23(3): 385–391.

Gjerde, K. M., H. Dotinga, S. Hart, E. J. Molenaar, R. Rayfuse and R. Warner (2008) *Regulatory and Governance Gaps in the International Regime for the Conservation and Sustainable Use of Marine Biodiversity in areas beyond National Jurisdiction*, Marine Series No. 1. Gland, Switzerland: IUCN. Available at 〈http://data.iucn.org/dbtw-wpd/edocs/EPLP-MS-1.pdf〉 (accessed 3 February 2012).

Gjerde, K. M. (2010) "Modalities for Advancing Cross-Sectoral Cooperation in Managing Marine Areas Beyond National Jurisdiction", 12th Global Meeting of the Regional Seas Conventions and Action Plans, Bergen, Norway, 20–22 September 2010. United Nations Environment Programme Working Paper 8, UNEP (DEPI)/RS.12/8.

Group of 77 (2011) "Statement on Behalf of the Group of 77 and China by Minister Diego Limeres, Deputy Permanent Representative of the Permanent Mission of Argentina to the United Nations, at the Ad Hoc Open-Ended Informal Working Group to Study Issues Relating to the Conservation and Sustainable Use of Marine Biological Diversity beyond Areas of National Jurisdiction", New York, 31 May. Available at 〈http://www.g77.org/statement/getstatement.php?id=110531〉 (accessed 3 February 2012).

Hourigan, T. F., J. Boutillier, M. Clark, J. Hall-Spencer (2008) "The Status of Cold-Water Coral Communities of the World: A Brief Update", in C. Wilkinson (ed.), *Status of Coral Reefs of the World: 2008*. Townsville, Australia: Global Coral Reef Monitoring Network and Reef and Rainforest Research Centre, pp. 57–66.

Hughes, T. P., D. R. Bellwood, C. Folke, R. S. Steneck and J. Wilson (2005) "New Paradigms for Supporting the Resilience of Marine Ecosystems", *TRENDS in Ecology and Evolution*, 20(7): 380–386.

IBRD/World Bank (2009) *The Sunken Billions: The Economic Justification for Fisheries Reform*. Washington, DC: The World Bank. Available at 〈http://siteresources.worldbank.org/EXTARD/Resources/336681-1224775570533/SunkenBillionsFinal.pdf〉 (accessed 3 February 2012).

Kaluza, P., A. Kölzach, M. T. Gastner and B. Blasius (2010) "The Complex Network of Global Cargo Ship Movements", *Journal of the Royal Society Interface*, 7(48): 1093–1103.

Kay, R. and J. Alder (1999) *Coastal Planning and Management*. London: E & FN Spon.

Kimball, L. (2005) *The International Legal Regime of the High Seas and the Seabed beyond National Jurisdiction*, CBD Technical Series No. 19. Montreal, Canada: Secretariat of the Convention on Biological Diversity.

Koslow, T. (2007) *The Silent Deep: The Discovery, Ecology, and Conservation of the Deep Sea*. Sydney: UNSW Press.

Koslow, J. A., G. W. Boehlert, J. D. M. Gordon, R. L. Haedrich, P. Lorance and N. Parin (2000) "Continental Slope and Deep-Sea Fisheries: Implications for a Fragile Ecosystem", *ICES Journal of Marine Science*, 57: 548–557.

Leary, D., M. Vierros, G. Hamon, S. Arico and C. Monagle (2009) "Marine Genetic Resources: A Review of Scientific and Commercial Interest", *Marine Policy*, 33: 183–194.

Mora, C. and P. F. Sale (2011) "Ongoing Global Biodiversity Loss and the Need to Move beyond Protected Areas: A Review of the Technical and Practical Shortcomings of Protected Areas on Land and Sea", *Marine Ecology Progress Series*, 434: 251–266.

Morato, T., W. W. L. Cheung and T. J. Pitcher (2006) "Vulnerability of Seamount Fish to Fishing: Fuzzy Analysis of Life-history Attributes", *Journal of Fish Biology*, 67: 1–13.

Orr, J. C., V. J. Fabry, O. Aumont, L. Bopp, S. C. Doney, R. A. Feely, A. Gnanadesikan, N. Gruber, A. Ishida, F. Joos, R. M. Key, K. Lindsay, E. Maier-Reimer, R. Matear, P. Monfray, A. Mouchet, R. G. Najjar, G.-K. Plattner, K. B. Rodgers, C. L. Sabine, J. L. Sarmiento, R. Schlitzer, R. D. Slater, I. J. Totterdell, M.-F. Weirig, Y. Yamanaka and A. Yool (2005) "Anthropogenic Ocean Acidification over the Twenty-first Century and Its Impact on Calcifying Organisms", *Nature*, 437: 681–686.

OSPAR (2010) "OSPAR Network of Marine Protected Areas: MPAs in Areas beyond National Jurisdiction", ⟨http://www.ospar.org/content/content.asp?menu=00180302000011_000000_000000⟩ (accessed 3 February 2012).

Pauly, D. et al. (2002) "Towards Sustainability in World Fisheries", *Nature*, 418: 689–695.

Pimental, D., R. Zuniga and D. Morrison (2005) "Update on the Environmental Costs Associated with Alien Invasive Species in the United States", *Ecological Economics*, 52: 274–288.

Ramsar Convention Secretariat (2007) *Coastal Management: Wetland Issues in Integrated Coastal Zone Management. Ramsar Handbooks for the Wise Use of Wetlands*, 3rd edition, vol. 10. Gland, Switzerland: Ramsar Convention Secretariat.

Rayfuse, R. (2010) "Moving Beyond the Tragedy of the Global Commons: The Grotian Legacy and the Future of Sustainable Management of the Biodiversity of the High Seas", in D. Leary and P. Pisupati (eds), *The Future of International Environmental Law*. Tokyo: United Nations University Press, pp. 201–224.

Riser, S. C. and K. S. Johnson (2008) "Net Production of Oxygen in the Subtropical Ocean", *Nature*, 451: 323–325.

Sissenwine, M. P. and P. M. Mace (2007) "Can Deep-Water Fisheries Be Managed Sustainably?", in *Report and Documentation of the Expert Consultation on Deep-Sea Fisheries in the High Seas*, FAO Fisheries Report 838, pp. 61–111.

Smith, K. L. Jr, H. A. Ruhl, B. J. Bett, D. S. M. Billett, R. S. Lampitt and R. S. Kaufmann (2009) "Climate, Carbon Cycling, and Deep-Ocean Ecosystems", *PNAS*, 106: 19211–19218.

Sorensen, J. (2002) *Baseline 2000 Background Report: The Status of Integrated Coastal Management as an International Practice*. Boston: University of Massachusetts. Available at ⟨http://www.uhi.umb.edu/b2k/baseline2000.pdf⟩ (accessed 3 February 2012).

TEEB (The Economics of Ecosystems and Biodiversity) (2010) *The Economics of Ecosystems and Biodiversity: Mainstreaming the Economics of Nature: A Synthesis of the Approach, Conclusions and Recommendations of TEEB*. Available at ⟨http://www.teebweb.org/⟩ (accessed 3 February 2012).
Thia-Eng, C. (1993) "Essential Elements of Integrated Coastal Zone Management", *Ocean and Coastal Management*, 21: 81–108.
Thia-Eng, C. (1998) "Lessons Learned from Practicing Integrated Coastal Management in Southeast Asia", *Ambio*, 27(8): 599–610.
Toropova, C., I. Meliane, D. Laffoley, E. Matthews and M. Spalding (eds) (2010) *Global Ocean Protection: Present Status and Future Possibilities*. Brest, France: Agence des aires marines protégées; Gland, Switzerland, Washington, DC, and New York: IUCN WCPA; Cambridge: UNEP-WCMC; Arlington, VA: TNC; Tokyo: UNU; New York: WCS.
Turley, C. (2000) "Bacteria in the Cold Deep-Sea Benthic Boundary Layer and Sediment–Water Interface", *FEMS Microbiology Ecology*, 33: 89–99.
United Nations (1982) *United Nations Convention on the Law of the Sea*. Division for Ocean Affairs and the Law of the Sea. Available at ⟨http://www.un.org/depts/los/convention_agreements/convention_overview_convention.htm⟩ (accessed 3 February 2012).
United Nations (2002) *Plan of Implementation of the World Summit on Sustainable Development*. In *Report of the World Summit on Sustainable Development, Johannesburg, South Africa, 26 August–4 September 2002*. A/CONF.199/20. New York: United Nations. Available at ⟨http://www.un.org/jsummit/html/whats_new/whatsnew.html⟩ (accessed 3 February 2012).
UNU-IAS (2012) "Bioprospecting Information Resource", ⟨http://www.bioprospector.org/bioprospector/⟩
Van den Hove, S. and V. Moreau (2008) *Deep-Sea Biodiversity and Ecosystems: A Scoping Report on Their Socio-economy, Management and Governance*. DEP/1021/CA, February. Cambridge: UNEP World Conservation Monitoring Centre.
Van Dover, C. L. (2010) "Mining Seafloor Massive Sulphides and Biodiversity: What Is at Risk?", *ICES Journal of Marine Science*, 68: 341–348.
Venter, J. C., K. Remington, J. F. Heidelberg, A. L. Halpern, D. Rusch, J. A. Eisen, D. Wu, I. Paulsen, K. E. Nelson, W. Nelson, D. E. Fouts, S. Levy, A. H. Knap, M. W. Lomas, K. Nealson, O. White, J. Peterson, J. Hoffman, R. Parsons, H. Baden-Tillson, C. Pfannkoch, Y. H. Rogers and H. O. Smith (2004) "Environmental Genome Shotgun Sequencing of the Sargasso Sea", *Science*, 304(5667): 66–74.
Vierros, M., F. Douvere and S. Arico (2006) *Implementing the Ecosystem Approach in Open Ocean and Deep Sea Environments*. United Nations University Institute of Advanced Studies report.
Vierros, M., B. Cicin-Sain, S. Arico and C. Lefebvre (2011) "Preserving Life: Halting Marine Biodiversity Loss and Establishing Networks of Marine Protected Areas in 2010 and Beyond", in A. Djoghlaf and F. Dodds (eds), *Biodiversity and Ecosystem Insecurity – A Planet in Peril*. London: Earthscan, pp. 55–70.

Watling, L., R. Waller and P. J. Auster (2007) "Corner Rise Seamounts: The Impact of Deep-Sea Fisheries", *ICES Insight*, 44: 10–14.

Watson, R. and T. Morato (2004) "Exploitation Patterns in Seamount Fisheries: A Preliminary Analysis", in T. Morato and D. Pauly (eds), *Seamounts: Biodiversity and Fisheries*. Vancouver, BC: Fisheries Centre, University of British Columbia, pp. 61–66.

Worm, B. et al. (2009) "Rebuilding Global Fisheries", *Science*, 325: 578–585.

Yooseph, S., G. Sutton, D. B. Rusch, A. L. Halpern, S. J. Williamson, K. Remington, J. A. Eisen, K. B. Heidelberg, G. Manning, W. Li, L. Jaroszewski, P. Cieplak, C. S. Miller, H. Li, S. T. Mashiyama, M. P. Joachimiak, C. van Belle, J.-M. Chandonia, D. A. Soergel, Y. Zhai, K. Natarajan, S. Lee, B. J. Raphael, V. Bafna, R. Friedman, S. E. Brenner, A. Godzik, D. Eisenberg, J. E. Dixon, S. S. Taylor, R. L. Strausberg, M. Frazier and J. C. Venter (2007) "The Sorcerer II Global Ocean Sampling Expedition: Expanding the Universe of Protein Families", *PLoS Biol*, 5(3): 432–466.

Zewers, K. E. (2008) "Bright Future for Marine Genetic Resources, Bleak Future for Settlement of Ownership Rights: Reflections on the United Nations Law of the Sea Consultative Process on Marine Genetic Resources", *Loyola University Chicago International Law Review*, 5(2): 151–176.

12
The role of indigenous peoples in global environmental governance: Looking through the lens of climate change

Kirsty Galloway McLean, Ameyali Ramos Castillo and Sam Johnston

Introduction

Broadening participation in international governance has been a prominent characteristic of the last 40 years. This change is illustrated in the rising influence of unelected bodies, which are in the broadest sense non-governmental (private sector, civil society groups and local communities). Increased participation of non-governmental actors in international governance is thought to accomplish several objectives, including more effective and efficient development, increased equity, legitimacy, transparency and accountability, and enhanced diversity and resilience. Enabling constructive participation in governance at the global level has been seen as one of the most important tasks for policy-makers concerned with improving the effectiveness of global governance.

An important aspect of this broadening participation has been the increased engagement of local and indigenous communities. Although there is no single definitive definition of "indigenous peoples", they are typically considered to be those peoples who have historically belonged to a particular region or country, before its colonization or transformation into a nation-state, and who may have different – often unique – cultural, linguistic, traditional and other characteristics from those of the dominant culture of that region or state.[1] The United Nations Permanent Forum on Indigenous Issues estimates that there are over 370 million indigenous peoples in 70 countries worldwide (UNPFII, 2011).

Green economy and good governance for sustainable development: Opportunities, promises and concerns, Puppim de Oliveira (ed.),
United Nations University Press, 2012, ISBN 978-92-808-1216-9

The recent rate of proliferation of indigenous peoples in global governance is notable. Over the past two decades, indigenous organizations have begun internal capacity-building efforts to gain a more sophisticated understanding of the global governance process and have used this experience to lobby for and gain seats in global governance discussions. For instance, parallel indigenous forums alongside UN conferences, which were considered innovations only 15 years ago, are now a routine element of intergovernmental negotiations.

Over just the past few decades, indigenous peoples have mobilized and transformed into a group with significant influence in setting international standards and considerable unified activity in transnational networks and fund-raising, as well as intergovernmental and non-governmental organizations (Kingsbury, 1998). Indigenous groups have begun to acquire salience for international governance, not only because they inhabit regions of interest (for example, biodiversity hotspots and resource-rich regions) but also because they hold knowledge that can provide valuable contributions to the knowledge base of international governance.

International policy context

The international community now recognizes that effective global action requires meaningful local participation in international policy-making and implementation. But this was not always the case. International interest in indigenous issues began formally only in the late 1970s, when the United Nations Economic and Social Council appointed a Special Rapporteur, Mr José Martínez Cobo of Ecuador, to study patterns of discrimination against indigenous peoples around the globe. In 1975, the World Council of Indigenous Peoples was founded in Canada and was tasked with dealing with the economic, cultural, political and social rights of indigenous peoples. In 1982, the United Nations Sub-Commission on Prevention of Discrimination and Protection of Minorities (UNSCPD) responded to reports documenting a wide range of human rights issues by appointing a Working Group on Indigenous Populations. Subsequently, based on the findings of the UNSCPD, the International Labour Organization (ILO) promulgated the Convention Concerning Indigenous and Tribal Peoples in Independent Countries (ILO Convention No. 169) in 1989. ILO 169 remains one of the most important operative international laws guaranteeing the rights of indigenous peoples. Among other provisions, it requires that special safeguards be put in place to protect the rights of indigenous peoples concerning the natural resources pertaining to their lands, including their rights to participate in the use, management and conservation of these resources.

The adoption of *Agenda 21*, the Programme of Action for Sustainable Development, by the United Nations Conference on Environment and Development (UNCED) in Rio in 1992 then set the international stage for indigenous peoples' engagement in global governance. Agenda 21 contains a series of recommendations specifically addressing the relevance of traditional knowledge to the implementation of sustainable development policies and programmes. These recommendations address a wide range of sustainable development issues: human health, land resources, deforestation, desertification and drought, sustainable agriculture and rural development, marine resources, freshwater resources, the role of farmers, the role of science, education, public awareness and information, and information for decision-making.

Recommendation 35.7 in the chapter on Science for Sustainable Development is perhaps one of the most significant recommendations on indigenous peoples' traditional knowledge (UNCED, 1992):

> Countries, with the assistance of international organizations, where required, should: ... (h) Develop methods to link the findings of the established sciences with the indigenous knowledge of different cultures. The methods should be tested using pilot studies. They should be developed at the local level and should concentrate on the links between the traditional knowledge of indigenous groups and corresponding, current "advanced science", with particular focus on disseminating and applying the results to environmental protection and sustainable development.

Since then, issues relating to indigenous peoples and traditional knowledge have been addressed in a number of international agreements focusing on different development issues. For example, the Convention on Biological Diversity (CBD), which entered into force in 1993, contains innovative and far-reaching provisions on traditional knowledge (CBD, 1992: Article 8(j)):

> Each contracting Party shall, as far as possible and as appropriate ... (j) Subject to national legislation, respect, preserve and maintain knowledge, innovations and practices of indigenous and local communities embodying traditional lifestyles relevant for the conservation and sustainable use of biological diversity and promote their wider application with the approval and involvement of the holders of such knowledge, innovations and practices and encourage the equitable sharing of the benefits arising from the utilization of such knowledge innovations and practices.

The adoption of the CBD marked the first time that a binding international instrument not only acknowledged the relevance of traditional knowledge to the resolution of global problems but also placed an obligation on governments to respect, preserve and maintain it. Developments under this Convention continue to promote the rights of indigenous peoples in this regard. For example, a major recent accomplishment under the CBD was the adoption in 2010 of the Nagoya Protocol on Access to Genetic Resources and the Fair and Equitable Sharing of Benefits Arising from their Utilization. The purpose of the Nagoya Protocol is to effectively implement one of the three core objectives of the Convention: the fair and equitable sharing of benefits arising from the utilization of genetic resources – an issue of great importance to the holders of traditional knowledge.

Encouraged by the milestones set by the CBD, in 2000 the Economic and Social Council established the United Nations Permanent Forum on Indigenous Issues as part of the International Decade of the World's Indigenous Peoples, with a mandate to discuss indigenous issues related to economic and social development, culture, the environment, education, health and human rights.

The contribution of indigenous peoples to cultural diversity has been recognized in various United Nations Educational, Scientific and Cultural Organization (UNESCO) instruments, including the 2001 Declaration on Cultural Diversity and the 2003 Convention for the Safeguarding of the Intangible Cultural Heritage.

The International Treaty on Plant Genetic Resources for Food and Agriculture entered into force in 2004, featuring as its centrepiece a "multilateral system for access and benefit-sharing", which guarantees facilitated access for certain categories of plant genetic resources for food and agriculture in return for benefit-sharing. In terms of traditional knowledge, the Treaty recognizes "the enormous contribution that the local and indigenous communities and farmers of all regions of the world, particularly those in the centres of origin and crop diversity, have made and will continue to make for the conservation and development of plant genetic resources which constitute the basis of food and agriculture production throughout the world" (FAO, 2009a: Article 9.1) and requires contracting Parties to protect and promote farmers' rights, including specific reference to the protection of traditional knowledge, the sharing of benefits, and the right to participate in making decisions at the national level on matters related to the conservation and sustainable use of plant genetic resources for food and agriculture.

Indigenous peoples' prominence in international governance culminated in 2007 when the United Nations General Assembly adopted the landmark Declaration on the Rights of Indigenous Peoples outlining the rights of the world's indigenous people and outlawing discrimination against them. Although the Declaration is not legally binding, it does set out the individual and collective rights of indigenous peoples, as well as their rights to culture, identity, language, employment, health, education and other issues. The Declaration emphasizes the rights of indigenous peoples to maintain and strengthen their own institutions, cultures and traditions and to pursue their development in keeping with their own needs and aspirations.

As indigenous peoples have gained more recognition in international treaties, international bodies have begun demonstrating increased engagement with indigenous peoples. For example, the World Intellectual Property Organization established the Intergovernmental Committee on Intellectual Property and Genetic Resources, Traditional Knowledge and Folklore in September 2000. Primary themes addressed by this Committee include the intellectual property questions raised by access to genetic resources and benefit-sharing; the protection of traditional knowledge; and protection of expressions of folklore. Negotiations are currently under way regarding an international legal instrument (or instruments) under this framework.

In 2001, the Commission on Human Rights appointed a Special Rapporteur on the rights of indigenous peoples. The World Bank Operational Policy and Bank Policy on Indigenous Peoples (OP/BP 4.10) of 2005 demands, wherever possible, the active participation of indigenous peoples in the development of their projects. The United Nations University Institute of Advanced Studies (UNU-IAS) established a research programme on traditional knowledge (the "Traditional Knowledge Initiative") in 2007 in preparation for developing a research institute focusing on traditional knowledge; and a special inter-agency United Nations Indigenous Peoples' Partnership was established in 2010.

In recent years, international knowledge institutions – such as the Millennium Ecosystem Assessment, the Arctic Climate Impact Assessment, the Global International Waters Assessment, and the Intergovernmental Panel on Climate Change – have also contributed to opening up spaces for indigenous peoples to participate in global governance processes by consolidating and legitimizing support for indigenous peoples' contributions, and by expanding indigenous participation within their own processes. The Millennium Ecosystem Assessment, for instance, deliberately sought to engage with local and indigenous peoples and encouraged them to adapt the assessment to their own conceptual frameworks and policy needs. Although to a lesser extent, the Intergovernmental Panel on Climate Change has also created opportunities for indigenous peoples to participate in their assessment reports as lead authors and contributing authors. As these international knowledge institutions have become increasingly important as powerful sources of expert authority in international governance, the ability to effectively engage with these institutions has proven invaluable for indigenous peoples.

These advances in international thinking, knowledge creation and action on indigenous issues and rights have been motivated by the growing affirmation of indigenous rights around the world, by strengthened commitments to equitable government on the part of national authorities and by the growing recognition that indigenous peoples have valuable information and insight to inform decision-making.

Despite the broad coverage of this range of global governance instruments, there are still some important gaps – most clearly evidenced in the lack of a legal guarantee to indigenous peoples, as communities, to their traditional lands with which they have deep, often spiritual, ties and upon which they rely for their livelihoods. As discussed in Chapter 2 of this volume, another important deficiency is the absence of any reference to cultural rights in the Millennium Development Goals.

International governance through local engagement

Together with the trend to encourage indigenous participation in governance at the international scale, there has been a progression towards more systematic approaches addressing direct engagement with the local level. Programmes where international donors establish an international mechanism to directly support small local-scale projects have been seen as fundamental for successful sustainable development. Many of these programmes provide direct financing and technical assistance to indigenous communities, allowing them to identify their own development priorities, hire assistance, manage project funds and implement the projects. Among the many donor organizations that now have such programmes are the Small Grants Programme of the Global Environment Facility (GEF), the Community-Driven Development Programme of the World Bank, the International Fund for Agricultural Development, community-based adaptation activities under the United Nations Framework Convention on Climate Change (UNFCCC) and the Equator Initiative of the United Nations Development Programme (UNDP).

Indigenous communities are particularly useful in an implementation or operational context, because they can provide implementation tailored to specific conditions and effectively balance social, economic and environmental pillars. This is especially true with regard to the management of natural resources, which is often best handled by indigenous and/or community organizations whose livelihoods directly depend on these resources, and who are free from many of the conflicting demands and bureaucracies of national governments. For example, many local projects facilitate small-scale agriculture through better soil management and harvesting techniques and through improved markets and connections, which directly affects local food security and diet. Projects often develop local infrastructure, such as water and sanitation systems, schools and health clinics, that directly supports education and health goals.

Direct engagement with the local scale has much to offer the global governance process. Leadership for the international and national levels often emerges from such "grassroots" activity. In many cases, the legitimacy of international policies and decision-making depends on local experiences and local perceptions. A number of international programmes are already benefiting from the local contributions of indigenous peoples in areas as varied as information collection and dissemination, policy implementation, monitoring and assessment, and policy development. These local experiences also demonstrate the complexity of the core challenges to sustainable development, which require many parallel actions, something that is very evident at the local level.

A critical question facing international governance is how to link the ad hoc nature of these local activities to global goals and needs.

Adapting to climate change: Global challenges need local inputs

Because of the nature of the challenge of climate change – it is a complex global issue; it is not just radically affecting ecological systems and other environmental impacts, but also influencing economic systems, infrastructure and the movement of human populations; and there is clear evidence of the impact of "bottom-up", place-based local action – it is an excellent lens through which to analyse indigenous peoples' engagement in global governance processes. As climate initiatives have begun to shift from an emphasis on global systems to more focused studies of the implications of climate change at the local level, they have become increasingly open to the idea that indigenous and other local people have valuable information about local impacts, vulnerabilities and adaptation/mitigation that could inform decision-making.

For indigenous peoples, the challenges of living with a variable and changing climate are not new. Indigenous peoples have been guardians of the environment for thousands of years and possess a broad knowledge base of the complex ecological system in their own localities (Gadgil and Folke, 1993; Schmidt and Peterson, 2009). Indigenous peoples' ability to predict and interpret environmental change through their traditional knowledge has been vital to their livelihoods, survival and well-being, and it has been the foundation for the development of social, political and governance structures. These knowledge systems are based on observing and experimenting with nature and contain a store of knowledge developed over time and passed on through generations.

Traditional knowledge is central in indigenous peoples' ability to respond to and manage environmental change. Traditional knowledge is holistic in outlook and adaptive by nature and is vast with respect to the environment. It provides indigenous peoples with the tools necessary to monitor the status of a resource, to protect certain species by temporarily restricting harvest, and to use integrated farming systems in order to maintain ecosystem process and function during periods of environmental change (Berkes et al., 2000). Indigenous peoples' traditional knowledge is continually being produced and maintained through complex socio-political and governance processes and helps them adapt to unpredicted environmental feedbacks.

Indeed, the Intergovernmental Panel on Climate Change (IPCC, 2007) has noted that societies have a long record of adapting to the impacts of weather and climate through a range of practices that include crop diversification, irrigation, water management, disaster risk management and insurance. In Colombia, for example, shamans of the Tukano people rely on their traditional knowledge of local biodiversity and climate to schedule hunting expeditions during periods of species abundance and to limit them during droughts and other unexpected environmental changes (Berkes et al., 2000). In the Puno region of Peru, indigenous peoples use their traditional knowledge about the environment and about wildlife (for example, the frequency of rains, the flowering of certain plants, the appearance of certain animals, the mating of animals, the incidence of plagues) to determine when to plant and when to harvest (Claverias, 2000). Many other indigenous peoples throughout the world rely on their traditional knowledge as a buffer against environmental variation, allowing them to identify, predict and adapt accordingly.

Research has documented that, although well-designed, top-down, scenario-driven approaches to adaptation have a role to play in reducing vulnerability to climate change, these approaches often fall short in addressing the specific needs and concerns of the most vulnerable people. In particular, these approaches are often based on limited access to credible and reliable information about climate trends in fragile ecosystems – such as islands, mountains and coasts – the very ecosystems where most of the world's indigenous peoples reside.

For many communities, there is a marked disconnect between their local traditional knowledge-based adaptation practices and public policies, which can result in undermining traditional knowledge and practices from indigenous and marginalized peoples. When considering factors that have an impact on a community's ability to cope with changing environmental conditions, close attention must be paid to the overarching political governance systems that may lead to the marginalization of indigenous peoples and local communities.

In the climate change context, research has found that adaptation programmes and policies designed to reduce vulnerability and enhance adaptive capacity are more successful when developed in cooperation with local representatives, because the community is likely to trust them and find the interventions consistent with local values and aspirations (Barnett and Campbell, 2010; Ford et al., 2006). This is especially true among indigenous communities where there is a long history of distrust between communities and governments.

Engagement with local peoples also improves the likely outcomes of decision-making and policy implementation by enabling the identification of key stakeholders and institutions and facilitating knowledge transfer (Huq and Reid, 2007). In addition, local knowledge and perceptions influence people's decisions on whether or not to act (Alessa et al., 2008) and on which adaptive measures to take over both the short and the long term (Berkes and Jolly, 2001). Working with local communities also often results in adaptations (particularly those relying on traditional knowledge) that are low cost (at least from a fiscal standpoint) and highly effective. Comprehensive estimates of adaptation costs, however, are sorely lacking. Even small adjustments to livelihood practices may require associated changes in the enabling environment (for example, information availability, institutional role, infrastructure use), and low normalized costs can still be high in absolute terms.

It is becoming more and more clear, therefore, that global interventions could greatly benefit from working with indigenous peoples to identify and document trends in regional and local climate changes, to understand their long-term implications for local peoples, and to develop effective and appropriate adaptation responses based on traditional knowledge.

The example of indigenous peoples and climate change mitigation

Let us examine, as an example of increasing global interest, the important role that indigenous peoples can play in reducing global greenhouse gas emissions or mitigation efforts.

The recognition that deforestation, particularly in the tropics, contributes 19–20 per cent of global greenhouse gas emissions led to a collective agreement between UNFCCC Parties that a key climate mitigation priority should be to conserve and enhance forests and other sinks and reservoirs of greenhouse gases (UNFCCC, 1992: Article 4.1(d)). Consequently,

UNFCCC Parties introduced REDD+ (Reducing Emissions from Deforestation and Forest Degradation) as an important mechanism for tackling climate change. The IPCC in its most recent assessment noted that reducing deforestation is the mitigation option with the largest and most immediate carbon stock impact in the short term per hectare and per year globally (IPCC, 2007). McKinsey & Co. (2009) calculated that it would cost around EUR 9 per tonne of carbon dioxide equivalent (tCO_2e) to generate credits from reducing forest loss and degradation, whereas carbon capture and storage on power plants would cost around EUR 40–55/tCO_2e and solar would cost around EUR 37/tCO_2e. This study also estimated that reducing forest loss and degradation could contribute as much as 6 gigatonnes of CO_2e per year or one-third of the required total global reduction in greenhouse gas emissions between now and 2020. Over USD 5 billion has been committed to REDD projects in the past few years and promises of many more billions have been made. As of September 2011, the main global REDD database had 480 registered projects in 36 countries amounting to USD 3.35 billion (REDD+, n.d.). The vast majority of these projects are on indigenous lands and/or territories.

According to the World Bank, indigenous peoples legally own more than 11 per cent of the world's forests (Sobrevila, 2008). In Asia and the Pacific, 25 per cent of forest land is owned by local communities and indigenous peoples and an additional 3 per cent is designated for use by communities and indigenous peoples (Larson et al., 2010). Papua New Guinea has more than 25.51 million hectares under community or indigenous ownership (RRI, 2009) and Australia reports approximately 90.78 million hectares (over 11.5 per cent) of land as indigenous owned (ANRA, 2010). Similarly, in Latin America the forested area owned by local communities and indigenous peoples is also 25 per cent, and an additional 8 per cent is forested public land designated for community/indigenous use (Larson et al., 2010). Mexico is at the forefront of community forestry, with more than 38.71 million hectares owned by communities/indigenous peoples, and, in Brazil, community and indigenous groups own approximately 109.13 million hectares (RRI, 2009). Agreements regarding the 4.7 million hectare "Great Bear Rainforest" in Canada provide a governance framework between First Nations and the provincial government that includes implementation of new logging regulations using ecosystem-based management. Based on a conservative assumption that, after harvesting, about 23 per cent of the carbon would remain locked in lumber, logging the area that has been protected by this agreement under regular forest legislation that applies elsewhere in the province would result in about 153 million tonnes of CO_2 being released (Holt, 2009).

The value of agroforestry systems as carbon sinks has recently been recognized as an important component of climate change mitigation

(Nair et al., 2009). In agroforestry systems, carbon can be sequestered from the atmosphere and stored in soils or vegetation. According to recent estimates, of the 960 million hectares of land under cultivation, 10–15 per cent is managed by traditional farmers (Alteri and Nicholls, 2008). This global population of smallholder farmers has been identified as the first target for policies to intensify production in mixed systems – effectively increasing carbon density and refilling depleted soil carbon reserves (Obersteiner et al., 2010). For smallholder agroforestry systems in the tropics, potential carbon sequestration rates have been estimated to range from 1.5 to 3.5 Megagrams of carbon per hectare per year (Montagnini and Nair, 2004).

In Mexico, indigenous Mayan communities are introducing timber species within their agricultural systems as crop–tree combinations to enhance carbon storage as part of a pilot carbon project. This project has successfully increased carbon sinks in several Mayan communities while at the same time promoting indigenous livelihoods (Nelson and de Jon, 2003). In eastern Zambia, two-year rotations of agroforestry species in rural indigenous communities sequestered 26–78 Megagrams per hectare of carbon in the soil. A similar project in southern Malawi sequestered 123–149 Megagrams per hectare in the soil (0–200 cm depth). (Makumba et al., 2006). Other projects like this are being implemented in various indigenous communities around the world with similar results.

Many other traditional agricultural activities that indigenous peoples rely on lead to high rates of carbon accumulation in the soil – such as no-till farming, crop residue retention, growing cover crops in the rotation cycle, and adopting complex farming systems. These technologies are increasingly being recognized as important, cost-effective and equitable terrestrial mitigation solutions that have the potential to enhance existing carbon sinks and to reduce net CO_2 emissions.

Not only are indigenous peoples and local communities owners of forest land, but they are also key players in ground-breaking ways to reduce greenhouse gas emissions. In Australia, the Western Arnhem Land Fire Abatement Project (WALFA) uses traditional fire management practices of aboriginal land owners together with modern scientific knowledge to reduce the extent and severity of wildfires in fire-prone tropical savannah and, as a result, the overall annual greenhouse gas emissions of Australia by around 36 per cent (Whitehead et al., 2008). Under this project, each year traditional owners have agreed to generate 100,000 tonnes of carbon credits in return for offset payments from ConocoPhillips of USD 1 million per annum (indexed to 2005) for 17 years.

This successful example of indigenous peoples collaborating with the private sector not only contributes environmental benefits but also provides important economic, biodiversity and sociocultural opportunities. In addition to providing ecosystem service benefits, which include mitigating greenhouse gas emissions, sustaining biodiversity and habitat rehabilitation (Edwards and Russell-Smith, 2009), WALFA provides significant sociocultural benefits to traditional land owners by offering employment opportunities for indigenous people skilled in land management and customary obligations to land and natural resources who would otherwise have little or no prospect of mainstream employment (Whitehead et al., 2009). Projects such as WALFA also enable the revival of cultural heritage, develop cross-cultural confidence and the expertise necessary for economic activities such as tourist enterprises and improve the health and overall well-being of local communities (Burgess et al., 2005).

In addition, projects such as WALFA have valuable scale-up potential for more global application. Managing fires more effectively could provide important mitigation opportunities for indigenous communities in other countries, as well as additional economic, biodiversity and sociocultural benefits. Global fire emissions averaged over 1997–2009 were 2.0 petagrams of carbon per year, with contributions from Africa (52 per cent), South America (15 per cent), Equatorial Asia (10 per cent), the boreal region (9 per cent) and Australia (7 per cent) (van der Werf et al., 2010). The largest contributor (44 per cent) to fire carbon emissions were fires in savannahs and grasslands. Almost half of this is considered to be due to savannah burning (both wildfires and managed fires), making it the single largest source of pyrogenic emissions (Koppmann et al., 2005). It is also believed to be a significant source of aerosol and trace gas inputs to the global atmosphere. Within the tropics, 42 per cent of emissions are estimated to come from Africa, 29 per cent from Asia, 23 per cent from South America and 6 per cent from Oceania (FAO, 2009b). Significant portions of these landscapes are under traditional communal land tenure and the responsibility for controlling the use of fire is often in the hands of local communities. Preliminary research suggests that indigenous communities in grassland ecosystems of Latin America (for example, Brazil, Bolivia, Venezuela – Bilbao, 2010; McDaniel et al., 2005; Mistry et al., 2005), Africa (for example, South Africa, Tanzania, Namibia, Botswana, Ghana, Mozambique – Appiah et al., 2010; Butz, 2009; Shaffer, 2010[2]) and Asia (for example, Russia and Kazakhstan – UNDP-GEF, 2009) provide the right conditions for developing WALFA-like community-based fire abatement approaches to generate carbon credits (Sejo et al., 2011).

Integrating traditional knowledge and "Western" science

Effective global governance relies on the best available knowledge base, and the urgent need to respond to the pressures of climate change has put a premium on the generation, interpretation and use of information within communities, regions, countries and globally. In recent years, there has been an increasing realization that the observations and assessments of indigenous groups provide valuable local-level information, offer ground-truths of global models, and are providing the basis for local community-driven adaptation strategies that are already being implemented.

Although indigenous knowledge is often defined in contrast to scientific or "Western" knowledge, it should not be seen as a rigid, static repertoire of traditions that is unable to incorporate innovations (Cleveland and Soleri, 2007). Traditional knowledge is actually flexible and adaptive and, by virtue of its diverse and empirical nature, can easily integrate skills and insights from other knowledge systems as well as from experimental practice.

Unfortunately, attempts to compare and contrast traditional ecological knowledge with scientifically acquired data often imply that indigenous peoples' way of knowing is inadequate in contrast with Western scientific methods (Sillitoe, 2007). In climate change debates, traditional knowledge is viewed as having the potential to help communities adapt to climate change, but uncertainty remains about whether or not (or how) it can be integrated with modern science, especially at the policy and planning level (Nyong et al., 2007; Macchi et al., 2008).

There can be challenges in integrating traditional and scientific knowledge. For example, even though indigenous peoples and scientists may seem on the surface to be observing the same phenomenon in the same environment, in actual fact the nature of their observations may differ quite profoundly. For example, when looking at changing weather in the Arctic, indigenous observers base their conclusions on multiple environmental and social factors (for example, wind speed, direction and variability, combined with temperature and precipitation, as well as the need for shelter and safety when travelling with or without family), which they consider in an integrated manner. In contrast, scientific research may isolate a single environmental variable (for example, temperature or wind speed) or focus on mean values and reach broader conclusions based upon an extrapolation from this different data set (Weatherhead et al., 2010). Both types of knowledge may be criticized for possible shortcomings (for example, unsystematic observations or lack of quantitative method in the development of traditional knowledge, versus a reductionist approach with consideration of too few variables, inappropriate choice of parameter to be measured, or expansive extrapolation from data of limited scope in scientific practices) but, faced with the challenge of climate change and the numerous surprises and unknowns as yet before us, creating a constructive dialogue between indigenous peoples and scientists will be an important step towards decision-making based on the best available knowledge.

Those who advocate the integration of indigenous knowledge in climate policy believe that this will lead to the development of more effective mitigation and adaptation strategies that are cost effective, participatory and sustainable (Robinson and Herbert, 2001; Hunn, 1993). Because traditional knowledge is the result of ongoing human interaction with the local environment, as ecosystems shift and alter, so does the resultant knowledge gained from consistent interaction with those ecosystems (Berkes, 1999; Menzies, 2006). Thus, indigenous knowledge systems are in a continual state of change – an adaptive quality that is especially relevant when responding to something as unpredictable as climate change.

Integration of local traditional knowledge and expertise with government and scientific data is proving to be a valuable and capable means of collecting both small- and large-scale transboundary data related to climate change. In the United States, the Swinomish Climate Change Initiative combined Coast Salish cultural knowledge with US government scientific expertise, with results that included identifying the extent of impacts, processes contributing to impairment, and areas of water quality concern. In the Arctic, remote sensing (for example, Landsat, AMSR-E) and other scientific data (for example, meteorology, modelling) are being combined with the indigenous knowledge of Sami reindeer herders to "co-produce" data sets to improve decision-making, herd management and adaptation strategies (Maynard et al., 2011). Rainmakers in the Nganyi community of western Kenya have collaborated with meteorological scientists to make integrated forecasts that are being disseminated by both indigenous and modern methods (Awuor, 2008). In terms of undertaking mitigative action, the WALFA project uses traditional fire management practices of aboriginal traditional owners in northern Australia in conjunction with modern scientific knowledge to reduce the extent and severity of wildfires in fire-prone tropical savannah regions. These are just a few of many initiatives where integration of traditional knowledge and scientific method has resulted in useful data for the development of sound climate change policies.

There are also various examples of technical tools and technologies that are being combined with indigenous knowledge to enhance adaptive capacity to climate change. Many indigenous youth are prioritizing getting training in modern technologies such as Global Positioning System. Indigenous youth in the Arctic, for instance, are using this technology to track animal movements and to determine when and where to hunt. Models that facilitate this type of capacity-building include the University of the Arctic, which comprises a network of about 100 universities and colleges throughout the Arctic. These universities are linked through distance learning and enable indigenous students from around the circumpolar world to learn geographic information systems, LANDSAT classification and other scientific techniques – techniques that are helping indigenous peoples in the region better prepare for climatic and environmental changes (University of the Arctic, 2012).

As evidenced in previous examples, it is apparent that long-term, respectful collaborative relationships between communities, governmental agencies and academic institutions may help strengthen the adaptive capacity of indigenous and non-indigenous peoples on the global scale. However, in order for these relationships to be successful, it is important to ensure that they recognize and respect the rights of the indigenous communities involved. Genuine respect for and connection with indigenous communities is fundamental to effective community engagement and equitable integration between traditional knowledge and science research. This includes careful analysis and understanding of the local context, leaders, networks, culture and environment. Programme design and implementation should integrate indigenous knowledge, and mechanisms should be designed in such a way that they do not undermine customary rights to lands and natural resources.

This means that indigenous peoples must take a proactive role at the national level of climate change governance – establishing their place as national providers of "climate knowledge" – and make the case for funding their essential climate response activities so compellingly that they cannot be passed over. It is also important to provide local communities with access to relevant technologies and information so that they can identify and monitor conditions, as well as provide guidance and suggestions for effective actions. A key feature of successful engagement is the use of existing formal and informal social networks and expertise to ensure that any integration of traditional knowledge and science is relevant and inclusive.

Sharing traditional knowledge and scientific knowledge is key to further developing knowledge essential to fighting climate change. However, it is necessary to get free, prior and informed consent from indigenous peoples and their communities before doing any research to further develop such projects, so that they can participate fully in the process.

Recent experience of policy-makers and practitioners confirms the importance of carefully designed, well-implemented strategies of integration of traditional knowledge and science as key components of effective climate adaptation and mitigation initiatives. However, many challenges remain to be overcome in successfully integrating traditional knowledge and science and engaging indigenous communities in the face of unprecedented climate change.

Ways forward: Climate governance challenges and opportunities

The range of climate change adaptation activities undertaken by indigenous peoples reflects the reality that indigenous cultures face different internal and external challenges. From a temporal perspective, most indigenous peoples' adaptation plans are still primarily responding directly to current climate variability (although, through the application of traditional knowledge, they incorporate learning from past adaptations to historical climates). Although the short-term plans for adaptation to current climate variability can also increase resilience to long-term climate change, indigenous peoples will require investment and planning responses that go beyond these short-term activities.

Further work is needed to address responses to observed medium- and long-term trends in climate and anticipatory planning is required in response to model-based scenarios of long-term climate change. Urgent attention is also needed in forming long-term adaptation strategies to empower the extremely vulnerable communities – those living in drought-prone, flood-prone, low-lying and coastal areas – to help them continue to develop robust coping mechanisms and to address forced environmental migration and its associated issues.

Another important challenge facing indigenous-led projects is the strong competition they face for funds and resources. Outcomes from many of these climate change projects provide compelling evidence of their success but, like other such initiatives, there is always a risk of the competitive element spreading resources too thinly and non-selectively. Development agencies need to respond to these proposals and plans quickly, inclusively and in a well-coordinated manner.

"Soft" adaptation measures (such as those that make use of traditional indigenous knowledge) can be more difficult to identify, design and gain support for at national level than those that involve hard infrastructure, but they remain vital to the effective implementation of adaptive activities in indigenous and marginalized communities. Also vital is developing and structuring the national and global policy environment in a way that ensures that the views of indigenous peoples are incorporated in larger-scale planning. Local capacity-building – building local knowledge and strengthening local organizations – is another essential component in enabling robust adaptation planning within indigenous and marginalized communities. A holistic approach, integrating social and natural sciences and indigenous peoples' traditional knowledge in the co-generation of solutions, can help face the future challenges of climate change.

Another challenge at the global level will come when assessing which local activities may benefit from scaling-up and wider application to guide risk reduction in other communities. This will require robust guidance in the interpretation of results and specific attention to sampling and care in scaling up qualitative findings (van Aalst et al., 2008).

Barriers that need to be addressed to support indigenous peoples in implementing climate change initiatives include restrictions on access to their land owing to unresolved land claims, disruption of intergenerational knowledge transmission, loss of languages, and paucity of methodological guidelines for the integration of traditional knowledge into various branches of science.

It is essential that the global community take the necessary measures to ensure the full and effective participation of indigenous and local communities in monitoring the impacts of climate change and in formulating and implementing mitigative and adaptive responses to those impacts. In this context, it should be recalled that indigenous peoples have made a unanimous call for implementation of their fundamental human rights and status as affirmed in the United Nations Declaration on the Rights of Indigenous Peoples (2007, and have continued to make it clear that these rights must be fully recognized and implemented in all decision-making processes and activities, including those related to climate change – for example, the 2009 Anchorage Declaration (see Galloway McLean et al., 2009) and the 2011 Sevvetijärvi Declaration (see IPCCA, 2011).

Projects in which Western scientists can learn from indigenous and other marginalized communities should also be encouraged. Public policy must consider the different levels and realities of indigenous peoples and marginalized populations, including their participation in the development of these policies. The United Nations Declaration on the Rights of Indigenous Peoples must be used as the foundation for any negotiations with indigenous peoples, including those relating to climate change.

Implications for global governance

Climate change simultaneously addresses numerous topics – health, diversity, poverty, development – and cannot be effectively addressed under the current convention arrangements and or the current disciplinary silos. Many adaptation initiatives are inextricably intertwined with related sustainable development activities, such as disaster management planning and income diversification strategies. A review of adaptation literature from indigenous and marginalized communities reveals that most strategies typically feature practical ongoing processes that respond to many factors or stresses, rather than discrete measures that are implemented to address climate change specifically. Consistent with typically holistic indigenous worldviews, most of the climate change adaptation plans implemented by indigenous peoples span more than one sector, combining, for example, ecosystem management with biodiversity conservation and livelihood diversification, or watershed improvements with increased agricultural capacity (Galloway McLean, 2010).

It will be essential in future to continue to enhance synergies between conventions, agreements and disciplines to promote cross-cutting themes. Specifically, it is important to address the strong relationship between diversity (culture, knowledge, biological) and sustainable development processes. The challenge to integrate different sources and types of knowledge is another most pressing issue.

Through their culture of intergenerational transmission of knowledge over thousands of years, indigenous peoples are unique repositories of learning and knowledge about developing and implementing successful initiatives to cope with local-level stressors such as climate change, and effectively responding to major environmental changes such as natural disasters. Historically, indigenous peoples have played a fundamental role in the conservation of biological diversity and the protection of forests and other natural resources, and, currently, their traditional knowledge on climate change can also substantively enrich the scientific knowledge and adaptation activities of others.

Notes

1. See, for example, the use of the term in documents issued by the United Nations (e.g. Declaration of the Rights of Indigenous Peoples), the International Labour Organization (e.g. ILO Convention No. 169) and the World Bank (e.g. Operational Policy 4.10 – Indigenous Peoples).
2. Also personal communications in November 2011 from Dr Nigel Crawhall, Indigenous Peoples of Africa Coordinating Committee (IPACC), and Dr Margaret Jacobsohn, Trustee of Integrated Rural Development and Nature Conservation (IRDNC).

REFERENCES

Alessa, L., A. Kliskey, P. Williams and M. Barton (2008) "Perception of Change in Freshwater in Remote Resource-Dependent Arctic Communities", *Global Environmental Change*, 18: 153–164.

Altieri, M. and C. Nicholls (2008) "Los Impactos del Cambio Climático sobre las Comunidades Campesinas y de Agricultores Tradicionales y Sus Respuestas Adaptativas", *Agroecología*, 3: 7–28.

ANRA (Australian Natural Resources Atlas) (2010) *Land Use Patterns in Australia*. Canberra: Australian Government.

Appiah, M., L. Damnyag, D. Blay and A. Pappinen (2010) "Forest and Agrosystem Fire Management in Ghana", *Mitigation and Adaptation Strategies for Global Change*, 15(6): 551–570.

Awuor, C. (2008) "Community Based Adaptation in Africa (CBAA) Project Planning Meeting 5–6 March 2008", International Development Research Centre/African Centre for Technology Studies, Nairobi.

Barnett, J. and J. Campbell (2010) *Climate Change and Small Island States: Power, Knowledge and the South Pacific*. London: Earthscan.

Berkes, F. (1999) *Sacred Ecology: Traditional Ecological Knowledge and Resource Management*. Philadelphia: Taylor & Francis Press.

Berkes, F. and D. Jolly (2001) "Adapting to Climate Change: Social-ecological Resilience in a Canadian Western Arctic Community", *Conservation Ecology*, 5(2): U514–U532.

Berkes, F. J., J. Colding and C. Folke (2000) "Rediscovery of Traditional Ecological Knowledge as Adaptive Management", *Ecological Applications*, 10(5): 1251–1262.

Bilbao, B. (2010) "Indigenous Use of Fire and Forest Loss in Canaima National Park", *Human Ecology*, 38(5): 663–673.

Burgess, C. P., F. H. Johnston, D. M. Bowman and P. J. Whitehead (2005) "Healthy Country – Healthy People? Exploring the Health Benefits of Indigenous Natural Resource Management", *Australian and New Zealand Journal of Public Health*, 29(2): 117–122.

Butz, R. (2009) "Traditional Fire Management: Historical Fire Regimes and Land Use Change in Pastoral East Africa", *International Journal of Wildland Fire*, 18: 442–450.

CBD (Convention on Biological Diversity) (1992) "Text of the Convention on Biological Diversity", ⟨http://www.cbd.int/convention/text/⟩ (accessed 1 February 2012).

Claverias, R. (2000) "Conocimientos de los Campesinos Andinos sobre los Predictores Climáticos: Elementos para su verificación" [Andean Peasants' Climate Forecast Knowledge: Elements to Verify This Knowledge], unpublished paper.

Cleveland, D. A. and D. Soleri (2007) "Extending Darwin's Analogy: Bridging Differences in Concepts of Selection between Farmers, Biologists, and Plant Breeders", *Economic Botany*, 61(2): 121–136.

Edwards, A. C. and J. Russell-Smith (2009) "Ecological Thresholds and the Status of Fire-sensitive Vegetation in Western Arnhem Land, Northern Australia: Implications for Management", *International Journal of Wildland Fire*, 18: 127–146.

FAO (Food and Agriculture Organization) (2009a) *International Treaty on Plant Genetic Resources for Food and Agriculture*. Rome: FAO. Available at ⟨http://www.planttreaty.org/content/texts-treaty-official-versions⟩ (accessed 4 February 2012).

FAO (Food and Agriculture Organization) (2009b) "Grasslands: Enabling their Potential to Contribute to Greenhouse Gas Mitigation". A submission by FAO to the UNFCCC. Rome: FAO.

Ford, J. D., B. Smit and J. Wandel (2006) "Vulnerability to Climate Change in the Arctic: A Case Study from Arctic Bay Canada", *Global Environmental Change*, 16(2): 145–160.

Gadgil, M. F. and C. Folke (1993) "Indigenous Knowledge for Biodiversity Conservation", *Ambio*, 22(2–3): 151–156.

Galloway McLean, K. (2010) *Advance Guard: Climate Change Impacts, Adaptation, Mitigation and Indigenous Peoples – A Compendium of Case Studies*. Darwin: United Nations University – Traditional Knowledge Initiative.

Galloway McLean, K., A. Ramos-Castillo, T. Gross, S. Johnston, M. Vierros and R. Noa (2009) *Report of the Indigenous Peoples' Global Summit on Climate Change, 20–24 April 2009, Anchorage, Alaska*. Darwin: United Nations University – Traditional Knowledge Initiative.

Holt, R. F. (2009) *Ecosystem-based Management in the Great Bear Rainforest: Defense for Climate and Species*. Vancouver: ForestEthics.

Huq, S. and H. Reid (2007) *Community-based Adaptation: A Vital Approach to the Threat Climate Change Poses to the Poor*. London: International Institute for Environment and Development.

Hunn, E. (1993) "What Is Traditional Ecological Knowledge?", in N. Williams and G. Baines (eds) *Traditional Ecological Knowledge: Wisdom for Sustainable Development*. Canberra: Center for Resource and Environmental Studies, Australian National University, pp. 13–15.

IPCC (International Panel on Climate Change) (2007) *AR4 Synthesis Report, Summary for Policymakers. IPPC Fourth Assessment Report*. New York: Cambridge University Press.

IPCCA (Indigenous Peoples' Biocultural Climate Change Assessment Initiative) (2011) "Press Release: Indigenous Leaders Call on the IPPC to Respect Indigenous Knowledge". Available at ⟨http://pubs.iied.org/G03151.html⟩ (accessed 4 February 2012).

Kingsbury, B. (1998) "'Indigenous Peoples' in International Law: A Constructivist Approach to the Asian Controversy", *American Journal of International Law*, 92: 414–457.

Koppmann, R. et al. (2005) "A Review of Biomass Burning Emissions, Part I: Gaseous Emissions of Carbon Monoxide, Methane, Volatile Organic Compounds, and Nitrogen Containing Compounds", *Atmospheric Chemistry and Physics Discussions*, 5: 10455–10516.

Larson, A., D. Barry, R. G. Dahal and C. Colfer (2010) *Forests for Peoples: Community Rights and Forest Tenure Reform*. London: Earthscan.

Macchi, M., G. Oviedo, S. Gotheil, K. Cross, A. Boedhihartono, C. Wolfangel and M. Howell (2008) *Indigenous and Traditional Peoples and Climate Change*. IUCN.

McDaniel, J. et al. (2005) "Smokey Tapir: Traditional Fire Knowledge and Fire Prevention Campaigns in Lowland Bolivia", *Society and Natural Resources*, 18: 921–930.

McKinsey & Company (2009) *Pathways to a Low-Carbon Economy: Version 2 of the Global Greenhouse Gas Abatement Cost Curve*. Brussels: McKinsey & Company.

Makumba, W., F. K. Akinnifesi, B. Janssen and O. Oenema (2006) "Long-term Impact of a Gliricidia–Maize Intercropping System on Carbon Sequestration in Southern Malawi", *Agricultural Ecosystems and the Environment*, 118: 237–243.
Maynard, N. G., P. Burgess, A. Oskal, J. M. Turi, S. D. Mathiesen, I. G. E. Gaup, B. Yurchak, V. Etylin and J. Gebelein (2011) "Eurasian Reindeer Pastoralism in a Changing Climate: Indigenous Knowledge & NASA Remote Sensing", NASA Technical Report, Washington, DC.
Menzies, C. R. and C. Butler (2006) "Introduction: Understanding Ecological Knowledge", in C. R. Menzies (ed.), *Traditional Ecological Knowledge and Natural Resource Management*. Lincoln: University of Nebraska Press, pp. 1–20.
Mistry, J., A. Berardi, V. Andrade, T. Kraho, P. Kraho and O. Leonardos (2005) "Indigenous Fire Management in the Cerrado of Brazil: The Case of Kraho of Tocantins", *Human Ecology*, 33(3): 365–386.
Montagnini, F. and P. Nair (2004) "Carbon Sequestration: An Unexploited Environmental Benefit of Agroforest Systems", *Agroforestry Systems*, 61: 281–295.
Nair P. K. R., B. M. Kumar and V. D. Nair (2009) "Agroforestry as a Strategy for Carbon Sequestration", *Journal of Plant Nutrition and Soil Science*, 172: 10–23.
Nelson, K. C. and B. H. J. de Jon (2003) "Making Global Initiatives Local Realities: Carbon Mitigation Projects in Chiapas", *Global Environmental Change*, 13: 19–30.
Nyong, A., F. Adesina and B. Osman Elasha (2007) "The Value of Indigenous Knowledge in Climate Change Mitigation and Adaptation Strategies in the African Sahel", *Mitigation and Adaptation Strategies for Global Change*, 12(5): 787–797.
Obersteiner, M., H. Böttcher and Y. Yamagata (2010) "Terrestrial Ecosystem Management for Climate Change Mitigation", *Current Opinion in Environmental Sustainability*, 2: 271–276.
REDD+ (n.d.) "Voluntary REDD+ Database", ⟨http://reddplusdatabase.org/⟩ (accessed 4 February 2012).
Robinson, J. B. and D. Herbert (2001) "Integrating Climate Change and Sustainable Development", *International Journal of Global Environmental Issues*, 1(2): 130–148.
RRI (Rights and Resources Initiative) (2009) *Tropical Forest Tenure Assessment: Trends, Challenges and Opportunities*. Washington, DC, and Yokohama: Rights and Resources Initiative and International Tropical Timber Organization.
Schmidt, P. and M. Peterson (2009) "Biodiversity Conservation and Indigenous Land Management in the Era of Self-Determination", *Conservation Biology*, 23(6): 1458–1466.
Sejo, F. et al. (2011) "Introduction", *Fire Ecology*, 7(1): 1–4.
Shaffer, L. (2010) "Indigenous Fire Use to Manage Savanna Landscapes in Southern Mozambique", *Fire Ecology*, 6(2): 43–58.
Sillitoe, P. (2007) "Local Science v. Global Science: An Overview", in P. Sillitoe (ed.), *Local Science vs Global Science: Approaches to Indigenous Knowledge in International Development*. New York: Berghahn Books.
Sobrevila, M. (2008) *The Role of Indigenous Peoples in Biodiversity Conservation: The Natural and Often Forgotten Partners*. Washington, DC: World Bank.

UNCED (United Nations Conference on Environment and Development) (1992) *Agenda 21: Earth Summit – The United Nations Programme of Action from Rio*. Available at ⟨http://www.un.org/esa/dsd/agenda21/res_agenda21_00.shtml⟩ (accessed 4 February 2012).

UNDP-GEF (United Nations Development Programme – Global Environment Facility) (2009) "Improving the Coverage and Management Efficiency of Protected Areas in the Steppe Biome of Russia. A Project Document".

UNFCC (United Nations Framework Convention on Climate Change) (1992) "United Nations Framework Convention on Climate Change". Available at ⟨http://unfccc.int/key_documents/the_convention/items/2853.php⟩ (accessed 4 February 2012).

University of the Arctic (2012) "Thematic Networks", ⟨http://www.uarctic.org/⟩ (accessed 4 February 2012).

UNPFII (United Nations Permanent Forum on Indigenous Issues) (2011) "About UNPFII and a Brief History of Indigenous Peoples and the International System", ⟨http://www.un.org/esa/socdev/unpfii/en/history.html⟩ (assessed 4 February 2012).

Van Aalst, M., T. Cannon and I. Burton (2008) "Community Level Adaptation to Climate Change: The Potential Role of Participatory Community Risk Assessment", *Global Environmental Change*, 18(1): 165–179.

Van der Werf, G. R., J. T. Randerson, L. Giglio, G. J. Collatz, M. Mu, P. S. Kasibhatla, D. C. Morto, R. S. DeFries, Y. Jin and T. T. van Leeuwen (2010) "Global Fire Emissions and the Contribution of Deforestation, Savanna, Forest, Agricultural and Peat Fires (1997–2009)", *Atmospheric Chemistry and Physics Discussions*, 10: 16153–16230.

Weatherhead, E., S. Gearhead and R. G. Barry (2010) "Changes in Weather Persistence: Insight from Inuit Knowledge", *Global Environmental Change*, 20(3): 523–528.

Whitehead, P. J., P. Purdon, J. Russell-Smith, P. M. Cooke and S. Sutton (2008) "The Management of Climate Change through Prescribed Savanna Burning: Emerging Contributions of Indigenous People in Northern Australia", *Public Administration and Development*, 28: 374–385.

Whitehead, P. J., J. Russell-Smith and P. M. Cooke (2009) "Fire Management Futures: New Options for Environmental and Socioeconomic Benefit", in *Culture, Ecology and Economy of Fire Management in Northern Australia: Rekindling the* Wurrk *Tradition*. Melbourne: CSIRO Publishing, pp. 379–394.

13
Global environmental health governance for sustainable development

Jamal Hisham Hashim and Zailina Hashim

Definition of health

According to the World Health Organization (WHO, 2006):

> Health is a state of complete physical, mental and social well-being and not merely the absence of disease or infirmity.
>
> The enjoyment of the highest attainable standard of health is one of the fundamental rights of every human being, without distinction of race, religion, political belief, economic or social condition.
>
> The health of all peoples is fundamental to the attainment of peace and security and is dependent upon the fullest co-operation of individuals and States.

This means that, because health is a fundamental human right, it is the responsibility of the state to ensure that every resident of the state enjoys a basic level of health status and accessibility to basic health services.

In 1974, Blum (1981) proposed an "Environment of Health" model, which was later referred to as the "Force Field and Well-being Paradigms of Health" (see Figure 13.1). According to Blum, four major determinants contribute to the health and well-being of humans. These determinants or "force fields" are heredity, healthcare services, behaviour or lifestyles and the environment, all of which must be taken into account when addressing the health status of an individual and the greater community. Many

---

Green economy and good governance for sustainable development: Opportunities, promises and concerns, Puppim de Oliveira (ed.),
United Nations University Press, 2012, ISBN 978-92-808-1216-9

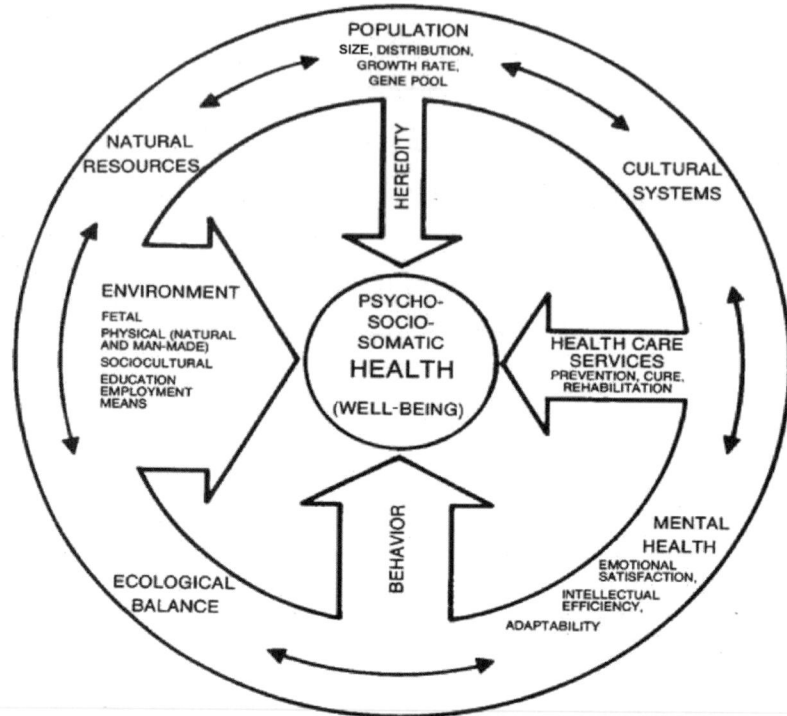

Figure 13.1 The "Environment of Health" model of H. L. Blum.

were initially sceptical about Blum's assertion of the importance of the environment in shaping human health. This was maybe because environmental deterioration in the late twentieth century had not yet reached a point where it had serious implications for human health. Yet, in that period, the Earth has begun to show stresses from rapid development in the form of urbanization and industrialization that do not seem to be sustainable in the long term.

The size of each determinant signifies its relative significance in influencing human health. Thus, the most important determinant is the environment, followed by lifestyles and heredity. Medical care, which is a major focus of public expenditure and intervention, has the least impact on health and well-being. An argument can be made here that the greatest impacts on the improvement in the general health of the masses can be more effectively and efficiently achieved through improvements in environmental health conditions such as sanitation, safe water supply, food hygiene and disease vector control than through improving public access to the latest medical care technology. At least, this statement is undeniably true for many developing nations, if not for the developed world as well.

The science of public health

> Public health ... emerged in the mid-19th century in several countries (England, continental Europe, and the USA) as part of both social reform movements and the growth of biological and medical knowledge (especially causation and management of infectious disease) [Porter, 1997]. Farr, Chadwick, Virchow, Koch, Pasteur, and Shattuck helped to establish the discipline on the basis of four factors: (1) decision making based on data and evidence (vital statistics, surveillance and outbreak investigations, laboratory science); (2) a focus on populations rather than individuals; (3) a goal of social justice and equity; and (4) an emphasis on prevention rather than curative care. All these elements are embedded in most definitions of public health. (Koplan et al., 2009: 1993)

The definition of public health that has best stood the test of time is that proposed by Winslow (1920) some 90 years ago:

> Public health is the science and the art of preventing disease, prolonging life, and promoting physical health and efficiency through organized community efforts for the sanitation of the environment, the control of community infections, the education of the individual in principles of personal hygiene, the organization of medical and nursing service for the early diagnosis and preventive treatment of disease, and the development of the social machinery which will ensure to every individual in the community a standard of living adequate for the maintenance of health; organizing these benefits in such a fashion as to enable every citizen to realize his birthright and longevity.

Public health initially developed as a branch of medical science, which focuses on the five levels of disease prevention. These are (1) health promotion; (2) specific protection; (3) early diagnosis and prompt treatment; (4) disability limitation; and (5) rehabilitation. Later, it expanded to include knowledge and practical inputs from related and supportive disciplines such as ecology, entomology, medical microbiology, sanitary and safety engineering, nutrition, veterinary science, food science and many others, which further enriched the field.

Thus, public health focuses on the science and art of preventing disease, promoting health and prolonging life not only through governmental interventions but also through organized community efforts and the understanding and application of a multidisciplinary approach. Public health in theory and in practice is mainly guided by the principles set forth in the Constitution of the World Health Organization (WHO) during the creation of the international body in 1948 (WHO, 1948, 2006). These principles are:

- Health is a state of complete physical, mental and social well-being and not merely the absence of disease or infirmity.
- The enjoyment of the highest attainable standard of health is one of the fundamental rights of every human being without distinction of race, religion, political belief, economic or social condition.
- The health of all peoples is fundamental to the attainment of peace and security and is dependent upon the fullest co-operation of individuals and States.
- The achievement of any State in the promotion and protection of health is of value to all.
- Unequal development in different countries in the promotion of health and control of disease, especially communicable disease, is a common danger.
- Healthy development of the child is of basic importance; the ability to live harmoniously in a changing total environment is essential to such development.
- The extension to all peoples of the benefits of medical, psychological and related knowledge is essential to the fullest attainment of health.
- Informed opinion and active co-operation on the part of the public are of the utmost importance in the improvement of the health of the people.
- Governments have a responsibility for the health of their peoples which can be fulfilled only by the provision of adequate health and social measures.

We can see that public health in its definition, theory and practice embodies the concept of sustainable development. In principle, sustainable development is development that also safeguards human health and well-being. Development that inflicts significant damage to the environment, which subsequently compromises human health and well-being, cannot be sustained over time. In other words, a healthy population is a prerequisite for a productive and creative society, which is needed to sustain national development.

What is global health?

The traditional effort of maintaining a healthy population within the national boundary in which they reside may no longer be adequate and protective. This is because threats to human health such as infectious diseases and pollution do not seem to respect national boundaries. This is evidenced in health issues such as the severe acute respiratory syndrome (SARS), avian influenza and H1N1, transboundary air and river pollution, and nuclear hazards such as Chernobyl and Fukushima. These global health concerns led to a growing interest in the science and discipline of global health.

The term "global health" is relatively recent. It "is derived from public health and international health, which, in turn, evolved from hygiene and tropical medicine. However, although frequently referenced, global health is rarely defined" (Koplan et al., 2009: 1993).

The Institute of Medicine of the National Academies in the United States defines global health as "health problems, issues, and concerns that transcend national boundaries, may be influenced by circumstances or experiences in other countries, and are best addressed by cooperative actions and solutions" (IOM, 1997: 2). This means health problems or issues that are international or transboundary in nature, which calls for concerted efforts that are international, interdisciplinary and multidisciplinary in approach to mitigate and control the health outcomes.

The Consortium of Universities for Global Health defines global health as "an area for study, research, and practice that places a priority on improving health and achieving equity in health for all people worldwide. Global health emphasizes transnational health issues, determinants, and solutions; involves many disciplines within and beyond the health sciences and promotes interdisciplinary collaboration; and is a synthesis of population-based prevention with individual-level clinical care" (Koplan et al., 2009: 1995).

Global health may refer to a health problem that stems from a global phenomenon such as climate change that is causing widespread changes in global disease patterns, especially of communicable diseases. It may also refer to a local or regional health issue that may spread globally. Examples of this would be the Chernobyl nuclear disaster, the swine flu H1N1 or SARS. The magnitude of the problems may not be large or widespread but the ability of these problems to spread across borders and continents makes them truly global in impact. However, we should not restrict global health to health-related issues that transcend international borders. Rather, the global context refers to any health issue that concerns many countries or is affected by transnational determinants, such as urbanization, or solutions such as polio eradication.

Global environmental health

According to the WHO, environmental health "is comprised of those aspects of human health, including quality of life, that are determined by physical, chemical, biological, social, and psychosocial factors in the environment. It also refers to the theory and practice of assessing, correcting, controlling, and preventing those factors in the environment that can potentially affect adversely the health of present and future generations" (WHO, 1993). Since environmental health aims to protect not only present but also future generations, its scope should be in line with that of sustainable development, which defines development as that which meets the needs of both the present and future generations.

Assessing health impacts from the environment, and correcting, controlling and preventing the impacts from being realized, is the main strategy and approach in environmental health. Environmental health is regarded as one of the sub-disciplines of public health. It is closely associated with occupational health, which is another sub-discipline of public health. Both environmental health and occupational health deal with health threats originating from human environment. Whereas the former deals with human ambient or general environment, the latter deals with human work environment.

Global environmental health, which is the main topic of this chapter, deals with environmental health issues that transcend national boundaries. Global environmental disruptions and changes have translated into impacts on human health that are both acute in nature, such as water-borne diseases owing to poor sanitation, as well as those that are chronic, such as skin cancers from exposure to arsenic in groundwater or exposure to excess ultraviolet light owing to depletion of the stratospheric ozone layer. Clearly, environmental health is not just a local public health issue but also a global public health concern.

The scope of environmental health

The scope of environmental health is truly extensive. The WHO Expert Committee on the Planning, Organization, and Administration of National Environmental Health Programmes (WHO, 1970: 10–11) proposed that its scope should include or relate to the following:

(1) Water supplies, with special reference to the provision of adequate quantities of safe drinking water that are readily accessible to the user,... giving due consideration to other essential uses of water resources.
(2) Waste-water treatment and water-pollution control, including ... domestic sewage,... and the control of the quality of surface water ... and ground water.
(3) Solid-waste management, including sanitary handling and disposal.
(4) Vector control, including the control of arthropods, molluscs, rodents, and other alternative hosts of disease.
(5) Prevention or control of soil pollution by human excreta and by substances detrimental to human, animal or plant life.
(6) Food hygiene, including milk hygiene.

(7) Control of air pollution.
(8) Radiation control.
(9) Occupational health, in particular the control of physical, chemical, and biological hazards.
(10) Noise control.
(11) Housing and its immediate environment, in particular the public health aspects of residential, public, and institutional buildings.
(12) Urban and regional planning.
(13) Environmental health aspects of air, sea, or land transport.
(14) Accident prevention.
(15) Public recreation and tourism, in particular the environmental health aspects of public beaches, swimming pools, camping sites, etc.
(16) Sanitation measures associated with epidemics, emergencies, disasters, and migrations of populations.
(17) Preventive measures required ensuring that the general environment is free from risk to health.

Even though the relationship between the environment and human health has been recognized since the mid-1970s, environmental health issues continue to plague human populations even today. The United Nations Environment Programme (UNEP, 2002) suggests that poor environmental quality is directly responsible for some 25 per cent of ill health worldwide. According to the WHO (2009), the five leading environmental health risks – indoor smoke; unsafe water, sanitation and hygiene; outdoor air pollution; global climate change; and lead exposure – were responsible for 8.7 per cent of all global deaths and 8.0 per cent of global DALYs (disability-adjusted life years) in 2004. These percentages were higher in low- and middle-income countries, at 9.6 per cent and 8.6 per cent, respectively (Table 13.1). Environmental degradation tends to have a greater impact on the health of populations in low- and middle-income countries than on those in high-income countries. This is because the environment is usually poorer in developing nations, their populations are more vulnerable to environmental threats owing to poorer nutrition and health status, and they are also less capable of adapting to a changing environment.

This clearly delivers the message that, although the environment supports lives, it can also adversely affect health and destroys lives when its integrity and sustainability are being compromised through unplanned and haphazard developments.

Global environmental health and sustainable development

Through our understanding of ecology and the biological sciences, we know that humans are the most adaptable creatures on the Earth. They

Table 13.1 Deaths and DALYs attributable to five environmental risks and to all five risks combined, by region in 2004

Risk	World	Low- and middle-income countries	High-income countries
Percentage of deaths			
Indoor smoke from solid fuels	3.3	3.9	0.0
Unsafe water, sanitation, hygiene	3.2	3.8	0.1
Urban outdoor air pollution	2.0	1.9	2.5
Global climate change	0.2	0.3	0.0
Lead exposure	0.2	0.3	0.0
All five risks	8.7	9.6	2.6
Percentage of DALYs			
Indoor smoke from solid fuels	2.7	2.9	0.0
Unsafe water, sanitation, hygiene	4.2	4.6	0.3
Urban outdoor air pollution	0.6	0.6	0.8
Global climate change	0.4	0.4	0.0
Lead exposure	0.6	0.6	0.1
All five risks	8.0	8.6	1.2

Source: WHO (2009).
Note: DALYs = disability-adjusted life years (i.e. years of productive life lost owing to disability).

are the most intelligent, mobile and ubiquitous among the higher organisms. Yet in some ways they can also be very vulnerable. As human degrade their environment, the physical changes to the environment first show their impacts on the lower plants and animals, for example the effects of acid rain on plants and of DDT on birds. Subsequently, as the extent and intensity of environmental pollution escalate, the seriousness of the effects of environmental pollution on humans becomes more obvious. Of increasing concern are the potential chronic effects of cumulative toxicants in the environment such as heavy metals, halogenated organics and polycyclic aromatic hydrocarbons. Among the health effects of these toxicants are cancer and their effects on critical organs such as the kidneys and liver.

The irony is that the chronic impacts of today's pollution will be on future generations because these chronic health effects may take 20 to 50 years or even longer to manifest themselves. Thus we have situations where, in their quest for rapid development, parents are polluting and harming their own children and grandchildren. Can we allow such situations to continue unchecked? The other question concerns what we can do to minimize such health effects.

We have argued earlier that a healthy population is a prerequisite for a productive and creative society, which is needed to sustain national development. Similarly, uncontrolled and unsustainable development that overexploits the natural environment and its resources is the main cause of our present environmental health problems. Unimpeded consumption of fossil fuel reserves has led to serious worldwide air pollution in megacities, which causes severe respiratory and cardiovascular health problems. In addition, over-consumption of fossil fuels has led to excess greenhouse gas emissions, which have resulted in global warming and climate change. Climate change has resulted in health-related problems such as the increased incidence of heat stress and of vector-borne and waterborne diseases.

The Brundtland Report (WCED, 1987) challenged us with the question of the sustainability of an economic and industrial development trajectory based on relatively cheap and accessible sources of fossil fuels. Environmental damage and ecosystem disruption were beginning to take their toll on the Earth's valuable and depleting natural resources such as forests, fresh water, and terrestrial, aquatic and marine lives. At the same time, the world's population was growing exponentially and still is. This population growth continues to exert tremendous pressures on the Earth's limited and depleting natural resources.

The dynamic changes in human population, depleting natural resources and disrupted ecosystems are beginning to have a serious impact on human health, changing morbidity and mortality trends. Even though global economic development has helped alleviate health problems related to poor sanitation (such as waterborne and food-borne diseases), some glaring deficiencies in health remain, especially in the developing world. Globally, 1.1 billion people lack access to safe drinking water, and 2.6 billion people lack proper sanitation (WHO and UNICEF, 2005). An estimated 24 per cent of the global disease burden and 23 per cent of all deaths can be attributed to environmental factors. Globally, about 1.5 million deaths per year from diarrhoeal diseases are attributable to environmental factors of contaminated water, poor sanitation and poor hygiene. Another 1.5 million deaths annually from respiratory infections are attributable to the environment, mainly indoor and outdoor air pollution (Pruss-Ustun and Corvalan, 2006).

The growing world population will continue to exert tremendous pressure on depleting natural resources unless some drastic actions are taken to slow down this consumption pattern. In 2009, the world population was 6.8 billion and was projected to reach 8.1 billion by 2025. What is more alarming is that most of this growth is occurring in the developing countries. The total fertility rate, which is the average number of children born to a woman in her lifetime, is 2.6 worldwide. It ranges from 1.7 in the developed countries to 4.6 in the least developed countries. By 2050, the population of Africa is expected to double to 2 billion (Population Reference Bureau, 2009). We have already mentioned that deaths and

DALYs attributable to environmental risks are already more pronounced in the developing countries (Table 13.1). Coupled with the high population growth rates that will be seen in these countries, the health consequences may be quite devastating if the prevailing conditions are allowed to continue. Therefore, the question of vulnerability and sustainability is even more acute and crucial in the developing world.

Fossil fuels such as petroleum, coal and natural gas, as well as earth minerals, are fast depleting owing to over-extraction and over-consumption. Fossil fuels, which are non-renewable energy resources, are being exhausted while renewable energy sources such as wind, solar and geothermal power are still not viable enough to fill the void left by the depleting non-renewable energy. Fossil fuels are chemical energy that has been harnessed from solar energy. This surplus energy is being stored in the Earth's crust. High population growth and increasing rates of energy consumption over the past century have very much depleted these energy sources; we cannot possibly maintain the current rate of energy consumption, let alone cater for future growth in energy demand.

Global environmental change and health impacts

Environmental health, as with the other disciplines of environmental sciences, has often been inappropriately labelled as being anti-development. This is a serious misperception of the aim of environmental sciences among the public, businesses and governments, and it needs to be rectified. Any form or degree of economic development cannot be maintained in an unhealthy society. Impacts of the environment on human health can lead to serious impediments to the nation's development processes. Such impediments may be caused by:

- Poor inventive and creative capabilities (for example, the effect of neurotoxins such as lead on children's IQ development)
- Reduced academic performance of schoolchildren and students (for example, increased school absenteeism owing to sickness related to air pollution, such as asthma, respiratory tract infections and conjunctivitis)
- Low productivity (for example, a high incidence of sickness causing high work absenteeism)
- High health maintenance costs (for example, the high cost of medical care for environmentally related diseases such as cancer, cardiovascular diseases and cataract)
- Loss of productive age (for example, reduced lifespan from chronic diseases such as respiratory and cardiovascular diseases owing to air

pollution and from cancer and nephrotoxicity owing to heavy metal poisoning)
Therefore, a well-planned national environmental health programme should not impede economic development. On the contrary, it should boost economic development by providing a country with a healthier and more productive workforce, who will not only initiate a high rate of economic growth but also be able to sustain it over a long period of time.

Stratospheric ozone depletion and climate change are two global environmental disruptions stemming from unsustainable development with serious health implications.

Stratospheric ozone depletion and health

Stratospheric ozone depletion, which was first observed over the Antarctic, is now also clearly visible over the Arctic. Unusually long-lasting cold conditions in the Arctic lower stratosphere led to persistent enhancement in ozone-destroying forms of chlorine and to unprecedented ozone loss, exceeding 80 per cent at 18–20 kilometres altitude (Manney et al., 2011). The stratospheric ozone layer filters the sun's harmful ultraviolet-B radiation. Among the health effects of increased UV-B radiation on humans is an increased incidence of skin cancers and cataracts. Although mitigations against ozone depletion have been generally successful, the same cannot be said of efforts to mitigate climate change.

The introduction of chlorofluorocarbons (CFCs) and other ozone-depleting substances (ODS) as propellants and refrigerants was thought to be something that would be harmless to human health because CFC is an inert and non-reactive gas with a low mammalian toxicity. However, owing to its non-reactiveness, it remains unchanged in the troposphere for a significantly long time. This allows it to reach the upper stratosphere, where it then reacts with the ozone layer and destroys it (Andino, 1999). The ozone layer, which acts as a filter for the harmful UV-B radiation, now allows an excess of UV-B radiation to penetrate through to the lower troposphere and cause harmful health effects. This would be an example of a good thing turning bad on humans. This demonstrates how complex and sensitive the Earth system is and how little we know about it. Once damage such as this has been inflicted on the Earth system, reversing it can even be harder.

The health effects and costs from ozone depletion can be quite staggering. West et al. (2005) predicted that an estimated 5–20 per cent depletion of the ozone layer by 2050 would result in an increased prevalence of cortical cataract by 1.3–6.9 per cent above expected levels among the population of the United States. This will translate into 167,000–830,000 additional cases of cortical cataract by 2050. Because of the high prevalence of cataracts in older persons, this increase could represent an excess cost of USD 563 million to USD 2.8 billion (at a 2003 cost of USD 3,370 per cataract operation).

The US Environmental Protection Agency (US EPA, 2006) also estimated the incremental incidences of basal cell carcinoma, squamous cell carcinoma and cutaneous malignant melanoma, as well as deaths from non-melanoma skin cancer, based on the increased levels of UV-B radiation under various ODS control initiatives, namely the Montreal Protocol of 1987 and the subsequent London Amendments of 1990, Copenhagen Amendments of 1992 and Montreal Adjustments of 1997. The largest incremental is for squamous cell carcinoma. The number of excess squamous cell carcinoma cases among the US population based on the Montreal Protocol control scenario would be 26,627,765 between 2015 and 2050. However, the more stringent controls accorded by various amendments would lead to a drop in numbers to 924,516 cases based on the London Amendments, to 186,009 cases based on the Copenhagen Amendments, and to 105,993 cases based on the Montreal Adjustments. Thus, we can see the tremendous health benefits in terms of the number of cancer cases avoided through an intervention on unsustainable development and a potential environmental disaster.

Climate change and health

Greenhouse gases such as carbon dioxide (CO_2), methane, nitrous oxide, CFCs and ozone prevent long-wave radiation from the Earth from escaping through the atmosphere into space. This produces the greenhouse effect, which leads to the phenomenon known as global warming, which drives climate change. The major greenhouse gas is CO_2, which comes mainly from fossil fuel combustion, cement production and land-use changes such as deforestation (Friedlingstein et al., 2010).

According to the Intergovernmental Panel on Climate Change (IPCC, 2007), climate change "refers to any change in climate over time, whether due to natural variability or as a result of human activity. This usage differs from that of the United Nations Framework Convention on Climate Change (UNFCCC), where climate change refers to a change of climate that is attributed directly or indirectly to human activity that alters the composition of the global atmosphere and that is in addition to natural climate variability observed over comparable time periods" (IPCC, 2007: 2, fn1).

Global average surface temperature has increased since 1861. Over the twentieth century, it has increased by about 0.74 ± 0.18 degrees Celsius. Since the late 1950s, overall global temperature increases in the troposphere and in surface temperature have been 0.13 degrees Celsius per decade. The 1990s was the warmest decade, with 1998 being the warmest year since 1861. The greatest warming effects occur over the tropical and subtropical regions. Among the environmental impacts of climate change would be rising atmospheric temperatures, changes in precipitation patterns, rising sea levels and ocean heat content (IPCC, 2007).

Among the health impacts of climate change will be thermal stress from heat waves. Decreased precipitation may cause severe droughts that trigger forest fires, leading to respiratory problems; give rise to famine and hunger; reduce surface water flow; and pollute drinking water sources. Increased precipitation and rising sea water cause flooding of low-lying areas, leading to population displacement, accidental deaths, and the spread of waterborne, vector-borne and zoonotic diseases (Figure 13.2).

The long-term impacts of climate change on human health are sometimes obscured by the shorter-term impacts from environmental changes brought about by economic development and urbanization. These combined impacts are probably at play in the Mekong Delta of Cambodia and Viet Nam, which is believed to be one of the areas significantly affected by climate change (Figure 13.3). Both environmental and climate changes will trigger environmental drivers such as population growth, sea-level rise and extreme weather events. These environmental drivers will then generate risk factors such as water pollution and vector habitat change, which will subsequently give rise to waterborne and vector-borne diseases, respectively.

As the Seventeenth Conference of the Parties (COP17) to the UNFCCC came to a close in Durban, South Africa, in early December 2011, countries across the globe were still debating the most effective mechanism to combat climate change, even though they almost unanimously agreed that the impacts of climate change are real and impending. At least 120 countries have backed the European Union's roadmap, which would see countries set a deadline of 2015 to sign a new global treaty with legally binding carbon emission targets. It would come into force from 2020 to replace the Kyoto Protocol, which expires in 2012 (*The Guardian*, 9 December 2011). Major carbon emitters such as the United States, China, India and Russia, which together produce 4,912 Teragrams of oxidized carbon (Tg-C), or 53.7 per cent of the world's total of 9,139 Tg-C in 2010, are reluctant to endorse this roadmap because it would seriously curtail their economic and industrial growth. The African continent, which is predicted to suffer significantly from the consequences of climate change, is responsible for only 326 Tg-C emitted, or 3.6 per cent of the world's total (CDIAC, 2011). This reflects a serious equity issue whereby the more affluent developed and developing countries have

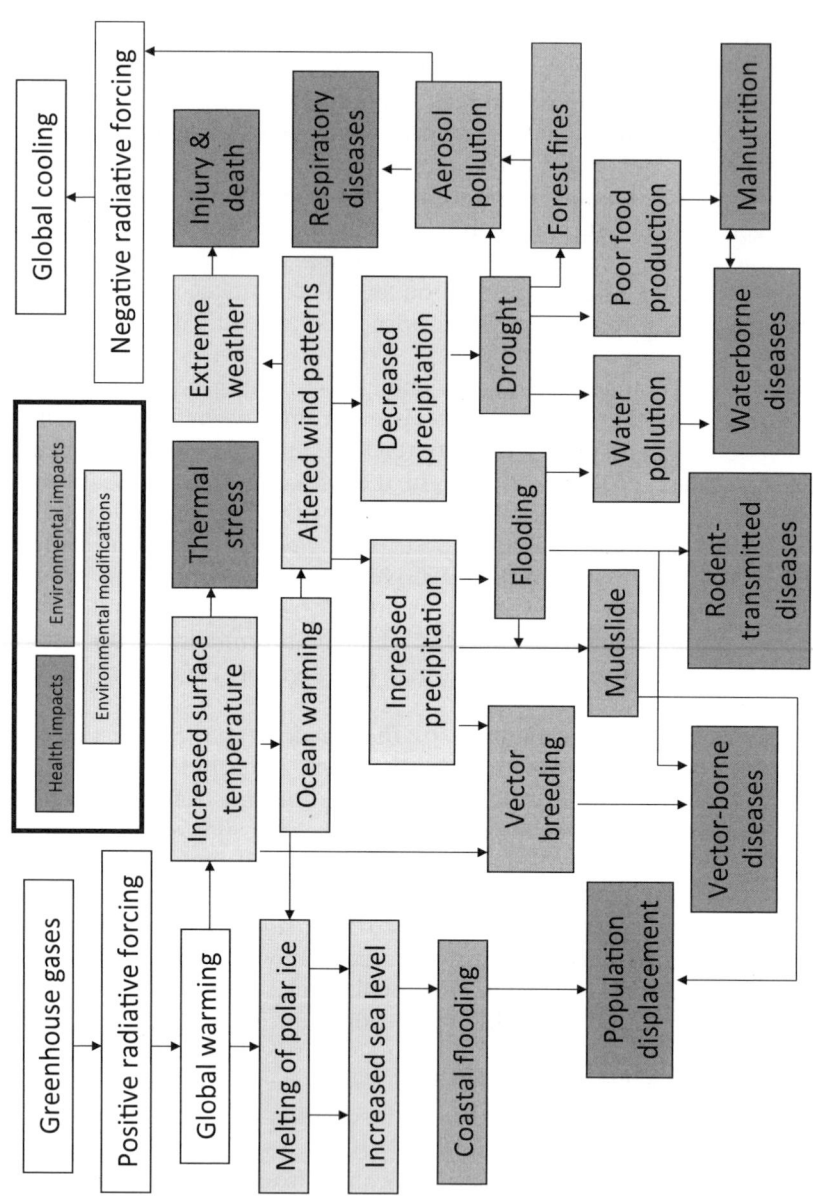

Figure 13.2 Health effects of global climate change.

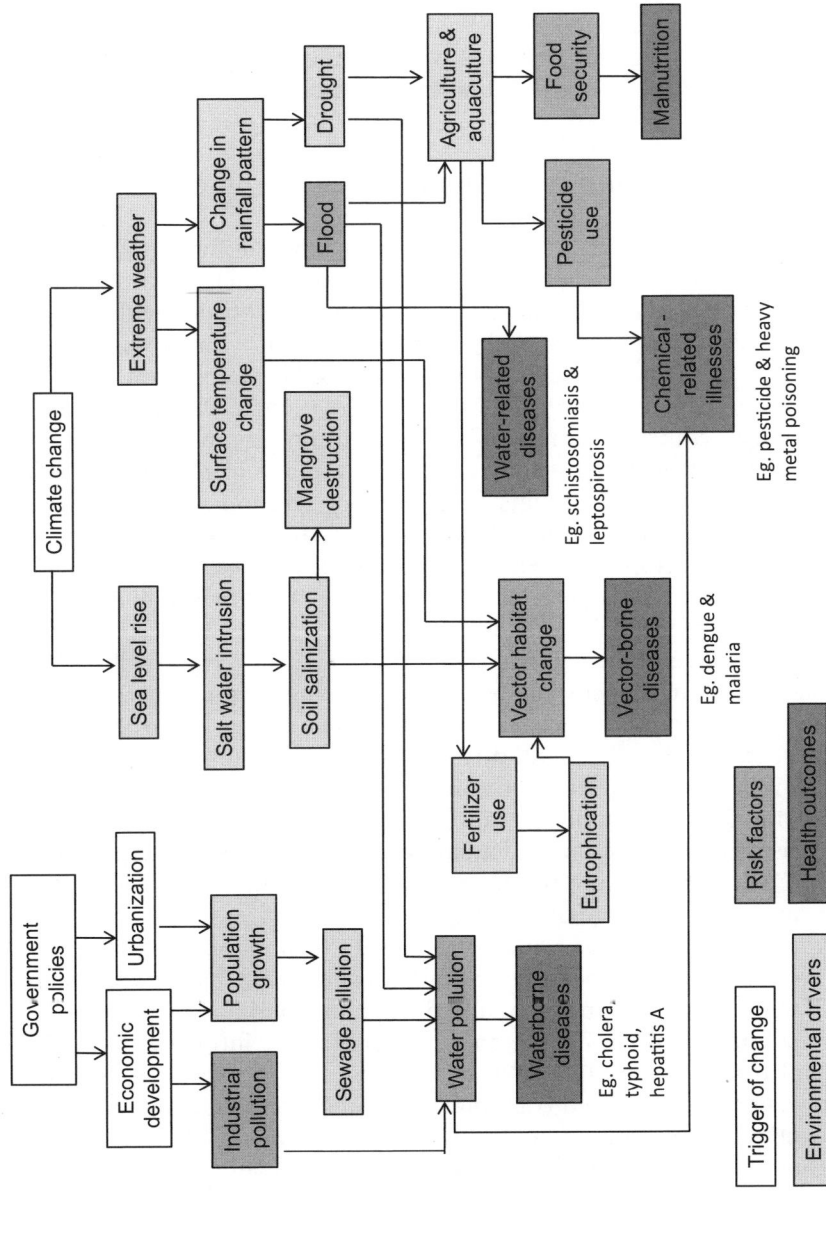

Figure 13.3 A theoretical assessment of the combined impacts of environmental and climate change on the environment and human health in the Mekong Delta.

much to gain economically from unrestricted carbon emissions, whereas the poorer nations in Africa have much to lose from the impacts of climate change. The developed and developing worlds are also better endowed to invest in climate change adaptation measures such as flood control and land irrigation schemes whereas the poorer nations are left to fend for themselves against the onslaught of climate change.

Environmental health for sustainable development

Good environmental health governance as outlined by the WHO as early as 1970 (see above) has helped to reduce much of the world's environment-related disease morbidity and mortality burden with respect to preventable communicable diseases associated with contaminated water and food as well as vector-borne diseases. However, even as traditional environmental health issues are being overcome through technology, organized community initiatives, health promotion and behavioural change, new environmental health challenges emerge to plague us. These include increasing health threats from outdoor and indoor air pollution and from environmental chemicals such as lead, arsenic and pesticides, as well as the health consequences of global climate change.

To make development sustainable in the long run, environmental conservation and environmental health governance should be incorporated into national development plans (Figure 13.4). Each nation will have a national aspiration, which will be defined through its various national economic, agricultural, industrial, environmental, energy and social policies. These national policies will drive its national development plans. For example, if a country aspires to be an industrialized country, it must have a well-defined energy policy, because no country can develop its industrial infrastructure without an adequate and efficient energy supply. Most countries would have a mixed energy supply policy that sources supplies from a mix comprising fossil fuels such as coal and gas and renewable energy sources such as solar and wind power. Such an energy policy will allow a country to spearhead its national development plans, which may include agricultural expansion, industrialization, commercialization, education, communication, health and transportation infrastructures. All these will bring positive or beneficial outcomes to society such as infrastructural growth, improved communication and transport, and increased employment, among others. At the same time, however, there may also be negative or undesirable outcomes such as the depletion of natural resources and pollution. In order for the overall national development plans to be sustainable, the positive outcomes need to be maximized while the negative outcomes are minimized.

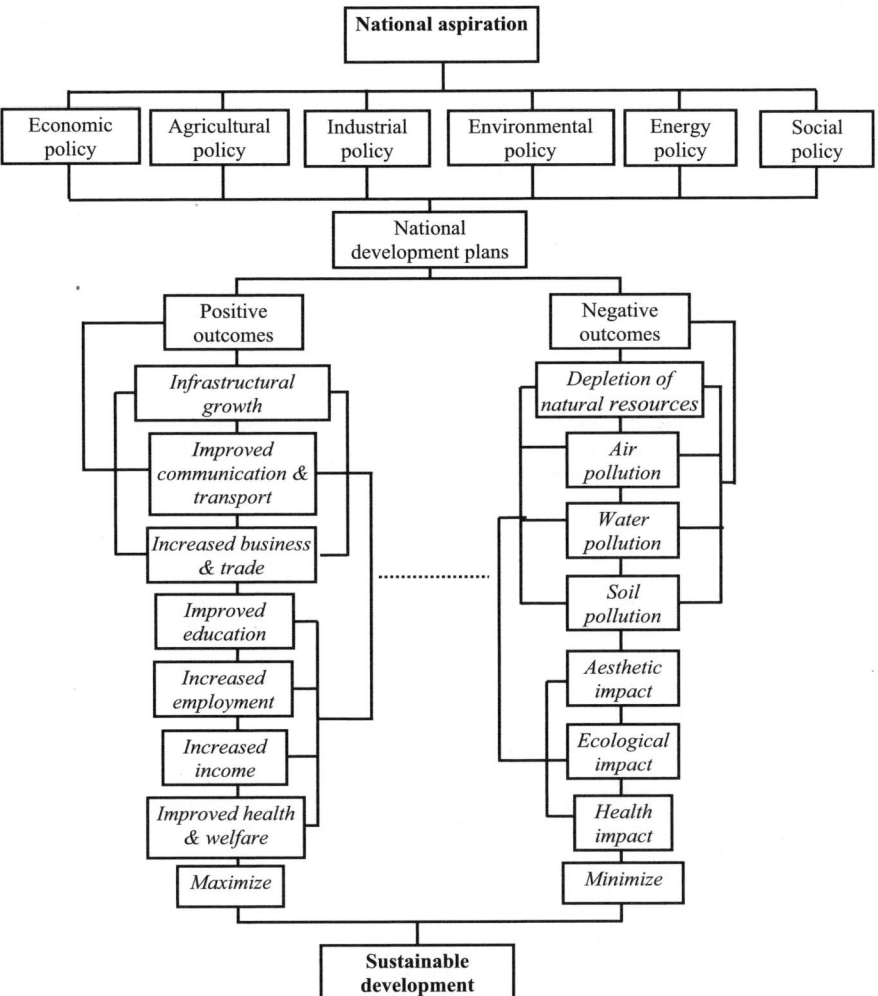

Figure 13.4 Environmental health governance within a national development plan.

REFERENCES

Andino, J. M. (1999) "Chlorofluorocarbons (CFCs) Are Heavier Than Air, So How Do Scientists Suppose That These Chemicals Reach the Altitude of the Ozone Layer to Adversely Affect It?", *Scientific American*, 21 October.
Blum, H. L. (1981) *Planning for Health*. New York: Human Sciences Press.
CDIAC (Carbon Dioxide Information Analysis Center) (2011) "Preliminary 2009 and 2010 Global and National Estimates of Carbon Emissions from Fossil-fuel

Combustion and Cement Manufacture". Available at ⟨http://cdiac.ornl.gov/trends/emis/perlim_2009_2010_estimates.html⟩ (accessed 7 February 2012).

Friedlingstein, P., R. A. Houghton, G. Marland, J. Hackler, T. A. Boden, T. J. Conway, J. G. Canadell, M. R. Raupach, P. Ciais and C. Le Quéré (2010) "Update on CO_2 Emissions", *Nature Geoscience*, 3: 811–812.

IOM (Institute of Medicine) (1997) *America's Vital Interest in Global Health: Protecting Our People, Enhancing Our Economy, and Advancing Our International Interests*. Washington, DC: The National Academies Press.

IPCC (Intergovernmental Panel on Climate Change) (2007) "Summary for Policymakers", in S. Solomon, D. Qin, M. Manning, Z. Chen, M. Marquis, K. B. Averyt, M. Tignor and H. L. Miller (eds), *Climate Change 2007: The Physical Science Basis. Contribution of Working Group I to the Fourth Assessment Report of the Intergovernmental Panel on Climate Change*. Cambridge and New York: Cambridge University Press.

Koplan, J. P., T. C. Bond, M. H. Merson, K. S. Reddy, M. H. Rodriguez, N. K. Sewankambo and J. N. Wasserheit (2009) "Towards a Common Definition of Global Health", *Lancet*, 373: 1993–1995.

Manney, G. L., M. L. Santee, M. Rex, N. J. Livesey, M. C. Pitts, P. Veefkind, E. R. Nash, I. Wohltmann, R. Lehmann, L. Froidevaux, L. R. Poole, M. R. Schoeberl, D. P. Haffner, J. Davies, V. Dorokhov, H. Gernandt, B. Johnson, R. Kivi, E. Kyrö, N. Larsen, P. F. Levelt, A. Makshtas, C. T. McElroy, H. Nakajima, M. C. Parrondo, D. W. Tarasick, P. von der Gathen, K. A. Walker and N. S. Zinoviev (2011) "Unprecedented Arctic Ozone Loss in 2011", *Nature*, 478: 469–475.

Population Reference Bureau (2009) *2009 World Population Data Sheet*. Washington, DC: Population Reference Bureau.

Porter, R. (1997). *The Greatest Benefit to Mankind: A Medical History of Humanity*. New York, USA: W. W. Norton & Company.

Pruss-Ustun, A. and C. Corvalan (2006) *Preventing Disease Through Healthy Environments: Towards an Estimate of Environmental Burden of Disease*. Geneva: World Health Organization.

The Guardian (2011) "Durban COP17: Connie Hedegaard Puts Pressure on China, US and India", 9 December.

UNEP (United Nations Environment Programme) (2002) *Global Environment Outlook 3 Synthesis: Past, Present and Future Perspective*. London: Earthscan.

US EPA (United States Environmental Protection Agency) (2006) *Human Health Benefits of Stratospheric Ozone Protection: A Peer Reviewed Report*. Washington, DC: US EPA.

WCED (World Commission on Environment and Development) (1987) *Our Common Future* [Brundtland Report]. Oxford: Oxford University Press.

West, S. K., J. D. Longstreth, B. E. Munoz, H. M. Pitcher and D. D. Duncan (2005) "Model of Risk of Cortical Cataract in the US Population with Exposure to Increased Ultraviolet Radiation Due to Stratospheric Ozone Depletion", *American Journal of Epidemiology*, 162: 1080–1088.

WHO (World Health Organization) (1948) *Preamble to the Constitution of the World Health Organization as Adopted by the International Health Conference*, New York, 19–22 June, 1946; signed on 22 July 1946 by the representatives of 61

States (*Official Records of the World Health Organization*, no. 2, p. 100) and entered into force on 7 April 1948.

WHO (World Health Organization) (1970) *National Environmental Health Programmes: Their Planning, Organization, and Administration. Report of a WHO Expert Committee*. Geneva: World Health Organization.

WHO (World Health Organization) (1993) "Environmental Health Definition", developed at a WHO consultation in Sofia, Bulgaria. As reported in US Department of Health and Human Services (1998) "An Ensemble of Definitions of Environmental Health", ⟨http://www.health.gov/environment/DefinitionsofEnvHealth/ehdef2.htm⟩ (accessed 7 February 2012).

WHO (World Health Organization) (2006) "Constitution of the World Health Organization", *Basic Documents*, 45th edn, Supplement, October.

WHO (World Health Organization) (2009) *Global Health Risks: Mortality and Burden of Disease Attributable to Selected Major Risks*. Geneva: WHO Press.

WHO (World Health Organization) and UNICEF (United Nations Children's Fund) (2005) *Water for Life: Making It Happen. WHO/UNICEF Joint Monitoring Programme for Water Supply and Sanitation*. Geneva: WHO Press.

Winslow C.-E. A. (1920) "The Untilled Fields of Public Health", *Modern Medicine*, 2: 183–191.

14

Good governance in cities for promoting a greener economy

Jose A. Puppim de Oliveira, Aki Suwa, Osman Balaban, Christopher N. H. Doll, Ping Jiang, Magali Dreyfus, Raquel Moreno-Peñaranda, Puspita Dirgahayani and Erin Kennedy

Introduction

Most of the world's population lives in urban areas today. Besides population, cities concentrate disproportionate amounts of the world's economy and the decision-making power in most countries. Thus, the challenges and opportunities for creating a greener economy and the institutional framework for sustainable development rest necessarily, or mostly, on how cities are developed and managed. Moreover, cities are centres of knowledge and innovation (both technological and institutional) that can make viable a greener economy and better governance within and beyond the cities.

The advent of the "new economy" based on the spread of information, technologies and efficient logistics initially was thought to disperse economic activities and reduce the need for a physical presence for certain activities (for example, work). However, the globalization of economic, political and social activities led to the need for a greater concentration of activities to generate economies of scale, and also concentrated decisions in large organizations to manage activities at the global scale (Sassen, 2000). These organizations required the concentration of physical structures and personnel, thus also creating a demand for services. Thus, cities grew in political and economic importance with globalization, instead of losing relevance.

The world today is much more connected and decisions are concentrated in large organizations, generally based in cities. The scale of some

Green economy and good governance for sustainable development: Opportunities, promises and concerns, Puppim de Oliveira (ed.),
United Nations University Press, 2012, ISBN 978-92-808-1216-9

organizations and the reach of their operations, including supply chain tiers, can influence the economy and politics globally. Some cities concentrate more of these organizations than other cities. Thus, a city's influence on economic, social and political systems, as well as its environmental consequences, can go beyond the city's boundaries. Besides the city economy, cities have huge influences on the regional and global environment and on regional and global economic, social and political systems. The scale of those influences can range from local (city level) to regional (areas beyond the immediate boundaries of the city), national and global.

Urban growth not only increases the number of people living in cities but also intensifies the opportunities and challenges in cities. Perhaps the most important opportunity linked to urban growth is the increase in the importance of the urban economy. With the processes of urbanization and rural–urban transformation, the economy in cities, especially in cities of developing countries, has been shifting from traditional artisanal crafts and markets to modern industry and service sectors. At present, a significant part of the world's economic activities and resources is concentrated in cities. Driven by the concentrated resources (for example, energy, human and finance) and huge markets, urban economies have developed very quickly since the nineteenth century. For instance, economic activities located in cities account for 55 per cent of gross national product in the least developed countries, 73 per cent in middle-income countries, and 85 per cent in the most developed countries (UN-HABITAT, 2006). In addition, 75 per cent of global economic production takes place in cities (Work Bank, 2009). The main objective of urban economies is to enlarge productive outcomes by concentrating markets for labour, goods and capital. This kind of economic development in cities can significantly promote the whole nation's economy and increase people's incomes, living standards and job opportunities. That is to say, rapidly growing cities bring economic prosperity not just to their inhabitants but to the whole country owing to spillover effects.

On the other hand, rapid urban growth habitually has entailed serious social and environmental challenges, such as urban poverty, various forms of pollution, vulnerabilities to natural events and climate change impacts. The negative and unsustainable outcomes of current urban economies, which are based on high production and consumption, as described in Chapter 5, have become more visible and attracted more attention since the 1990s. Cities today are responsible for 67 per cent of total global energy consumption and more than 70 per cent of greenhouse gas emissions (UN-HABITAT, 2008), and these trends significantly intensify the severity of two of the great challenges of our time: climate change and energy security. In order to keep up with rapid urban expansion and urban population growth, more resources as well as more consumption and production are required. The ever-increasing production and consumption in cities result in serious environmental problems in terms of air, water and land pollution and the degradation of ecosystems. Populations that do not have access to efficient resources and facilities in cities will suffer most from localized environmental problems and unhealthy living conditions. This constitutes another dark side of urban development – "social inequity", which can be regarded as just the result of the unbalanced and uneven structure of urbanization, especially in many developing countries.

The role of cities in promoting a green economy involves particularly the idea of greening the city economy, which also includes city decisions that go beyond the administrative boundaries of cities. The institutional framework for more sustainable development is intrinsically linked to the way cities operate and "think". The large concentration of decisions with a massive scale and far-reaching impacts puts cities in the centre of the discussions about sustainable development. Understanding how the economy and politics of the city function and how the city is connected to a larger world (regional, national, global) is fundamental to understanding how to create institutional mechanisms to move the world towards a green economy.

Cities and sustainable development

The urbanization process

Urbanization is one of the key defining features of humanity as a whole. The progressive shift of people from rural areas and activities into towns and cities is a complex process inextricably tied to economic development and technological change. Cities have existed for millennia but only relatively recently (the past 200 years) have large proportions of the human population moved into cities. Cities are fundamentally the result of surplus. Without a surplus of food production, all people would be occupied in the basic activity of subsistence and without a surplus; there would be no need for people to congregate in order to manage it. A surplus of food frees people from the land and allows them to engage in other activities, some of which produce goods, many of which are traded.

From this origin, cities have gradually evolved to incorporate larger numbers of people and wider ranges of activities. Although improving transport and trade enabled products to be brought from further afield, the volumes were such that a city was essentially reliant on the resources in its hinterland. It was not until the industrial revolution that a series of interrelated processes were set in motion to produce the urbanization we see today. The combination of a superabundance of energy in the form of fossil energy with innovations designed to exploit its potential to do mechanical work spurred the largest socio-spatial transformation the planet has ever witnessed. Increases in food production and the mechanization of that process freed yet more people to work in industry and services in new cities. Although this process was essentially no different from processes over the centuries, the scale and speed of this process were remarkable. In some places, it was so rapid that it often occurred more quickly than it could be managed, and it is this feature – the sheer speed of development – that poses a critical problem for sustainable development in the coming decades.

Impacts at different scales (local, regional, global)

Urbanization, although a global process, has gained more traction in some places than others. Being inextricably linked with economic development, it is no surprise to discover that the richest countries in the world are also among the most urbanized. However, the global disparity in wealth across the world is also matched by levels of urbanization. As such, it becomes rapidly apparent that not all cities are alike. They do not confront the same challenges, nor do they pose the same threat to the environment. It has been shown that, generally, as cities develop they first become centres of energy consumption relative to the national average and then become entities of efficiency, displaying lower levels of per capita energy use than the national average (IEA, 2008). Cities in China may be set on high- or low-carbon pathways of intensive development as a function of their geographical location and their activities (Dhakal, 2009). Yet even cities in developed countries display different levels of per capita emissions depending on their function (Onishi and Kobayashi, 2011). Cities may be concentrated on certain industries providing goods to other cities or internationally or be specialized in the service sector. In this sense, cities cannot be considered as stand-alone entities; they are dynamic and interconnected to their regions and countries but also to other cities and countries.

This broad relationship of the city to its surrounding areas can be explained in the following way. Early on, in the development stage, cities are more polluting because there is a lack of pollution in the hinterlands and rural areas. As countries develop, cities become more adept at both cleaning their environment and exporting pollution outside their boundaries, and often outside their own county. Combining this with economic development brings about greater efficiencies in city life and can begin to provide services that are cleaner at the per capita level, more so than in rural areas that have the same needs. Therefore cities can be seen as moving from being areas of relative pollution to relative efficiency.

Yet, with greater connectivity and speed of capital flows, innovations in one place can find themselves adopted or adapted in another location very quickly. Cities may be said to simultaneously embody efficiencies and externalities. It is the nature of this balance, not just over levels of development but over city size, density and economic function, that make cities such a complex area of study. The green economy in cities would seek to mitigate both of these impacts through the development process and throughout the many scales of impact from local to global.

Is the city a good place to foster a green economy?

The growing size and importance of cities across the globe make the city arguably the single most important entity for fostering the green economy. Cities are often a better spatial unit by which to conceive of such activities given the diverse nature of cities, because their management can be more responsive to urgent problems and free from competing national interests. Across the range of development, we see that cities play an increasingly important role in the implementation of policies regarding global environmental issues such as climate change and biodiversity loss. The green economy provides another platform for ambitious cities to promote their green credentials.

The green economy will take on a different character in different cities depending on their level of development and spatial organization. It is important to recognize that cities face different challenges. Although urbanization is increasing at a global scale, when this is differentiated by region, the picture that emerges is unique to each city. Cities in developed countries seek to grow by generating new jobs and industry; some cities are declining as they lose the battle for investment and talent. African and Asian cities are growing rapidly and their path of development will be crucial to the form that urbanization takes in this century. Every city has a role to play, whether adopting reforming measures for its economy, greening its sectors or seeking an entirely different path.

For those cities that are embarking on their development, it is crucial to understand that infrastructure lasts at least 30 years but often much longer. Once in place, many management options become channelled into seeking technical solutions of propulsion and retrofitting rather than basic design. Therefore, it is crucial to understand the relative importance of the different tools available to cities if the green economy is to become a precursor to sustainable development.

Institutional framework for governance in cities

Cities are ideally suited to experiment with and implement green initiatives (UNEP, 2011). They are human settlements that host a considerable number of people and economic activities. This concentration of people and their productive and consumptive behaviours have a significant impact on the environment in terms of, for example, air pollution, greenhouse gas emissions, waste production and water waste. It is therefore necessary to tackle the problem of the degradation of the environment that is brought about by the development of cities, while at the same time defining policies that are socially and economically oriented.

The study of cities as a favourable setting for the development of green economies is even more pertinent when considering the innovation capacity of urban centres (UNEP, 2011). In fact, the concentration of people, business activities and academic institutions favours the creation and circulation of knowledge, competition and, thus, the emergence of new ideas or technological products enabling the greening of economic activities.

Within this context, city governments have a major role to play. They hold important powers, in terms of legal competency and resources, in sectors that are relevant for the development of a green economy, such as transportation, waste management, urban planning, buildings, water management and welfare. Thus, through planning and cross-sectoral actions, local councils may elaborate policies aiming at creating "eco-cities" or "low-carbon" cities that have limited carbon emissions and resource consumption. However, local governments are also limited in their constitutional powers and they are not the only actors that can foster the development of a green economy at the city level.

Other administrations at the regional or state level, including international agencies and investors, private companies and businesses, non-governmental organizations (NGOs), citizens and influential individuals, are other key stakeholders in the economic and social life of a city (Bulkeley and Betsill, 2005; Corfee-Morlot et al., 2009). These urban contributors aspire to influence the definition of local policies in order to promote their own individual and collective interests and values. As such, the governance of cities occurs at multiple levels and contains vertical and horizontal dimensions (Corfee-Morlot et al., 2009). The vertical dimensions correspond to the traditional legal approach where local governments are at the bottom of the state administrative organization and where the central government possesses the supreme authority. Relations between the different authorities are usually strictly defined by laws as well as by their powers. The horizontal dimensions focus on actors intervening at the city scale. These can be, among others, local governments, civil society stakeholders, companies or individuals. Relations between them are not necessarily formalized; they are constantly evolving (for example, local governments networks, lobbies and local assemblies) and their influence over one another very much depends on the local environment.

Urban governance aims at connecting these dimensions and ensuring territorial cohesion from a political, economic and social perspective. Promoting a green economy in cities involves technological and behavioural changes, which requires the participation of all of the stakeholders. A key challenge is therefore to establish a governance scheme in which all of the different local interests are expressed and taken into account as well as represented to external agents, such as international agencies, other public authorities and/or private investors. This scheme varies from one urban context to another and is largely path dependent.

Physical, historical, political, social and economic factors are relevant when searching for an appropriate governance system. From a physical perspective, some cities are compact, concentrating people and activities within a limited area, whereas other cities face urban sprawl. Cities are also diverse in political and legal terms. From one country to another, depending on the depth of decentralization, local governments have different competencies and resources. This affects their level of autonomy in defining local policies. Moreover, in a strong administrative state, cities often have close relations with the central authorities and will base their action on national policies or will seek support from the authorities. Where state institutions are weaker, cities appear to be more independent and seek external or alternative support. Finally, cities have different socioeconomic structures. Some cities are instrumental economic centres that attract investment and talented populations whereas others are marked by economic backlash or social crisis because they are unable to cope with the rapidity of the urbanization process. This is particularly true for cities in developing countries, which are emerging as important actors in the global market economy but also have to deal with other priorities such as poverty eradication.

There is, therefore, no one-size-fits-all model of good governance. International agencies such as the World Bank, the United Nations Human Settlements Programme (UN-HABITAT) and the United Nations Economic and Social Commission for Asia and the Pacific are now working to develop indicators to assess current structures of urban governance and their efficiencies (see, for instance, UN-HABITAT, 2002). Four major principles are commonly put forward to assess good governance: effectiveness and efficiency; equity; participation; transparency and accountability. Efficiency refers to the delivery of public services and the promotion of local economic development and, in the context of the green economy, the protection of the environment and the promotion of social welfare. Equity means to ensure equal access to essential services. Participation refers to freedom of association and inclusion in the decision-making process. Transparency and accountability give citizens the ability to monitor the activity of decision-makers and actors who are contributing to policy-making. The ability to monitor may be either direct or through legitimate intermediate institutions or representatives.

The difficulty in assessing urban governance is considering these principles in light of the local environment's current situation, which may affect the four principles in different and unknown ways. Added to the question of the variety of urban contexts, governance is difficult to draw out because it is a dynamic process that regularly witnesses the emergence of new actors and policies. Governance must therefore be flexible enough to allow for new interests and solutions to emerge.

In many countries, informal economies represent an important share of cities' financial flows and have major impacts in terms of job creation and environmental degradation. Famous examples include the numerous local waste management companies that are owned by criminal organizations in the southern regions of Italy. In the first instance they appear to create job opportunities locally and are economically advantageous for contracting with the local government. In the long run, however, practice shows that the environmental requirements included in the public procurements are ignored within informal economies and the final outcome is often a higher rate of degradation than before.

Multilevel governance is therefore a challenging framework for the greening of city policies. It is essential to involve the different actors in the decision-making process and to coordinate their actions in order to achieve positive implementation of the policies (Bulkeley and Betsill, 2005).

Looking at the vertical dimension, the relationship between the national level and the local level is key. Many city projects need to be endorsed by a national policy in order to be fully effective. For instance, the devolution of powers and the greater autonomy of local governments from the central state allow city governments to adopt tax incentives for the use of clean energies or to levy taxes on polluting activities. Therefore, subsidiary power needs to be promoted in all sectors.

The relationship between cities and international stakeholders may also be important. Projects defined by international agencies or foreign private investors may contradict national urban policies and possibly affect the legitimacy of other public authorities. The rules defined for the regulation of these projects may also be limited in their scope and ignore other sectors' policies (Osmont et al., 2008). The permanence of the governance scheme defined by internationally funded projects after the withdrawal of the investors is also problematic. It is therefore necessary to connect the local–global initiatives with the national context. This can be achieved through the local governments, which have gained increased political weight with the growing economic value of a city's activities.

As for the horizontal dimension, it is necessary to create partnerships between the different actors. To that end, it is important that the green economy is mainstreamed in the local political agendas and that every department in municipal councils acknowledges this objective. The benefits of a green economy at the city level must be clearly identified. This involves developing the capacity of the different actors through local structures of information and debates. For example, relations between locally elected staff and communities can be strengthened through participatory democracy tools, such as local citizen assemblies. As for the relationship with private actors, legal frameworks such as public–private partnerships are useful instruments to bring local authorities and companies together to negotiate (Osmont et al., 2008). They encourage companies to participate in the creation of a common good while at the same time undertaking profit-making activities. Lastly, it is important to consider the networks of local authorities (Bulkeley, 2010). These networks allow for information-sharing and can provide resources for the enhancement of local capabilities. Regulatory frameworks that allow for cooperation between neighbouring communities are also useful to overcome the barrier of municipal boundaries (when an issue does not fit administrative divisions) and to find the most efficient method of action in each sector.

The institutions and actors involved in the greening process of cities are numerous and varied. The challenge is to coordinate their actions and to find the most appropriate system of governance in the particular context of each city.

Linking the green economy to urban processes: Economic processes in cities

The way out of urban development vs. environmental degradation is not to stop urban growth, which would be almost impossible in some cases, but to reconcile and harmonize the opportunities and challenges resulting from urban growth. Indeed, urbanization can lead to a greener economy, because cities have many advantages in being more economically efficient and environmentally friendly. History has proven that urbanization can be managed in a way that promotes both the economy and human well-being. The recent global debate on transitioning towards a greener economy may be a great opportunity to reconcile the opportunities and the challenges of urban development and to pursue long-term sustainable development in cities. A green economy is defined by the United Nations Environment Programme (UNEP) as one that "focuses on improving human well-being and reducing social inequity over the long term, while not exposing future generations to significant environmental risks and ecological scarcities" (2011: 552). Therefore the concept of a green economy, if achievable, could help to solve many of the environmental and social problems pertaining to urban development. Cities may indeed offer significant opportunities for achieving a greener economy. The concentration of people, resources, knowledge and economic activities in urban areas, if properly managed, can provide economies of scale and efficiency gains that reduce the use of resources and energy and thereby promote "doing more with less" (ICLEI, 2011: 2). In this sense, the transition from the traditional economy to a green economy could be achieved by reducing resources and energy consumption in cities, thereby improving the key components of urban development and other services generally offered in cities.

We will analyse the opportunities for and the obstacles to a greener economy in cities by looking at the specific economic processes that take place in cities: transformation of space (urban development); production and consumption; circulation (trade and transportation); and the production of ecosystem services, social services and knowledge-based activities. Understanding how to green those processes can have huge social, economic and environmental impacts on the cities and beyond.

Transformation of space: Urban development

Among the most significant key components of an urban economy is the physical and spatial development of cities. Urban development transforms the natural environment and resources into built superstructures and infrastructure, and this transformation places significant stress on the remaining natural environment. The way we build our cities also determines, or at least affects, how we spend and distribute or redistribute our economic resources. Urban forms and the spatial distribution of urban functions in cities play a critical role in this respect. Sprawled cities, where low density is the norm and different urban functions are distantly located, increase the consumption of energy and natural resources, both terrestrial and aquatic. Besides, the cost of urban development is high in dispersed cities because relatively large land areas are provided with urban infrastructure and utilities. For instance, 70 per cent of the cost of water supply systems goes towards pipes, and 30 per cent of urban energy consumption goes towards the pumping of water and the collection of waste water (Suzuki et al., 2010). Therefore a smaller land-use area can result in lower operating costs for a city's utilities. Similar conclusions can also apply to the transportation infrastructure. Compact cities with high-density and mixed-use urban quarters result in energy savings; low levels of land-use change and the preservation of surrounding agricultural and forests lands result in reduced infrastructure costs and the protection of water resources.

The density and the land use of an urban area are key factors in the amount of energy that a city will consume. This is particularly true for transport-related energy consumption. It has been verified that there is an indirect relationship between urban density and energy consumption, which means that energy consumption will be higher in a less dense city that is sprawled over a larger area of land (Kirby, 2008). Compact urban forms help to increase the density, and thereby reduce transport-related energy consumption. It has been argued that, with more compact development, a 20–40 per cent reduction in the miles driven by private cars can be achieved (Ewing et al., 2008). For instance, in Portland in the United States, per capita vehicle trips have been reduced by 17 per cent simply by promoting compact urban growth since 1990, and emissions of greenhouse gases (GHGs) were kept at 1990 levels despite a 16 per cent growth in population (Condon et al., 2009). Urban form also influences the amount of natural environment and resources that is converted into urban environments. A good example of this is a comparison of the built-up areas of Atlanta in the United States and Barcelona in Spain. Both cities had approximately the same population in 1990 – 2.5 million and 2.8 million, respectively. When looking at the built-up areas of the two cities, however, the amount of land used for urban development was 26 times greater in the dispersed city of Atlanta, which occupied 4,280 km^2 in 1990 (Bertaud and Poole, 2007; Suzuki et al., 2010).

Another advantage of compact mixed-use cities for the purpose of achieving a green economy is that, in cities where travel distances and travel times are shorter, public and non-motorized transportation systems could be provided easily and cost effectively. The effective and extensive provision of public and non-motorized transport options could help to increase access by the urban poor and low-income citizens to various urban facilities and especially to job markets. It has been shown that, in cities where affordable and convenient public transportation systems and safe cycling and pedestrian routes do not exist, it is mostly urban poor and low-income families who suffer from exclusion from urban life, spending long hours on city roads and in high-traffic areas. Tiwari (2002) argues that the urban poor in Delhi are also the "transport poor", and that their well-being is dependent on short trip lengths, non-motorized modes of transportation and public transportation.

A key component of urban development that can promote the transition to a green economy is the superstructure, more specifically the buildings. The construction and building sector deeply affects every single person's daily life. The building sector is one of the main contributors to carbon emissions, utilizing approximately 40 per cent of global energy consumption; it consumes 12 per cent of all fresh water and generates 40 per cent of the total volume of waste (Rode et al., 2011). One of the key goals of the green urban economy is to promote energy and resource efficiency in the building sector and to provide high-quality, healthy and affordable buildings for urban residents. Providing adequate housing for approximately 80 million new urban residents every year is a great emerging opportunity for the economy. Investments in the green economy in the areas of construction and the building sector could expand many industries in cities, given the strong interlinkages of the building sector with other sectors. For example, the adoption of new materials, technologies and appliances for saving energy could promote the development of the manufacturing, transportation and construction industries; the adoption of more solar, wind and biomass energy could encourage the utilization of renewable energy; and recycling waste could develop waste management. Greening the construction and building sector could also provide more sustainable production and consumption for the whole urban community and significantly increase people's welfare. In developing countries, more job opportunities may be produced with this kind of green sustainable development and, just as importantly, more healthy, safe and affordable housing will be available, which could substantially eradicate poverty and inequity in cities.

Consumption and production in cities

Perhaps the greatest current challenge for cities is to be able to create economic opportunities but not at the expense of aggravating environmental degradation and inequality inside and outside city boundaries. In an increasingly urbanized world challenged by global environmental change and pervasive poverty, cities are looking for new pathways to provide human well-being while using natural resources sustainably. Developing a green economy for urban areas is a response to those challenges. Such an approach should take into account sustainable production and consumption issues, because cities consume vast amounts of resources to meet increasing demand for goods and services by their residents and for their daily functioning, which can lead to environmental loss and economic exploitation in the supply areas. Sustainable consumption and production should aim to transform current environmental challenges faced by cities into economic opportunities, by boosting demand for more sustainable products and technologies, by improving the environmental performance of products throughout their lifecycle, by helping consumers to make informed choices, and by promoting awareness and lifestyle changes that help individuals to adapt their urban life to today's challenges (as analysed in Chapter 5). In addition, in order to build up more sustainable production–consumption networks, cities should not just see themselves as consumers of distant natural resources. By enhancing their own local ecosystem services, urban areas can provide well-being for their residents while reducing their consumption footprints, and thus creating opportunities for greening both their economies and their landscapes. From heat island control to flood mitigation, from local food provisioning to water purification, managing local ecosystems properly so as to increase their functionality will create innovative economic opportunities for clean development and ultimately render cities and local economies visibly greener.

Consumption and production for a green urban economy

One of the most noticeable aspects of urban functioning is consumption. Whereas cities occupy only approximately 2 per cent of the Earth's surface, they consume 75 per cent of its resources (UNDESA, 2010). Urban production and consumption processes are among the main causes of appropriation of environmental goods and services from ecosystems (MA, 2005). It has been acknowledged that more affluent cities tend to appropriate higher shares of natural resources outside their boundaries (Folke et al., 1997). Although urban consumption is linked to unprecedented economic and social opportunities for city dwellers, the gap between urban and rural living standards and consumption levels increases as countries become more urban (World Bank, 2008). Furthermore, many urban residents live in poverty, vulnerable to environmental impacts and unable to benefit socially and economically from the opportunities of urban life.

Urbanization has brought even deeper changes to human lifestyles, including consumerism (Davis, 2000). Increasing disposable incomes translate into greater demand for environmental goods and services, which is often met by unsustainable production processes. Food consumption in urban areas illustrates clearly how cities can contribute to unsustainable production–consumption patterns. For example, rising living standards, particularly in the urban centres of the developed and rapidly developing world, have been associated with shifts in diets. Increasing meat consumption (see, for example, FAO, 2006) is connected to the expansion of livestock-rearing and the environmental impacts of deforestation, GHGs and biodiversity loss. Wild species are also victims of unsustainable urban consumption patterns. Pets, foods and ornamental or medicinal species of plants and animals are being put at risk to satisfy urban demand (TRAFFIC, 2008; Wilkie and Carpenter, 1999).

Sustainable consumption and production and the role of cities

The concept of sustainable consumption and production (SCP) has long been proposed as a pathway for reducing environmental impacts and creating human well-being, as examined in Chapter 5. Yet there are several, sometimes contradictory, definitions of what constitutes SCP, which in turn leads to different implications for a green economy and in particular for the role of urban areas.

In 1994, the Oslo Symposium on Sustainable Consumption emphasized resource-use efficiency and pollution reduction in the provision of basic human well-being as fundamental aspects for achieving SCP (Robins and Roberts, 1998). Although this approach points to important issues for tackling urban ecological footprints in the provision of basic goods and services for inclusive urban development, further linkages are needed to economic mechanisms for achieving a green economy in cities through SCP.

In 2003, the Marrakech Process emerged as a response to renewed interest in SCP issues worldwide, and it materialized in the Johannesburg Plan of Action of the World Summit on Sustainable Development. Its goals are as follows:

- To assist countries in their efforts to green their economies
- To help corporations develop greener business models
- To encourage consumers to adopt more sustainable lifestyles. (UNDESA, n.d.)

The Marrakech Process represents an advance over previous approaches because it links SCP to economic drivers and touches upon issues of lifestyle change, which are both crucial aspects for SCP in cities.

More recently, the European Environmental Agency has developed an approach to SCP based on increased resource-use efficiency, enhanced ecosystem resilience and greater human well-being (European Environmental Agency, 2010). The incorporation of the resilience concept, understood as preventing overexploitation of natural resources so as to allow nature to replenish itself by not exceeding its carrying capacity, is particularly relevant for urban areas, because cities consume enormous quantities of ecosystem goods and services located in areas outside their boundaries. The approach also considers the equitable distribution of the environmental and economic benefits and costs of economic activities for achieving SCP, which is in turn relevant for developing green economy approaches for cities, because economic and ecological inequality remain pervasive in urban areas across the world.

Overall, SCP initiatives have been successful in highlighting the need for deep changes in current consumption and production patterns worldwide as a precondition for sustainable development and thus for a green economy. Although not focusing exclusively on cities, most of the aspects highlighted by SCP approaches are relevant for fostering a green economy in urban areas, especially those related to reducing ecological footprints and increasing socioeconomic and environmental equity.

Growing greener cities: Urban areas providing green goods and services

Ecosystems and local biodiversity can provide fertile ground for innovation, leading to a boost in the local economy that provides well-being for urban residents and contributes to reducing the urban footprint. For example, it is acknowledged that urban agriculture can provide multiple benefits for city residents, from access to fresh produce to community-building or innovative employment opportunities (Pearson et al., 2010). In aquatic urban ecosystems, sustainable aquaculture and good fisheries management can contribute positively to a green economy by providing local foods, creating employment and fostering technological innovation while reducing ecological footprints (Costa-Pierce et al., 2005).

Rethinking cities as providers of goods and ecosystem services through the sustainable management of their local resources for fulfilling urban lifestyles and reducing footprints has resulted in some interesting concepts. The concept of "continuous productive urban landscapes" (CPULs) is emerging as a powerful planning framework that can in turn be linked to fostering green urban economy opportunities in local food production–consumption networks. From the CPULs perspective, the city adopts a compact form so that its environs can be used for urban agriculture (Viljoen, 2005). According to the CPULs approach, growing food in and around cities can significantly decrease the need for industrialized production, extensive packaging and long distribution chains from productive spaces (rural areas) to consuming ones (cities).

Likewise, the concepts of *satoyama* and *satoumi* (analysed in Chapter 6) can provide inspiration for the integration of urban ecological production and consumption when rethinking the modern, sustainable city. Both concepts refer to "a dynamic mosaic of managed socio-ecological systems producing a bundle of ecosystem services for human well-being" (JSSA, 2010: 13). Although they were created for rural landscapes, there are lessons that modern cities can learn regarding how to enhance sustainable production–consumption networks by increasing the local circulation of goods and services in a way that is ecologically sustainable and economically restorative. For instance, it has been noted that *satoyama* landscapes in peri-urban areas can become important hotspots for ecological restoration and increased ecological production in order to meet urban demands for food, energy and cultural services while revitalizing areas with declining populations. The *satoumi* concept can provide valuable insights for the planning of modern, sustainable coastal cities (Yanagi, 2005).

Overall, urban ecosystems can be linked to processes leading to the development of a greener economy for cities by decreasing urban footprints and increasing local circulation of material and economic resources. Yet more work needs to be done in order to fully integrate local ecosystems into a sustainable economy, including aspects related to the provision of ecosystem services (and biodiversity) fundamental for human well-being, such as climate regulation or water provision. Initiatives based on payment schemes for ecosystem services in cities are one response to these challenges.

Circulation: Trade and transportation

Transportation is fundamental to a city's economy. At the most basic level it involves the movement of two things: goods and people. It is particularly vital in contributing to urban economic productivity through better accessibility and the efficient movement of people (rich and poor, high- and low-skilled), resources and goods within the city area as a countermeasure to the spatial mismatch of labour and workplace, housing and services, and producer, retailer and consumer. Transport provides a functional linkage between the various land uses in the city. The availability of transport infrastructures, on the other hand, also influences the location of activity centres, including industrial, commercial and residential areas. An improved transportation infrastructure system is expected to save travel time and to increase the cost-effectiveness of overall urban mobility. In supporting trade, urban freight transport is responsible for the distribution of materials or products with an origin and/or a destination within the city area as well as those that are only passing through the city area. An improved transportation system allows reliable, quick and low-cost freight movements. Additionally, the transport sector is a source of investment and urban employment induced by urban transport infrastructure development and by management itself, including green transport as a business field (Dalkmann and Sakamoto, 2011).

Especially in the context of developing countries, the economic role of informal transport modes – including rickshaws, bicycle wagons, three-wheelers, motorcycle taxis and small vans – is significant as a source of mobility and employment, particularly for the urban poor. In fact, these modes provide flexible, door-to-door transportation and fill a gap by providing relatively lower-cost transportation (Cervero and Golub, 2007). Because of their small size, these vehicles are able to enter narrow streets or passageways and to reach neighbourhoods that cannot be entered by conventional buses or trucks. Policies that restrict the use of informal transportation, which provides niche services in circulating people and goods as well as generating employment for urban poor, may unintentionally disrupt the economic activity of a city (CDIA, 2011).

Beyond the city limits, one needs to distinguish between the benefits to the city and the impacts of the city to the surrounding area. At the hinterland scale, the transport sector is a means to rebalance the economy and to reduce regional inequalities. It expands markets and enables the equitable distribution of goods to different markets. By opening access to new markets, it invites new investments, innovations and wider employment opportunities.

In both developed and developing countries, cities appropriate enormous quantities of resources from around the world. Indeed, cities cannot function without this process; therefore transportation links to and from the city are vital to its function and development. These imports have been principally facilitated through maritime transport. More recently, air transport has become a popular means of transportation, especially for perishable goods that would spoil during a long journey at sea. These two modes of exurban transport have a profound impact on the urban economy. Efficient exurban transport systems to the city (road and rail) play a large part in deciding which goods a city may import. The efficiency of maritime transport has increased hugely over time and frequently the greatest cost is incurred in getting goods to and from the ports. This is particularly acute in developing countries, where cities far from the coast encounter vey high transaction costs in moving goods.

The recognition that importing goods by air will play a central role in city development has led to the prediction that cities may become planned around airport hubs. The "aerotropolis" model of urban development places the airport at the centre of the city, arguing that airports will be the next great determinant of urban form, just as highways and the automobile were in the twentieth century, at least in the United States (Karsada and Lindsay, 2011). When viewed from this perspective, it is increasingly clear that cities are planned not just with their internal function in mind but also with respect to their connections to the wider world. With the exception of port cities, much of this infrastructure is outside the control of the city government. The aerotropolis model provides a compelling means of internalizing control of the city's links and at one level may provide a centripetal force to the city, constraining sprawl. However, this model comes at the cost of the environmental impacts of air transport and its increasing use.

Being a means to improve the socioeconomic goals of a city as well as an industry in itself, urban transport in developing countries is facing difficulties in becoming green and equitable while pursuing productivity.

Transportation has a series of conflicting goals that need to be aligned to generate a green economy:
- The greenness of the transport sector essentially comes down to two things: (i) the extent to which transport trips degrade the environment (land, water and air resources); (ii) the extent to which trips can be reduced through sensible planning. The goals include an improvement in energy efficiency, a reduction in air pollution and GHG emissions, increased use of renewable resources, reduced use of non-renewable resources and, overall, improved public health.
- The equity of transport is represented by a high degree of spatial accessibility, affordability and barrier-free facilities, which allow all types of urban dweller to perform their daily activities effectively, efficiently and safely.
- The goals of an economical transport system are, first, to maximize the city's economic productivity, indicated by, among other things, minimizing transport costs and duration, dynamizing the city economy, and generating jobs and income to the population in the city and beyond; and, second, to encourage more investments, urban employment and other sources of local revenues from the development of the transport sector itself. To align these goals, the measure should be one or a mix of the three pillars of transport policy options: avoid, shift and improve (Dalkmann and Brannigan, 2007: 393). The rest of the section describes each option based on priority.

The first priority is to promote a shift to efficient modes. For the movement of people, the use of public transport and non-motorized modes needs to be encouraged by improving the design of the city-wide public transport network, providing priority systems for public transport to increase its speed, improving multimodal connectivity and ensuring the safety, security, convenience (barrier-free) and affordability of public transport. The problem is that most public transport systems are not financially sustainable and are heavily subsidized. Increasing ridership to achieve cost recovery, not to mention profit, requires "soft" measures to change people's preferences for private modes, which are relatively indifferent. One way is to push private mode users out of their vehicles and shift them to public transport by implementing stringent measures such as road pricing, a vehicle ownership quota system, and other travel demand management policy instruments. Besides being useful to curb motorization, these economic instruments have the potential to be earmarked for financing the transit system. Such an innovative financing mechanism could keep public transport services affordable, particularly for urban poor who need the services the most, so that they are not excluded from full participation in urban socioeconomic activities. It should be highlighted here that a healthy business model for regulators and operators is essential in delivering affordable and reliable public transport services.

For the movement of goods, there is an increasing trend of shifting from land transport, particularly lorries, towards multimodal transport (land, rail, air and water) for freight shipment. Transportation and logistics are continuing to integrate in response to economic globalization, speed-to-market product delivery, agile manufacturing and business practices, and integrated supply chain management (Rondinelli and Berry, 2000). In particular, cheap maritime transport costs have amplified the effect of comparative advantage and variable labour costs at a global scale. Furthermore, reorganization of informal modes of land transport should be carried out. Their functions as gap-fillers would remain beneficial for the city's economy.

Because overall demand for transport activity is growing rapidly and increasingly motorized (cars and motorcycles for passenger transport and lorries for freight transport), the second priority is to improve the efficiency of road vehicles through technological improvements such as fuel-efficient vehicles, alternative power sources (Dalkmann and Sakamoto, 2011) and efficient driving methods (for example, reducing idling). Although technology can do a lot, again it raises the equity issue of cost. On the one hand, a green urban economy can be stimulated through investment in and promotion of green technologies but, on the other hand, these have to be considered as only part of the solution, recognizing that not everyone can afford them. A green and equitable transport sector should without doubt incorporate elements of low-emission transportation modes accessible to the entire community in the city and at a cost that all can afford.

Third, because travel is a derived demand of urban activities, urban transport systems should be integrated with land-use development to allow the efficient movement of people and goods. City planning can have a major impact but, if it is ill considered, a path dependency is set in train where sustainable options become harder and more costly to implement. Thus, it is increasingly necessary to make city-planning moves ahead of market forces. For passenger transport, the concept of transit-oriented development – mixed-use compact land-use development around transit nodes – has the potential to reduce motorized trip rates and to promote the use of the greenest mode of transport: walking and cycling.

Specifically for freight movements, multimodal freight transport facilities in a city need to be expanded. This would also support trade activities beyond a city's boundary. However, this will attract new activities into the surrounding areas, change land uses, increase density and generate more intensive local and cross-town traffic. Such activities are likely to be much greater in a global city logistics region, where a more complex producer environment exists along with the large market and higher-income economy (O'Connor, 2010). Logistic operational inefficiencies are caused by conflicting needs for fluid movement, a lack of supporting urban facilities, coinciding with intra-city traffic peak hours, cost issues, and the increasing pressure of environmental protection and resource conservation. One way to ease the frictions between people and freight activities in urban traffic is by consolidating the locations of logistics infrastructures (parking spaces, loading/unloading facilities, multimodal transfer points) with buildings (industries, retail outlets, offices and housing), coupled with regulations to reduce friction with other road users through spatial and time restrictions (Muñuzuri et al., 2004; Zanni and Bristow, 2010).

It should also be noted that, from the bigger picture, current consumer lifestyles and vested interests are a pervasive obstacle in all sectors. This cannot be underestimated in a capitalist society, where a healthy economy is dependent on the endless circulation of goods to meet consumers' preferences. Moreover, one needs to look not solely at the transportation of those goods but also at their entire lifecycle. Serious consideration needs to be given to the extent to which consumption-miles can be reduced through local production of food and other goods.

Cities are generally applying two-pronged transport policies, which increase the penetration of cleaner vehicles for passengers and freight and, at the same time, promote a shift towards more efficient modes. However, the integration of land-use and transport measures can be found in only a few cities worldwide, for example Curitiba in Brazil. In terms of efficient logistics operations, enterprises are pursuing the implementation of new approaches, such as environmentally oriented supply chain cooperation, which aims to reduce the consumption of materials, water and energy through the whole supply chain by cooperating with suppliers and consumers. More recently, a circular economy has been promoted in Chinese cities (Zhu et al., 2010), for example, for e-scrap in the ICT and electronics industries (Park et al., 2010). Using such practices, economic systems could and should operate according to (re)cycling principles in support of natural systems. However, it remains debatable whether or not such approaches can bring competitive advantages, although there are indications that a win–win benefit can be achieved and preferential policies from the government (subsidies or other forms of incentives) can help to encourage more enterprises to adopt them (Zhu et al., 2010).

In conclusion, a major impediment to the adoption of green transport is the cost of implementing green transport solutions at a scale that covers the whole city. This is a particularly serious issue in rapidly developing cities that find themselves pressed financially but also having to respond to mobility challenges, which may lead to the selection of the quickest but least sustainable (environmentally and socially) options. Nonetheless, transport is a complex sector involving a wide array of activities and stakeholders, which reach beyond city boundaries. Thus, the transport sector is strategic enough to create a window of opportunity to invite more private investments driven by green policies to finance the shift to green transport in a city, if an appropriate regulatory framework is in place.

Ecosystem, social and knowledge services

Some of the most important parts of a city economy are those not captured directly by the market economy or by prices, such as ecosystem services, social services (for example, community based, social capital) and knowledge-based activities (human and intellectual capital). Because these are not reflected in the gross domestic product (GDP) of cities and countries, they are generally underestimated or completely ignored by policy-makers; at worst, they are interpreted as a negative asset or as trade-offs for pursuing other "development" policies that reflect the traditional way to measure GDP, such as building houses, factories or roads.

Thus, a greener city economy has to deal with the way we value and manage such resources. One of the biggest obstacles to attracting the attention of policy-makers or to incorporating these resources into policy processes is that the services provided by these resources are not completely translated into direct monetary values. Even though the economic valuation of environmental resources has been around for several decades (Barde and Pearce, 1991) and several efforts have been made to quantify and raise awareness about the value of ecosystems and environmental resources (TEEB, 2010), many of the methodologies are not robust enough and some of the values cannot be fully captured by economic valuation techniques. Social capital too has been recognized as an important asset, for example, to make governments more effective (Putnam, 1993).

The greening of the city economy includes both the city economy and the influence the city may have beyond its boundaries. Urban ecosystems provide a series of benefits to the local population such as recreation, culture-based services (traditions based on biodiversity, etc.), the provision of water and food, flood control services, and energy and climate change mitigation (carbon and heat island management). Moreover, many of these services are fundamental to the well-being of the poorest population, who have little access to human-made concrete-based infrastructure. Preserving the quantity and quality of these services is key for a green economy and for poverty eradication in the city.

However, cities have an influence on the environment, populations and economy of regions beyond the city boundaries and even in distant places. A large proportion of the resources needed for city activities is provided by external ecosystems and many of the impacts of cities (positive and negative) affect the environment and the well-being of people living outside the cities. For example, many financial institutions that provide capital for activities beyond city boundaries are located in cities, particularly the large cities of the developed world. If those institutions worked for greening the economy, it would produce significant impacts. Cities are also responsible for a large part of the GHGs produced worldwide. Those GHGs influence many urban, rural and forest environments in distant places, affecting the services they can provide to local populations. Thus, we have to create mechanisms to green those links to facilitate the movement of the green economy to places beyond the city boundaries (similar to the "negative" externalities of cities). There are some good examples of devices already being used, such as the ecological value-added tax in Brazil, where resources are transferred to municipalities that conserve natural spaces and water reservoirs (Puppim de Oliveira, 2003).

Other city resources that are difficult to assess monetarily but that are key to a greener economy are those related to human, social and intellectual capital. Cities are centres for making decisions that have big impacts. Cities generally concentrate large amounts of qualified human resources (human capital), because urban citizens tend to be better educated. Cities have the connectedness that social movements (social capital) and organizational innovative capacity (intellectual capital) need to blossom. Universities and think-tanks are mostly located in cities. Cities also concentrate decision-makers such as politicians (all parliaments are in cities), government officials, chief executive officers of companies and the headquarters of social organizations or NGOs. Cities are hubs for new technical and institutional ideas and innovation that could change the world. Allied with the concentration of capital and decision-making power, this intellectual capital could create huge changes towards the greening of the global economy. How this innovation potential can be used to green the economy in cities and elsewhere is still not clearly understood or quantifiable. However, this is no excuse not to act and move towards a greener economy that help to eradicate poverty and protect the environment.

Challenges in moving towards a green economy

Even though there are good examples of green initiatives in cities, mainstreaming the green economy in the diverse economic activities described above faces tremendous challenges, particularly in developing countries where poverty alleviation is one of the priorities. These challenges range from legal and governance barriers to financial and technical aspects, as discussed below.

Law-related challenges and barriers

At the city level, two major barriers from a legal perspective limit the capacity of local governments to foster a green economy:

Legal uncertainty and a lack of implementation

Cities have to work together with civil society and the private sector to achieve a greener economy. They need to attract investors willing to contribute to sound environmental projects with a high probability of economic or political returns. Against this background, legal certainty is a primary challenge for governments. In fact, potential project leaders and investors need to assess the risks associated with their activities in order to manage them. An uncertain legal framework blurs the development scenario of a project and thus affects the evaluation of potential economic benefits.

To some extent, legal certainty depends on the national authorities responsible for enhancing the rule of law. Courts are key actors in ensuring that parties to a contract have their rights protected and in constraining public authorities to obey the laws. However, local governments are crucial actors as regards two legal aspects. First, they are critical players in the implementation of international, national and local norms. Second, their role is essential in the adoption of local regulations that create incentives to attract private stakeholders to work together towards the same objective. An important step at the local level is therefore to provide as much information as possible on the local regulatory context and to create a safe environment for investments.

National legal frameworks and obsolete policies

City governments are bound by national legislation, which in many countries governs most of the relevant areas for the development of a green economy. The regulation of property rights, land use, infrastructure and the use of natural resources must be based on norms defined at the national level. This hinders cities from negotiating freely with potential external partners. For instance, a national law in Thailand prohibits foreign investors from owning land in the country.

Finally, climate change literature draws attention to the mainstreaming of mitigation and adaptation goals into existing policy frameworks to use financial and human resources more efficiently and effectively as well as to guarantee continuity in priorities instead of radical change (Biesbroek et al., 2009). This also applies to policies and strategies for a green economy. Interventions to achieve a green economy are argued to be more effective when they build upon local strengths and appropriate local policies (Chapple, 2008). However, this is not a straightforward issue, because in some cases policies and regulations that have been in use for a long time may prevent the introduction and implementation of new and up-to-date policies and regulations. This blocks the flexibility needed to integrate new information and the development of new technologies. Besides, old policy and legal frameworks may not be compatible with the new concepts, strategies and implementation tools. In such cases, reforms need to be made to the existing institutional arrangements and policy frameworks prior to incorporating the new concepts and measures.

Governance-related challenges and barriers

Governance-related challenges are numerous and very much contingent on the local context and structure of the city.

Low decentralization and lack of power and capacity at the local level

The degree of decentralization in a country may hinder cities' initiatives towards a greener economy. In fact, most of the policies and strategies to achieve a green economy need to be implemented at the local level, which is the jurisdiction of subnational governments and local authorities. The existence of strong and capable political authorities at the local level is a requirement for harmonizing the economic and environmental agendas. In many countries, however, most of the responsibilities, resources and capacity to implement actions towards a green economy still belong to national governments rather than subnational and city governments. This results in a major obstacle, which may be termed an "implementation deficit" (Bulkeley, 2006). Targets, policies and strategies defined at international and national levels cannot be implemented sufficiently at the local level owing to the deficiencies of city governments in administration, finance and service delivery. If fiscal power remains in the hands of higher-level authorities and local governments are given no taxation autonomy, local authorities will not be able to create financial incentives such as preferential tax treatment, discount rates or abatements to attract investors. In order to push the environmental agenda forward by realizing a green economy, local governments have to be strengthened through institutional reforms towards more decentralization.

Limited coordination (vertical and horizontal) between government bodies and divisions

Urban and environmental challenges are generally tackled by a departmental or a sectoral approach through which different divisions of local and national governments deal with the main issues. Sectoral approaches have certain advantages in tackling challenges, such as the specialization of divisions and personnel and a reduction in the duplication of tasks. However, sectoral approaches may end up with limited coordination and cooperation between governmental bodies and divisions and thereby prevent the development and implementation of integrated policies. The realization of a green economy calls for the effective coordination and integration of the efforts and activities of all governmental bodies and divisions. Therefore institutional reforms need to be undertaken to promote more integrated public policy-making. One solution might be to create an organization or a committee to deal with issues pertaining to a green economy by facilitating and increasing communication between different governmental bodies and economic sectors. Such an organization or a committee could also function as a holder and transmitter of the institutional memory and facilitate budget-sharing among local governmental bodies in order to coordinate initiatives for a green economy.

Lack of awareness of policies to achieve a green economy

Particularly in developing countries, awareness of the need to push environmental agendas forward is yet to be developed. This applies not only to the general public but also to policy- and decision-makers. Local governments could play a crucial role in the transition to a green economy because the local level is the most appropriate level for the implementation of policies and strategies. However, local governments in many countries suffer from lack of social capital in terms of aware and knowledgeable experts and active civil society. An understanding of how a conventional economy can be transformed into a green economy that reduces the consumption of resources has to be advanced among policy-makers, public officials and professionals, for example through formal or informal initiatives in education for sustainable development (as discussed in Chapter 5).

Financial and economic challenges and barriers

With or without political commitment to a green economy or to putting mandatory standards in place, a lack of financial resources at the local level often limits the capability of a city in promoting greener growth. Aside from that, green technologies or infrastructures may require higher investment and might not provide any guarantee of financial returns within a reasonable period of time. Moreover, policy-makers may not be able to provide incentives or subsidies that are attractive enough for private sectors and individual households to invest or change their behaviour.

Although private financing is a strong potential source for financing change, a city's economic structure is made up of several types of companies, including companies whose interests lie mostly within the "brown" economy, "greener" companies, which take their corporate environmental responsibilities more seriously, and "green" businesses, which produce alternative green products. "Brown" companies are sometimes quite influential in the policy-making process and react to changes. They may also be linked to political interests. In many countries, for example, fossil fuels are subsidized, and the removal of the subsidies is not political viable because many people depend on the subsidies to buy their energy needs. On the other hand, "greener" companies need greater economic justifications to expand their green practices, and "green" businesses may encounter difficulties in becoming mainstream in the market, particularly in the early stages, without suitable economic incentives from the public sector.

Challenges and barriers to new technologies

Overcoming technical barriers is vital for achieving the goal of a green economy. Many countries, both developed and developing, have suffered from a lack of technical capacity in the process of moving to a green economy. Generally, there are three kinds of technical barriers.

A lack of technologies is the first obstacle. For example, clean technologies can be used for reducing carbon emissions and environmental pollutants, but most of these clean technologies are new, advanced and expensive. Investors have to bear the high costs and risks of utilizing, operating and maintaining the clean technologies. Furthermore, old technologies have been in use for long periods, which also prevents new technologies from being utilized initially.

A lack of regulations and standards is another technical barrier. Without integrated and sound regulations and standards, there will be obstacles to the process of implementing a green economy at city, national and even international levels.

Another barrier is the lack of effective systems to support the development of a green economy. A single technology cannot make a significant difference to an old economy. Only a system that integrates different technologies and allows them to work smoothly and effectively can effect real changes towards a green economy. If there is not enough awareness, professional skill and experience among those who run the systems, the obstacles may become more serious.

Sociopolitical challenges and barriers

Achieving a green economy in practice may be more difficult than is predicted by the conceptualizations and estimations. As discussed in Chapter

4, many green initiatives will conflict with other developmental goals in the short and medium term and will never be implemented. They also may face resistance from small, but powerful, corporate or political interests, or even conflict with poverty alleviation strategies, such as the provision of subsidized fuel to poor families.

Citizens also need to understand more about what the green economy means and that it is fundamentally different from "business as usual". A green economy will be a qualitatively better but not necessarily a quantitatively bigger economy. If the green economy is to achieve the accompanying aim of poverty eradication, it is necessary to ensure that all sections of society are included. However, the development paths of many developing countries have mirrored those of developed countries, which got richer by increasing their environmental footprint. It is not immediately clear how the development path can be reoriented or, indeed, the extent to which it needs to be if low-carbon energy supplies and production systems can be effectively installed at capacity and social change instinctively rejects mass consumerism. It may take generations to achieve a situation where greater environmental awareness from a young age, combined with concepts such as collaborative consumption, may lead to less material consumption overall. Much of this entails a wider societal transition and cities, although they are the unit of analysis for this chapter, face different challenges to implementing the green economy owing to the nature of their economic activities and the behaviour of their citizens. Thus, some cities will be able to go further than others in achieving these reforms, and those that do will serve as models for others to follow.

The huge number of cities in the world means there is a large potential for innovative solutions to emerge from their varying geographical, developmental and cultural contexts. When allied to the growth in intercity networks of learning and sharing of best practices, the ability to diffuse and test various strategies and deal with the uncertainty of climate change is greatly enhanced. Several networks exist, with the alliance between the C40 Cities Climate Leadership Group and the Cities Program of the Clinton Climate Initiative being one of the most prominent. Cities and their leaders, however, need to be open to sharing and to recognize that solutions can come from anywhere, even from less developed cities. Likewise, adopting innovative strategies can be an effective way to promote the city, especially in developing nations.

Opportunities and solutions for a green economy

Even with all the challenges described above, cities still offer several opportunities and solutions for achieving a greener economy.

Law-related opportunities and solutions

An efficient legal regime oriented to the green economy is a key instrument for cities, because it defines the governance context, financial tools and sanctions in the event of a breach of the rules. Depending on their power remit, city governments may use different approaches to foster a green economy within their territory.

Green public procurements

Local governments are responsible for the provision of important public services that have a huge potential to contribute to a green economy. Waste and water management, transportation and buildings are essential social and economic activities with important environmental impacts. In this context, urban authorities may include environmental objectives (for example, to construct buildings with green roofs) in their contracts with external service providers. As long as competition rules are enforced, local governments can also choose their partners in tenders based on environmental or social criteria. The development of guidelines for urban green procurements and the reform of procurement rules may be necessary in order to foster this practice. Cities in Brazil, São Paulo for example, have achieved some success in this area, developing programmes such as the "merenda escolar" (school meal), by means of which schools can contract local small producers (family farmers) of fresh and naturally processed organic foods to supply mandatory school food services, thus contributing to local employment in the formal economy and to sustainability in the food chain. Through the organization of tenders, local authorities also have the power to dismantle local markets by awarding different contracts to different zones or sectors, thus facilitating the entry of new operators and potentially more innovation.

Defining standards for emissions and industrial processes

City governments have the power to enact local regulations. If they have the political power and the enforcement capacity to do so, they may define emissions standards (for example for GHGs and pollutants), land use, building codes and energy efficiency standards or mandate the phasing out of certain noxious industrial processes or technologies. However, in order to be more efficient, such mechanisms must be inspected and followed by sanctions in the event of non-compliance.

Overcoming administrative boundaries through cooperation agreements

City governments as a legal entity have the capacity to enter agreements with other local authorities to share responsibility for the provision of essential services. Thus they may overcome administrative boundaries and create economies of scale that are more attractive for private partners. They may also tackle environmental issues spread over several communes. To do this, a third entity is usually created. It is awarded the necessary powers to negotiate with the stakeholders and its action plan is defined by the representatives of the different public authorities.

Governance-related opportunities and solutions

Governance-related solutions range from institutional solutions to policy instruments.

Institutional reform towards more decentralization

Decentralization refers to a reform in the organizational structure of governments that gives more autonomy and power to local governments and provides them with sufficient capacity to deliver. In this sense, decentralization could be an opportunity to overcome the "implementation deficit" at the local level arising from the lack of resources and capacity of local governments. Several countries have successfully implemented decentralization policies and empowered the political authorities at the local level. Indonesia is an interesting example in Asia, where most of the power has been given to local governments in line with the diversity of their cultural and historical backgrounds. The decentralized system in Indonesia provides cities and localities with autonomous governance that is observed to be an advantage in promoting sustainable low-carbon development, especially through various pilot and experimental projects (LCS-RNet, 2010).

International network of cities and local governments for information exchange

Local governments can take a leading role in achieving the transition to a green economy in cities mainly because of their proximity to the implementation level of policies and strategies. In addition, local governments are the political authorities that are closest to citizens. They can create significant change not just by effective implementation of policies but also by motivating, encouraging and leading citizens and stakeholders at the local level. In order to do this, however, they need to develop their capacities in terms of knowledge, information and experience of appealing and effective solutions that have been developed and put in place in different parts of the world. International networks of cities and local governments could play a crucial role in this respect. Through joining such networks, cities and local governments could increase synergies and facilitate knowledge and information exchange. Currently there are several networks, such as ICLEI – Local Governments for Sustainability, the

C40 Cities Climate Leadership Group and CITYNET, that are facilitating interaction between cities and local governments all over the world. The thematic and geographical coverage of such networks needs to be expanded so as to include green economy concepts and cities that are currently excluded.

Co-benefits of policies for green economy

Green economy refers to a process through which more outcomes are achieved by using fewer inputs or by consuming less. In this sense, policies for a green economy can generate several benefits simultaneously, especially in terms of resource savings. For instance, prevention of urban sprawl is regarded as a strategy for a green urban economy because energy consumption for transportation and infrastructure utilities and the cost of providing these utilities are lower in compact cities. Developing countries, which need to tackle many problems with limited resources, could benefit from such policies and achieve cost-effectiveness. Therefore, a co-benefits approach can be an encouraging factor and an opportunity to shift the mindset of policy-makers towards a green economy by indicating a more optimal use of limited resources. However, more research is required to make clear the co-benefits of green economy policies.

Opportunities in sustainable construction: Green building councils, standards and certification systems

There are great opportunities in the building sector to mitigate GHGs, because energy consumption for heating, cooling and lighting in buildings is high. Recently, there have been attempts to apply the principles of sustainable development to the entire cycle of construction activity. This has led to the development of concepts of sustainable construction and green buildings. Green buildings are regarded as one of the best strategies for mitigating global warming and reducing the environmental footprint of cities. There is no doubt that sustainable construction and green buildings offer significant opportunities to achieve a green economy: they both aim to reduce resource consumption and environmental pollution originating from buildings.

In many developed countries since 2000, green building councils have been established in order to promote sustainable construction and green buildings through guidelines and certification systems. Guidelines and certification systems for green buildings can assist in raising awareness of environmental issues and in creating economic development through diversification of construction activities. In order to encourage and scale up the implementation of sustainable construction, guidelines for green buildings could be mandatory in public sector buildings (Chapple, 2008).

Financial opportunities and solutions

As an entry point, public intervention becomes critical. Thus, the change towards a green economy starts from optimizing public financing. The aims are two-fold.

The first aim is to reform the public budget allocation process. Public funding may be limited, but budgets from several development sectors can be combined to support green growth. The role of public funding is to empower local stakeholders, including investors and taxpayers, in developing a greener city. It should act as a stimulus to accelerate the process of institutional reform towards participatory urban planning and development. A participatory budgeting process in Porto Alegre in Brazil, which has brought equitable public spending with greater accountability, could be a model to adopt. Moreover, public funding mobilization should explicitly reflect the city's development visions and priorities for a green economy to gain public trust in the city's commitment. From there, a city can expect greater public participation.

The second aim is to attract private financing for green policies by reducing the risks or increasing the rewards, particularly for land developers, energy companies, construction sectors, public service operators (public transport, waste management, water, etc.), freight transporters and industries. This can be achieved by adopting fiscal instruments such as financial incentives and instruments (for example, feed-in tariffs) to offset the higher cost of green technology installation and clean energy usage, and incentives or disincentives (for example, preferential tax treatment or exemption) to prevent urban conversion of agricultural land or to encourage land developers to build green open spaces.

As for "brown" businesses, internalizing the environmental costs into taxation, fees and charges is one possible instrument. In the long run, however, it will be necessary to establish market conditions that favour "greener" and "green" businesses, so that these companies can have comparative advantages over "brown" companies. Since citizens comprise the market, it is necessary to influence their preferences in terms of green lifestyles, for example by reforming environmentally harmful subsidies (such as fuel subsidies) and conversely adopting greener subsidies (such as subsidies on public transport operations), and by adopting progressive taxes on electricity consumption, vehicle ownership and other environmentally harmful urban activities.

To increase the market share of green products, the public sector may need initially to be the main purchaser, starting by adopting energy efficiency measures in government buildings and daily operations. In addition to earmarking green taxes, other financial sources from national, bilateral and international funding can be utilized to support municipalities in this matter, including climate financing (Glemarec, 2011).

Recognition mechanisms: Competitive awards for green, innovative cities

Since many cities host significant industrial development, as well as educational and research centres (including R&D), their role in sustainable innovation change can be fundamental for achieving a green economy. Making the transition from unsustainable technologies and urbanization models that place a high burden on the environment and/or the wellbeing of people can be facilitated by developing policy instruments that lead to innovation in eco-design and improved product performance. Cities can favour the adoption of a green economy by assisting the establishment of green technology hubs, sponsoring academic opportunities in green innovation through the institutions located within their boundaries, and implementing innovative urbanization and urban regeneration mechanisms. Recognition of such efforts, especially at the international level and in a competitive fashion, can encourage cities to move their green economy agenda forward.

Economic mechanisms: Payment for ecosystem services in urban areas

Economic compensation for stakeholders providing environmental goods and services otherwise not captured by the market mechanism has been proposed as a means of improving sustainability and economic development (TEEB, 2010). Although most such experiments have been undertaken in rural areas, cities can be promising spaces to develop innovative economic incentives for a green economy. The establishment of special urban environmental protection areas as a way of preserving threatened peri-urban ecosystems while providing economic incentives for local populations can be a powerful mechanism to slow down suburbanization encroachment.

Technical opportunities and solutions

Technical barriers cannot be tackled purely by technical solutions. Only under a comprehensive strategy, which must include solutions from the legal, institutional and financial systems, can the technical barriers be overcome and the green economy developed.

The priority is to make sure that the policies are sound and suitable for enhancing the utilization of appropriate technologies, and that strengthened institutions can supervise and encourage the implementation of technical operations. Reasonable financial measures are also needed to provide funding, tax exemptions and subsidies for utilizing green technologies. Furthermore, a good market mechanism must be set up to provide investors with the incentive to invest in new green technologies with lower financial risks.

In order to avoid difficulties in adopting and operating technologies, it is very important that regulations and standards are integrated at the city, national and international levels. Integrated regulations and standards can accelerate the utilization of technologies, allow more cities to gain access to advanced technologies, and remove existing obstacles to technology transfer between cities. More national and international collaboration is needed to promote the integration of regulations and standards.

Socioeconomic opportunities and solutions

Consumption–production networks: Rural–urban partnerships

Since cities obtain most of their environmental goods and services from outside their boundaries, establishing SCP networks among supplying regions and consumer centres can move urban areas forward into a green economy while contributing to rural sustainability and well-being. One of the challenges that remain for the achievement of a truly green urban economy is to make sustainable products affordable and thus mainstream while improving livelihoods in the producing regions. There have been some interesting experiences in this respect regarding food products; for example, the establishment of community-supported agriculture programmes in which local and peri-urban producers can sell directly to consumers results in higher returns for the producers and lower prices for the consumers, while improving local producers' capacities in marketing and distribution.

Cultural change: Towards more sustainable lifestyles

Urbanization is increasing rapidly worldwide, and so is the demand for all sorts of environmental goods and services associated with urban lifestyles – food, energy, fibres, fuel, water, minerals, etc. Yet, as has already been mentioned, consumerism – or extravagant consumption and wasteful resource-use patterns to satisfy ever-growing individual needs – is also an ingredient of modern city life. Lifestyle changes need to be realized in order to achieve a green economy that provides well-being for all. By making these changes affordable, attractive and desirable, cities can make their economies greener. One example of lifestyle change is the use of bicycles for transportation. Whereas for years it seemed inevitable that in the course of development cities had to sweep away bicycles in favour of motorized vehicles, many cities worldwide are increasingly developing human-powered vehicles as a response to environmental challenges, which in turn is creating new business opportunities.

Conclusion

The world cannot move towards a green economy without cities. Greening the economy of cities is a necessary condition for achieving a greener world economy that leads to poverty eradication. Governance within and beyond cities needs to be steered to direct cities' huge resources of physical, financial, human, social, natural and intellectual capital towards the objective of a greener economy.

Technological change is a critical component of urbanization; as such, there are many opportunities available to stimulate areas of the green economy. However, the impact of technology is ultimately a social process. No single technological innovation will set us on the path to a green economy without a corresponding shift in public understanding and acceptance of sustainable development. The urbanization process brings with it changes in consumer tastes, attitudes and perspectives. None of these are negative in themselves, but experience has shown that consumption increases with economic development. However, although the imperative to change consumption patterns is an important component of the green economy, the consumer cycle also plays a central role in how we understand the functioning of the economy in its present form. Arguments about consumption have generally focused on the morality of consumption, the right of less economically developed cities to have access to goods and services, paths of development and fundamentally what we consider to be human well-being. Indeed, change in individual and collective behaviour through a different kind of formal and informal education is essential to achieve the objective of mainstreaming green economy principles in the city economy.

The green economy has emerged as a central theme because of a deep-seated recognition that the aspiration of sustainable development will fail if we do not get the economy right. Whether this is pragmatic realism or a fundamental failure of the concept to oust economic primacy is an issue outside the remit of this chapter. What is important is to recognize that, if the green economy is to be a prerequisite for sustainable development, then it will have to be different from our current understanding of the economy. A green economy goes beyond simply greening parts of the conventional economy. It will require a broader understanding of how the economy functions, including the appropriate pricing of environmental externalities. The challenge to understanding the effect of cities lies in realizing how much a city's activities rely on these externalities both within and outside its borders; a problem compounded by deficiencies in city-level statistics even for population data (Montgomery, 2008). In this respect, some degree of scrutiny must be applied to city activities that claim to be green. There are many activities that superficially look and feel like they are making a difference. For example, the use of electric vehicles obviates the need for fossil fuels, but what is the environmental impact of the manufacture of the batteries, or, indeed, of the mode of electricity generation that powers the cars? In more complicated scenarios, efficiency savings could be reinvested in activities that might reduce or even eliminate the initial savings. Only when the full lifecycle and larger-scale effects of such activities are considered can we start to assess the green credentials of cities and the initiatives that support them. Cities are highly complex entities. They cannot exist in isolation and are therefore underpinned by a host of internal and external linkages. Very often these linkages are invisible at the city level but are precisely those that need to be considered when we talk of cities and the green economy.

REFERENCES

Barde, J. P. and D. W. Pearce (1991) *Valuing the Environment: Six Case Studies*. London: Earthscan.

Bertaud, A. and R. W. Poole (2007) "Density in Atlanta: Implications for Traffic and Transit". Policy Brief 61, Reason Foundation, Los Angeles. Available at ⟨http://reason.org/studies/show/density-in-atlanta-implication⟩ (accessed 9 February 2012).

Biesbroek, R., R. Swart and W. Van der Knaap (2009) "The Mitigation–Adaptation Dichotomy and the Role of Spatial Planning", *Habitat International*, 33(3): 230–237.

Bulkeley, H. (2006) "A Changing Climate for Spatial Planning", *Planning Theory and Practice*, 7(2): 203–214.

Bulkeley, H. (2010) "Cities and the Governing of Climate Change", *Annual Review of Environment and Resources*, 35: 229–253.

Bulkeley, H. and Betsill, M. (2005) "Rethinking Sustainable Cities: Multilevel Governance and the 'Urban' Politics of Climate Change", *Environmental Politics*, 14: 42–63.

CDIA (Cities Development Initiative for Asia) (2011) *Informal Public Transportation Networks in Three Indonesian Cities*. Cities Development Initiative for Asia. Available at: ⟨http://www.cdia.asia/wp-content/uploads/Informal-Public-Transportation-Networks.pdf⟩ (accessed 9 February 2012).

Cervero, R. and A. Golub (2007) "Informal Transport: A Global Perspective", *Transport Policy*, 14(6): 445–457.

Chapple, K. (2008) *Defining the Green Economy: A Primer on Green Economic Development*. Berkeley: Center for Community Innovation, University of California-Berkeley.

Condon, P. M., D. Cavens and N. Miller (2009) *Urban Planning Tools for Climate Change Mitigation*, Policy Focus Report. Cambridge, MA: Lincoln Institute of Land Policy. Available at ⟨http://www.lincolninst.edu/pubs/1573_Urban-Planning-Tools⟩ (accessed 9 February 2012).

Corfee-Morlot, J., L. Kamal-Chaoui, M. G. Donovan, I. Cochran, A. Robert and J.-P. Teasdale (2009) "Cities, Climate Change and Multilevel Governance", OECD Environment Working Paper No. 14. Paris: Organisation for Economic Co-operation and Development.

Costa-Pierce, B. A., A. Desbonnet, P. Edwards and D. Baker (2005) *Urban Aquaculture*. Wallingford: CABI Publishing.

Dalkmann, H. and C. Brannigan (2007) *Transport and Climate Change: Module 5a, Sustainable Transport: A Sourcebook for Policy-makers in Developing Cities*. Eschborn: Deutsche Gesellschaft für Technische Zusammenarbeit (GTZ).

Dalkmann, H. and K. Sakamoto (2011) "Transport: Investing in Energy and Resource Efficiency", in United Nations Environment Programme, *Towards a Green Economy: Pathways to Sustainable Development and Poverty Eradication*, pp. 374–411. Available at ⟨http://www.unep.org/greeneconomy/GreenEconomyReport/tabid/29846/Default.aspx⟩ (accessed 8 February 2012).

Davis, D. S. (2000) *The Consumer Revolution in Urban China*. Berkeley and Los Angeles: University of California Press.

Dhakal, S. (2009) "Urban Energy Use and Carbon Emissions from Cities in China and Policy Implications", *Energy Policy*, 37(11): 4208–4219.

European Environmental Agency (2010) *Towards a Set of Indicators on Sustainable Consumption and Production (SCP) for EEA Reporting*. ETC/SCP Working Paper 1/2010, European Topic Centre on Sustainable Consumption and Production.

Ewing, R., K. Bartholomew, S. Winkelman, J. Walters and D. Chen (2008) *Growing Cooler: The Evidence on Urban Development and Climate Change*. Washington, DC: The Urban Land Institute.

FAO (Food and Agriculture Organization of the United Nations) (2006) *Livestock's Long Shadow: Environmental Issues and Options*. Rome: FAO. Available at: ⟨http://www.fao.org/docrep/010/a0701e/a0701e00.HTM⟩ (accessed 9 February 2012).

Folke, C., A. Jansson, J. Larrson and R. Costanza (1997) "Ecosystem Appropriation by Cities", *AMBIO*, 26: 167–172.

Glemarec, Y. (2011) *Catalysing Climate Finance: A Guidebook on Policy and Financing Options to Support Green, Low-Emission and Climate-Resilient Development*. New York: United Nations Development Programme.

ICLEI – Local Governments for Sustainability (2011) "Briefing Sheet: Green Urban Economy", ICLEI World Secretariat, Bonn. Available at ⟨http://local2012.iclei.org/fileadmin/files/ICLEI_Green_Urban_Economy_Briefing_Sheet_20110215.pdf⟩ (accessed 9 February 2012).

IEA (International Energy Agency) (2008) *World Energy Outlook 2008*. Paris: International Energy Agency.

JSSA (Japan Satoyama Satoumi Assessment) (2010) *Satoyama-Satoumi Ecosystems and Human Well-Being: Socio-ecological Production Landscapes of Japan (Summary for Decision Makers)*. Tokyo: United Nations University Institute of Advanced Studies. Available at ⟨http://www.ias.unu.edu/sub_page.aspx?catID=111&ddlID=1418⟩ (accessed 8 February 2012).

Karsada, J. D. and G. Lindsay (2011) *Aerotropolis: The Way We'll Live Next*. New York: Farrar, Straus & Giroux.

Kirby, A. (2008) *Kick the Habit: A UN Guide to Climate Neutrality.* Nairobi: United Nations Environment Programme.

LCS-RNet (International Research Network for Low Carbon Societies) (2010) *Towards Sustainable Low-Carbon Development and Green Growth in Indonesia and Asia: Synthesis Report – Key Findings from the Dialogue between Policy-makers and Researchers.* Bogor, Indonesia: LCS-RNet.

MA (Millennium Ecosystem Assessment) (2005) *Millennium Ecosystem Assessment: Current State and Trends.* Washington, DC: Island Press. Available at: ⟨http://www.millenniumassessment.org/en/Condition.aspx⟩ (accessed 4 January 2011).

Montgomery, M. R. (2008) "The Urban Transformation of the Developing World", *Science*, 319: 761–764.

Muñuzuri, J., J. Larrañeta, L. Onieva and P. Cortés (2004) "Solutions Applicable by Local Administrations for Urban Logistics Improvement", *Cities*, 22(1): 15–28.

O'Connor, K. (2010) "Global City Regions and the Location of Logistics Activity", *Journal of Transport Geography*, 18(3): 354–362.

Onishi, T. and H. Kobayashi (2011) *Low Carbon Cities: The Future of Urban Planning*, Master's program in sustainable urban regeneration series. Tokyo: Gakugei Shuppan-Sha.

Osmont, A., C. Godblum, J.-F. Langumier, E. LeBris, C. De Miras and C. Musil (2008) *Urban Governance: Questioning a Multiform Paradigm. Analyses and Proposals of the Working Group on Urban Governance.* Paris: Ministère des Affaires Etrangères et Européennes.

Park, J., J. Sarkis and Z. Wu (2010) "Creating Integrated Business and Environ mental Value within the Context of China's Circular Economy and Ecological Modernization", *Journal of Cleaner Production*, 18(15): 1494–1501.

Pearson, C., S. Pilgrim and J. Pretty (eds) (2010) *Urban Agriculture: Diverse Activities and Benefits for City Society.* London: Earthscan.

Puppim de Oliveira, J. A. (2003) *Economic Instruments for Environmental Management: Lessons from National and International Experiences.* Salvador, Brazil: Center for Advanced Studies in Environmental Issues.

Putnam, R. (1993) *Making Democracy Work: Civic Traditions in Modern Italy.* Princeton, NJ: Princeton University Press.

Robins, N. and S. Roberts (1998) *Consumption in a Sustainable World.* Workbook prepared for the OECD Workshop on Consumption in a Sustainable World, Kabelvaag, Norway, 2–4 June.

Rode, P., R. Burdett and J. C. Soares Goncalves (2011) "Buildings: Investing in Energy and Resource Efficiency", in United Nations Environment Programme, *Towards a Green Economy: Pathways to Sustainable Development and Poverty Eradication*, pp. 331–374. Available at ⟨http://www.unep.org/greeneconomy/GreenEconomyReport/tabid/29846/Default.aspx⟩ (accessed 8 February 2012).

Rondinelli, D. and M. Berry (2000) "Multimodal Transportation, Logistics, and the Environment: Managing Interactions in a Global Economy", *European Management Journal*, 18(4): 398–410.

Sassen, S. (2000) *Cities in a World Economy*, 2nd edn. Thousand Oaks, CA: Pine Forge Press.

Suzuki, H., A. Dastur, S. Moffatt, N. Yabuki and H. Maruyama (2010) *Eco² Cities: Ecological Cities as Economic Cities*. Washington, DC: World Bank. Available at ⟨http://issuu.com/world.bank.publications/docs/9780821380468⟩ (accessed 9 February 2012).
TEEB (The Economics of Ecosystems and Biodiversity) (2010) "The Economics of Ecosystems and Biodiversity", ⟨http://www.teebweb.org⟩ (accessed 9 February 2012).
Tiwari, G. (2002) "Urban Transport Priorities: Meeting the Challenge of Socio-economic Diversity in Cities: A Case Study of Delhi, India", *Cities*, 19(2): 95–103.
TRAFFIC (2008) *What's Driving the Wildlife Trade? A Review of Expert Opinion on Economic and Social Drivers of the Wildlife Trade and Trade Control Efforts in Cambodia, Indonesia, Lao PDR, and Vietnam*, East Asia and Pacific Region Sustainable Development Discussion Papers, East Asia and Pacific Region Sustainable Development Department. Washington, DC: World Bank. Available at ⟨http://siteresources.worldbank.org/INTEASTASIAPACIFIC/Resources/226262-1223319129600/wildlife_fullreport.pdf⟩ (accessed 9 February 2012).
UNDESA (United Nations, Department of Economic and Social Affairs), Population Division (2010) *World Urbanization Prospects, the 2009 Revision*. New York: UNDESA.
UNDESA (United Nations, Department of Economic and Social Affairs), Division for Sustainable Development (n.d.) "Sustainable Consumption & Production Patterns (SCP) (& the Marrakech Process)", ⟨http://www.un.org/esa/dsd/dsd_aofw_scpp/scpp_index.shtml⟩ (accessed 14 February 2012).
UNEP (United Nations Environment Programme) (2011) *Towards a Green Economy: Pathways to Sustainable Development and Poverty Eradication*, ⟨http://www.unep.org/greeneconomy/⟩ (accessed 8 February 2012).
UN-HABITAT (United Nations Human Settlements Programme) (2002) *The Global Campaign on Urban Governance*. Nairobi: UN-HABITAT Publisher.
UN-HABITAT (United Nations Human Settlements Programme) (2006) *State of the World's Cities 2006/7*. London: Earthscan.
UN-HABITAT (United Nations Human Settlements Programme) (2008) *State of the World's Cities 2008/2009*. London: Earthscan.
Viljoen, A. (ed.) (2005) *Continuous Productive Urban Landscapes (CPULs): Designing Urban Agriculture for Sustainable Cities*. London: Architectural Press.
Wilkie, D. S. and J. F. Carpenter (1999) "Bushmeat Hunting in the Congo Basin: An Assessment of Impacts and Options for Mitigation", *Biodiversity and Conservation*, 8(7): 927–955.
World Bank (2008) *World Development Report 2009: Reshaping Economic Geography*. Washington, DC: World Bank. Available at ⟨http://econ.worldbank.org/WBSITE/EXTERNAL/EXTDEC/EXTRESEARCH/EXTWDRS/EXTWDR2009/0,,menuPK:4231145~pagePK:64167702~piPK:64167676~theSitePK:4231059,00.html⟩ (accessed 9 February 2012).
World Bank (2009) "The World Bank Urban & Local Government Strategy: Concept & Issues Note". Available at ⟨http://www.wburbanstrategy.org/

urbanstrategy/sites/wburbanstrategy.org/files/Urban%20Strategy%20Concept%20Note%20FINAL.pdf) (accessed 9 February 2012).

Yanagi, T. (2005) "Sato-Umi: A New Concept for Coastal Sea Management". A Report of the Research by the Research Institute for Applied Mechanics, Kyushu University, Japan.

Zanni, A. M. and A. L. Bristow (2010) "Emissions of CO_2 from Road Freight in London: Trends and Policies for Long Run Reductions", *Energy Policy*, 38(4): 1774–1786.

Zhu, Q., Y. Geng and K.-H. Lai (2010) "Circular Economy Practices among Chinese Manufacturers Varying in Environmental-Oriented Supply Chain Co-operation and the Performance Implications", *Journal of Environmental Management*, 91(6): 1324–1331.

Conclusion

15

Key issues and lessons learned for moving towards a greener economy and creating better governance for sustainable development

Jose A. Puppim de Oliveira

This chapter

This last chapter highlights the main issues raised by the individual chapters regarding how to move forward the agenda of institutional frameworks for sustainable development and the green economy in the context of sustainable development and poverty eradication. The book has presented several analyses that help us to understand how much progress has been achieved in some areas and what still needs to be done. This chapter provides an integrated analysis of the issues that cut across the different perspectives, pointing out the main obstacles to greening the economy and to creating a system to govern environmental resources in a more equitable and sustainable way at the different scales. The chapter reveals the main points that are essential to reforming the political and economic institutions at the various levels identified by the previous chapters, in order to move the sustainability agenda speedily and smoothly forward in the next few years.

Key issues and lessons learned

This section discusses the main lessons from the previous chapters. It also points out some of the shortcomings in the economic and political institutions hindering the creation of a greener economy that boosts environmentally sustainable development and fights poverty. It highlights the

Green economy and good governance for sustainable development: Opportunities, promises and concerns, Puppim de Oliveira (ed.),
United Nations University Press, 2012, ISBN 978-92-808-1216-9

importance of addressing these shortcomings from different perspectives to advance a more integrated approach to a greener economy and governance.

There are trade-offs in the green economy

Even though the concept of the green economy is not new, experiences up to now have generally been on an ad hoc basis and lacking in scale. For example, we still do not have one application of the green economy at the country or regional level that simultaneously covers several sectors. The case of payments for ecosystem services to mitigate deforestation in Costa Rica is one of the few examples at a larger scale (the country level), but it is still limited to the forestry sector. Moreover, some of the large-scale examples, such as ethanol in Brazil, initially had different objectives than that of sustainable development or poverty alleviation (Puppim de Oliveira, 2002).

The recent interest in bringing the green economy back to policy discussions at the highest level with a focus on poverty alleviation could lead to new experiments in practice. However, there are several potential obstacles to the implementation of green economy initiatives, as discussed in the previous chapters. For example, when analysing experiences in three southern African countries, Resnick, Thurow and Tarp (Chapter 4) argue that green growth is difficult to achieve in those countries because general socioeconomic objectives, such as job creation and poverty alleviation, may clash with environmental sustainability. There is no straightforward way of pulling off a win–win situation that achieves economic growth, poverty alleviation and environmental protection at the same time. The authors claim that, as with many other economic reforms, the reforms needed to promote green growth require short-term sacrifices to achieve long-term objectives and may face tremendous opposition from some groups, including the poor.

Chapter 7 also discusses the governance challenges for the green economy to work in Africa. After making an assessment of sustainable development governance in African countries since Rio-92, Afful-Koomson concludes that there are major governance obstacles to mainstreaming sustainable development objectives in African economies. In many countries, decisions lack the participation and the voice of important stakeholders or transparency. Afful-Koomson argues that institutions to support good governance need to be established to make the green economy deliver the expected benefits in poverty alleviation and environmental sustainability in the continent.

It is still difficult in most cases to integrate the different objectives of a green economy with one another. Measuring economic outcomes and linking them to social and environmental aspects is not an easy task, and efforts have been made to provide new systems to report economic and social progress that presents this reality (Stiglitz et al., 2009). In practice, there are significant trade-offs that prevent the green economy from becoming a reality in many situations for both rich and poor countries at present. Aligning diverse objectives and short-term interests with long-term goals, such as poverty alleviation and climate change mitigation, may be possible on a small scale or in certain conditions or localities. However, any large-scale cross-cutting initiatives will probably face enormous implementation challenges and may require tremendous financial and technical efforts, as well as strong political support at the national and international levels. Gaining such backing does not seem feasible in the short term, especially in the present global financial institutions and with the current governance structures at the various levels. In order to create a greener economy, an institutional framework needs to be in place to regulate the economy, but most of today's economy is unregulated, remaining informal or beyond the control of existing mechanisms like a large part of international financial systems. Thus, the green economy probably needs to be preceded by a larger reform in the economic institutions and regulatory organizations.

The political economy may prevent change

The authors in this book mention another set of obstacles related to the political economy in implementing sustainable development policies. Achieving a greener economy involves huge distributional implications from the economic and social costs and benefits at all levels. In aggregate, society is expected to accrue significant economic, social and environmental benefits in the medium and long term with a green economy. However, some will lose a lot in order to allow others to gain a little. Some of the losers from the green economy are politically influential and are likely to put a lot of political pressure on various stakeholders to prevent or change green economy policies.

For example, reducing climate change by the rate necessary to avoid a collapse in the many of the Earth's supporting systems entails an enormous shift from our dependence on fossil fuels towards the use of renewable energies. This, in turn, will leave potential winners and losers. Geothermal energy is one sustainable alternative already available to many countries, as discussed in Chapter 8. However, if renewables become an alternative, oil-producing countries may lose their major – and in some cases only – source of hard currency, which is used to finance basic public services. Many of these countries, such as Nigeria and Angola, are still poor and may be big losers if financial mechanisms are not put in place to ease the transition. A change to renewables without any compensation may also spur resistance in the oil companies, which are some of the largest corporations in the world and have a lot of political clout. Chapter 4 analysed how large mining and energy corporations may resist the various low-carbon green growth policies in southern African countries, because those policies go against the corporations' interests. Financing the implementation of alternative mechanisms has faced difficulties, as in the Ecuadorian proposal for compensation in exchange for leaving the oil reserves in the Yasuni National Park unexploited to protect its rainforest, biodiversity and inhabitants. Large-scale schemes, such as REDD+ discussed in Chapter 2, may also need significant amounts of resources that may not be readily available. Identifying those trade-offs at the global, national and local levels would help to make explicit what obstacles would be likely to appear and what needs to be done to move the green economy and sustainability agenda forward in a particular context.

Equity concerns are still not at the centre of discussions on the green economy

Environmental quality is closely linked to human well-being, as the Millennium Ecosystem Assessment (MA, 2005) demonstrated in the case of ecosystem services. However, neither the costs nor the benefits related to the environment are distributed evenly: some individuals, groups and countries are affected differently by changes in the environment. There are important equity implications when we discuss the health of the environment or the gains from environmental improvement. Climate change is a good example of how unevenly the causes and consequences of the changes in climate are distributed. Even though we are all responsible for the problem (through the principle of "common but differentiated responsibilities"), the richest are those who have polluted most, but the poorest are more likely to suffer from the harshest consequences because they are generally more vulnerable and lack the resources to adapt quickly.

Discussions on the green economy tend to consider the idea of economic growth as the main outcome, with little emphasis on equity aspects, even though the outcomes of decisions and development processes have important equity implications. Thus, if more sustainable, fairer development is the long-term objective of development processes around the world, equity should be brought to the centre of discussions on the green economy and the institutional framework for sustainable development.

Understanding how development processes have an impact on equity and how to change governance to have fairer outcomes for the most vulnerable and powerless groups in several arenas is an issue covered in this book. Equity issues have been discussed directly or indirectly in several chapters (for example, Chapters 2, 3, 4, 9 and 12). The authors argue that the well-being of several disadvantaged societal groups, communities and regions around the world is threatened by environmental degradation for which they are not directly responsible. Chapter 9 discusses these issues regarding biodiversity. The authors argue that new mechanisms to improve the governance of biological resources could have a positive impact on the most vulnerable communities that depend on those resources. Overconsumption to heat the economy in some parts of the world, sometimes in the same locality, leads to negative impacts in other parts, generally where the most vulnerable groups work or live, such as the poor or indigenous peoples. Those groups are also generally powerless to make the necessary changes in resource governance to change the course of actions.

Discussions on technology need to be broadened beyond the "technological fix"

Unlike in the 1950s and 1960s, when stresses on our environment started to become a social and political concern, technical knowledge and technological solutions are today much more advanced. In the past, the implementation of solutions was hindered because basic technical knowledge and tools were not available. For example, when the problem of Minamata disease emerged in Japan in the 1950s, the health effects of mercury and other heavy metals were mostly unknown. Today, we have a huge amount of information about those effects and the technology to tackle such problems. In the 1960s, we also did not have the basic technologies for effective desulphurization and denitrification to control air pollution, which are widespread today.

Technology is readily available to provide sustainable solutions in many situations. Chapter 8, for example, looks at the tremendous untapped potential of geothermal energy in many countries. Geothermal energy could be an affordable source of sustainable energy for many people who do not have access to basic energy supplies, thus improving social conditions in many parts of the world. Many developing countries, such as El Salvador and Kenya, have started to exploit this potential. A greater effort to develop technical capacity in some developing countries could also have a significant impact on the production of clean energy, and consequently on the social improvements needed to achieve the Millennium Development Goals.

However, many of the solutions for sustainability problems lie in the economic, social and political viability of the technological solutions that are widely available today. Moreover, the availability of technologies and their distribution became the main driver to find solutions to unsustainability problems. In the context of a green economy, this has ethical foundations and equity implications, as discussed in Chapter 3. The authors examine the gaps in the proposed "green technological revolution" aimed at providing a "technological fix" for sustainability problems. They argue that there is a lack of understanding of the value of sufficiency to complement efficiency in discussions on the green economy. Most of the technological solutions are based solely on the optimization of economic efficiency, which has equity implications because the efficiency gains are not distributed evenly.

Another set of discussions concerns access to technological development and the sharing of its benefits. Many technological developments are based on natural assets in different parts of the globe. How these benefits are or should be shared is directly or indirectly addressed in several chapters, such as Chapters 9 and 11. The authors in Chapter 9 analyse the huge benefits that biodiversity can bring to society, including the potential for new technologies to produce new pharmaceutical products and cosmetics. Even though the Nagoya Protocol on Access and Benefit-sharing provides a framework for improving the equity aspects of bio-prospecting, there are still governance gaps. For example, Chapter 11 examines one of the most untapped resources on Earth in terms of knowledge: the oceans. Oceans are also one of the least regulated resources in terms of both access to manage the resources per se (for example, fisheries) and the knowledge based on those resources. Bio-prospecting in the sea has developed rapidly, but there is a gap in the governance of both the benefits from the resources and the risks.

Good governance with governments, but beyond international organizations and national governments

Most of the discussions on what is called the institutional framework for sustainable development are focused on global governance, especially the reform of the United Nations system. Chapter 10 has a thorough discussion on the reforms needed in the international governance system to produce more efficient, fairer outcomes from international environmental processes. These discussions emphasize the role of international organizations and national governments, and, to a lesser extent, non-governmental actors, in the governance mechanisms. Even though these discussions are important for strengthening the international system, because the national governments are legitimate representatives of the people living within their borders, many other actors have been active in influencing governance at various levels. However, complexity in the governance of many issues may require a broader set of actors than those commonly explored by the traditional governance literature, particularly if we want to strengthen the link to implementation.

Many of the chapters in this book contribute to identifying and analysing important stakeholders in several policy processes on diverse issues at different scales. Chapter 12 examines the role of indigenous peoples in global environmental governance. They are present in several countries around the world and have contributed to many global processes, but their views are still not represented by many national governments. Strengthening their role and their "traditional" knowledge could make a rich contribution to international discussions as well as to innovations in implementation. Local authorities and subnational governments are another set of actors whose involvement in global governance has grown. Chapter 14 looks at how cities, where most of the world's population lives, have a huge potential to tackle global environmental issues, particularly climate change. The governance of cities will determine the future of the green economy because cities are the backbone of the economy of most countries and their influence goes well beyond their boundaries.

The importance of values and traditional knowledge systems is not fully recognized

The transition to a more sustainable society will need a radical change in the values of mainstream society: West and East, North and South. This implies a change in the ways we think and do things in all aspects of our personal and professional lives. Different knowledge systems need to emerge and transform "Western"-style society. On the one hand, some "Western" values have contributed a lot to making the world better, for example by stressing the importance of freedom and the rule of law and even by allowing the emergence of ecological concerns and the idea of sustainable development. Western science was a key factor in identifying the limits of the planet and warning of climate change. However, other aspects of Western values were responsible for leading us towards unsustainable lifestyles and poorly regulated systems for governing the Earth's natural resources, both locally and globally.

Several chapters in this book raise the importance of bringing a different set of values to society in order to make changes towards a more sustainable development path. Chapter 5 analyses how education could be a tool in transforming the unsustainable production and consumption patterns in modern societies. This would be a necessary condition for achieving the objectives of the green economy. Education for sustainable development would need to be incorporated into the existing educational structures, focusing the learning process on values compatible with sustainable development, such as equity and justice, and local sustainable innovation. Certain of these new values are embedded in some traditional knowledge systems. Many traditional societies produce and consume in a much more sustainable way and have maintained a close link with nature for many generations. At the international level, as Chapter 12 analyses, indigenous groups with their traditional knowledge systems have added new knowledge and values to the global environmental processes, but they still need to be strengthened in these processes and supported at the local and regional levels because some of them are under threat. Agricultural systems that use natural resources in a sustainable manner could provide an alternative to the large-scale agricultural systems that are dependent on many external inputs. Looking at socio-ecological production landscapes, the authors in Chapter 6 examine how those landscapes are under threat owing to the loss of traditional knowledge and socioeconomic transformations such as emigration or population ageing. They claim that an international effort to revive those traditional knowledge systems could provide an alternative mechanism to boost a greener economy.

Innovation capacity needs to be at the centre of the search for the sustainable solutions

Discourses on limits push for a stronger political commitment by countries, major groups and international organizations to develop a credible institutional framework for guiding us to more sustainable development and steering the mainstream economy to a greener path that could eradicate poverty. However, we need more innovation capacity to generate the tools and mechanisms to transform broad concepts into practical results for advancing the implementation of such commitments. Several chapters in this book, such as Chapters 3, 5 and 14, stress the importance of putting innovation, both technical and non-technical, at the centre of the debates on the green economy and governance.

The experience and the capacity of societies to innovate locally is essential to generate viable solutions to local and global problems. Two main points related to this should be highlighted from the previous discussions. The first point is to create mechanisms to identify and generate innovative solutions, both technological and institutional, that can have large positive impacts on societies. Those innovations have to cut across sectors and regions and lead to radical impacts on the way societies use environmental resources and distribute their benefits. Incremental small changes towards sustainable development are still important, but it is only with more radical changes that we can achieve the proposed international goals, such as reductions in greenhouse gas emissions or the preservation of biodiversity, in order to avoid future unsustainable paths. Thus, in addition to the effective implementation of individual projects and programmes, innovative initiatives with a much larger impact are necessary.

The second point is to create governance mechanisms that facilitate the dynamic exchange of knowledge and resources locally and globally to generate and diffuse the innovative solutions needed for radical changes. We have to create mechanisms that facilitate the development of local innovation capacities in order to scale up innovations. Because many of the solutions to global concerns emerge at the local level, we need local and global efforts to create the capacity to innovate locally and spread those innovations globally to those who need them. Local groups must be able to adopt the best technologies for their local needs, absorb new technologies and create the institutional mechanisms to increase their benefits. Thus, we need to understand the global mechanisms that facilitate the diffusion of knowledge and resources to enable the development and dissemination of good local solutions to other localities in a fair, effective and efficient manner. An international forum or agency on sustainable innovation that could coordinate efforts to govern, promote, identify and diffuse sustainable innovations, both technological and institutional, would be essential to accelerate the implementation of the sustainable development agenda.

Final remarks

The Earth is under pressure and needs dramatic changes in the way we use and abuse its carrying capacity. Unlike the report of the Club of Rome (Meadows et al., 1972), which forewarned of environmental ramifications in decades ahead, this time some tipping points have already been reached, as in the case of climate change, which may have irreversible consequences. Apart from the population almost doubling in the last 40 years, the level of consumption of many natural resources has increased several fold (UNEP, 2011). Yet, even with such large increases, many of the pressing social problems in many countries, such as poverty, continue to indicate an unequal utilization of resources. Another difference from the 1970s is our access to knowledge about the sustainability problems we face today. We know much more about local and global environmental problems and their consequences today than we knew in the 1970s, when environment-related sciences were emerging and the links between environmental, social and economic issues were still mostly unknown. We also lacked the tools and technology we have today. Nevertheless, we have not been able to create governance mechanisms, at either the global or the national level, to make the necessary changes to steer our societies and economies towards a more sustainable path. Even though governance over our environmental resources has evolved and decision processes linked to sustainable development issues have been more participatory and transparent in some aspects, we have not reached the point of making the radical changes we need.

In this context, the discussions on the green economy and the institutional framework for sustainable development are timely. There is an urgent need to decouple the economy from the use of natural resources (UNEP, 2011), so that economic growth will not pile more stress on our limited resources. Moreover, besides being greener, the economy should help to solve pressing social problems such as poverty. We also need appropriate institutions and organizational structures at the international level to be more efficient, transparent and effective in making decisions and implementing them. As pointed out earlier, these discussions are not new in practice or in the literature.

Even though recent discussions have benefited from the accumulation of empirical and theoretical knowledge in past decades, they have not produced the kind of conceptual originality and tools necessary to put the green economy on the mainstream political, social and economic agenda. Much of past and present discussions on the green economy are based on the mainstream market-based economic system and the values that are embedded in it. This system was responsible for creating the problems in the first place, and it is unlikely to be the solution. The chapters in this book show the differences between intentions and results when the green economy is put into practice, as in the analyses of southern Africa in Chapter 4. They also indicate the lack of discussions on important topics such as equity and changes in values. On the other hand, discussions on governance remain mostly in the international sphere; discussions at the national and subnational level are unconvincing, but they are also a key factor in implementation, as well as in specific issues discussed in this book, such as the governance of oceans or the role of indigenous peoples.

The way economies function and political organizations respond determines how sustainable we are at the local, national and global levels. Reforming economic and political institutions is indeed a necessary condition if we want to move towards a more sustainable world, in which we maintain our environment and eradicate many of our social problems, such as poverty. We know a lot about the green economy and governance, but there is a lack of political will to move the agenda forward, which may also depend on larger reforms in economic and political systems. We also lack the tools to carry out changes. However, emerging new discussions on the green economy and governance offer some positive signs that changes may be possible. Nevertheless, a "golden bullet" that would automatically solve all problems is unlikely to exist. We need to discuss and analyse specific issues in depth to come up with solutions that are politically legitimate, socially acceptable and economically viable.

REFERENCES

MA (Millennium Ecosystem Assessment) (2005) "Millennium Ecosystem Assessment", ⟨http://www.maweb.org/⟩ (accessed 9 February 2012).
Meadows, D. L., D. H. Meadows, H. Donella, J. Randers and W. Behrens (1972) *The Limits to Growth*. New York: Universe Books.
Puppim de Oliveira, J. A. (2002) "The Policymaking Process for Creating Competitive Assets for the Use of Biomass Energy: the Brazilian Alcohol Programme", *Renewable & Sustainable Energy Reviews*, 6(1–2): 127–138.
Stiglitz, J. E., A. Sen and J.-P. Fitoussi (2009) *Report by the Commission on the Measurement of Economic Performance and Social Progress*, ⟨http://www.stiglitz-sen-fitoussi.fr/en/index.htm⟩ (accessed 9 February 2012).
UNEP (United Nations Environment Programme) (2011) *Decoupling Natural Resource Use and Environmental Impacts from Economic Growth*, A Report of the Working Group on Decoupling to the International Resource Panel. Fischer-Kowalski, M., Swilling, M., von Weizsäcker, E. U., Ren, Y., Moriguchi, Y., Crane, W., Krausmann, F., Eisenmenger, N., Giljum, S., Hennicke, P., Romero Lankao, P., Siriban Manalang, A., Sewerin, S. Available at ⟨http://www.unep.org/resourcepanel/Publications/Decoupling/tabid/56048/Default.aspx⟩ (accessed 9 February 2012).

Index

10 Year Framework of Programmes (10YFP), 153
2001 Declaration on Cultural Diversity, 248

Abuja Declaration on Fertilizer for an African Green Revolution, 82
abundance, 49, 56–57, 64, 73, 84, 86, 252, 289
accountability, 25, 33, 147–148, 202, 209–210, 213–217, 245, 292–293, 316
acid rain, 274
Adam Smith, 49, 55, 62
adapting to climate change, 251
adaptive management, 235
aerosol, 256
affordable housing, 297
Africa, 7, 12–13, 15–17, 27, 38, 71–80, 82, 84–89, 105, 121, 169, 171, 175–177, 256, 262, 275, 279, 282, 290, 328, 330, 336
Africa Roundtable for SCP, 153
African Development Bank Group (AfDB), 139
African National Congress (ANC), 77
African palm oil, 85
African Union Commission (AUC), 139
Agenda 21, 3, 10–12, 17, 21, 24, 42, 94, 103, 116, 151–153, 247, 266
Agricultural Input Subsidy Program (AISP), 81–83

agriculture, 31, 38, 53, 72, 74, 80, 82, 85, 117, 119, 122–123, 126–127, 139, 150, 184, 189, 201, 223, 247–248, 250, 300, 318
agrobiodiversity, 185
agroforestry, 185, 254–255
agro-processing, 74
agro-sylvo-pastoral systems, 120
Aichi Prefecture, 119, 127–128
Andean *ayni*, 121
Ankeniheny-Zahamena Corridor (CAZ), 126–127
Antarctica, 233
Antarctic, 224, 228, 233, 236, 237, 277
Antarctic Treaty System, 228, 236
anti-reform coalitions, 72
anthropocene, 212
apartheid, 77
aquaculture, 170, 300
aquifers, 82
archipelagic State, 231
architecture of international environmental governance, 206–207
Arctic Climate Impact Assessment, 249
Argentina, 38
Arndt, 78, 84–86, 89, 90
Asahi Kasei Chemicals Corporation, 126
Asia, 7, 27, 48, 71, 105, 110–111, 155, 175, 177, 237, 254, 256, 290, 292, 314

Asian Institute of Technology (AIT), 110–111
Atlanta, 296
atmosphere, 35, 127, 172, 223, 255, 256, 278
attitudes, 98, 319
automobile industry, 9
avian influenza, 270

bacteria, 224, 230
Bali, 37, 176
Bali Action Plan, 37
balneology, 169–170
Baltic Sea, 237
Barcelona, 296
Baringo, 169
base of the pyramid, 97
behaviour, 83, 833, 94, 102, 112–113, 205, 267, 282, 291–292, 296, 310, 312, 319
Beijing Olympic Games, 170
benefit-sharing, 222, 231–235, 238, 248–249
benthic communities, 226
benthic ecosystems, 227
Bingu wa Mutharika, 81
bioenergy, 164
biodiversity
  conservation, 27, 126, 181, 183–186, 189–190, 262
  hotspots, 184, 187, 246
  targets, 39, 183, 186–188, 190
biofuels, 72, 73, 84–86, 88, 96, 224
biogeochemical cycles, 223
biomass, 5, 63, 125–126, 161, 164, 172, 182, 226, 297
biosphere, 54–55, 59, 62
biotechnology, 224
birds, 274
BirdLife International, 124
blue ling, 223
Blum, 267–268
Bolivia, 256
bottom of pyramid, 97
bottom-up, 129, 251
Botswana, 27, 140, 256
Brazil, 3, 10, 27, 37, 38, 85, 94, 119, 131, 254, 256, 305, 307, 316, 328
Bretton Woods, 215
BRIC, 27
Brundtland Report, 4, 10, 24, 27, 275
buildings, 170, 173, 177, 291, 297, 305, 313, 315–316

businesses, 8, 11, 50, 64–65, 73, 78, 80, 105, 276, 291, 311, 316
business model, 54, 63, 65, 299, 303
bush meat, 182

C40 Cities Climate Leadership Group, 312, 315
calcareous organisms, 227
Cambodia, 123–124, 131, 279
Canada, 85, 104, 110, 162, 167, 173, 177, 246, 254
cancer, 223, 242, 272, 274, 277–278
capability approach, 57
capacity-building, 103, 120, 131, 139, 175–177, 183, 201, 231–233, 238, 246, 258, 260
capacity factor, 164–165
capitalist, 6, 62, 305
carbon dioxide, 35, 80, 127, 170, 174, 223, 254, 278
carbon stocks, 182
carbon tax, 73, 80, 209
carcinoma, 278
Caribbean, 13, 27
Cartagena, 11
cashews, 84
Caspian Sea, 237
cassava, 85
cataracts, 277–278
Catskill Watershed, 182
Cebu, 104, 106, 108, 173
cement, 278
Centre for Trade and Sustainable Development (ICTSD), 37
central governments, 149
CEPAL, 169
certification, 29, 107, 315
Charles Maier, 49, 55
Chernobyl, 270–271
China, 15, 27, 37–38, 85, 112, 167–168, 170, 173, 175, 177, 180, 232, 279, 289
chlorofluorocarbons (CFCs), 277–278, 283
ciconia boyciana, 125
circular economy, 305
cities, 3, 6–8, 15, 19, 27, 152, 214, 286–320, 333
city governments, 291, 293, 308–309, 313
CITYNET, 315
civil society, 8, 11–12, 30, 62, 78, 95, 103, 105, 120, 160, 210, 245, 291, 308, 310

Clean Development Mechanism, 13, 152, 173–174
clean energy, 34, 37, 161, 316, 331
climate change, 3–4, 10, 12, 19, 26, 29–31, 33–37 47, 66, 78, 96, 125, 139, 165, 172–173, 175, 177, 181–182, 200, 222, 226–228, 245, 249–262, 271–275, 277–287, 290, 306, 308, 312, 329–330, 333, 335
Clinton Climate Initiative, 312
Club of Rome, 8, 335
child labour, 97
coal, 5, 59–60, 72–73, 75, 77–80, 86, 88, 163–164, 276, 282
coal-fired plants, 77
Coast Salish, 258
coastal area, 18, 221, 226, 233–238
co-developers, 100
Colombia, 252
Colorado, 205, 206, 209, 211, 217–218
Colorado State University, 206, 218
Columbia University, 160
Copenhagen Amendments, 278
co-producers, 97, 100
co-production, 147
Commission on Biofuels, 85
Commission on Human Rights, 249
common but differentiated responsibilities, 30, 330
common heritage of mankind, 231
communist, 6, 49
Communities of Practice, 102, 113–115
Community Based Adaptation, 31
community engagement, 98, 108–109, 259
community trust, 65
comparative advantages, 74, 84, 204, 316
compensatory mitigation, 127, 128
compliance, 30, 187–188, 201–202, 209, 214, 217, 313
ConocoPhillips, 255
Conference of Parties, 35
conflicts, 35, 49, 96, 185, 210
Congress of South African Trade Unions (COSATU), 78
Conservation International (CI), 126–127
Consortium of Universities for Global Health, 271
consumers, 30, 75, 79, 88, 97, 100, 107, 125, 297–299, 305, 318
consumer behaviour, 94, 113

consumption and production, 16, 17, 19, 94–96, 98, 100, 102, 104, 113–115, 123, 152, 158, 297–299
continental shelf, 225
continuous productive urban landscapes (CPULs), 300
Convention Concerning Indigenous and Tribal Peoples in Independent Countries, 246
Convention for the Protection of the Marine Environment of the North-East Atlantic, 229
Convention on Biological Diversity, 3, 10, 15, 29, 39, 119, 129–131, 183, 185, 188–189, 191, 221, 227–229, 232–236, 247–248
Convention on International Trade in Endangered Species, 39, 184
Convention for the Safeguarding of the Intangible Cultural Heritage, 248
cook stoves, 161
cooking fuels, 161
cooling, 170, 171, 173, 177, 315
coral reefs, 224, 226
corporate governance, 143
corruption, 97
crab, 223
crop residue retention, 255
cultural diversity, 25, 182–183, 248
cultural heritage, 248, 256
Cuyahoga River, 50

Dakar, Senegal, 153
DALYs (disability-adjusted life years), 273–274, 276
DDT, 274
debt crisis, 51
decision-making, 26, 53, 97, 99, 126, 129, 140, 143, 144–146, 149–150, 204–205, 209, 211, 213–214, 216–217, 247, 250–251, 253, 258, 261, 286, 293, 307
decentralization, 141, 154, 292, 309, 314
Declaration on the Rights of Indigenous Peoples, 248, 261
deforestation, 10, 12, 29, 34, 35, 73, 85–86, 126–127, 172, 187, 247, 253, 254, 278, 298, 328
Dehesa, 120
Delaware, 64
Delhi, 296
deliberative democracy, 100
de-localization, 96

deep sea, 222–233, 237, 239
Democratic Progressive Party (DPP), 81, 83–84
dialogue, 65, 100–101, 114, 205, 207, 232, 257
diarrhoeal diseases, 275
disease vector control, 268
DNA sequencing, 234
donors, 27, 31, 77, 81, 250
Dorward and Chirwa, 82–82, 89
drinking water, 169, 272, 275, 279
drivers of global environmental change, 207
droughts, 81, 172, 252, 279

early diagnosis, 269
Earth System, 200, 206, 209–212, 217–218, 277
Earth System Governance Project, 200, 206, 209, 218
East African Rift Valley, 169
eco-cities, 291
ecological
    imperialism, 58
    injustice, 57–58
    modernization, 55
Eastern Europe, 27, 162, 175
ecologically and biologically significant areas (EBSAs), 236
Eco Mark Africa, 153
Economic and Social Council (ECOSOC), 25, 137–139, 203–204, 207, 246, 248
economic development, 4, 6, 8–10, 16, 24, 27, 49–51, 61–62, 73, 100, 120, 152, 161, 163, 173, 177, 199, 275–277, 279, 287–289, 292, 315, 317, 319
economy–environment, 9
ecosystem approach, 188, 221, 228, 235
ecosystems, 6, 13–14, 16–18, 27–30, 39–40, 53, 66, 96, 107–108, 117, 121, 123–128, 131, 138, 181–185, 187, 190, 224, 226–227, 229, 234, 236, 238, 252, 256, 258, 265, 275, 288, 298, 300–301, 306–307, 317
ecosystem disruption, 275
ecosystem network, 128
ecosystem services, 19, 34, 36, 39, 53–54, 104, 117, 121, 126–127, 181, 184, 188, 190, 213, 295, 298, 300, 301, 306, 328, 330
ecotourism, 186
Ecuador, 246, 330
education
    formal and non-formal, 95

Education for Sustainable Development (ESD), 17, 94–96, 98–108, 112–114, 310, 333
El Salvador, 167–169, 174, 176, 178, 331
electric vehicles, 320
electricity, 58, 64, 71–73, 76–80, 86, 88–89, 160–161, 164–169, 171–173, 176–177, 316, 320
Elinor Ostrom, 14
employment, 27, 28, 34, 53, 73, 76–78, 86–88, 102, 104, 125, 128, 150–151, 155, 249, 256, 282, 300–303, 313
energy
    energy consumption, 65, 161, 163, 170, 173, 177, 276, 287, 289, 295–297, 315
Energy Sector Management Assistance Program (ESMAP), 160
enthalpy, 172
Environment of Health model, 267–268
environmental
    assessment, 202, 226, 228
    colonialism, 58
    degradation, 7, 10, 13, 23, 34, 52, 96, 117, 151, 155–156, 227, 273, 293–294, 297, 331
    effects, 30
    governance, 13–15, 18–19, 142–143, 152, 199–200, 202, 203, 206–209, 218, 245, 333
    health, 19, 267–268, 271–273, 275–277, 282–283
    health risks, 273
    injustices, 16
    management, 9, 152, 185, 189, 237
    migration, 260
    problems, 6, 8–12, 16, 19, 200, 234, 288, 335
    regulations, 50
    resources, 14, 306, 327, 334, 336
    standards, 9
    stewardship, 52, 190
    values, 13, 208, 210
Environmental Impact Assessment (EIA), 8, 228, 232, 235–238
enzymes, 224, 230
epistemic community(ies), 97, 150, 154
Equator Initiative, 31, 186, 250
equity, 23–24, 34, 40, 47, 49–66, 130, 155, 161, 183, 186, 209, 210, 222, 228, 230, 232–235, 238, 245, 269, 271, 279, 292–293, 303–304, 330–332, 334, 336
ESKOM, 77, 78

Ethiopia, 131, 169
Europe, 27, 72, 120, 143, 162, 170, 171, 269
European Environmental Agency, 299
European Patent Office (EPO), 37
European Union, 78, 84, 173, 279
extremophiles, 224

fair-trade, 107, 125
feminism, 6, 8
fertilizers, 7, 71–72, 82, 83, 86, 88, 124–135, 171
fibre, 181–182, 318
Fiji, 131
Finland, 38, 167, 203
finance, 34–36, 61, 72, 75, 87, 138, 170, 173, 199, 287, 306, 309, 329
financial crises, 23, 33, 148
fish farming, 169, 170, 172
fisheries, 123, 221, 223, 227–229, 231, 234, 236, 300, 332
flood mitigation, 298
floods, 172
flooding, 81, 125, 279
food
  crisis, 81
  hygiene, 268, 272
  needs, 81
  production, 96, 107, 221, 224, 288–289, 300
  security, 30–31, 36, 86, 124, 128, 139, 251
Food and Agriculture Organization (FAO), 81, 85, 221, 223, 226, 236, 248, 256, 298
Food Security and Sustainable Development (FSSD), 139
footprint, 52, 55, 298–301, 312, 315
forestry, 117, 119, 123, 125–126, 184–185, 254, 328
forests, 36, 73, 124–127, 182, 189, 253–254, 262, 275, 296
fossil fuels, 5, 37, 53, 59, 66, 72, 85, 120, 125, 163, 172, 177, 275, 276, 282, 311, 320, 329
France, 119, 167, 201
freedom, 18, 57, 61, 63, 101, 225, 228, 231, 293, 333
fruit, 182
Fukushima, 270

gender equality, 25, 27, 28, 58, 120
G-77, 232
GC/GMEF, 202–204

General Assembly, 25, 28, 39, 47, 103, 137–138, 190, 201, 204, 231–232, 238, 248
genes, 224, 230
genetic diversity, 123, 182
genetic manipulation, 123
genetic resources, 182–185, 222, 224, 230–233, 238, 248–249
geographic information systems, 259
geothermal energy, 17, 160–178, 329, 331
geothermal (ground source) heat pumps (GHPs), 169, 170–173, 177
German Federal Ministry for the Environment, Nature conservation and Nuclear Safety (BMU), 153
Germany, 56, 167, 201
Global Biodiversity Outlook, 29, 41, 226
global carbon cycle, 223
global commons, 18, 215, 218, 222, 225, 233, 237–238
Global Environment Facility (GEF), 31, 36, 250, 256
Global Environmental Health, 19, 267, 271–273
Global Environment Outlook, 226
global health, 15, 270–271
Global International Waters Assessment, 226, 249
Global Positioning System, 258
globalization, 5, 23, 33, 122, 126, 145, 286, 304
global warming, 10, 82, 96, 172, 176, 275, 278, 315
Ghana, 17, 27, 82, 131, 256
Gokase River, 126
good governance, 14, 23–25, 28, 32, 39, 47, 137, 143, 286, 292, 328, 332
Governing Council for the United Nations Environment Programme (GCUNEP), 138
government institutions, 141, 149
grasslands, 256
grassroots innovation, 63, 97, 100
Great Bear Rainforest, 254
Greenland, 29
Gross Domestic Product (GDP), 26, 38, 54, 80, 84, 212–213, 216–217, 306
Gross National Product, 57, 287
Greenhouse Gas(es) (GHG), 35–37, 72–73, 78–80, 82, 85–86, 126, 169, 172, 173, 253–256, 275, 278, 287, 291, 296, 298, 303, 307 313, 315, 334

greenhouse(s), 169–172
Grenada, 131
green
  buildings, 315
  economy, 3, 5, 12–18, 30, 33, 45, 47–48,
    52–59, 61–65, 71, 94–95, 97–102, 106,
    112–115, 117–118, 121, 123, 127,
    129–132, 136–137, 142, 150–156, 184,
    186, 188–190, 199, 218, 288, 290–292,
    294–297, 299–300, 303, 306–319,
    327–336
  growth, 14–16, 71–73, 75–78, 82, 85–89,
    94–95, 99, 130, 316, 328, 330
  jobs, 71, 87, 151
  procurement, 187, 313
  revolution, 7, 31, 82
  society, 94, 112–113
  technological revolution, 53, 58, 332
  technology, 61, 316–317
groundwater, 82, 170, 272
growth linkages, 74–75, 87
Guatemala, 167–169, 174

health
  child, 28
  definition of, 267
  reproductive, 28
H1N1, 270–271
habitats, 128, 222, 224, 226, 235
Hakone Vision Factory, 211, 215–217
healthcare services, 267
heating, 63, 160, 169–177, 315
heat island, 298, 306
heat waves, 279
herbal medicinal, 186
heredity, 267–268
High-Level Panel on Global Sustainability, 33
hollowing-out, 145
Honey Bee Network, 63
horticulture, 169–171
Hugo Grotius, 225
human
  capital, 51, 53, 75, 307
  development, 10, 12, 56–57, 61, 131, 161, 213, 222
  Human Development Index, 10, 213
  rights movements, 6
  security, 65
  well-being, 15, 18, 71, 119, 121, 129–130,
    181–183, 187–190, 212, 237, 294–295,
    297, 299–301, 319, 330

Hungary, 38, 167
hunger, 25, 28, 32, 279
hydropower, 62, 77, 79, 164, 169, 172
hydrothermal vents, 224, 227
hygiene, 268–269, 271–275

ICLEI, 295, 314
ICTs, 27, 33
infectious diseases, 182, 270
invasive species, 226
IFSD, see also Institutional Framework for
  Sustainable Development, 13–15, 19,
  200, 204, 209, 211, 216–218
implementation of global agreements, 15
inequity, 23, 34–35, 288, 295, 297
India, 9, 27, 37–38, 49, 54, 61–63, 66, 82, 121,
  131, 185, 189, 279
indicators, 25, 27, 39–40, 107, 110, 120, 146,
  165, 184, 188, 292
indigenous
  forums, 246
  knowledge, 150, 154, 247, 257–260
  people, 3, 14, 18, 140, 245–262, 331, 333, 336
  ownership, 254
Indonesia, 15, 111–112, 167, 169, 174, 176, 314
industrial revolution, 5–6, 37, 61, 289
innovation systems, 63
innovative measures, 23
informal economies, 293
information technologies, 213, 286
Institutional Framework for Sustainable
  Development (IFSD), 3–4, 12–15, 19,
  136, 151, 153, 199–201, 204, 206,
  209–211, 216–218, 286, 330, 332, 336
institutions, 4, 9, 14, 17, 38, 63–65, 97–100,
  105, 109–110, 119, 136–155, 175–176,
  183, 186, 188, 201, 204–206, 209–218,
  234, 238, 249, 253, 259, 291–294, 307,
  317, 327, 329, 336
intellectual capital, 306–308, 319
intellectual property rights (IPRs), 37–38
inter-cropping, 82–83
interest group, 73, 75, 80, 147
Intergovernmental Committee on
  Intellectual Property and Genetic
  Resources, Traditional Knowledge and
  Folklore, 249
Intergovernmental Panel on Climate
  Change (IPCC), 29, 33, 163–164,
  171–172, 249, 252, 254, 261, 278

Intergovernmental Science-Policy Platform on Biodiversity and Ecosystem Services, 188
international agency(ies), 291–293
International Decade of the World's Indigenous Peoples, 248
international environmental governance, 18, 200, 202, 203, 207–209, 218
International Environmental Governance Architecture Research Group, 200, 218
International Geothermal Association (IGA), 176
International Human Dimensions Programme on Global Environmental Change (IHDP), 200, 218
International Institute for Applied Systems Analysis (IIASA), 161–162
International Labour Organization (ILO), 210, 246, 262
International Seabed Authority, 227
International Treaty on Plant Genetic Resources for Food and Agriculture, 184, 248
inter- and intra-generational equity, 50
Intergovernmental Panel on Climate Change (IPCC), 29, 33, 35, 163, 249, 252, 254, 278–279
intergovernmental system, 207, 214
International Monetary Fund (IMF), 25–26, 81
International Organization for Standardization, 29
irrigation, 82, 120, 124, 171, 252
islands, 221, 225, 252
Italy, 85, 167, 202, 293
invertebrate, 227

Japan, 7, 15, 20, 38, 56, 118–121, 125–129, 167, 211, 218, 232, 331
Japanese Cedar (*Cryptomeria japonica*), 126
Japanese Cypress (*Chamaecyparis obtusa*), 126
Japanese Medaka fish, 125
Japan *Satoyama Satoumi* Assessment (JSSA), 120–121, 300
jatropha, 73, 84–86
Jevon's Paradox, 52, 56
Johannesburg, 12, 152–152, 160, 201, 221, 299
Johannesburg Plan of Implementation (JPOI), 153, 221–222

Jose Martinez Cobo, 246

Kazakhstan, 256
Kenya, 27, 82, 87, 167–169, 171–172, 174, 176, 202–203, 258, 331
Kenya Flower Council, 171
Kibera Community Youth Programme, 87
Kyoto Protocol, 11
knowledge systems, 100, 251, 257–258, 333–334

labour productivity, 5
labour unions, 8, 78, 80
Lake Naivasha, 171
land rights, 27
LANDSAT, 25–259
landscapes, 17, 117–132, 182, 256, 298, 300, 334
land use, 85, 120–122, 124, 278, 295–296, 301, 304–305, 308, 313
Laos, 112
Latin America, 7, 13, 27, 176, 254, 256
leadership, 28, 30–33, 209, 222, 251, 312, 315
learning processes, 17, 95, 98, 100, 102, 114
legitimacy, 114, 207, 210, 213–217, 245, 251, 293
legumes, 83
life-long learning, 98, 105, 107–109
livelihoods, 29–30, 58, 63, 96, 109, 111, 117–118, 123, 190, 223, 226, 250, 255, 318
lifestyles, 112, 152, 247, 267, 268, 298–300, 305, 316, 318, 333
load factors, 77, 79
lobbies, 292
local assemblies, 292
local communities, 14, 18, 30, 36, 87, 97, 100, 102, 105, 110, 112–113, 119, 123–124, 127, 129, 130–132, 150, 155, 185–186, 189, 190, 245, 247, 253–256, 259, 261
local governments, 126, 191–194, 308–310, 313–315
local innovation, 97, 113, 335
London Amendments, 278
London smog, 50
loss of biodiversity, 4, 29, 39, 53, 226
low-carbon, 48, 71, 78, 97, 151–155, 289, 291, 312, 314, 330
low-carbon technologies, 154
low-income citizens, 296
low-income countries (LIC), 167–168, 171–173

lower-middle-income countries (LMC), 167–168, 171–173
Love Canal, 50
Lund University, 218

macro-economy, 82
Madagascar, 126–127
Madrid Protocol, 236
Mahatma Gandhi, 61, 66, 99
mainstreaming, 13, 33, 39, 105, 112, 139, 153, 155, 202–203, 208, 237, 307–308, 319, 328
maize, 81–82, 86
major groups, 11, 140, 214, 217, 334
Malawi, 16, 27, 72, 73–74, 76, 80–84, 86, 89, 131, 255
Mali, 27
Malmo, 105–107
marine ecosystems, 14, 187, 229, 236
marine protected areas (MPAs), 221, 228, 229, 232, 235, 238
marine resources, 18, 221, 237, 247
Marine Stewardship Council, 29, 214
market-based mechanisms, 173
Marrakech Process, 152, 299
Marrakech Task Force on Cooperation with Africa, 153
Mauritius, 27
Mayan communities, 255
MDGs (see Millennium Development Goals)
mechanization, 289
medical care, 268, 276
Medicinal plants, 189–190
medicines, 223
Mekong Delta, 279, 281
melons, 171
Mexico, 37–38, 167, 201, 254–255
microbe, 106, 224, 230
micro-organisms, 230
Mid-Atlantic Ridge, 224, 229
Middle Eastern, 72
middle-income countries, 167, 273, 287
Millennium Development Goals (MDGs), 12, 24–25, 27–28, 32, 38–40, 103, 152, 160–161, 169, 171, 173, 175–177, 212, 217, 250, 331
Millennium Ecosystem Assessment, 15, 117, 121, 181, 192, 226, 249, 330
Millennium Summit in New York, 12
Minamata, 7, 331

mining, 60, 73, 77, 80, 88, 126, 127, 150, 227, 330
Ministry of the Environment of Japan (MOEJ), 118–119, 131
minority rights, 25
mitigate, 12, 78, 182, 271, 277, 290, 315, 328
Miyazaki Prefecture, 126
Monitoring, 36, 98, 103, 121, 123, 184, 202, 210, 235, 251, 261
monoculture, 122–124, 128
Montreal Adjustments, 278
Montreal Protocol on Substances that deplete the Ozone Layer, 29
Mozambique, 16, 72–74, 76, 84–86, 89, 256
multidisciplinary, 53, 269, 271
Multilateral Environmental Agreements (MEAs), 26, 199, 203
multilateral environmental diplomacy, 136, 142
Multilateral Fund, 29
multilateral regime, 14, 152, 207
multilevel governance, 293
multilateral treaty system, 207

Nairobi, 87, 203–204
Nairobi-Helsinki Outcome, 203–204
Nakicenovic, 161–163
Nagoya Protocol on Access to Genetic Resources and the Fair and Equitable Sharing of Benefits Arising from Their Utilization, 185, 232, 248
Nairobi-Helsinki Outcome, 203–204
National Biofuels Policy and Strategy (NBPS), 85
National Councils for Sustainable Development (NCSD), 137, 139, 140–142, 151–152
National Park, 7, 125, 330
natural capital, 53
natural gas, 164, 276
natural sciences, 260
nature-based tourism, 185
negotiation, 35, 136–137, 144, 152, 186, 200, 202, 210, 233, 246, 249, 261
neo-Keynesian, 147–148
neo-liberalism, 143
Nepal, 131, 185
networks, 64, 104–105, 111–113, 131, 143, 146, 148–150, 152–153, 156, 209, 210, 221, 246, 259, 292, 294, 298, 300, 312, 314–315, 318

New Partnership for Africa's Development (NEPAD), 82, 139, 153
new public management (NPM), 143, 146
Nganyi community, 258
Nicaragua, 167–169, 174
nitrogen, 26, 39, 81
Nobeoka City, 126
non-communist manifesto, 49
non-compensatability, 96
non-government organizations (NGOs), 11, 100, 102, 108, 120, 127, 130, 138, 140, 291, 307
non-state actors, 140, 145, 149, 151, 210, 214, 216–217
non-timber forest products, 185
North African, 72
North East Atlantic Fisheries Commission, 229, 236
Northwest Atlantic Fisheries Organization, 229
nuclear energy, 8, 37, 163–164
nuclear hazards, 270
nuclear power, 59–61, 104, 108, 110

occupational health, 272–273
ocean, 12, 14, 15, 18, 29, 172, 190, 221–238, 332, 336
  acidification, 29, 222, 226
  dumping, 225
  fertilization, 227, 237
  heat content, 279
  open, 18, 222–223, 225, 229, 235, 237, 239
Oceania, 27, 256
oil imports, 84
Olkaria geothermal power station, 171
operating costs, 171, 295
orange roughy, 223
oreos, 223
organic fertilizers, 82–82, 88, 124
organic food, 107, 125, 313
Organisation for Economic Co-operation and Development (OECD), 37–38, 52, 71, 82, 163, 167–168, 172–173
Oriental Stork, 125
oryzias latipes, 125
Oslo Symposium on Sustainable Consumption, 299
OSPAR Convention, 229, 236
outsourcing, 147
Our Common Future, 10, 48, 50–51
oxygen, 223

ozone-depleting substances (ODS), 11, 29–30, 39, 278

pacifism, 6, 8
Pakistan, 112
Papua New Guinea, 167, 174, 254
Pastoral groups, 121
patents, 37, 224, 230
payment(s) for ecosystem services, 36, 317, 328
payments for environmental services, 185
pecuniary benefits, 189
pesticide, 7, 106, 125, 138, 282
petroleum, 276
Philippines, 104, 106, 111–112, 167, 174
phosphorus, 81
planning, 39, 49, 97, 101, 107, 257, 260–261, 272–273, 291, 300–301, 303–304, 316
plants, 35, 50, 59, 66–67, 77, 123, 151, 189, 165, 171, 252, 254, 274, 298
Poland, 38
polar, 224, 227
polar oceans, 227
political governance, 143, 253
pollution, 6–10, 12, 26, 29, 39, 50, 53, 82, 85, 123, 225–228, 270, 272–277, 279, 282, 287–291, 299, 303, 315
Polokwane, 78
Portugal, 85
poverty
  alleviation, 4, 13, 16, 33, 71, 107, 111–112, 183–189, 307, 312, 328–329
  eradication, 3, 4, 12, 108, 136, 151, 199, 292, 306, 312, 319, 327
  traps, 187, 189
polymetallic sulphide, 227
Porto Alegre, 316
precautionary approach, 183, 228, 235, 238
precautionary principle, 25
primary energy, 58, 66, 163–164, 170, 173, 175, 177
private sector, 30, 35, 38, 60, 87, 88, 97, 109, 111, 120, 130, 140–141, 147, 149, 154–155, 245, 255, 308, 310
privatization, 147, 231
Promotion of Sustainability in Postgraduate Education and research (Pro-SPER.Net), 104–105
pro-poor, 48, 75, 86, 109, 112, 155
protected areas, 123, 187, 190, 221, 225, 229
proteins, 223–224

public–private governance networks, 210
public–private partnerships, 87, 147, 214, 294
public sector reforms, 143
public transportation, 53, 296
Puno, 252
purification, 181, 298

quasi-markets, 148

Rachel Carson, 7, 66, 138
radioactivity, 95
Ramsar Convention, 184, 234
rationality, 14, 129
ray species, 223
Rebound Effect, 52, 56
redfish, 223
REDD+ (Reducing Emissions from Deforestation and Forest Degradation), 35–36, 39–40, 126–127, 187, 254, 330
refugees, 58
Regional Centres of Expertise (RCE), 103, 105–107, 110, 112–114
Regional Fisheries Managements Organisations (RFMOs), 229, 236–237
regulation, 33, 50, 147–148, 155, 181–182, 184, 210, 223, 227–228, 237, 254, 293, 301, 305, 308, 311, 313, 318
rehabilitation, 256, 269
renewables, 59, 66, 77, 79, 163–164, 329–330
remote sensing, 258
renewable energy, 25, 34, 39, 41, 53, 59, 64–65, 73, 88, 152, 163–165, 169–170, 172–173, 175–177, 276, 282, 297
research and development (R&D), 34, 38, 82, 105, 185, 317
resilience, 30, 96, 108, 148, 224, 245, 260, 299
respiratory infections, 275
Resource and Poverty Response Mapping Management (REPORMA), 106–107
resource-efficient, 48, 153–155
Rio+10, 12, 152
Rio+20, 3, 12–13, 16–17, 23, 25, 33–34, 40, 48, 136–137, 140, 152, 184, 199, 200, 204, 209, 222, 237–238
Rio+40, 156
Rio Conventions, 11, 24
Rio Declaration, 24, 153
Rio de Janeiro, 3, 10, 47, 94, 183
risk reduction, 261

risk society, 95–96, 99
river pollution, 270
Romania, 38
roundnose grenadier, 223
rules, 14, 23, 32, 40, 121, 132, 190, 225, 227–228, 293, 313
rule of law, 24, 28, 32, 308, 333
rural electrification, 169
rural population, 150, 182
Russia, 6, 27, 167, 256, 279

safe water, 268, 273–274
Sahelian, 121
Sami reindeer herders, 258
sanitation, 6, 10, 28, 31, 163, 251, 268–269, 272–275
Sargasso Sea, 230
Saskatchewan, 104, 108, 110
Satoyama
    International Partnership for the *Satoyama* Initiative (IPSI), 119–120, 130–131
    Satoyama Initiative, 17, 118–119, 121–122, 129–132
savannah burning, 256
scenarios, 79, 162–163, 188, 260, 320
science of public health, 269
science–policy interface, 202
scientific, 30, 50–51, 57, 63, 119, 122, 144, 201–202, 211, 223, 225–226, 228, 230, 233, 235–236, 248, 255, 257–259, 262
scientific knowledge, 122, 201, 255, 257–259, 262
schools, 8, 31, 105–111, 128, 169, 171, 251, 313
seabed, 222, 224, 227, 229, 231, 237, 239
seamounts, 224, 226, 229, 234
secretariat, 25, 131, 234, 236
Second World War, 7, 55
seeds, 8, 81, 82–83
SEPLs, 119–121, 123, 125, 128132
severe acute respiratory syndrome (SARS), 270–271
shamans, 252
shark, 223
shipping, 225–227, 234
shrimp, 223
Silent Spring, 7, 55, 66, 138
sinks, 253–255
Skane, 107–108
Slovakia, 131

Small Grants Programme of the Global Environment Facility (GEF), 31, 36, 250, 256
smallholders, 81, 86, 88
small scale, 31, 121, 250, 329
social capital, 306–307, 310
social governance, 143
social inclusion, 63
social inclusiveness, 4, 65
social media, 213
social networks, 64, 259
socially inclusive growth, 151
socio-ecological production landscapes, 117–119, 121, 131
soil erosion, 123
soil fertility, 73, 81, 118, 122
solar, 35, 37, 59, 61–63, 66, 71–72, 79, 87, 164–165, 172, 254, 276, 282, 297
Solar Electric Light Company, (SELCO), 63–64
solar photovoltaic (PV), 37, 59
solid-waste management, 59, 272
Sorghum, 85
South Africa, 12, 16, 27, 38, 72–74, 76–80, 84, 86–88, 256, 279
South Korea, 27, 38, 111, 175, 177
Soviet Union, 6, 162
space heating, 160, 169–170, 172–173, 177
Special Rapporteur on the rights of indigenous peoples, 249
species, 39, 87, 120, 123–126, 128, 182, 184, 190, 223, 224, 226–228, 230, 234–235, 238, 252, 255, 298
species extinctions, 226
sponges, 224
sprawled cities, 295
stakeholder participation, 235
stakeholders, 16, 18, 25, 47, 80, 86, 95, 97–98, 100, 102–103, 107, 110, 127, 129, 137, 139, 140–142, 145, 149–152, 156, 185, 188–189, 190, 206, 208, 234–235, 237, 253, 291–293, 306, 308, 314, 316–317, 328–329, 333
Stern Review, 13, 82
Stockholm Conference, 9, 138
strategic environmental assessment (SEA), 228, 235–237
stratospheric ozone depletion, 277
stratospheric ozone layer, 218, 272, 277
structural adjustment, 75, 87, 89
Subsidiary Body on Scientific, Technical and Technological Advice (SBSTTA), 119

subsidy, 73, 81–84, 89
sufficiency, 51, 58, 61, 62, 332
sugar, 73
sugar cane, 73, 85–86
sulphur, 81
sustainable consumption and production (SCP), 94–95, 97–98, 102, 114–115, 152, 297, 299
sustainable development, 6, 10, 13, 24–26, 48, 103, 130, 136, 141, 151, 156, 199, 200, 201, 205, 213, 215–216, 272, 247, 251, 253, 319, 334
Sustainable Development Goals (SDGs), 212, 217
sustainable development governance, 136–138, 142–143, 146, 149–150, 156, 199, 201, 216, 328
sustainable economy, 19, 210, 301
Sustainable Energy Utility (SEU), 64–65
sustainable growth, 143
sustainable use of biological diversity, 247
Sweden, 9, 38, 105, 107, 138, 167
swine flu, 271
Swinomish Climate Change Initiative, 258
Switzerland, 167, 201

Tanzania, 27, 82, 256
technological innovation, 47, 56, 223, 300, 319
technological processes, 144
Technology and Economic Assessment Panels, 30
Thailand, 112, 308
The Economics of Ecosystems and Biodiversity (TEEB), 13, 53, 126
three pillars, 4, 24, 32–33, 35, 112, 114, 141, 151, 199, 211, 213, 303
tidal energy, 164
timber, 125–126, 181–182, 184–185, 255
tomatoes, 171
top-down, 252
Towards a Green Economy, 52, 98, 132, 288, 307, 309, 311, 315–316, 319
toxins, 82, 96, 276
trade-off, 4, 8–9, 52, 72–73, 75–77, 79, 86–89, 117, 118, 144, 188, 306, 328–330
trade unions, 56, 78, 140
traditional knowledge, 63, 97, 121–122, 233–235, 247–249, 251–253, 256–261, 333–334
traditional societies, 49, 334

tragedy of the commons, 14, 225
training, 34, 103, 107, 110–112, 175–178, 234, 258, 302, 308
transboundary, 145, 215, 233, 258, 270–271
transboundary air, 270
transformative governance, 107, 200, 204–205, 211–212
transformative learning, 17, 95, 98, 100–102, 106, 112–114
transitional countries, 170, 176
transparency, 30, 214, 245, 292–293, 328
trapaeng, 123–124
tropical medicine, 271
Tukano people, 252
Tunisia, 171
Turkey, 38, 137, 167–168, 173, 178
Type II partnership, 141, 152

ultraviolet-B radiation, 277
UN Commission on Sustainable Development (UNCSD), 3, 138, 139, 141, 142
UN Conference on Environment and Development (UNCED), 3–5, 94, 247, 276
UN Conference on the Human Environment, 9, 66, 138
UN Conference on Sustainable Development (UNCSD), 3, 11, 138–139, 141–142, 199, 204, 215
UN Conference on Trade and Development (UNCTAD), 13
UN Convention on the Law of the Sea (UNCLOS), 225, 228, 230–232, 238–239
UN Convention to Combat Desertification, 3
UN Decade of Education for Sustainable Development (UN DESD), 103
UN Declaration on the Rights of Indigenous Peoples, 248, 261
UNDESA, 52–54, 58, 62, 117, 122, 298–299
UN Development Programme (UNDP), 10, 25, 31, 131, 160, 250, 256
unemployment, 78, 150
UN Economic Commission for Africa (ECA), 137
UNEP's Governing Council / Global Ministerial Environment Forum (GC/GMEF), 202
UNESCO, 18, 38, 103, 125, 248
UN Environment Programme (UNEP), 9, 13, 14, 26, 29–30, 33, 37, 52–53, 71, 130, 138, 184, 186, 199–204, 210, 216, 273, 291, 295, 335–336
UN Framework Convention on Climate Change (UNFCCC), 25, 28, 31, 34–35, 37, 173–174, 177, 180, 200, 204, 250, 253–254, 279
UN General Assembly (UNGA), 103, 137–139, 190, 201, 204, 231–232, 238, 248
UN Human Settlements Programme (UN-HABITAT), 287, 292
UN Permanent Forum on Indigenous Issues (UNPFII), 245, 248
UN Sustainable Development Council, 215
UN Trusteeship Council, 201
Universiti Sains Malaysia (University of Science, Malaysia), 104, 106, 111
Universitas Gadjah Mada (Indonesia), 111
University of Cebu, 104
University of East Anglia, 124
UN Secretary General, 25, 47
unsustainable consumption, 98, 102, 114
United Democratic Front (UDF), 81
United Kingdom, 85, 124, 145
United Nations Global Compact, 111
United Nations University Geothermal Training Programme (UNU-GTP), 15, 17, 168, 175–178
United Nations University Institute for Natural Resources in Africa (UNU-INRA), 17, 137
United Nations University Insititute of Advanced Studies (UNU-IAS), 15–19, 104, 106, 114, 118, 132, 186, 224, 249
United Nations University International Institute for Global Health (IIGH), 15, 19
United Nations University World Institute for Development Economics Research (UNU-WIDER), 15, 16
United Nations Millennium Summit, 160
United Nations Sub-Commission on Prevention of Discrimination and Protection of Minorities (UNSCPD), 246
United States, 7, 38, 49, 55, 62, 64, 66, 145, 148, 161–162, 167, 173, 177, 206, 226, 258, 271, 277, 279, 296, 302
upper-middle-income countries (UMC), 167–168, 172–173
urban agriculture, 300

350 INDEX

urban areas, 5, 84, 122, 286, 295, 297–300, 317–318
urban and regional planning, 273
urban footprint, 300–301
urban growth, 287, 294, 296
urban poor, 76, 296, 301–303
urbanization process, 288, 292, 319
US Environmental Protection Agency (US EPA), 278
USM, 106
UV-B, 277–278

value orientation, 98–99, 104, 106–109
Van de Walle, 76
Viet Nam, 279
vulnerable marine ecosystems (VMEs), 229, 236

W. W. Rostow, 49
Washington Consensus, 31
water, 28, 29, 31, 36, 63, 64, 72, 82–83, 85, 87, 112, 123, 126, 10, 163, 169–173, 177, 181–182, 210, 221–224, 226, 231, 234–235, 239, 249, 251–252, 258, 268, 272–275, 279, 282, 288, 291, 295–298, 301, 3003–307, 313, 316, 318
  pollution, 6, 7, 10, 12, 85, 272, 279
  purification, 181, 298
watershed, 49, 126, 182, 262
waterways, 82
Weberian, 146
well-being, 6, 15, 18, 55, 63, 66, 71, 76–78, 94, 109, 117, 119, 121, 129–130, 132, 181–183, 186–190, 212, 221, 235, 237, 251, 256, 267–270, 294–307, 318–319, 330–331
Western Arnhem Land Fire Abatement Project (WALFA), 255–256, 258
Western Europe, 161

Western Siem Pang (WSP), 123–124
White-shouldered Ibis (WSI), 124
wildlife, 138, 252
wild tubers, 182
wind, 5, 64, 79, 164–165, 169, 172, 174, 237, 257, 276, 282, 297, 306
women, 24, 28, 31–32, 39, 141, 171
Working for Water programme, 87
World Bank, 25–27, 31, 34, 71, 75, 77, 78, 81–82, 85, 89, 143, 160–162, 165, 167, 227, 249–250, 254, 262, 292, 298
World Bank Operational Policy and Bank Policy on Indigenous Peoples (OB/BP), 249
World Café, 18, 200, 205–207, 210–211, 217, 219
World Comission on Environment and Development (WCED), 10, 24, 48, 50–51, 54, 275
World Council of Indigenous Peoples, 246
World Development Report, 165
World Energy Council (WEC), 162–163
World Environment Organization, 201, 203, 218
World Geothermal Congress (WGC), 176
World Health Organization (WHO), 25, 201, 210, 267, 270
World Intellectual Property Organization, 249
World Summit on Sustainable Development, 24, 103, 152, 160, 221–222, 237, 299
World Trade Organization, 25, 208
Worm-Fert, 106

Yokkaichi, 7

Zambia, 27, 255